Diary of
Henry Eugene Maul
Prisoner of War

Published by
LuLu Press, Inc.
700 Park Offices Drive
Durham, North Carolina 27709

Halstead, Diana Maul, 1951 –
Maul, Henry Eugene, 1924 – 1997
Diary of Henry Eugene Maul, Prisoner of War / Diana Maul Halstead.
ISBN: 979-8-218-02110-8
1. World War II–Non-Fiction. 2. American History–Non-Fiction. 3. Alton, Illinois–Non-Fiction. 4. World History–Non-Fiction. 5. Prisoners of War–Non-Fiction.

Cover design artist Diana Maul Halstead

www.TheKriegiesDaughter.com
@TheKriegiesDaughter

Manufactured in the United States of America.

July 2022

Introduction

Our dad, Henry Eugene "Gene" Maul, was born in Alton, Illinois, March 11, 1924, to Bertha Marie Schneider and Henricus (Henry) Charles "Happy" Maul. He had two sisters, Virginia "Quinny" Lee Maul Munger, April 4, 1927, and Mary Jane Maul Painter Hinton, December 13, 1931.

Dad was greatly influenced (and angered) by the attack on Pearl Harbor, December 7, 1941. At the time, he was a senior at Marquette High School in Alton, Illinois, his and our hometown. Shortly after his 18th birthday and graduating from high school, he enlisted in the Army Air Force June 30, 1942. Dad trained with Boeing School of Aeronautics, advancing to American Air Training in the fall.

Growing up, and even as an adult, my sisters and I were asked to never ask our dad about the war, or his time spent as a prisoner. Of course, we didn't know much when we were younger...other than our dad made a point of watching every-single-movie-ever-made about World War II. I still remember the times I woke up at night as a child and going into the living room to sit with my dad...while he was watching one of his movies.

Dad was a member of the 96th Bomb Group and the 338th Bomb Squadron flying as the waist gunner in a B-17 42-38-62 'Laura Jane'. Dad and his crew completed 8 missions before being shot down flak (flak were the primary fire launches of linear shrapnel that can deplete any armor and kill the target with a single, or a maximum of 2 hits) May 8th, 1944. The 'Laura Jane' crash landed and exploded. Thankfully, our dad's crew all bailed from the plane with one casualty.

Dad landed in a tree, which broke his ribs during his fall. The crew was captured by German scouts who marched them to Dulag Luft in Oberusal, where their intake as POWs would take place, and then on to Auswertestelle West (evaluation Center West), prior to being taken to "solitary" confinement of 200-250 men. Dad went on to Stalag Luft III, where he spent most of his time, in the Province of Silesia, 90 miles southeast of Berlin, in a stand of trees south of Sagan.

As I look back on my dad's life and reflect on my own son's young life when he was 19, I cannot imagine what his mother or father, my grandparents, went through when they were informed their son was missing in action, later being told he was a prisoner of war.

In January 1945, Dad was part of one of the several prisoner "forced marches" from Stalag Luft IV in Kiefheide, in -13° temps, to Nürnberg. A few weeks later he marched again and finally liberated May 12, 1945.

It has humbled me to learn what men can endure. World War II POWs endured starvation, disease, illness, poor hygiene, little water, intense solitude, loneliness and…capture They endured because they did it as a group.

With 200 men literally locked in their small barracks for hours on end, with many of the men forced to sleep on the cold ground…but probably more comfortable than sleeping on the 6 wood slats provided in lieu of a mattress.

The men formed a community with one leader and were very organized. Each man helped the other to keep moral high. When a new POW came, he was welcomed, and the long-standing POWs were eager to hear news about home.

Most Americans back home had no idea what their family or loved ones were experiencing. I hope you read some of the cigarette packs. That give an idea how out-of-touch loved one's were about POWs. One mother wrote that she hoped her son would "be able to go out often and enjoy the nightlife…that German's really know how to entertain visitors." A girlfriend/fiancée wrote to her POW that she was breaking up the with him because he "gave up" and allowed himself to be captured instead of fighting on.

With hard work and good leaders, moral was kept high. Still, a lingering thought was always there…would Hitler order all POWs killed.

Men and women are greatly influenced by war, whether they participate or not, whether they agree or not.

May we always keep our heads high, understand the cost of freedom, and allow no man to walk alone.

Diana Maul Halstead

The Kriegie's Daughter

Table of Contents

POW's referred to themselves as Kriegies.

Kriegie: *Kriegie is short for the German word "Kriegesgefangenen", meaning prisoner of war.*

Dad, Daddy, Father

Our Father was the most loving and happy Fathers a child could hope for. Given the uncertainly he had from his exposure to the war and the effects it had on his loved ones, friends, family, church, and community, he was a kind and generous man.

Following Father's graduation from Marquette High School, he was supported spiritually and morally by his devout beliefs. He was the proud older brother to his two younger sisters, and a wonderful influence to our family throughout his life. His Mother, Grandmother Bertha, lived to be 98 years old. Grandma told me at our Father's funeral, that for his 21st birthday, she sent him a German chocolate cake (with nuts and coconut icing) surrounded and packed in a tin of popcorn. It was very important to her that he receive it, so she got specific instructions from the Red Cross on how to pack and send the cake expeditiously. Because he was a prisoner of war, he received it many months later. Dad said that he eventually really enjoyed the cake & popcorn and shared it with his fellow POW's. Receiving packages and letters from family, friends, and his priest were highlights of his stay.

Father's high moral standards encouraged him to see the best in people. He got up every morning and made my sisters and me breakfast of whatever we wanted but...there was a set menu of whatever we wanted. Our Mother was always served first, with coffee in bed...every morning. He always made sure that we safely got to school and safely returned home.

One of our favorite things to do as kids was to ride bikes. Our Father taught us how to ride safely and stay out of trouble, which was important since we lived in a very hilly town.

He always took care of our Mother's and our cars, too. If it was chilly out, he would even warm-up all the cars each morning. He also made sure we each had full tanks of gas and checked the oil.

After working at his Father's shoe business, he started teaching people how to drive a car. He truly cared about everyone's happiness and safety. He was always truthful and carried himself with dignity and integrity.

Dad loved flying small private planes. His love for flying rubbed off me. What you can see when you are in the air is like Heaven. You feel like you are in God's Kingdom of rainbows and clouds.

What Diana has done to bring Dad's diary to life is truly amazing. To learn about our family and heritage through her research of our family ancestry has been the most enlightening experience. The friends and family that we have reached through this diary has been a wonderful journey for the three of us, Diana, Shelia, and me.

The discovery of the diary is now our family legacy and one of my most treasured possessions. It is sad that we were unable to share it with our Father while he was alive but understand how painful it must have been for him to "go back" to the memories of the war. We were totally unaware of the impact the diary would have on our lives and now cherish every page we get to read because Diana has preserved it for us and for future generations of our family and friends to read and share.

Our parent's wedding album was our family's "coffee table" book, and now this diary will be its replacement.

When my Father passed away November 7, 1997, we received hundreds of cards from my Father's friends and family; he was loved by so many. In 2004 we found a large memory box filled with the cards, our Father's funeral information, and the diary; a book we had never before seen. As we first turned the pages of the diary, it began shedding in our hands; it was so fragile. We were concerned that we would be unable to even try to preserve the diary and what he had written.

Our Father was an artist, a humble and grateful artist. All our lives, we never knew he was an artist until we saw his drawings. When we saw his drawings, we were so grateful to have this diary become a part of our lives to now share with others. I was fortunate enough to have inherited my Father's love of art. When I am painting, wonderful memories come to me. It's an ideal way to express yourself in silence.

As children, we spent many weekends on our Father's boat; he loved the river. When the Sunday paper came, our Father would take it on the boat with us. The first thing he would read was the comic strip "Beetle Bailey". Of course, as children, we had no interest in this Army cartoon but knew our Father loved it. We are honored to have inherited the same perseverance our Father had throughout this life, and grateful to share this memory now.

Cynthia

Cynthia Jeanne Maul-Franke-McNeill
(aka Cindi Carson)

The Process

What a journey this has been. What started out as a small project to prepare my dad's World War II diary for preservation, ended up being one of the most profound journeys I would ever embark, getting to know my dad, not as a father, but as a person.

Often times, as their children, we think of our parents as just that "our parents", mom or dad; their lives began when we were born and exist only for us. We sometimes forget they had lives before we were born.

Until about 10 years ago, I had no idea Dad's diary even existed. A little more than two years ago I was able to see it, touch it, read it...for the very first time. At first glance, I was blown away. Now, two 'plus' years later...I am still blown away by my dad's artwork, his poetry, his stories...his life.

Reflection is an expression used many times when processing my dad's words with his life as a soldier, and as a young man. It was like I had made a quilt of my dad's life having thought I completed the entire quilt, and then, finding I missed some/many pieces. My journey began when I started stitching the new pieces together, giving me the full picture of who my dad was, and who he became.

The dad I knew was the kind of person that always enjoyed a good time, from barbequing in the driveway or the back of our boat, the CinDeLa. He always enjoyed having a beer with buddies at the Alton Motorboat Club, square dancing with my mom at the Sportsman's Club, or just watching old World War II black & white movies. Later, my dad loved spending time with each of his five grandchildren and watching them grow. I know he would be so proud of how each of them has prospered. Cindy, Shelia, and I hope he would also be proud of us for the paths we chose. While they were not always easy, he instilled the belief in each of us that we could handle any task placed before us and become better for it.

My dad would be described as a quiet force. While he was not into small talk, if he had something to say, it would be wise to listen. Dad had no enemies, and many considered him a good friend. My dad's childhood and adult best friend was his first cousin, Bern Snyder. Uncle Bern and Dad had matching cabin cruisers, docked them next

to each other at Clifton Terrace Marina and then the Alton Motorboat Club. They helped each other with home renovations and more. It truly

warms my heart to know what great life-long friends Dad and Uncle Bern were.

Dad was one of those men that did whatever it took to provide for his family. When I was born, he was a part of my grandfather's shoes store, Maul's Shoes, in Downtown Alton. A few years later he started AADTA Driving School, teaching people how to drive (his patience level made this a perfect fit). Dad also worked nights at McDonnell Douglas, teaching people to drive during the day, sleeping in between. Like I said, whatever it took to keep his family fed and safe.

As I touched each page of Dad's diary, reading his poems, his thoughts, his anguish, it touched me in a way I had not planned. I was seeing a part of my dad I never knew existed. As children, my mother told us girls to never ask my dad about the war…we never did. Now, we know why.

Prior to sending Dad's diary to the preservationist, I decided to take mobile photos of each page, each cigarette wrapper, and the items my dad brought back after liberation. For years, my sister, Cindy, kept everything in a nice Chanel box that seemed pretty perfect for keeping his diary safe.

Today, the diary still has not been sent to the preservationist, but it is in an air-tight, water-tight, fireproof safe…and a large baggie.

While snapping photos of the contents of the Chanel box and reading my dad's writings, I started researching what my dad wrote about. One thing led to another…

It meant so much to me to share my experience of this "discovery of Dad" with both of my sisters, Cindy, and Shelia. With each new find, I would call or text them. How blessed we were to have been able to share so many stories of our dad, discovering how what we knew of our dad related to his time as a prisoner of war. Shelia, the youngest of the three of us, and my dad had a dear and close relationship. Sadly, Shelia was taken from us before the diary was completed, but she loved learning about Dad and his life. It is my hope that her two

sons, Daniel, and Thomas, will enjoy getting to know more about my dad and understand his relationship with their mom.

Shelia's sons, Cindy's two daughters, Courtney and Christin, and my son, Christopher, were all able to share great family times and create

beautiful memories with my dad, as he watched them each grow to become positive young people. For Dad's grandchildren, it wasn't just the camping, the shopping, the holidays, or birthday parties that made him smile; it was being included in their young lives.

It is my sincere hope that as you read through the pages of my dad's diary you see the same brave young man. May we remember that each soldier that fought or is fighting for our country, our freedom, walked a similar path. We owe each and every one of them our thanks and our respect.

May God bless you all,

Diana Maul Halstead

The Kriegie's Daughter

Excerpts of emails from Dad's childhood friends:

From Leo Hohnstedt

In 2004 I corresponded with one of my dad's childhood friends, Leo Hohnstedt, asking him about growing up with my dad, their friendship, and any information he knew of my dad leading up to his enlistment in the US Army Air Corps.

"Of course, you know Gene chose one of the most dangerous assignments, a gunner, or a bomber crew, flying missions over occupied Europe. Frightening flights into anti-aircraft fire, rockets, highly experienced fighter pilots in often superior aircraft and always the chance of engine trouble. Then his plane went down, and he was a prisoner of war, in the hands of an army facing defeat and retribution for their crimes.

Some civilians, and not just Germans, hated bomber crews because of the high-commands' decision to bomb urban populations, regardless of traditional military, economic targets. Course, today some regard the fire- bombing of Dresden and Hamburg as murder, unnecessary for military victory, but debilitating to post war Germany's ability to compete with the British Empire. Of course, the crews had no choice. It was fly the mission assigned or face court-martial and disgrace.

In any case, the SS and the Nazis had committed so many atrocities that most crews felt justified in bombing Germans and their factories and towns. Gene made fleeting reference to his imprisonment and forced march to the west as the Russian army pressed the Germans west. He just didn't want to talk about it!

Gene was well-liked by everyone. He always treated me as he had from kindergarten on, as an old friend. Besides going to school together at St. Mary's and Marquette we lived close to Haskell Park and would meet other classmates there, or at someone's house who lived nearby. Gene was a true friend. Although there were periods of time after the War when I did not see much of him, I knew that he always was the type that did not indulge in a lot of talk about things that needed to be done ... he just pitched in and helped see that they got done.

In high school I often was oblivious to the mainstream socializing, and can't say much about your dad's high school years, except that he often used to sit next to me during the weekly required hour of

rambling remarks by the priest whose title was Superintendent. The nuns owned and operated the school. They tolerated the "Superintendent" who was appointed by the bishop, even though at the time the diocese did not own the high school.

Gene brightened up my junior and senior years as we sat together in assembly. Father Smith was furious if anyone dared talk, eat, or chew gum while part of his captive audience. Gene would turn to me and ask if I wanted a "cough drop". We would eat Merck chloroform-loaded lozenges for an hour, and Gene checked frequently to inquire if I felt ok and didn't I want another cough drop. In other words, we carried on a conversation while everyone else waited, not patiently, but quietly.

And when the Japs hit PEARL HARBOR your dad's attitude changed. Now he really was quiet, at least around me. Often, we would see each other "downtown" on Saturday night. We would walk without conversation; we were waiting until we would finish school and go into service. As far as your dad was concerned, no conversation was required, and I respected that. After walking around we would go into Block's ice cream parlor, AND YOUR DAD WOULD FEED ALL HIS CHANGE INTO THE JUKE-BOX, PLAYING "LETS REMEMBER PEARL HARBOR" time after time."

Thank you, Leo!

From Rosemary Dodgen

On a whim I created a Classmates.com page for my dad with his Marquette High School graduating class. I emailed three classmates with a hope & a prayer of a reply since they would all be in their late 90's now. To my surprise, Rosemary Dodgen, responded to my email. I was speechless to read her email about my dad from so many years ago:

"Your dad was very quiet but enjoyed the chaos that was going on around him in the classroom. Our class was without a doubt, a wild bunch but had so much fun together. Our class was very cohesive. There were no separate groups, everyone hung out together, played together, and were best friends together."

Thank you, Rosie!

S/Sgt Henry E. "Gene" Maul

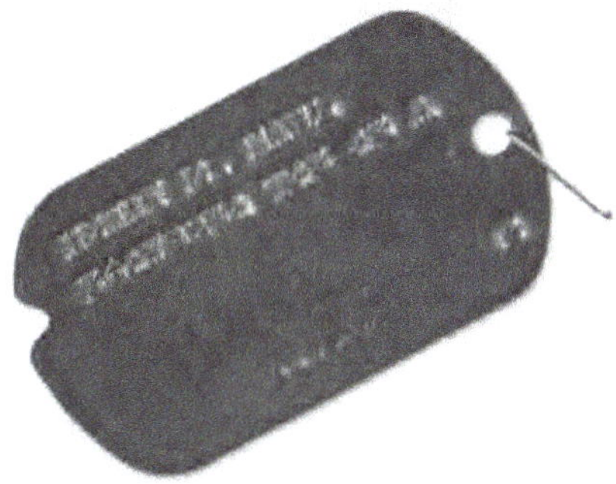

ID "Dog" Tag

American Air Flight Training ID

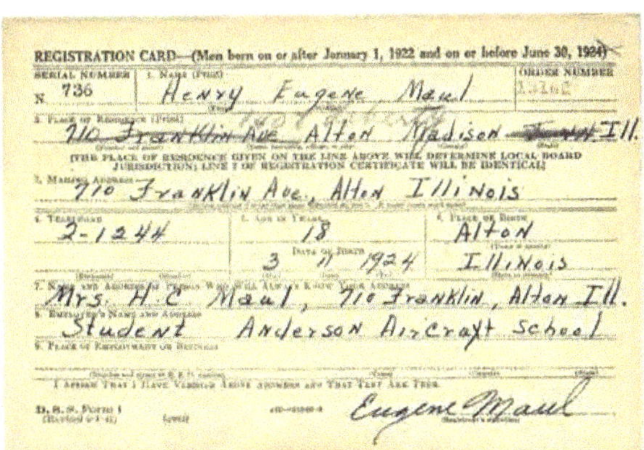
REGISTRATION CARD—(Men born on or after January 1, 1922 and on or before June 30, 1924)

SERIAL NUMBER N 736 — 1. NAME (Print) Henry Eugene Maul

2. PLACE OF RESIDENCE (Print) ~~710 Franklin Ave~~ Alton Madison ~~[illegible]~~ Ill.

[THE PLACE OF RESIDENCE GIVEN ON THE LINE ABOVE WILL DETERMINE LOCAL BOARD JURISDICTION; LINE 2 OF REGISTRATION CERTIFICATE WILL BE IDENTICAL]

3. MAILING ADDRESS 710 Franklin Ave., Alton Illinois

4. TELEPHONE 2-1244 — 5. AGE IN YEARS 18 — DATE OF BIRTH 3 11 1924 — 6. PLACE OF BIRTH Alton Illinois

7. NAME AND ADDRESS OF PERSON WHO WILL ALWAYS KNOW YOUR ADDRESS Mrs. H.C Maul, 710 Franklin, Alton Ill.

8. EMPLOYER'S NAME AND ADDRESS Student Anderson Aircraft School

9. PLACE OF EMPLOYMENT OR BUSINESS

I AFFIRM THAT I HAVE VERIFIED ABOVE ANSWERS AND THAT THEY ARE TRUE.

D. S. S. Form 1 — Eugene Maul

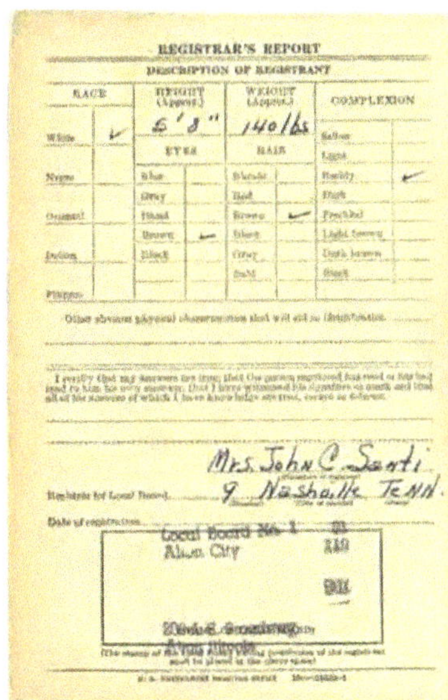
REGISTRAR'S REPORT

DESCRIPTION OF REGISTRANT

RACE		HEIGHT (Approx.)		WEIGHT (Approx.)		COMPLEXION	
White	✓	6'8"		140 lbs		Sallow	
		EYES		HAIR		Light	
Negro		Blue		Blonde		Ruddy	✓
		Gray		Red		Dark	
Oriental		Hazel		Brown	✓	Freckled	
		Brown	✓	Black		Light brown	
Indian		Black		Gray		Dark brown	
				Bald		Black	
Filipino							

Other obvious physical characteristics that will aid in identification

Mrs. John C. Santi

Registrar for Local Board 9 Nashville Tenn.

Date of registration

Local Board No. 1
Alton City

Registration Card

Henry Eugene Maul

Nationality: American
Service Numbers: 36478231
Highest Rank: Staff Sergeant
Job/Role: Waist Gunner

8 Completed Missions
Shot down May 8, 1944, in B-17 42-38062 'Laura Jane'
Lost by enemy aircraft; Crash landed
Prisoner of War

Units served with:

96th Bomb Group
The 96th Bomb Group flew B-17 Flying Fortress to targets across occupied Europe from May 1943 to April 1945

338th Bomb Squadron

Aircraft 42-38062 'Laura Jane'
B-17 Flying Fortress
Delivered Cheyenne 29/11/1943; Kearney 12/12/1943; Presque Is 19/12/1943
Assigned 338BS/96BG (BX-U) 25/12/1943; Failed to Return; Missing in Action Berlin 8/5/1943; Crashed at Ostenholz NW of Celle, Germany

Crew of B-17 #42-38062 'Laura Jane'
Shot Down May 8, 1944
Ostenholz, 18 Miles NW of Celle, Germany
Missing Air Crew Report 4566
Captured by German Scouts

George Bischoff
Second Lieutenant | Bombardier | Prisoner of War

Everett Bradeen
Technical Sergeant | Radio Operator | Prisoner of War

Louis Guillory
Technical Sergeant | Top Turret Gunner | Prisoner of War

Curtis Jensen
Staff Sergeant | Ball Turret Gunner | Prisoner of War

Elmer Kapinschke
Staff Sergeant | Right Waist Gunner | Prisoner of War

Frank King
Second Lieutenant | Pilot | Prisoner of War

William Lloyd
Staff Sergeant | Tail Gunner | Prisoner of War

Henry Maul
Technical Sergeant | Waist Gunner | Prisoner of War

William Reade
Second Lieutenant | Navigator | Killed in Action

James Smith
Second Lieutenant | Co-Pilot | Prisoner of War

Dad's Diary

A WARTIME LOG

WAR PRISONERS AID

AIDE AUX PRISONNIERS DE GUERRE

KRIEGSGEFANGENENHILFE

WORLD'S ALLIANCE OF YOUNG MEN'S CHRISTIAN ASSOCIATIONS
ALLIANCE UNIVERSELLE DES UNIONS CHRÉTIENNES DE JEUNES GENS
WELTBUND DER CHRISTLICHEN VEREINE JUNGER MÄNNER

[redacted]
GENÈVE (Suisse)
CENTRE INTERNATIONAL
37, Quai Wilson

Adresse Télégraph. : FLEMGO-GENÈVE
Compte de Chèques postaux : I. 331

June, 1944

Dear Friend,

As its title-page indicates, this "War-time Log" is part of a special remembrance from the folks at home. The other articles in the packet are more or less perishable, but this is intended to be kept as a permanent souvenir of the present unpleasantness.

If you do not want to keep a regular diary or even occasional notes on war-time experiences, these pages offer many other possibilities. If you are a writer, here is space for a short story. If you are an artist (some people are) you may want to cover these pages with sketches of your camp, caricatures of its important personalities, whether residents or authorities. If you are a poet, major or minor, confide your lyrics to these pages. If you feel that circumstances cramp your style in correspondence you might write here letters unmailable now, but safely kept to be carried with you on your return. This book might serve to list the most striking concoctions of the camp kitchen, the records of a camp olympic, or a selection of the best jokes cracked in camp. One man has suggested using the autograph of one of his companions (plus his fingerprints?) to head each page, followed by free and frank remarks about the man himself. The written text might be a commentary on such photographs as you may have to mount on the special pages for that purpose. The mounting-corners are in an envelope in the pocket of the back cover. Incidentally, this pocket might be used for clippings you want to preserve, or, together with the small envelopes on the last page, to contain authentic souvenirs of life in camp.

Perhaps you will discover some quite different use for this book. Whatever you do, let it be a visible link between yourself and the folks at home, one more reminder that their thoughts are with you constantly. If it does no more than bring you this assurance, the "Log" will have served its purpose.

Yours very sincerely,

WAR PRISONERS' AID OF THE Y.M.C.A.

PRINTED BY ATAR S. A., GENEVA
1944

A WARTIME LOG

A REMEMBRANCE

FROM HOME

THROUGH THE AMERICAN Y.M.C.A.

Published by

THE WAR PRISONERS' AID OF THE Y. M. C. A.

37 Quai Wilson

GENEVA — SWITZERLAND

THIS BOOK BELONGS TO

S/SGT Henry E. Maul

U.S. Army Air Force

A.S.N. 36478234 P.O.W. 1102

Stalag - Luft III. Bks. 1. Rm. 10

Germany

Y.M.C.A.

THIS BOOK BELONGS TO

S/Sgt Henry E. Maul
U.S. Army Air Force
A.S.N. 36478234 P.o.W. 1102
Stalag-Luft III. Bks: 1. Rm. 10
Germany

Y.M.C.A.

May 8, 1944, the day my dad's plane was shot down.

1

Army Air Force Patch

AAF

This drawing of my dad's is one of the B-17 Fly Fortress. On first glance, the drawing looks like a plane taking on enemy fire. On a deeper look, it is such an accurate drawing, it could only have been created by someone that intimately knew the plane. Dad didn't miss much from the Ball Turret Gunner underneath belly of the plane, the Bombardier in the front, the Waist Gunner window, Tail gunner, Flight Engineer area, and Radio Operator. The only thing missing are the humans manning the plane.

MEMORY

Rest old buddies rest ooo—
Now mild the silent movement while the
Millions turn grateful hearts your way
Your loves, your comrades, now in the stiring
Pause of aching tribute, my heart remembers
Careful days and nights we shared together
Pace by pace the heavy mile, side by side through tempest and hell,
Till God laid you in your final biraco and
send me marching further on,
Alone, alone old buddy, yea is but hardly alone for
Where I am you're glowing spirt, and where you
are does valor stand a watch
Under the sentry of the skies, you sleep, who will protect you
Now because you gave such gift to Courage and prosperity
That none deserves, such bliss full sleep as you
Rest old buddies rest
We dont forget.

THAT OLD GANG OF MINE

No one at the base, so it's a pretty certain sign
The Luftwaffe is shooting down that old gang of mine
The boys are singing jail songs the forgotten "Sweet Adeleine"
The Luftwaffe is shooting down that old gang of mine
There goes Jim, there goes John down to Stalag IV B
Now and then we meet again, and they don't seem the same
Oh! but I get that lone home feeling when I hear engine whine
The Luftwaffe is breaking up that old gang of mine

MEMORY

Rest old buddies rest ooo –
Now mild the silent movement while the
Millions turn grateful hearts your way
Your loves, your comrades, now in the stiring
Pause of aching tribute, my heart remembers
Careful days and nights we shared together
Pace by pace the heavy mile, side by side through tempest calor hell,
Till God laid you in your final biraco and
send me marching further on,
Alone, alone old buddy, yea is but hardly alone for
Where I am you're glowing spirit, and where you
are does valor stand a watch
Under the sentry of the skies, you sleep, who will protect you
Now because you gave such guilt, to courage and prosperity
That none deserves, such blissfull sleep as you
Rest old buddies rest
We don't forget.

THAT OLD GANG OF MINE

No one at the base, so it's a pretty certain sign
The Luftwaffe is shooting down that old gang of mine
The boys are singing jail songs the forgotten "Sweet Adeleine"
The Luftwaffe is shooting down that old gang of mine
There goes Jim, there goes John down to Stalag IV B
Now and then we meet again, and they don't seem the same
Oh! But I get that gone home feeling when I hear that engine whine
The Luftwaffe is breaking up that old gang of mine

Dad’s story is felt throughout this entire image...

At the very top of the image is what looks like a Bullet, but it’s not. The bullet-shaped image is actually Flak, the projectile that brought down my dad’s plane in one shot.

The very center of the image has a Cross within a Heart. My dad’s Faith in God kept him centered during his imprisonment. His mother, my grandmother, even sent him a Rosary to help him through difficult times.

Above the Heart Cross is the symbol of a New Dawn, the Air Force's notion that "the bomber will always get through" which ended up being tragically wrong. Gunners believed with every fiber of their being that they were an “Unstoppable Force”.

The main component of the image is my dad's Waist Gun, a key defense feature of B-17 formations, combining lateral areas with a gauntlet of massed firepower.

The background Stars, including the large star, depict Dad’s belief in his country, the United States of America.

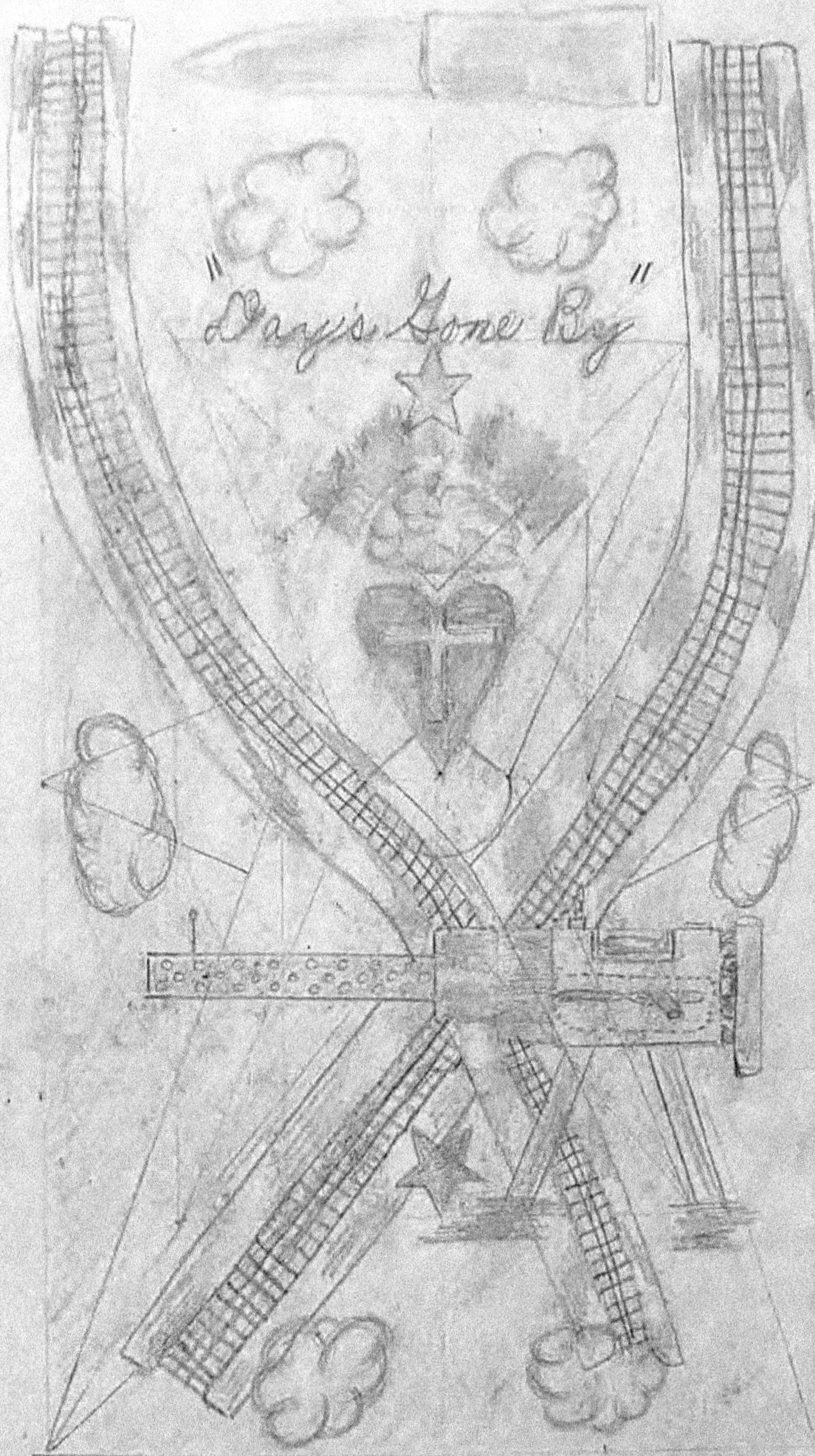
"Day's Gone By"

Getting ready for take-off...

The tail of the B-17 Flying Fortress. Again, the detail of the Tail Gunner area is amazing!

Czechoslovakia and Polish Air Force Emblems

WINGS OF THE CZECHOSLOVAKIA AIR FORCE

WINGS OF THE POLISH AIR FORCE

French and Royal Air Force Emblems

WINGS OF THE FRENCH AIR FORCE

WINGS OF THE ROYAL AIR FORCE

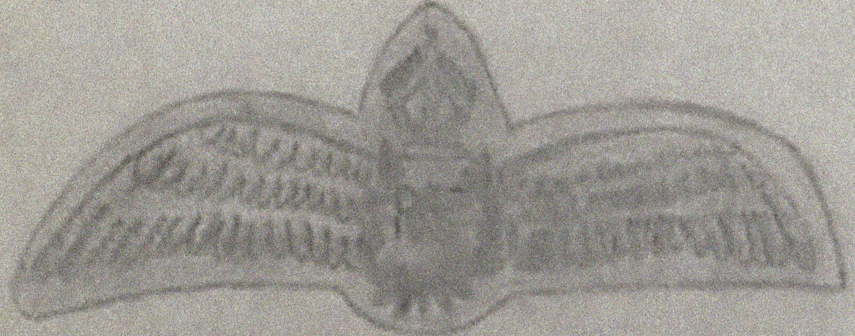

A self-portrait of my dad as a waist gunner.

Waist Gunners wore flak helmets, flak suits, oxygen masks, and an armor plate contoured to the curve of the fuselage below the windows. The armor plate was the waist gunner's only protection from the flak and bullets.

Standing at their guns, the gunner's body filled a larger target area than was the case for the rest of the crew, who were sitting or kneeling. Waist gunners incurred the largest number of casualties of all the **F**lying **F**ortress crew positions.

M-2-

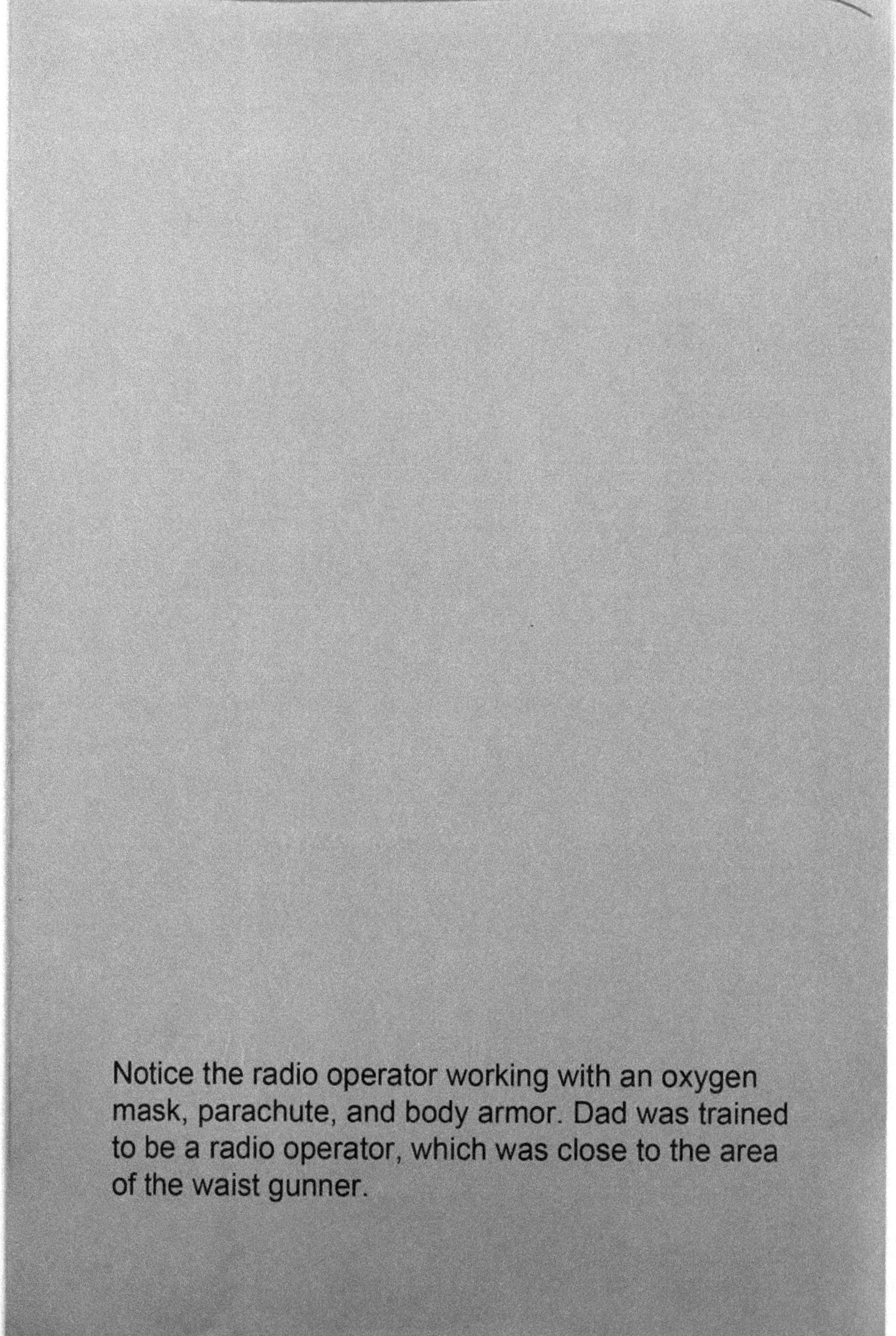

Notice the radio operator working with an oxygen mask, parachute, and body armor. Dad was trained to be a radio operator, which was close to the area of the waist gunner.

RADIO OPERATOR

21

A Gunner's Day

A Gunner's Day is Never Done
Up at Dawn before the Sun,
With the Roar of Engines in his Head
Wishing that He could've stayed in Bed,
Chow at Four, Fried eggs and Stuff
Won't have Time to eat too Much,
Briefing at Five, The Crew's are all There
Anxious to be up There in The Air,
See to your Chute, Ammunition and Guns
For you Know Boys its not for Fun,
Jerry will be there up in the Blue
Waiting For Someone May be You,
Take off at Six or maybe Six-Thirty,
Hope No one has a Gun that is Dirty,
Form with the Group at Twelve Thousand Feet,
See that Formation It Really Looks Neat,
Put on your Mask, the Air is getting Thin,
Off to the Battle Some with a Grin,
We're over the Water, Now test your Guns
Enemy Coast here Comes the Fun,
Flak at Six and Flak at Twelve
Watch out Boys They're giving us Hell,
Here comes Fighters Comin in Low,
They may be Ours, don't shoot Till you Know.
P.51's and P.38's,
Our escort is here They're Never Late,
They're Fighting Fools, Each man at his Ship,
Their is never a Jerrie that they Couldn't Whip.
The air is Cool just Fifty below,
Turn up your heat So you won't Freeze a Toe,
A Sharp Lookout Boys the Target is Near,
We don't care to meet The Enemy way over Here.

There is our Target, And plenty of Flak,
Bombs away Boys, And Now we Turn Back,
Coming out of the sun, Their enemy ships.
Aim True boys, we still got Plenty more trips.
There goes one Down, Another one Too,
Our Fighters Are Busy to see None get Thru
Theres flames in The Sky As Another goes Down.
The pilot bails out, he's Safe on the Ground.
There in the Tail the guns Start to Roar,
There's Blood on your guns, You shoot As Before,
Your ship has been Hit, But Still Flies thru the Air,
You think of your Loved ones And Whisper A Prayer
Smoke from the Target Leaps high in the Sky.
We'll show these DAMN Jerries, We Know how to Fly.
The Fighters Have Left us, The few that are Left,
Our fighters got Some, We got the Rest,
We've been up Eight hours, Two hours To Go.
Though we're doing Two Hundred It Seems Very Slow
England At Last, The Tail Gunner Turns,
We think of our Buddies that will never return,
We Fly over the Field, The Crew gives a Sigh.
We've finished Another. To do or to Die,
Wheels touch the ground, A Screech and a Bump
Our ship brought us Back over the Hump,
We're Tired and Dirty, Thirsty and Sore,
The Sun has gone Down An Hour Before.
First clean your guns, do it good, Boys.
For that gun is Life, his, mine and Yours.

A Sandwich and Coffee, your Chute to Turn In,
You're in the interrogation room, So turn on the "Gin,"
Two meals a day, Both in the Night,
Gets on your nerves, But you're still ready to Fight,
The mess hall is warm in the Cold of the Night,
You Sit down to Eat and Talk Between Bites.
You Talk of the Fighters, The foes and ours Too.

And also of the Boys who never got Through,
Of ships going down, Exploding in the Air,
The Bullets that missed your head, by only A Hair,
Your ships Full of Holes, guess Joes in his Bed,
He stopped A Flak Fragement, it Lodged in his Head,
Then head for your Sack AT TEN or AT One,
A Letter from Home, Another From Mom,
I love you She wrote, You Know you have Won,
But A Gunners DAY is Never Done,

A LOVELY HAND

LAST NIGHT I HELD A LOVELY HAND
A HAND SO SOFT AND NEAT
I THOUGHT MY HEART WOULD BURST WITH
JOY
SO WILDLY DID IT BEAT

NO OTHER HAND UNTO MY HEART
COULD GREATER SOLACE BRING
THAN THAT DEAR HAND I HELD LAST NIGHT
FOUR ACES AND A KING

A Gunner's Day

A Gunner's Day is Never Done
Up at Dawn before the Sun,
With the Roar of Engines in his Head
Wishing That He could've stayed in Bed.

Chow at Four, Fried eggs and Stuff
Won't have time to eat too Much,
Briefing at Five, The Crew's are all There
Anxious to be up There in the Air,

See to your Chute, Ammunition and Guns
For you know Boys its not for Fun,
Jerry will be There up in the Blue
Waiting for Someone may be You.

Take off at Six or Maybe Six-Thirty,
Hope No one has a Gun that is Dirty,
Form with the Group at Twelve Thousand Feet,
See That Formation It Really Looks Neat,

Put on your Mask, The Air is getting Thin,
Off to the Battle Some with A Grin,
We're over The Water, Now Test your Guns
Enemy Coast here comes the fun,

Flak at Six and Flack at Twelve
Watch out Boys They're giving us Hell,
Here comes Fighters comin in Low,
They may be Ours, don't shoot till you know.

P.51's and P.38's,
Our escort here They're Never Late,
They're Fighting Fools, Each Man at his Ship.
There is Never a Jerrie that they Couldn't Whip,

The air is Cool just Fifty below,
Turn up your heat So you won't Freeze a Toe,
A sharp Lookout Boys the Target is Near,
We don't care to meet The Enemy way over Here.

There is our Target, and plenty of Flak,
Bombs away Boys, And now we Turn Back,
Coming out of the sun, Their enemy ships.
Aim True boys, we still got Plenty more Trips,

There goes one Down, Another one Too,
Our Fighters are Busy to see None get Thru
Theres flames in The Sky as another goes down.
The pilot bails out, he's Safe on the Ground,

There in the Tail the guns Start to Roar,
There's Blood on your guns, You shoot as Before,
Your ship has been Hit, But still Flies thru the Air.
You think of your Loved ones and Whisper a Prayer.

Smoke from the target leaps high in the sky,
We'll show the damn Jerries we know how to Fly,
The Fighters have left us, the few that are left
Our Fighters got some, we got the rest.

We've been up Eight hours, Two hours To Go
Though were doing Two Hundred It Seems Very Slow.
England at last, The Tail Gunners Turns,
We think of our Buddies who will never return.

We Fly over the Field, The Crew gives a Sigh
We've finished another, To Do or To Die.
Wheels touched the ground, A Screech and a Bump,
Our ship brought us Back over the Hump.

We're Tired and Dirty, Thirsty and Sore,
The Sun has gone Down An Hour Before,
First clean your guns, do it good, Boys,
For that gun's Life, his, mine or Yours.

A sandwich and Coffee, your Chute you Turn In,
You're in the interrogation room, so turn on the "Gin,"
Two meals a day, Both in the Night.
Gets on your nerves, But you're still ready to Fight.

The mess hall is warm in the Cold of Night,
You sit down to Eat and Talk Between Bites.
You talk of Fighters, The foes and ours too,
And also of the Boys who never got through.

Of ships going down Exploding in the Air,
The Bullets that missed your head, by only a Hair.
Your ships full of Holes, guess Joes is in his bed,
He stopped a Flak Fragment, it Lodged in his Head.

Then head for your Sack at Ten or At One,
A Letter from Home, Another then From Mom,
I love you She wrote, You Know you have Woh,
But A Gunners Day is Never Done.

A Lovely Hand

Last night I held a lovely hand
A hand so soft and neat
I thought my heart would burst with joy
So wildly did it beat

No other hand unto my heart
Could greater solace bring
Than that dear hand I held last night
Four Aces and a King

Vanished Mission

Early in the morning
Before the sun did rise
We were awakened for a mission
That contained a great sunrise.

After a healthy breakfast
And a briefing of our flight
We took off in an airplane
That didn't returned that night.

High into the heavens
We climbed on our course
Soon to pound the enemy
With all our might force

Deep in enemy territory
We received quite a check
A direct hit with a burst of flak
And our plane began to rock

With our wings full of holes
Plus an engine out of commission
We we forced out of formation
To a less favorable position

Then came the fighters
From all over the sky
It was one against many
But we fought without a cry.

We all did our best
But t'was all in vain
A fighter got a lucky shot
And we started down in flame

The Pilot gare the warning
And we all bailed out
Only to be captured
By a group of German scouts.

They took us for a train ride
Far behind the danger zone

Unfinished Mission

Early in the morning
Before the sun did rise
We were awakened for a mission
That contained a great surprise.

After a healthy breakfast
And a briefing of our flight
We took off in an airplane
That didnt returned that night.

High into the heavens
We climbed on our course
Soon to pound the enemy
With all our mighty force

Deep in enemy territory
We received quite a shock
A direct hit with a burst of flak
And our plane began to rock

With our wings full of holes
Plus an engine out of commision
We we forced out of formation
To a less favorable position

Then came the fighters
From all over the sky
It was one against many
But we fought without a cry.

We all did our best
But t'was all in vain
A fighter got a lucky shot
And we started down in flame

The Pilot gave the warning
And we all bailed out
Only to be captured
By a group of German scouts.

They took us for a train ride
Far behind the danger zone
Our fighting days, are over
Still we can't return

Now we're in a prison camp
With one undying vision
To complete the other half
Of our unfinished misson

Kriegsgefang'ner Kelly

Kelly get your barrack bag
The shipping list is here
Were sailing on the first tide
For home and yester-year

But Kelly stirred no muscle
To join the homing folks
He was parked before a stove
Beside a Red Cross box

Kelly we're a sailing
The bitter war is done
It's off to the states, boy
To sweethearts and fun

But Kelly turned odea fear
His stubborness uncleft
I should sail for any where
With all this groceries left

It's a sad story they tell these days
Along the bowery streets
Of Kriegsgefang'ner Kelly
With his parcell full of meat

And some loved adventures
And some loved curly-locks
But Kriegsgefang'ner Kelly
Loved a faithful Red Cross Box

Kriegsgefang'ner Kelly

Kelly get your barrack bag
The shipping list is here
Were sailing on the first tide
For home and yester-year

But Kelly stirred no muscle
To join the homing folks
He was parked before a stove
Beside a Red Cross box

Kelly we're a sailing
The bitter war is done
It's off to the states, boy
To sweethearts and fun

But Kelly turned odesfear
His stubbornness uncleft
I should sail for any where
With all this groceries left

It's a sad story they tell these days
Along the bowery streets
Of Kriegsgefang'ner Kelly
With his parcell full of meat

And some loved adventures
And some loved curly-locks
But Kriegsgefang'ner Kelly
Loved a faithful Red Cross Box.

Dear Draft Dodger

I'm writing this short letter
And every word is true
Don't look away Draft Dodger
For it's addressed to you

You feel at ease and no danger
Back in your old home town
You've cooked up some pitiful story
So the draft board would turn you down

You never think of real men
Who leave home every day
You only think of their girl friends
That you can take while they're away

You sit at home and read your paper
You jump and yell "we'll win"
Just where do you get that "we" stuff
This war will be won by men

Well that's all Mister Slacker
I suppose your face is red
America is no place for your kind
I mean every word I said

So in closing dear draft dodger
Just remember what I say
Keep away from my girl, you bum
For I am coming home some day

Dear Draft Dodger

I'm writing this short letter
And every word is true
Don't look away Draft Dodger
For it's addressed to you

You feel at ease and no danger
Back in your old home town
You've cooked up some Pitiful story
So the draft board would turn you down

You never think of real men
Who leave home every day
You only think of their girl friends
That you can take while they're away

You sit at home and read your paper
You jump and yell "we'll win"
Just where do you get that "WE" stuff
This war will be won by men

Well thats all Mister Slacker
I suppose your face is red
America is no place for your kind
I mean every word I said

So in closing dear draft dodger
Just remember what I say
Keep away from my girl you bum
For I'm coming home some day

Out In The Blue

The city throbs with the pulse of life
With the commerce and industry ever at strife
With hustle and bustle and traffic roar
Far from distant sounds of war,
The park all clasped in their usual floral gown
And place Prevails in the old home town
The bomber roar and the sirene moan
Are things thank God ouit unknown
But way out here in the distant blue
There's a living hell that men go throug
As day by day and night by night
They're locked together in the worlds wor [illegible]
As courgeously striving they stagger and reel
Towards off the increasing enemies heel,
To spare all the loved ones they left home, b [illegible]
From the rapes and the bandage the Ge has in m
yet down in the cities if you seek you shall find
These who have choosen to stay home behind
Watching the fight from the silver screen
Sipping the whiskey calm, and serene
Laughing and joking and airing their views
Sleeping each night in their warm cozy bed
While their fellow men fall to the earth stone dead
Out in the blue of a foreign land
Death waves his scyth with unerring hand
Reaping the harvest so awful and grim
Which saten long ago has promised to him
The harvest of youth on the threshold of life
All trapped in the hold of titanic strife
Your husbands and sweethearts and also your sons
Gallantly fighting and maning their guns
Yet down in the cities if you seek you will find
Those who have choosen to stay home behind
With their sports each weekend in white flannel pants
A cinema show or maybe a dance
And when holding you close in un-uniformed arms
They whisper banalities and speak of your charms

Out In The Blue

The city throbs with the pulse of life
With the commerce and industry ever at strife
With hustle and bustle and traffic roar
For from distant sounds of war,
The park all clasped in their usual floral gown
And place prevails in the old home town
The bomber roar and the sirene moan
Are things thank God quit unknown
But way out here in the distant blue
There's a living hell that men go through
As day by day and night by night
They're locked together in the worlds worst fight
As courgeously striving they stagger and reel
Towards off the increasing enemies heel.
To spare all the loved ones they left home, behind
From the rapes and the bandage the foe has in mind
Yet down in the cities if you seek you shall find
These who have choosen to stay home behind
Watching the fight from the silver screen
Sipping the whiskey calm, and serene
Laughing and joking and airing their views
Sleeping each night in their warm cozy bed
While their fellow men fall to the earth stone dead
Out in the blue of a foreign land
Death waves his scythe with unnerving hand
Reaping the harvest so afful and grim
Which saten long ago has promised to him
The harrest of youth on the threshold of life
All trapped in the hold of titanic strife
Your husbands and sweethearts and also your sons
Gallantly fighting and maning their guns
Yet down in the cities if you seek you will find
Those who have choosen to stay home behind
With their sports each weekend in white flannel pants
A cinema show or maybe a dance
And when holding you close in un-uniformed arms
They whisper banalities and speak of your charms
They talk of there love and loyalty to you
As long as it keeps them out of the blue
While bom on a crest of a ghostly tide
Death goes around with an argentic stride
Whispering the name of some one you lore
As flights scream down from the skies above
To shower them bullets with murderous aim
On the men they been send out to kill and to main
Leaving them dying in dark falling smoke
To bleed and to cry out to die and to choke
Still in the city if you seek you will find
Those who have choosen to stay home behind
Stout hearted fellows with hearts of gold
Gold is yellow so we are told
Eager to share in the peace victory brings
Claiming their rights to lifes precious things
Proud of the fact they had nothing to lose
Their's was their choice and thus did they choose
When the battle is over and victory is won
When the hell and the bombing and gun fires done
When homeward they march these unfortunate few
To pick up the threads of the life once they knew
How well they will know when they march down the street
Which echoes these tramp of their military feet
That the values they placed on their homeland and you
Was settled and paid for out in the blue
Settled and proved far beyond any doubt
By them and their commrades who proudly set out
Who suffered the agony torture and pain
Of war in the air lover of foreign plain
Of freezing and thrust and blazing guns.
Who gamely and doggley struck it and won
To proud to the world, of God up above
That its you above all on the earth who they love
Still down in the city seek and you'll find
Those who have choosen to stay home behind
Proud of the fact they had nothing to loose
There was a choice and thus did they choose.

They talk of there love and loyalty to you
As long as it keeps them out of the blue
While born on a crest of a ghostly tide
Death goes around with an argantic stride
Whispering the name of some one you love
As fights stream down from the skies above
To shower them bullets with murderous aim
On the men they been send out to kill and to main
leaving them dying in dark falling smoke
To bleed and to cry out to die and to choke
Still in the city if you seek you will find
Those who have choosen to stay home behind
Stout hearted fellows with hearts of gold
Gold is yellow so we are told
Eager to share in the peace victory brings
Claiming their rights to lifes precious things
Proud of the fact they had nothing to lose
There's was their choice and thus did they choose
When the battle is over and victory is won
When the hell and the bombing and gun fires done
When homeward they march these unfortunate few
To pick up the threads of the life once they knew
How well they will know when they march down the street
Which echoes there tramp of their military feet
That the values they placed on their homeland and you
Was settled and paid for out in the blue
Settled and proved far beyond any doubt
By them and their commrades who proudly set out
Who suffered the agony, torture and pain
Of war in the air lover of foriegn plain
Of freezing and thirst and blazing guns.
Who grimely and doggley struck it and won
To proud to the world, of God up above
That its you above all on the earth who they love
Still down in the city seek and you'll find
Those who have choosen to stay home behind
Proud of the fact they had nothing to loose
There was a choice and thus did they choose

APPRECIATION

It seems like years have gone by
Since those days that we used to fly
When we'd leave England early each day
Then go sailing off in the sky far away
Our cares and worries were few
Although they griped plenty that's true
As we were always wanting a pass
To go to town for another glass
The food was good, so was the dough
We didn't appreciate it though
Untill oneday we didn't come back
As the Luftwaffe hit us a whack
Only then did we start to realize
We started to think, and opened our eyes.
The Red Cross is the one and right at first
To satisfy all, but for our thirst.
They feed and cloth and always try
To get anything that money can buy
A lovely photograph, or sports equipment
Always gives us a lot of enjoyment.
Prison camp life is always pretty slow
And it's hard to keep the morale from getting low
But when the food parcells arrive each week
The morale goes up to it's peak
Then there's trading to get what you crave
To get a fair exchange for all that you gave
And we all eat plenty, at least very well
But without the parcells it would be hell
There is one thing found to be true
That whenever this war is over
All of us Kriegies of well known ranks
Will express to Red Cross our heart felts.

Appreciation

It seems like years gone by
    Since those days that we used to fly
When we'd leave England early each day
    Then go sailing off in the sky far away
Our cares and worries were few
    Although they griped plenty that's true
As we were always wanting a pass
    To go to town for another glass
The food was good, so was the dough
    We didn't appreciate it though
Untill one day we didn't come back
    As the Luftwaffe hit us a whack
Only then did we start to realize
    We started to think, and opened our eyes.
The Red Cross is the one and right at first
    To satisfy all, but for our thirst.
They fee and cloth and always try
    To get anything that money can buy
A lovely photograph, or sports equipment
    Always gives us a lot of enjoyment.
Prison camp life is always pretty slow
    And it's hard to keep the morale from getting low
But when the food parcells arrive each week
    The morale goes up to it's peak
Then there's trading to get what you crave
    To get a fair exchange for all that you gave
And we all eat plenty, at least very well
    But without the parcells it would be hell
There is one thing for to be true
    That whenever this war is over
All of us Kriegies of well known ranks
    Will express to Red Cross our heart felts.

MY LAST LETTER

Miss you so much to-night, Darling
The day has been dreary and long
I year for your quick step, and laughter
And your lighted song
Miss you so much to-night, Darling
My tears will blind my eyes as I write
But I know that God in his mercy
Will see through darkness, come light

THAT SAME LITTLE GIRL

You're just the same little girl, that I new in school
You're just the same little girl, I'm the same little fool
With your pretty black hair, and your gorgeous eyes
You're the cause of my worries, my heartaches and sighs
You're the one that I think of each hour we're apart
You can say you don't love me just friendship that's all
But I find you near to me whenever I call
For you're the same little girl with those same little ways
And I'll make you love me one of this days.

What was his Name

What was his name, the lad so young
Who in silk and string his life had hung
OH! Yes it did, if I recall
The day he made that eternal Fall

What was his name, the lad so brave
Who Fought for their ship, their life to save
There were many fighters with one desire
To see a "Fort" go down on fire

So in they came, they did their best
There was the flame to do the rest
Over the phone came the Pilots shout
Okay boys, here's where we get out

My Last Letter

Miss you so much to-night, Darling
The day has been dreary and long
I yearn for your quick step, and laughter
And your lighted song
Miss you so much to-night, Darling
My tears will blind my eyes as I write
But I know that God in his mercy
Will see through darkness, comes light

That Same Little Girl

You're just the same little girl, that I knew in school
You're just the same little girl, I'm the same little fool
With your pretty black hair, and your gorgeous eyes
You're the cause of my worries, my heartaches and sighs
You're the one that I think of each hour we're apart
You can say you don't love me just friendship thats all
But I find you near to me whenever I call
Yes you're that same little girl with those same little ways
And I'll make you love me one of this days.

What was his Name

What was his name, the lad so young
Who in silk and string his life had hung
OH! Yes it did, if I recall
The day he made that eternal Fall

What was his name, the lad so brave
Who fought for their ship, their life to save
There were many fighters with one desire
To see a "Fort" go down on fire

So in they came, they did their best
There was the flame to do the rest
Over the phone came the Pilots shout
Okay boys, here's where we get out

B-24

OF A B-24 they all make fun.
They say she was made in 1901
There's something I can't deny
She looks like a box car in the sky.

The tail is short, the wing is long
I hear she was put together wrong
Maybe it was, but this I'll bet
They'll find a use for the damned thing yet.

They scheduled one, a mission to fly
The crew was unhappy, they were sure to die
With a grunt and a groan she takes off in the air
And those on the ground whisper a prayer

They were over the channel bound for "Calais"
The crew knew for sure it was Judgment day
No fighters, no flak came up from the ground
But the brave crews hearts began to pound.

She was full of rattles, groans and squeaks
An awful hissing, from oxygen leaks
They banked to the right and turned around
That shivering "Lib" was England bound

Number one quit with an awful noise,
And it really worried the "suicide boys"
No. three quits with a hell of a roar
And then they feathered Engine No. Four

The crew was worried and tried to leave
Just as the "Lib" gave her final heave
Then like a rock she spun to the ground
And never a body or piece was found

Only death in a cold, cold grave
For only that, your life you gave
Instead of dying in that infernal machine
You should have flown —
IN A "B-17".

B-24

Of a B-24 they all make fun.
They say she was made in 1901
There's something I can't deny
She looks like a box car in the sky.

The tail is short, the wing is long
I hear she was put together wrong
Maybe it was, but this I'll bet
They'll Find a use For the damned thing yet.

They scheduled one, a mission to Fly
The crew was unhappy, they were sure to die
With a grunt and a groan she takes off in the air
And those on the ground whisper a prayer

They were over the channel bound for "Calais"
The crew knew For sure it was Judgement day
No Fighters, No Flak came up from the ground
But the brave crews hearts began to pound.

She was Full of battles, Groans and squeaks
An awful Hissing, From oxygen leaks
They banked to the right and turned around
That shivering "Lib" was England Bound

Number one quit with an awful noise
And it really worried the "suicide boys"
No. three quits with a Hell of a roar
And then they Feathered Engine No. Four

The crew was worried and tried to leave
Just as a the "Lib" gave her Final Heave
Then Like a rock she spun to the ground
And never a body or piece was found

Only death in a cold, cold grave
For only that, is our life you gave
Instead of dying in that infernal machine
You should have flown –
In A "B-17".

Bombers Blues

My mama done told me
When I was in Khaki.
My mama done told me, son
Those big birds are pretty things
They'll give you a good ride
But when the ridings done
Those birds will get you
They're worrisome thing
Will Leave you to sing
The Blues in the night

Now the Pilots singing
Hear the alarm bell ringing
Bail out, bail out.
From Calais to Bourdeaux
From Frankfort to Brunswick
Where ever the big birds go,
I've been in some rough Flak.
And I've had some good times
But there is one thing I know
When they brief us for Berlin,
I'll go to my sack, Lay Flat on my back
And Sing The Blues in the Night

Bombers Blues

My mama done told me
When I was in khaki.
My mama done told me, son.
These big birds are pretty things
They'll give you a good ride
But when the ridings done
Those birds will get you
They're worrisome thing
Will leave you to sing
The Blues in the night

Now the Pilots singing
Hear the alarm bell ringing
Bail out, bail out.
From Calais to Bourdeaux
From Frankfort to Brunswick
Where ever the big birds go,
I've been in some rough flak.
And I've had some good times
But there is one thing I know
When they brief us for Berlin,
I'll go to my sack, lay flat on my back
And sing. The Blues in the Night.

Grace

Her name was Grace, one of the best
But there came one night I gave her the test
I looked at her with joy and delight
She is mine for the rest of the night

She looked so pretty, so sweet and slim
The night was dark, the lights were dim
I was so excited my heart missed a beat
For I knew that night I was in for a treat.

I saw her stripped, I saw her bare
I felt all around her every where
We started off, she screamed with joy.
For this was her first night with a boy

I got so high as quick as I could
I handled her well, the response was good
I turned her over, then on her side
Then on her back I tried

It was a great thrill, she was the best in the land
That twin engin bomber from the bomber command

Grace

Her name was Grace, one of the best
But there came one night I gave her the test
I looked at her with joy and delight
She is mine for the rest of the night

She looked so pretty, so sweet and slim
The night was dark, the lights were dim.
I was so excited my heart missed a beat
For I knew that night I was in for a treat.

I saw her stripped, I saw her bare
I felt all around her every where
We started off, she screamed with joy.
For this was her First night with a boy

I got so high as quick as I could
I handled her well, the response was good
I turned her over, then on her side
Then on her back I tried

It was a great thrill, she was the best in the land
That twin engine bomber From the bomber command.

Thoughts of a P.O.W.

There's barbed wire around us, and guns by the score
The thoughts of escape are, still as before
Our thoughts are at home, and our loved ones we miss
A longing for someone we used to kiss.

That someone is waiting, same as before
Though we haven't heard From her for months or more
We dream through the night, and yes thru the day
But our dreams and our thoughts are so far away

Our dreams will come true, we haven't a doubt
The gates will be opened, we'll be there to go out
We'll go marching Home when the day is here
Yes, we'll come marching home with nothing to fear

The worst part is over, a few don't come back
They were taken, by fighters and flak,
But we who are left, will come home to stay
And have you by our sides to start a new day.

P.O.W.s Dream

Oh! Lovely Lady so far away
A year has passed me here today
I dream each night that you may be
Shipped in a Red Cross parcel to me
I hope that you will forever stay
In my mind as you do today.

Thoughts of A P.O.W.

There's barbed wire around us, and guns by the score
The thoughts of escape are, still as before
Our thoughts are at home, and our loved ones we miss
A longing for someone we used to kiss.

That someone is waiting, same as before
Though we haven't heard from her for months or more
We dream through the night, and yes thru the day
But our dreams and our thoughts are so far away

Our dreams will come true, we haven't a doubt
The gates will be opened, we'll be there to go out
We'll go marching Home when the day is here
Yes, we'll come marching home with nothing to fear

The worst part is over, a few don't come back
They were taken, by fighters and flak,
But we who are left, will come home to stay
And have you by our sides to start a new day.

P.O.W.s Dream

Oh! Lovely Lady so far away
A year has passed me here today
I dream each night that you may be
Shipped in a Red Cross parcel to me
I hope that you will forever stay
In my mind as you do today.

A STORY TO TELL

The barracks were crowded in old four A,
The prisoners as usual were happy and gay
When in walks a gunner's, looking quite well
And says if you'll listen I've a story to tell

It deals with a fortress and her ten men crew
Who on tuesday morn into Germany flew
The weather was clear for bombing 'twas fine
We flew with our formation across the Rhine

We all reached our target, things were going well
When Flak hit our engines, and from formation we fell
Left alone in the sky, the fighters raised hell
But we got our share boys, ere our seventeen fell

They set us on fire, the rest you can guess
When we hit the silk, she sure was a mess
We landed in Germany, escape was in vain
The brought us to this Stalag, in a dirty old train

My story is ended, but that isn't all
There are plenty of others, to answer the call
Crews like ours who'll bomb right along
They'll finish the job, before very long
(We Hope)

A Story to Tell

The barracks were crowded in the four se.
  The prisoners as usual were happy and gay
When in walks a gunners, looking quite well
  Send says if you'll Listen I've a story to tell

It deals with a fortress and her ten men crew
  Who on Tuesday morn into Germany flew
The weather was clear for bombing T'was fine
  We flew with our formation across the Rhine

We all reached our target, things were going well
  When Flak hit our engines, and from formation we fell
Left alone in the sky, the fighters raised hell
  But we got our share boys, ere our seventeen fall

They set us on fire, the rest you can guess
  When we hit the silk, she sure was a mess
We landed in Germany, escape was in vain
  The brought us to this Stalag, in a dirty old train

My story is ended, but that isn't all
  There are plenty of others, to answer the call
Crews like ours who'll bomb right along
  They'll finish the job, before very long
(We Hope)

Combat Crew

Oh! You can't go to Heaven on a B-24
St. Peter would say.....Pull 50 more

Now the Pilot of the Bomber is the Boss
An occasional Gunner Is his only Loss.

Now the Co-Pilot....Is a Damn good man
He can Fly the Ship, But can he Land.

Now the navigator he charts the sky
His Famous words are...Where the Hell am I

Now the Bombardier has no bomb sight
So he censors mail Both day and Night

Now the Pilot called, said check the gear.
Said the Engineer....The Gear ain't here

Now the radio man was top of the world
When he wrapped his legs...Round the Gibson girl

Now the Nose Turrent Gunner Cried I want no more
I can't get through these double doors.

Now the top turrent gunner saw a 109
Cried Lets go Home, Don't you think its Time

Now the Ball Turrent gunner saw the 88's
Cried Oh St. Peter, Open up those Gates

Now the Tail Gunner yelled Loud and Long
Their coming in Ten Thousand Strong.

Now the Boys on the Ground They worked Last Night
They sweat us out on Every Flight

Now you've heard our story About A Combat Crew
As you can see It's not SNAFU.

Combat Crew

Oh! You can't go to Heaven on A B-24
St. Peter would say..... Pull 50 more

Now the Pilot of the Bomber is the Boss
An occasional Gunner Is his only Loss.

Now the Co-Pilot.... Is A Damn good man
He can Fly the Ship, But can he Land.

Now the Navigator he charts the Sky
His Famous words are ... Where the Hell am I

Now the Bombardier has No bomb sight
So he censors mail Both day and Night

Now the Pilot called, said check the gear.
Said the Engineer .... The Gear ain't here

Now the radio man was top of the world
When he wrapped his legs --- Round the Gibson Girl

Now the Nose Turrent Gunner Cried I want no More
I can't get through these double doors

Now the top turrent gunner saw a 109
Cried Lets get home, Don't you think its Time.

Now the Ball Turrent gunner saw the 88's
Cried Oh St. Peter, Open up those Gates

Now the Tail Gunner yelled Loud and Long
Their coming in ten Thousand Strong.

Now the Boys on the Ground They worked Last Night
They sweat us out on Every Flight

Now you've heard our story About A Combat Crew
As you can see It's not SNAFU

Tread Softly

You boast and rave of the things you've done
Of shooting down planes, that came out of the su[n]
You groan and moan of the rough times you ha[d]
But just stop and think, Jack, was it that bad
Now some day it will end, and you will return
To the ones that you love, and for whom you've yea[rned]
Oh! The Questions they'll ask, How proud you'll be
To tell how you fought for their liberty
But think of the Boys who were once alive
Who gave all, that the world might strive,
And to be a better place in which to Live
So stop and think Jack, what did you give?

Good Girl

Please don't ask me to marry you yet
Mother would just have a fit
Good gosh it was just today we met
Can't you be patient a bit
You know people would talk about things
I mean if they aren't in good taste
Besides I don't think a Girl, if she's nice
Would marry a men in such haste
I'll wed you tomorrow if you like
And share your toothbrush and comb
But if you keep teasing me darling
I'll get up, get dressed and go home

Tread Softly

You boast and rave of the things you've done
  Of shooting down planes, that came out of the sun
You groan and moan of the rough times you had
  But just stop and think, Jack, was it that bad?
Now some day it will end, and you will return
  To the ones that you love, and for whom you've yearned
Oh! The Questions they'll ask, How proud you'll be
  To tell how you fought for their liberty
But think of the Boys who were once alive
  Who gave all, that the world might strive,
And to be a better place in which to Live
  So stop and think, Jack, what did you give?

Good Girl

Please don't ask me to marry you yet
Mother would just have a fit
Good gosh it was just today we met
Can't you be patient a bit
You know people would talk about things
I mean if they aren't in good taste
Besides I don't think a Girl, if she's nice
Would marry a men in such haste
I'll wed you tomorrow if you like
And share your toothbrush and comb
But if you keep teasing me darling
I'll get up, get dressed and go home

A-Sad-Story

Now listen and I'll Tell you a story
Of a thing that happened to me
So Profit by my Experience
And don't cross over the sea

I was doing fine and dandy
With three good meals a day
But now I'm in a prison camp
And starving my rear away

I had no cares or worries
My mind was always at ease
Till some sergeant told me
I was going to fly in the breeze

They put me in a "17"
And flew me across
Telling me I had no say
Uncle Sam was my boss

But when I got to England
And saw the fix I was in
I thought all they told me
Surely must be a sin

Things went very well
For the First few months, but then
They told me I was flying
Right over old Berlin

The fighters came by droves
The Flak was thick as Hell
But things began to Happen
When the Pilot rang the bell

Now I thought I would be very smart
And walk right back to France
Through the whole German army
without giving them a chance.

But I found I wasn't good
When it came to trapping the Hun
For all they needed to capture me
Was one small boy with a gun.

So they put me in a box car
And shipped me off to camp
I asked for food and water
But they kicked me in the pants

Now I'm inside four high fences
Eating fish pate three times a day
And its looks very proably
For the duration thats where I'll stay

But I guess its all for the best
And will turn out good in the end
And Germany will find out
What's inside us American men.

But when the war is over
We will March through old Berlin
And the people will be singing
The "Yanks" have done it again.

A – Sad – Story

Now listen and I'll tell you a story
Of a thing that happened To me
So Profit by my Experience
And don't cross over the sea

I was doing fine and dandy
With three good meals a day
But now I'm in a prison camp
And starving my rear away

I had no cares or worries
My mind was always at ease
Till some sergeant told me
I was going to fly in the breeze

They put me in a "17"
And Flew me across
Telling me I had no say
Uncle Sam was my boss

But when I got to England
And saw the fix I was in
I thought All they told me
Surely must be a sin

Things went very well
For the First Few months, but then
They told me I was Flying
Right over old Berlin

The fighters came by droves
The Flak was thickas Hell
But things began to Happen
When the Pilot rang the bell

Now I thought I would be very smart
And walk right back to France
Through the whole German army
Without giving them a chance.

But I found I wasn't good
When it came to trapping the Hun
For all they needed to capture me
Was one small boy with a gun.

So they put me in a box car
And shipped me off to camp.
I asked for food and water
But they kicked me in the pants

Now I'm inside four high fences
Eating fish pate three times a day
And its looks veng probably
For the duration that's where I'll stay

But I guess its all for the best
And will turn out good in the end
And Germany will find out
What's inside us American men.

But when the war is over
We will March through old Berlin
And the people will be singing
The "Yanks" have done it again.

That's when I think About Her

When things are so rough
And the going gets tough
That's when I think about you, dear
When the lights are dim
When my chances seem slim
That's when I think about you, dear
When I linger at night
Under Prussian stars bright
I remember you there
With a rose in your hair
Just as you whispered goodnight, dear.
And I'll be singing this song, as I fly along
For that's when I think about you

My Six Bed Slats

Each night before I go to bed
I fix a pillow for my head
Now I lay my blankets neat
On which I hope to get some sleep

I lay down easy on my sack
The boards aren't right to fit my back
Up out of bed I go slowly
To move these slats to and fro

I get back in with a sigh
My head is low, my feet is high
So up out of bed again I go
To move the slats to and fro

This time I'm madder than before
So I grab my sack and sleep on the floor.

Thats when I think About Her

When things are so rough
And the going gets tough
Thats when I think about you, dear
When the lights are dim
When my chances seem slim
Thats when I think about you, dear
When I linger at night
Under Prussian stars bright
I rember you there
With a rose in your hair
Just as you whispered goodnight, dear.
And I'll be singing this song, as I fly along
For that's when I think about you

My Six Bed Slats

Each night before I go to bed
I fix a pillow for my head
Now I lay my blankets neat
On which I hope to get some sleep

I lay down easy on my sack
The boards aren't right to fit my back
Up out of bed I go slowly
To move these slats to and fro

I get back in with a sigh
My head is low, my feet is high
So up out of bed again I go
To move the slats to and fro
This time I'm madder than before
So I grab my sack and sleep on the floor

My Future With Her

It's just a year or so ago
We said so long, short and sweet you know
She said she'd wait for me
No matter how long the war would be

Soon the time will come for me to go home
And I will be like a King on a throne
I'll have her always by my side
For now she is my own sweet bride.

We'll have a car, a house, and a little ground
Just for two children to run around
I know how happy we will be
Just us four, the wife, two kids and me.

These our future dreams you see
That's the way I'd like to be.
Things will run smooth all the time
I'll be happy with her love, and her with mine.

My Future With Her

It's just a year or so ago
We said so long, short and sweet you know.
She said she'd wait for me
No matter how long the war would be
Soon the time will come for me to go hom
And I will be like a King on a throne
I'll have her always by my side
For now she is my own sweet bride

We'll have a car, a house, and a little ground
Just for two children to run around
I know how happy we will be
Just us for, the wife, two kids and me.

These our future dreams you see
That's the way I'd like to be
Things will run smooth all the time
I'll be happy with her love, and her with mine.

A Gunner's Prayer

I wish to be a Pilot
    And you along with me
But if we all were Pilots
    Where would the Air Force be

A pilots just a chauffeur
    It's his job to fly the ship
It was we who did the fighting
    Although we didn't get the fame

It takes guts to be a gunner
    To sit in the tail
When the Messerschmitts are coming
    And the slugs begin to whale

So if we all must be gunners
    Let us make a bet
We'll be the best Damn gunners
    That Jerrie ever met.

A Gunner's Prayer

I wish to be A Pilot
And you along with me
But if we All were Pilots
Where would the Air Force be

A pilots just a chauffeur
It's his job to fly the ship
It was we who did the fighting
Although we didn't get the fame

It takes guts to be a gunner
To sit in the tail
When the Messerschmitts are coming
And the slugs begin to whale

So if we All must be gunners
Let us make A bet
We'll be the best DAMN gunners
That Jerrie ever met.

My Buddies

They say they died in Glory
Whatever that may be—If
Dying in a burst of flame is Glory
Then its not for me

In the briefing room that morning
They sat with clear eyes, and strong hearts
Just one of those many gunners
Determined to do his part.

My buddies had guts alright
They sought not Glory nor Fame
They knew they had a job to do
And their crew all felt the same

But death had the final word
For in it's log, I wrote their names
And my buddied died that morning.
In Glory and in Flame

My Buddies

They say they died in Glory
Whatever that may be – if
Dying in a burst of flame is Glory
Then its not for me

In the briefing room that morning
They sat with clear eyes, and strong hearts
Just one of those many gunners
Determined to do his part.

My buddies had gust alright
They sought not Glory or Fame
They knew they had a job to do
And their crew all felt the same

But death had the final word
For in it's log, I wrote their names
And my buddied died that morning.
In Glory and in Flame

Our Queen B-17

For all the boys who loved her
Will tell you as well as I
She's the most graceful thing in the heavens
She's the Queen of the sky

She spreads her wings over most of the earth
But still keeps looking for the higher berth
And through all tricks and trouble known
She fights and fights to bring us home.

Way up there in the world of blues
She carries all her gallant crews,
Thru hoardes of Fighters, and ample Flak
Fighting always to bring us back

Now let me tell a story
One all the boys know well
A story of fighting men
Who ride the airy swell

The boys all retired early
For they knew the time ahead
When the G. I. C.Q. will come
To route them out of bed

We rised early in the morning
While the stars were still above
Rush off for our breakfast
And then to briefing make

We listened to the statistics
Of cargo and the rail
And pray to God our creator
That our mission will not fail

The ground crews are all waiting
As we ride along the ramp
The engines have been tested
And the Pilot runs his stamp

The air crew chores are finished
As quickly as can be
So they may relax a bit
Before they take off you see

The time has come, the engines roar
Our queen begins to move
She taxies out on the line
That puts her in the groove

A final checkup, the engines purr
They never miss a beat
She races down the runway
And soon is off her feet.

She climbs and soars above the roar
Of sisters on her side
And knows it is her solemn duty
To always be in stride

The mission starts and in our hearts
We know of fear and worry
Cause way below, The Flak
Gets up there in a hurry

The fighters come on doggedly
To try and break our wings
But Queenie fights and fights
To deliver her great stings

Success at last, the target passed
She's proudly winging on
To show her fame and fortune
To all the folks at home.

So when the war is over
She only asks for this
To show her your attention
And praise her with the best.

Thanks for the Memories

Thanks for the memories
Of flights to Germany
Across the cold North Sea
With blazing guns, we fight the Huns
For Air supremacy, how Lucky we are.
Thanks for the Memories
Of Me. 109's
Of Flak guns on the Rhine
We did our bit, and we got hit
And ended our good times,
we hated them so much
We drifted out of formation
We jumped and what a sensation
And now we sweat out the duration
Our job is done, we had our fun
So thanks for the Memories
Of days we had to stay
In Stalag luft IV A
The cabbage stew, which had to do
Till Red Cross parcel day
How Thankful we are.

Our Queen B-17

For all the boys who loved her
will tell you as well as I
She's the most graceful thing in the heavens
She's the Queen of the sky

She spreads her wings over most of the earth
But still keeps looking for the higher berth
And through all tricks and trouble known
She fights and fights to bring us home.

Way up there in the world of blues
She carries all her gallant crews
Thru hoardes of Fighters, and ample Flak
Fighting always to bring us back

Now let me tell a story
One all the boys know well
A story of fighting men
Who ride the airy swell

The boys all retired early
For they knew the time ahead
When the G.I. C.Q. will come
To route them out of bed

We rised early in the morning
While the stars were still above
Rush off for our breakfast
And then to briefing make

We listened to statistics
Of cargo and the rail
And pray to God our creator
That our mission will not fail

The ground crews are all waiting
As we ride along the ramp
The engines have been tested
And the Pilot runs his stamp

The aircrew chores are finished
As quickly as can be
So they may relax a bit
Before they take off, you see

The time has come, the engines roar
Our queen begins to move
She taxies out on the line
That puts her in the groove

A final checkup, the engines purr
They never miss a beat
She races down the runway
And soon is off her feet

She climbs and soars above the roar
Of sisters on her side
And knows it is her solemn duty
To always be in stride

The mission starts and in our hearts
We know of fear and worry
Cause way below, The Flak
Gets up there in a hurry

The fighters come on doggedly
To try and break our wings
But Queenie fights and fights
To deliver her great stings

Success at last, the target passed
She's proudly winging on
To show her fame and fortune
To all the folks at home.

So when the war is over
She only asks for this
To show her your attention
And praise her with the best.

Thanks for the Memories

Thank for the memories
Of flights to Germany
Across the cold North Sea
With blazing guns, we fight the Huns
For Air supremacy, how lucky we are.
Thanks for the memories
Of Me. 109's
Of Flak guns on the Rhine
We did our bit, and we got hit
And ended our good times, we liked them so much
We drifted out of formation
We jumped and what a sensation
And now we sweat out the duration
Our job is done, we had our fun
So thanks for the memories
Of days we had to stay
In Stalagluft IV A
The cabbage stew, which had to do
Till Red Cross parcel day
How thankful we are

POW's were given 2 chunks of coal per POW.

The coal was meant to keep the POW warm (which it did not) and used to cook with.

There was no vent for the make-shift stove so POW's used old milk cans to form a smokestack.

Our Milk CAN Chimney

Most of the time, POW's were locked in their barracks (200 men, fewer beds).

On occaision, POW's in Stalag Luft III were allowed to play football for exercise. (this was only in Stalag Luft III)

53
AND-THERE-WERE FOOTBALL-GAMES

With only one 2-minute cold shower every 2 months,
imagine how good it must have felt to stay
shaved and have a hair cut.

The Kriegie Emporium Boasts Six Tonsorial Artists

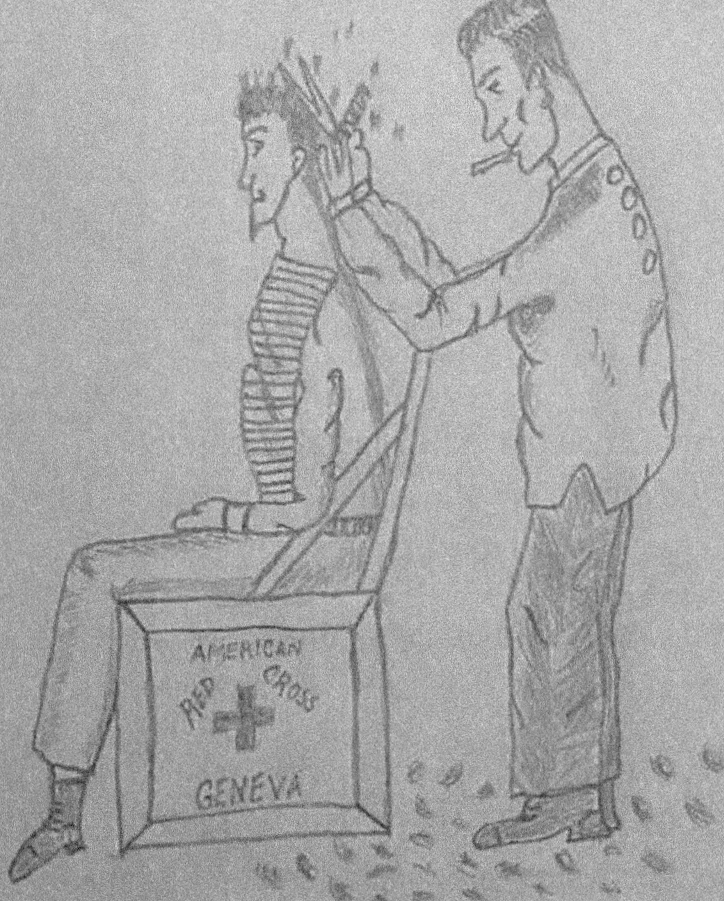

The Red Cross played a pivotal role in the lives of every POW and were welcomed on every visit.

The Red Cross, and parcels from home, were key in keeping POW"s moral high.

Germans were required to give POW"S 1800-2000 calories a day. About 200-500 of those calories were expected to come from parcels from home or Red Cross parcels.

POW's fell far short of the required daily caloric intake and starved.

SPAM
RED CROSS
The Full
Parcel Daze

German Prison Guards were usually men that were too old to fight the war or recovering from injuries suffered in battle.

For the most part, in Stalag Luft III guards left the POW's alone, causing little anguish. That didn't stop the POW's from wanting to have a laugh or two at the guards expense.

Brownie and His Cans

Other than the occaisional football game, POW's only recreations were writing, drawing, and reading. Most all POW's read every book in the library...many times.

Growing up, I never saw my dad read a book, or have any interest in books. This was because most all of his time during his 12 months as a POW was spent r-e-a-d-i-n-g.

Then There's the Library

This may be repetitive, but bears repeating...

The Red Cross was crutial to the POW's and and the Red Cross was always there, every step of the way, to help POW's in any way they could.

"RED CROSS CLOTHING"
OUR MOTTO!
"WE AIM TO PLEASE EVERYONE"

One of the ways POW's were able to feel the fresh air was the "early" morning roll calls.

-ROLL CALL-

The Mystery of the Missing "Kriegie"

SEARCH

Going Home

Mail Call

There were few good things to happen in the life of a POW, but occaisionally making their own beer was one of them. Like the coffee, it was not "flavorful" but it did reaise the spirits of the consumers.

"Brew Up"

The calendar begins May 8, 1944, the day my
dad's plane, the Laura Jane (on her 9th mission),
was shot down by enemy flak about 4:00 that afternoon.

May 8, 1944
Ostenholz, 18 Miles NW of Celle Germany
Missing Air Crew Report 4566
Captured by German Scouts

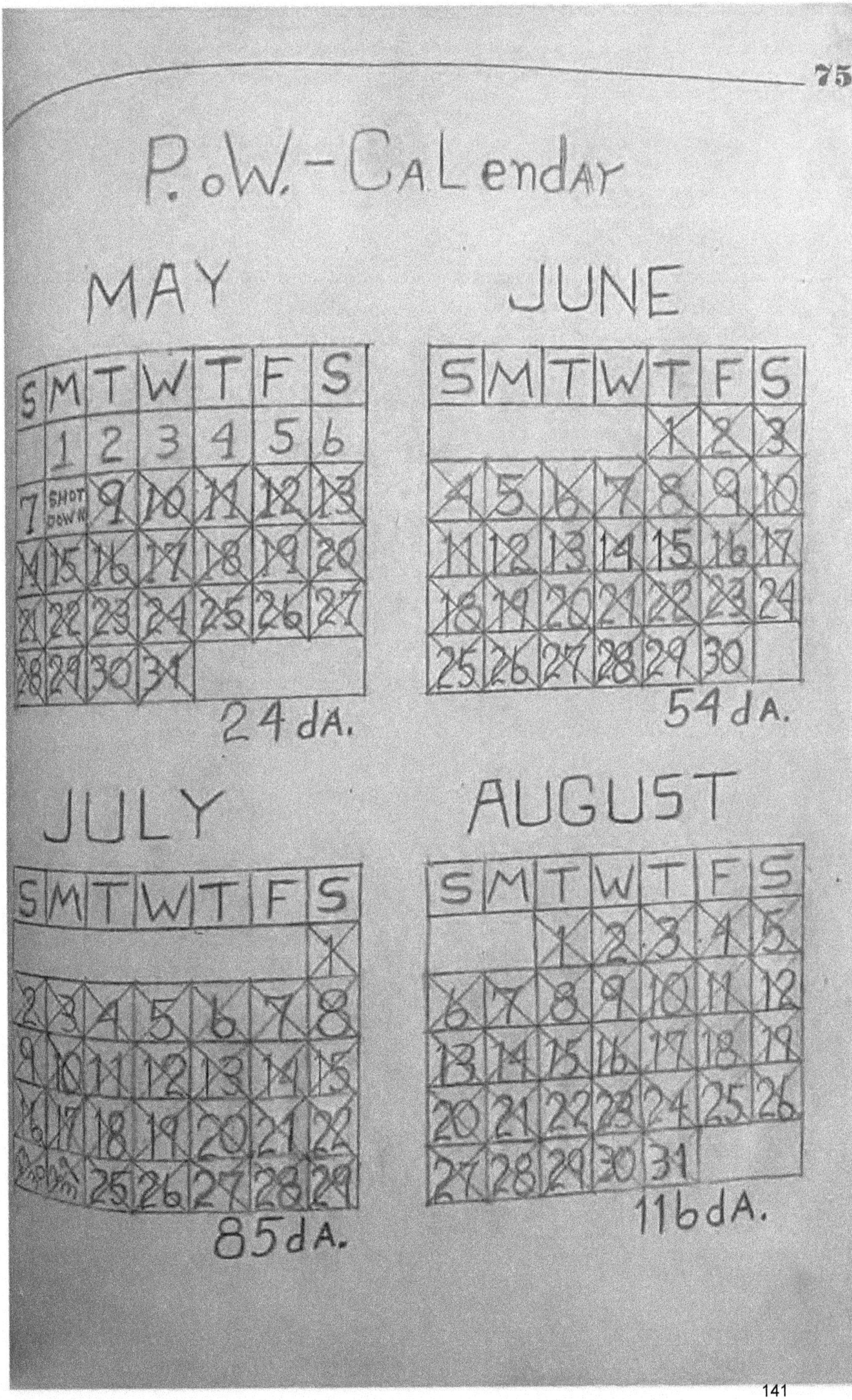

P.o.W.-Calendar

MAY

S	M	T	W	T	F	S
	1	2	3	4	5	6
7	SHOT DOWN	9	10	11	12	13
14	15	16	17	18	19	20
21	22	23	24	25	26	27
28	29	30	31			

24 dA.

JUNE

S	M	T	W	T	F	S
				1	2	3
4	5	6	7	8	9	10
11	12	13	14	15	16	17
18	19	20	21	22	23	24
25	26	27	28	29	30	

54 dA.

JULY

S	M	T	W	T	F	S
						1
2	3	4	5	6	7	8
9	10	11	12	13	14	15
16	17	18	19	20	21	22
[illegible]	[illegible]	25	26	27	28	29

85 dA.

AUGUST

S	M	T	W	T	F	S
		1	2	3	4	5
6	7	8	9	10	11	12
13	14	15	16	17	18	19
20	21	22	23	24	25	26
27	28	29	30	31		

116 dA.

SEPTEMBER

S	M	T	W	T	F	S
					1	2
3	4	5	6	7	8	9
10	11	12	13	14	15	16
17	18	19	20	21	22	23
24	25	26	27	28	29	30

146 dA.

OCTOBER

S	M	T	W	T	F	S
1	2	3	4	5	6	7
8	9	10	11	12	13	14
15	16	17	18	19	20	21
22	23	24	25	26	27	28
29	30	31				

177 dA.

NOVEMBER

S	M	T	W	T	F	S
			1	2	3	4
5	6	7	8	9	10	11
12	13	14	15	16	17	18
19	20	21	22	23	24	25
26	27	28	29	30		

207 dA.

DECEMBER

S	M	T	W	T	F	S
					1	2
3	4	5	6	7	8	9
10	11	12	13	14	15	16
17	18	19	20	21	22	23
24	25	26	27	28	29	30

238 dA.

My research shows Dad and about 80,000 men left Stalag Luft IV in Kiefheide, Germany January 31st, and marched until February 7th to Nürnberg.

The men were ill-equipped to march in the often -13°F temperatures. They were malnourished, consuming less than 2,000 calories a day, some for years, were not in good physical shape, and did not have proper clothing (including shoes) for the extreme weather.

Dad stayed in Nürnberg until he marched again leaving Nürnberg at 12:00AM April 4, 1945.(see dad's notes on The EXODUS page 345).

No X's on the calendar after March 10, 1945, but he was liberated May 12, 1945, just past his one year mark from his date of capture May 8, 1944.

JANUARY

S	M	T	W	T	F	S
	1	2	3	4	5	6
7	8	9	10	11	12	13
14	15	16	17	18	19	20
21	22	23	24	25	26	27
28	29	30	31	Left [illegible]		

269 dA

FEBRUARY

S	M	T	W	T	F	S
				1	2	3
Arrived [illegible]						
4	5	6	7	8	9	10
11	12	13	14	15	16	17
18	19	20	21	22	23	24
25	26	27	28			

297 dA.

MARCH

S	M	T	W	T	F	S
				1	2	3
4	5	6	7	8	9	10
11	12	13	15	16	17	18
18	19	20	21	22	23	24
25	26	27	28	29	30	31

APRIL

S	M	T	W	T	F	S
1	2	3	4	5	6	7
8	9	10	11	12	13	14
15	16	17	18	19	20	21
22	23	24	25	26	27	28
29	30					

106th Infantry Division

106th Infantry Division
(earlier version)

Hash Marks Displaying Time of Service

8th Army Air Force Shoulder Insignia

A Burst of Flak

You're flying in the sky so Blue
The Flak comes up so straight and true
It hits the plane and drives you back
The cause of it is a Burst of Flak

The fighters then come with a bloody thirst
To give you a taste of a 20 m.m. burst
It knocks your baddies on their back
And the cause of it was a burst of Flak

You grab your chute and head for the door
Cause your plane is disabled, your wounded and sore
As you hit the silk the sky goes black
And the cause of it all was a burst of Flak

You fall through the air and all is quiet
The ship goes down the faithful kite
Then you hit the ground with a sodden smack
The cause of it all was a burst of Flak

The farmers and soldiers come over the hill
With blood in their eyes and ready to kill
They lift you up and give you a smack
The cause of it all was a burst of Flak

They gather the crew and march you to town
Where the people watch you with a frown
They lock you up in a filthy shack
And the cause of it all was a burst of Flak

Dulag-Luft is the name of the hole
Where they ask you questions to see what you know
But the "Yanks" refuse with wits intack
And the cause of it all was a burst of Flak

A Burst of Flak

You're flying in the sky so Blue
The Flak coming up so straight and true
It hits the plane and drives you back
The cause of it is a Burst of Flak

The fighters then come with a bloody thirst
To give you a taste of a 20 m.m. burst
It knocks your buddies on their back
And the cause of it was a burst of Flak

You grab your chute and head for the door
Cause your plane is disabled. Your wounded and sore
As you hit the silk the sky goes black
And the cause of it all was a burst of Flak

You fall through the air and all is quiet
The ship goes down the faithful kite
Then you hit the ground with a sudden smack
The cause of it all was a burst of Flak

The farmers and soldiers come over the hill
With blood in their eyes and ready to kill
They lift you up and give you a smack
The cause of it all was a burst of Flak

They gather the crew and march you to town
Where the people watch you with a frown
They lock you up I a filthy shack
And the cause of it was a burst of Flak

Dulag-Luft is the name of the hole
Where they ask you questions to see what you know
But the "Yanks" refuse with wits intack
And the cause of it all was a burst of Flak

Then you go to the Barbed-wire Camp
Where you're only Friend is a Red Cross stamp
You sleep on the floor and it hurts your back
The cause of it all was a burst of Flak

We sit and think of our girls and wifes so true
And the boys still flying up in the blue
Of pillows and sheets that make their sacks
Where we never hear a burst of Flak

Barbed Wire Hotel

In North Western Germany
There's a beautiful spot
It's a barbed wire hotel
Where the meals are served hot

Fourth of a loaf of bread per day
A bowl of German stew
A small chunk of horse meat
A can of weak English brew

All these come free
It doesn't cost a cent
Your meals and sack
Both go with the rent

There you will meet Ober Leutenant Volts
But you will like him in spite of Hell
For he is the manager
Of the barbed wire Hotel.

Then you go to the Barbed-wire Camp
Where you've only Friend is a Red Cross stamp
You sleep on the floor and it hurts your back
The cause of it all was a burst of Flak
We sit and think of our girls and wifes so true
And the boys still flying up in the blue
Of pillows and sheets that makes their sacks
Where we never hear a burst of Flak

Barbed Wire Hotel

In North Western Germany
There's a beautiful spot
It's a barbed wire hotel
Where the meals are served hot
Fourth of a loaf of bread per day
A bowl of German stew
A small chunk of horsemeat
A can of weak English brew
All this comes free
It dosen't cost a cent
Your meals and sack
Both go with the rent
If you want to visit
This hotel so neat
Fly a mission over Germany
Where the Flak is thick
There you will meet Ober Leutenant Volts
But you will like him in spite of [illegible]
For he is the manager
Of the barbed wire Hotel.

The drawing on the opposite page was drawn by my dad during his time in Stalag Luft IV, which was in Keifheide, Germany. He left Luft IV and Keifheide January 31, 1944 in a march to Nürnberg. It took 8 days in freezing weather to make the journey, by foot.

When my dad was first captured he was in Stalag Luft III, which, if a prison camp can be praised, Luft III was one of the better camps with one two-minute cold shower every two months, occasional football playing, a library, and well organized by the POW's.

Stalag Luft IV was not well organized, there were no showers at all, no library, no activities other than 200 men being locked in their barracks for most of each day with nothing to do but draw, write, and talk.

"WELCOME HOME"

KRIEGSGEFANGENLAGER #4
KEIFHEIDE, GERMANY

Mail from home often took 2-3 months for the POW to receive. By then, even in my dad's case, the POW could have been moved to a new camp (or 2) creating even more delays. I suspect it took family and friends quite a bit of time to figure this out.

POW's were also only allowed to send 2 letters and 4 cards monthly.

Guards often confiscated packages for themselves that were sent from home.

OH HAPPY DAY
Friday At 1:01 PM.
"You've Got It"
Friday At 1:01 PM.
"You've Had It"

Prisoners of War often went from complete boredom to sheer freak-out because of the continual air raids. While they did get used to them, the volume could cause even experienced POW's to become a bit anxious.

S'MATTER FELLERS?
WHEEEYEW
-AIR-RAID-VIRGIN!

And to think Joe mailed that letter 2-3 months ago...

JOE SAYS "HE'S HAD MY PARCEL"
I GUESS THAT MEANS HE'S
RECEIVED IT!

POW's were given 2 "lumps" of coal in which to keep warm...and try to cook with. The POW's pooled their lumps of coal to make more heat for everyone. With winter temps at -13 F and the POW's not having proper clothing, I'm sure they were tempted to use the sides of the building for kindling.

I was impressed that my dad seemed to capture the true look of the wood barracks that matches many of the photographs.

COAL-SHORTAGE

According to my research, the men may have run for chow, but it was only out of desperation and starvation. The food, from the coffee, to the beer, to the slivers of meat were some of the most vial food the POW's would ever eat. So it is no wonder when the Red Cross brought chocolate for the POW's they relished in their treats.

Latrines were probably the most disgusting places in the camps. They were never cleaned making rat, lice, flea, and other problems even worse.

POW's so relied on letters from home to keep their spirits high. When a POW did not receive a letter from home in a while, other POW's share their's with him.

It was heartbreaking when a POW would receive a "Dear John" letter from a girlfriend or wife. In true POW spirit, they all banded together to console the heartbroken.

NO MAIL
TWO YEARS
MILK
MILK

"Sweating it out"
(Got to go!)

HAROLD W. SCULL
3 HUDSON ST.
CRIS FIELD Md.

LEWIS M RUSH
429 E. 6th
HUTCHINSON KAN.

ARTHUR H. WAY
CORDELL, MICH.

JAMES E. CLARK
19th Ave.
Meridian Miss.

HAROLD W. NININGER
213 SO. ELM ST
Mc Pherson, KANSAS
"Shorty"

ARMANDO FAZZONE
102 HERBERT ST.
Redbank N.J.
Ph-1996R
"Fuzzy"

DALE HELMER
133 MARSHALL St.
Coldwater Mich.

Claude W. Brown
10 South Maybelle
Tulsa. OKLA.

VINCENT GALLOZZI
174 W. Granada
Hershey PENN.
Ph 2527 "VINCE"

James H. DAVIS
7434 Leadale Drive
Wellston Hills Miso.

Kenneth E. Parker
Box #344
TUNICA Miss.

David F. Finkle
921 N.W. First Ave
Hampton Iowa
Dave

Anthony J. Delcizzi
372 Watertown St
Newton Mass
"Dell"

Edward J. Hunter
#2 Gandy St.
N.side Pitts. Pa
"Eddie"

Kenneth J. Mellon
R.R.2
Fredonia KAN.
Ph. 302-J "Mell"

Edwin R. Scott
839 Garden St
Olean. N.Y.
"Scotty"

EARL V. Muller
4320 Torrence Ave.
HAMMOND IND.
"Mull"

William N. Lloyd
R.R. 2
Commanche Tex
"Tex"

Albert J. Gardella
8801 Shore Rd.
Brooklyn N.Y.

Charles E. Patterson
56 Wyckoff Ave.
MANASQUAN N.J.

LAWANCE LANGWELL
RFD #1
MANISTIQUE, MICH.

Carl T. Fields 6th & Cherry St. Port Townson Wash.	Wade H. Prince 212 Maple St Rockville Center L.I. N.Y.	Don E. Halloway P.O. # 57 Battle Ground, IND.
Bernard D. Belletieve 906 Ave C. Brooklyn N.Y. "Benny"	Curtiss S. Jensen 5267 Everts Lane Pacific Beach (9) San Diego, Calif. "Shorty"	Wallace Tharp Col. Springs Colorado.
Fred Pitcher [Kinser] 132 2nd ST Anamosa Iowa	Louis Zommer Route 3 Box 447 Miami Fla. "Doke"	Lewis E. Chinn Beaver Dam Ky.
Buren F. Powell 917 Magoffen Ave. El Paso Tex.	Paul Chagnon 37 Lasayette Place Salem Mass	Albert H. Saltau 7615 Washington St K.C. Mo.
Otto Stange Brooq 246th St Bell Rose L.I. N.Y.	Charles P. Sierra 130-19-117th St Ozone Park. L.I. N.Y. "Chuck."	Robert W. Kleeman Elizabeth Colo.
John Jacoby 7781 Ritchie St Oakland Calif.	George E. Walter 128 Cooper St. Uppermontclair N.J.	Reyes V. Torres 3025 Cera St El Paso, Tex.
Gordon L. Lowe 210½ Depot St Greenville Tenn "Toten"	Frank R. Talia. 325 Parson St. Harrison N.Y.	Ted. A. Eikrem Alexander N. Dakota

W.B. Elliott 8625 N. Hurst Ave. Portland (3) Ore.	DAN. J. Reynolds 260 GEL Thorpe Ave Atlanta GA.	Pierre Collin 14 Rue Pierre Cu[illegible] E. Pinal (Vosges) Fran[illegible]
Louis D. Guillory % White Kitchen 537 St. Clai Borne Ave New Orleans La "Gil"	James J. Verdi 1235 Buttonwood St Phil. PA. Ph. Fre. 4730	Albert Grick Box 2 South Mont[illegible] Penn.
Glynn Matthews Box 941 Engleside Tex. (MATT)	Adolfo von W. Fouga. 642 Essex St. San Antonio, Tex. (AL)	Dan. V. Matlock Box 353 Monahans, Tex.
Carl R. Fegely Mertztown PA. RT. 1 (Goon)	Charles F. Cannon 546 S. Mc. Donough Montgomery Ala (Cannonball)	Eugene C. Arkett 100 Clover Ave. Elwood City Pa (Spark[illegible])
John B. Costalletty 1715 W. Dalena Milwaukee Wis. (Jockey)	Stanley F. Lepkowski 19 Hillside Ave. Schenectady N.Y.	Edward M. Gonzales P.O. Box 65 Del Mar. Calif.
Ralph Liedtke 1420 W. Chambers St. Milwaukee Wis.	Carrol E. Graves 95 Cleveland Ave S.E. Atlanta GA. (Good Buddy)	Joseph V. O'Donnell Jr. 133 Nysonset Ave. Dorchester Mass.
William A. Reynolds No 25 Beulah St. Pueblo Colo (Deacon)	Fred W. Bittner 635 2nd Ave Lyndhurst N.J.	Dwight F. Galyon 428 Monter St. Dennison Tex. (Red)

Elias Fay 171 New Jersey Ave. Brooklyn, N.Y.C. N.Y.	Dwight K. MacCrachem Ebensburg Pa. (Mac)	A.E. Brown 1718 Elizabeth St. Scranton, 4, Pa.
William Lee Rt. 1 Box 171 Mesa, Arizona	Thomas W. Cima Box 287 Edgemont Sta. E. St. Louis, Ill.	Charles L. Roberts 144 Avery St. Mt. Clemens Mich.
Dennis D. Fay Deer River New York.	Fred Korhonen 657 Florence St. Astoria, Oregon.	Fred G. Perkins Box 523 Hoscoe Pa. (Buck)
Frank Zywiczynski 3119 Glenwood ST Toledo, Ohio	George Diggins No 3 Oder ST. Marcus Hook, PA.	Charles L. Willard Route 1 Blevins PA. (Arkie)
Jack B. Pope Gen. Del. Mena, Ark	Darwin E. Marl 2721 Falton ST Everett Wash. Dody	Edward M. Waters 5324 Kansas Ave. N.W. Wash D.C.
Carl F. Glade 188 Guernsey Ave. Columbus, Ohio	Everett N. Howe 124 Buckingham Ave. Syracuse N.Y (Baldy)	Robert R. Robinson 431 7th Ave South Wis. Rapids, Wis. (Robbie)
Dale J. Johnson Washta, Iowa (Johnny)	Eugene A. Tomlin 2305-6th Ave. No. Birmingham Ala. (Pinky)	Angelo J. Aratari 27 Desinger Place Rochester N.Y. (Red)

Laurence Light P.O. Box 111 Llano Tex.	Carroll Middleton 209 S. Sterling St Streeter Ill. (Jr.)	Edwin W. Estridge Rt. 1 # 2 Bethune, S.C. (Colonel)
Robert L. Caryl Gainesville N.Y.	John R. Lemons Jr. 516 Park View Dalas Tex. (Tex)	Robert P. Marcell Rt. Box 190 Wausau Wis.
Raymond Wallach 1126 W. Pratt Blvd. Chicago Ill.	Baldimerio A. Estala 701 Nogalitos St. San Antonio, Tex.	Donald W. York Richland Mo.
R.A. Von Sternberg 10 - Bon Mar Road Pelham Manor, N.Y., N.Y.	James Radford 992 Bedla Pl. Memphis Tenn	Daniel G. Kricke 2216 Leland Ave. Chicago, Ill.
Sylvester A. Freeze 111-47-130th St. Ozone Park L.I. N.Y.	Bill J. Shelton 918 N. Washington Enid, Okla.	Eddie Fialkowski 2359 Trombly St Detroit, Mich.
Alexander Klecha 72 Albert St Garfield N.J. (Al)	Windsor E. Graham Lithonia Rt. 2 Georgia.	Ned R. Lewis 615 Bowman Ave. East Alton, Ill. (444[illegible]
James C. Smith 733 Salem Ave Elizabeth, N.J.		

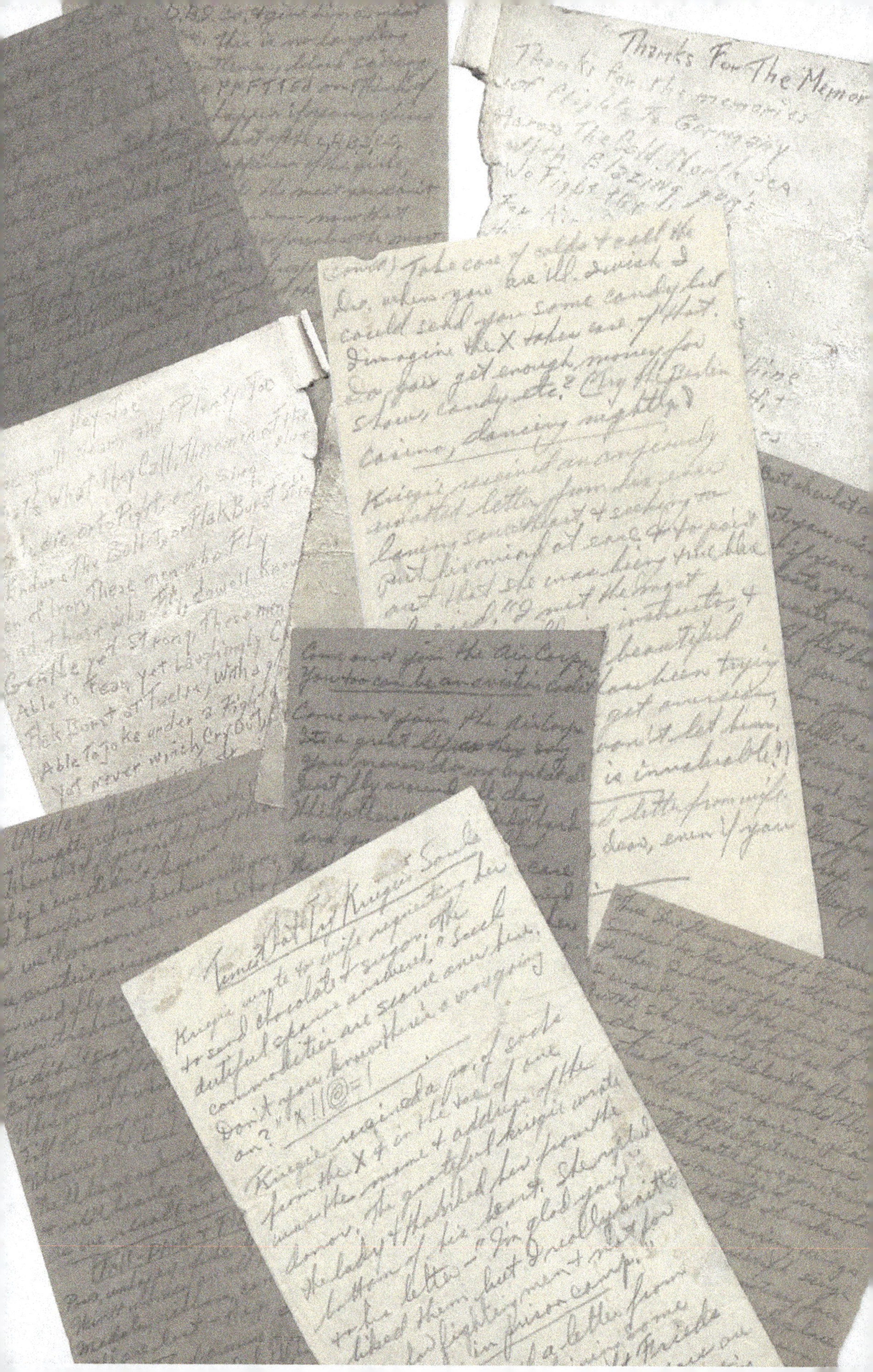
Thanks For The Memor
Come and join the Air Corps
Come and join the Air Corps

Musings and Cigarettes

A Kriegie wrote home for his bank balance. Six months later the reply came back “Guess”. said his Mother – He made his guess, six months later another reply came back “Wrong, guess again.”

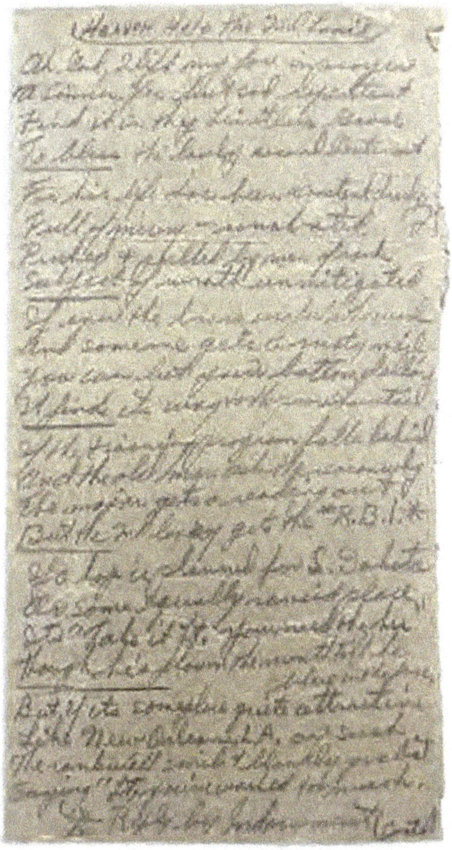

Heaven Help the 2nd Louie

Oh God, I lift my face in prayer
A simmer, Yes, but sad repentant
Find it in thy Limitless Good
To bless the lonely second lieutenant

For his life has been a constant drudgery
Full of misery – unabated
Pushed & pulled by men of rank
Subject of wrath unmitigated

If ever the brass snafu's the work
And someone gets a rusty nail,
You can bet your bottom dollar
It finds its way to the shavetail

If the training program falls behind
And the old man ask the reason why
The major gets a reading out
But the 2nd looey gets the *R.B.I.*

If a hop is planned for S. Dakota
Or some equally named place
Its "Take it Lt. You need the hrs"
Though he's flown the month till he blue in the face.

But if its someplace quite attractive
Like New Orleans, L.A. or Sarah
The rank will smile & blondly grabit
Saying "Lt, you've worked too much.

Reply by Indorsement

(contd)

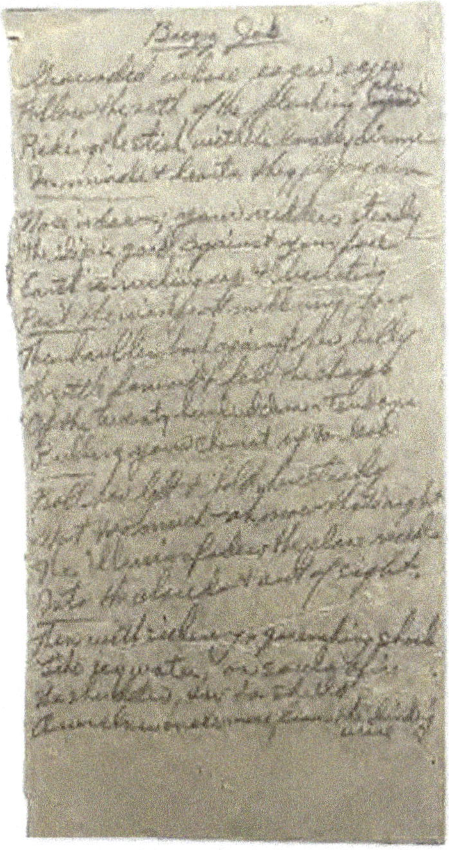

Buzz Joe

Grounded whose eager eyes
Follow the path of the flashing plane
Riding the stick with the lovely airmen
In minds & hearts they flying aim

Nose is down; your rudders steady
The ship is good against your face
Earth is reaching up & bursting
Past the wings that maddening pace

Then haul her back against her belly
Throttle forward & feel the charge
Of the twenty hundred demon tendons
Pulling your chariot up to God

Roll her left & hold her steady
Not too much – oh, now that's right
The illusion fades, the plane recedes
Into the clouds & out of sight.

Then with sickening, quenching shock
Like icy water, on souls afire
We shudder, try to shield
Ourselves once more from the binding wire.

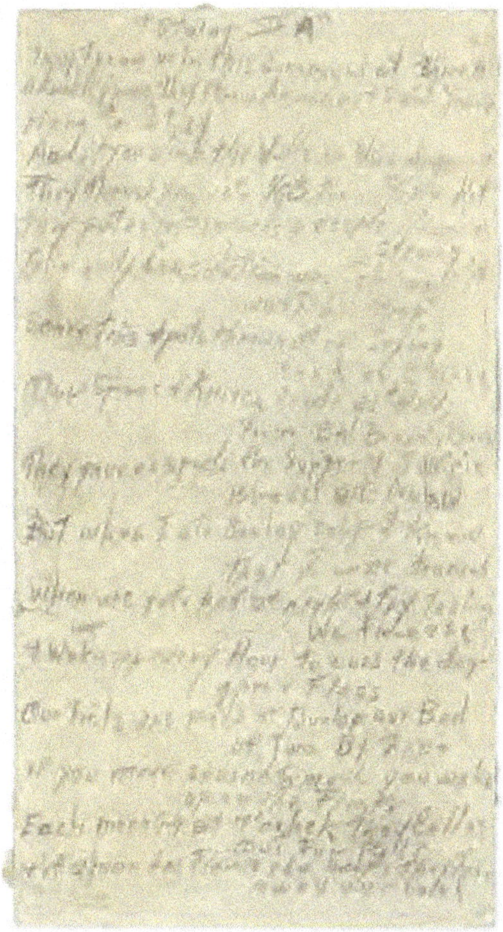

"Stalag III A"

They Threw us in this compound at "Three A"
A double fence they threw Around us & said you're Here to Stay
And if you climb the Walls or Wire do you cut
They threw you into 40B The Solitary Hut
They put us in Barracks a couple Hundred strong.
Our only Consolation was "oh well. It won't be long."
Some tins & pots throw at us saying Cook or Starve,
Our Spoons & Knives, Crude as Hell, from Bed Boards Carved
They gave us spuds for Supper & Jerrie Bread at Noon
But when I ate Barley soup I knew that I was doomed
When we go to bed at night & try to sleep We Freeze
& Wake up every Hour to cuss the dog gone Fleas
Our Ticts are made of Burlap our Bed of Two By Four
IF you move around to much you wake up on the Floor.
Each morning at 7'oclock they Call us out For Roll
& if a man has Flown the coop, They take away our coal.

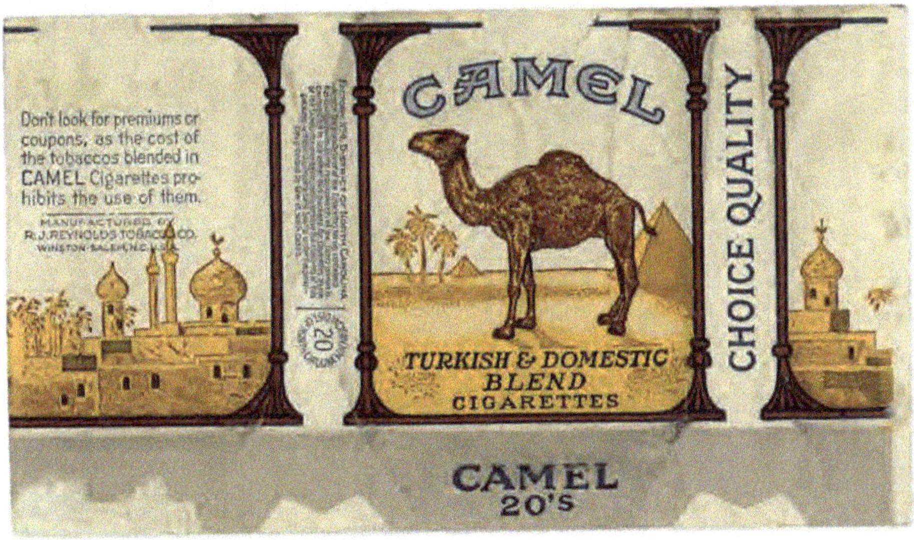

(quotes from other POW letters)

Darling, be home soon won't
You? Take care of Andy when
You are out drinking. He is
So wild. Can you buy beer
Or do they just sell wine?
Are the German girls good dancers?

Fiancé to P.O.W "Darling married
Your father. Love Mother.

Receiving a Red Cross Sweater a
P.O.W. wrote thanking donor
& received this reply "I'm sorry
You received it. I meant it
for someone in active service."

Darling, can I send you any money

I am glad you are true to me
but I want you to go out &
have a good time if you can.

Honey do you have your locker
& radio with you.

I'd send your golf clubs
but the P.O. won't allow it.

Here's a money order for $10.00
If you need more let me know.

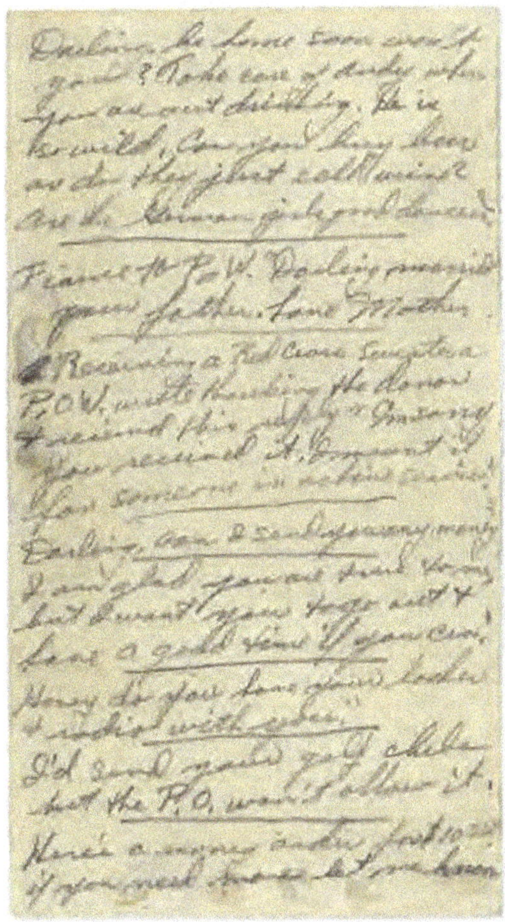

(quotes from other POW letters)

"I'm sorry, John, our Engagement is broken
I think its too bad you
didn't stay with the ship."

"Son, even though
you did bail out; we still
love you."

POW since 1941. "Darling
I have just had a baby.
but don't worry, Mother
forgives me. The American
officer is sending you
cigarettes.

(From POW wife). "How is your
Mother & Dad. I haven't
Been able to see them lately"

Wife of P.O.W writes "I am
Going to Kent in two weeks,
Do you mind? Write &
let me know.

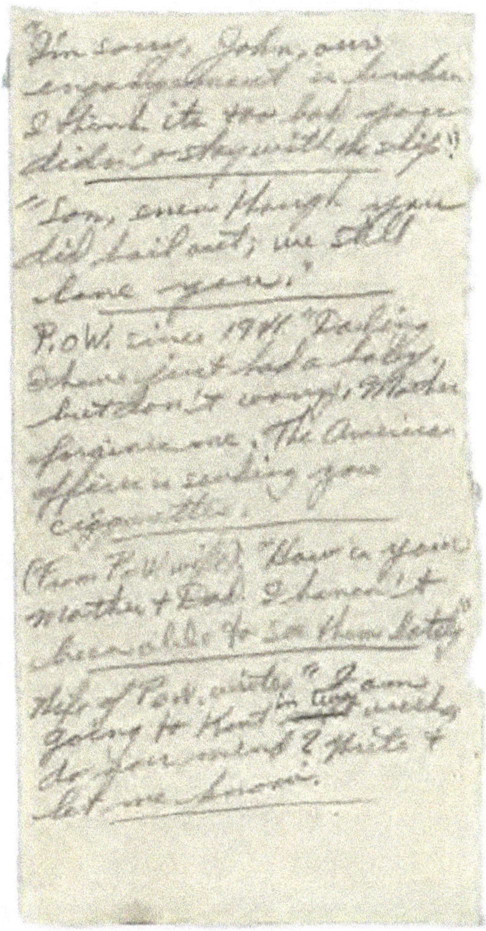

EXTRACTS From P.O.W. Letters

Darling, I was so glad you
was shot down before
flying became dangerous.

Darling, In your letter
you ask for slippers.
What color would you like?

Darling, The words after lousey
when describing your new
camp were censored.

To a P.O.W. shot down Jan 1943
"I'm sorry to hear you were
shot down so early in the war."

"Darling, I hope you are
staying true to me."

Darling, I have just been
in bed with bronchitis.
That's the name of a complaint
not a boyfriend.

First letter from Financee. "Dear
Sergeant. You were missing
for a month so I got married."

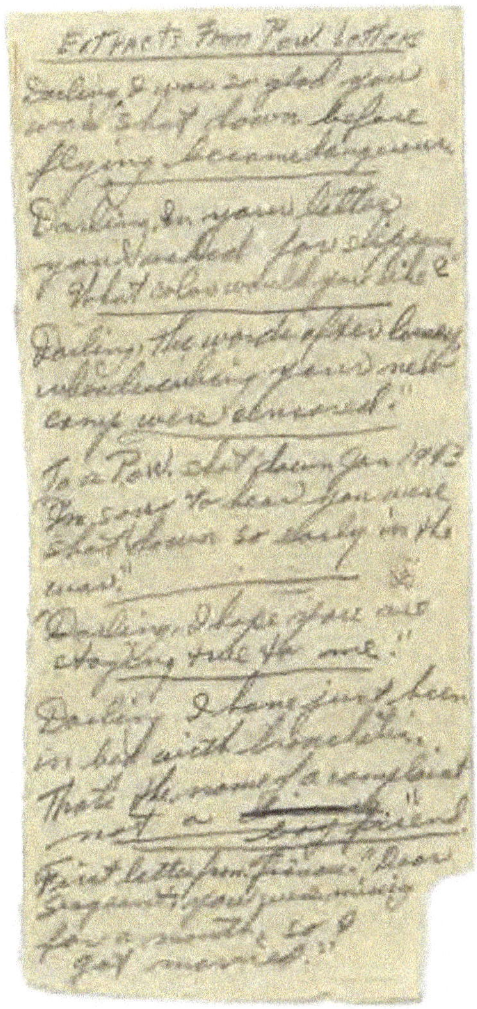
EXTRACTS From Pow letters
Darling I was so glad you
was shot down before
flying became dangerous
Darling In your letter
you asked for slippers
What color would you like?
Darling the words after lousey
when describing your new
camp were censored."
To a Pow. shot down Jan 1943
I'm sorry to hear you were
shot down so early in the
war."
Darling I hope you are
staying true to me."
Darling I have just been
in bed with bronchitis.
That's the name of a complaint
not a boyfriend.
First letter from fiancee. "Dear
Sergeant you were missing
for a month, so I
got married."

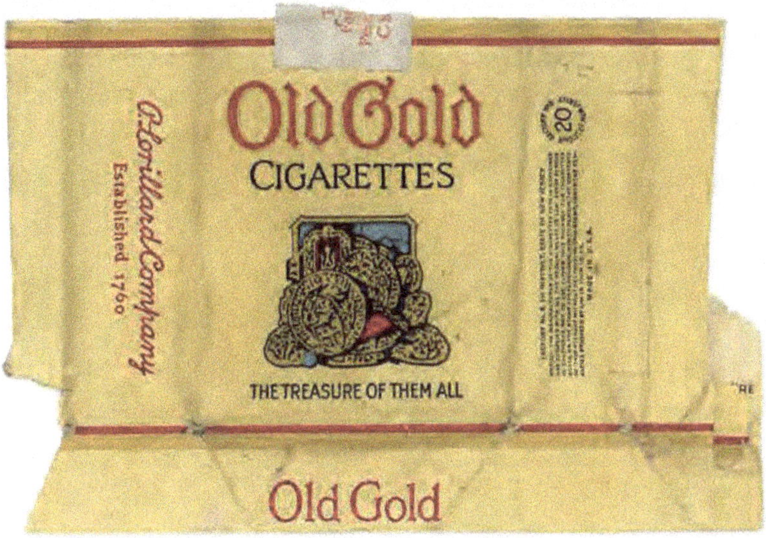

AN IDEA

"A man in this war is not willing to die
in a B-17, because he feels it is for a
cause; nor does he invite the fire of an
88mm Flack gun because he is
spiritually uplifted. The exaltation of battle
is known to be physical hysteria & mental
& Spiritual hoping. The men die in the Faith
that death cannot possibly come to them.
It is somehow an accident which happens
To others - not ever to them.

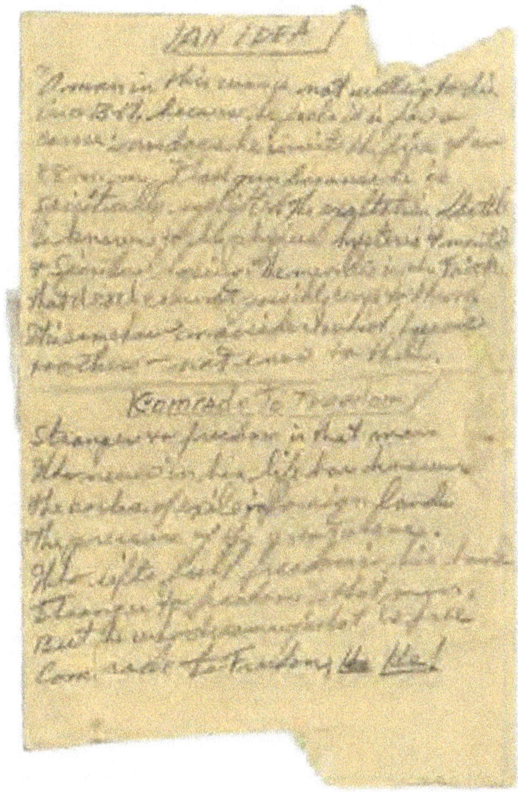

Comrade To Freedom

Stranger to freedom is that man
Who never in his life has known
The barbs of exile in foreign lands
The pressure of the great alone.
Who sifts full freedom in the hand
Stranger to freedom is that man,
But he who dreams of what is free.
Comrade to Freedom, He He!

How I Was Shot Down
(By Anonymus Kriegies)

-Flak at twelve o'clock
-Top turrent of B-17 (Fighter pilot)
-Fell out waist window (Gunner B-24}
-Ran out of Gas
-Here comes the P-SI's
-Eager Wingman (Fighter Pilot)
-Formation turned right - we turned left.
-Crash landed 1-mile from Switzerland
-Flak, our guns (Fighters over invasion front)
-Propagandized flak gunners.
-No rear view mirror
-One lucky shot
-I thought that was lands end
-Our escort was R.A.F. - PSIs
-We went to Big Bee
-I didn't see the fence post.
-Didn't think he had enough lead on me
-Let's make one more run
-Polesti, summer 1943
-Ju52 out of the sun
-I zigged when I should have zagged

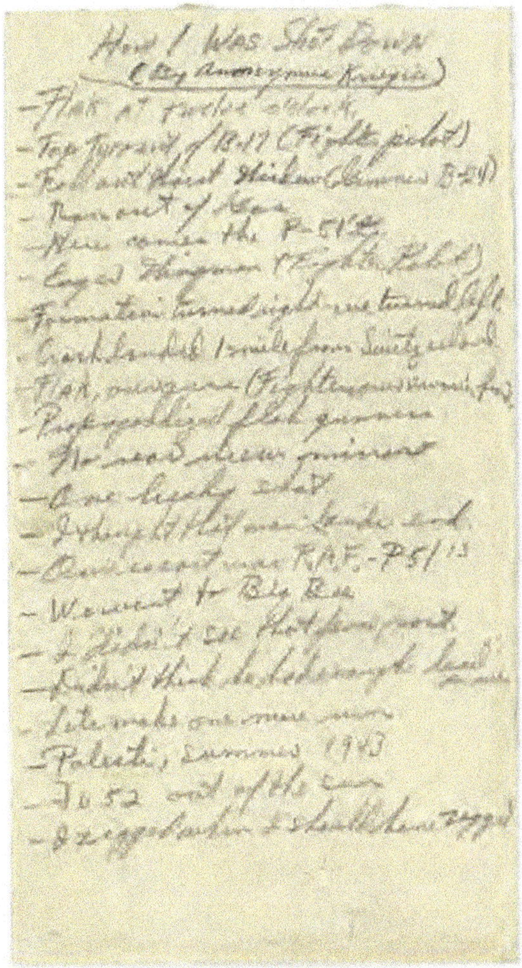
How I Was Shot Down
(By Anonymus Kriegie)
-Flak at twelve o'clock
-Top turrent of B-17 (Fighter pilot)
-Fell out waist window (Gunner B-24)
-Ran out of Gas
-Here comes the P-51's
-Eager Wingman (Fighter Pilot)
-Formation turned right we turned left
-Crash landed 1 mile from Switzerland
-Flak, our guns (Fighters over invasion front)
-Propagandized flak gunners
-No rear view mirror
-One lucky shot
-I thought that was lands end
-Our escort was R.A.F. - P51's
-We went to Big Bee
-I didn't see that fence post
-Didn't think he had enough lead on me
-Lets make one more run
-Polesti, summer 1943
-Ju52 out of the sun
-I zigged when I should have zagged

BA

They Say we Bomb their Railroads, This
we know is True.
Our Red Cross Parcels never come,
Their Trains cannot come through
Some days we had a little fun, Our Faces Filled
with Laughter
They bring their dogs upon the scene we
Head for the rafters
So when this war is over & our Enemy
we have Beat
I wouldn't be a bit surprised IF the
Dogs have Jerrie meat.

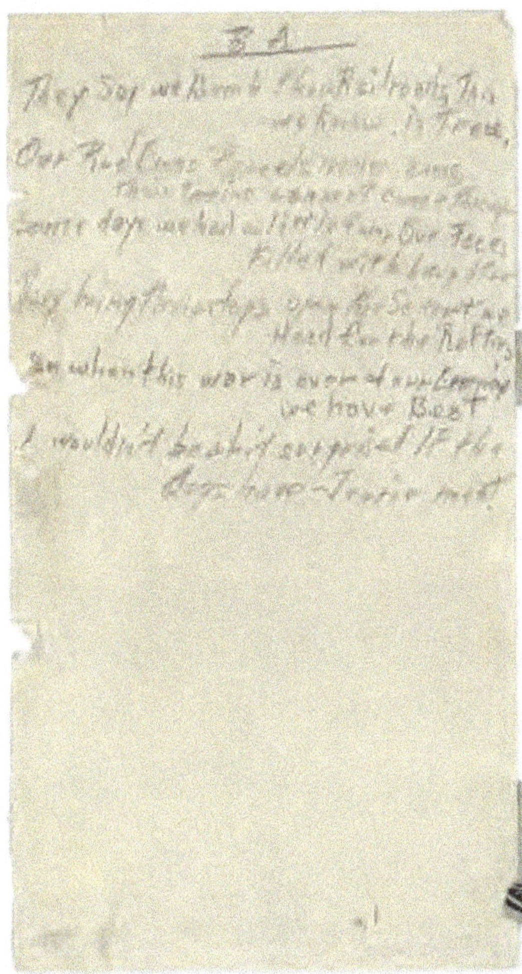

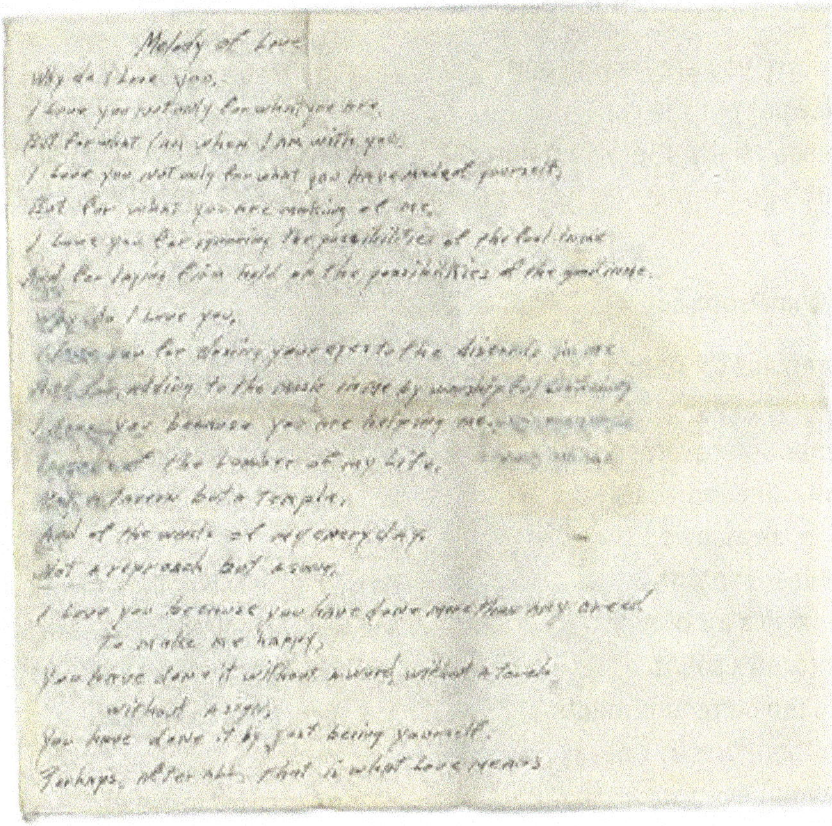

Melody of Love

Why do I love you?
I love you not only for what you are,
But for what I am when I am with you.
I love you not only for what you have made of yourself,
But for what you are making of me,
I love you for ignoring the possibilities of the fool in me
And for laying firm hold on the possibilities of the good in me.
Why do I love you?
I love you for closing your eyes to the discords in me
And for adding to the music in me by worshipful listening.
I love you because you are helping me
To make of the lumber of my life
Not a tavern but a temple,
And of the words of my every day
Not a reproach but a song.
I love you because you have done more than any creed
to make me happy,
You have done it without a word, without a touch,
without a sign,
You have done it by just being yourself.
Perhaps, after all, that is what love means.

She didn't go for that

She said, "Sorry you are leaving early."
On your way put out the cat."
"I'm not leavin', Baby, there's no hurry"
But she didn't go for that

Post War Prophecy

My postwar plans for happiness
Effect a million souls,
I'd like to mention several points
To define my aim and goals
I do not plan, as many do,
To live in sweet content
But aim to raise a lot of hell
Until my fortune's spent
I'll break all ten commandments
Yes, smash them one by one
Nice folks won't even speak to me
But boy, won't I have fun.
I'll pillage plunder, rape and steal,
Select a shapely frauline
And hide away for many months
With her as my companion
I'll refuse to be influenced
By religious sects or creeds.
I'll be looked upon in worse contempt
Than familiarity breeds.
I'll flirt with all the pretty dames
That I see in every drive.
If plans work out, I'll be the worst
Adulterous man alive
And when my violent program
Has scorched my soul well
I'll be prepared to pass away
And gently go to Hell!

If I Have to Go Back

Wherever this war's last battles spent,
And I am beckoned to freedom's track
Ca I take on a life of self content:
Can I stand it if I have to go back?

With nothing to do but loll around
An nothing to eat but steaks,
With nothing to drink but seven-crown
And no place to fish but in the lake,

No place to sit but the living room lounge
And no place to sleep but on a soft bed
With nothing to wear but a chalked striped shirt
And a pork-pie in on my head.

No place to go but to parties,
All dressed up in evening clothes
No one to date but good looking girls
And nothing to see but the shaws

Nothing to drive but an automobile
With nothing but gas in the tank
With a four digit no. in my checking account
And nothing but dough in the bank

Back to the same old civilian life
Doing just as I wish & please
Just going & coming whenever I like
Tied down to a life of ease.

Oh to be condemned to a life like that
What a pity, alas and alack!
Just how can I stand it
If I have to go back!

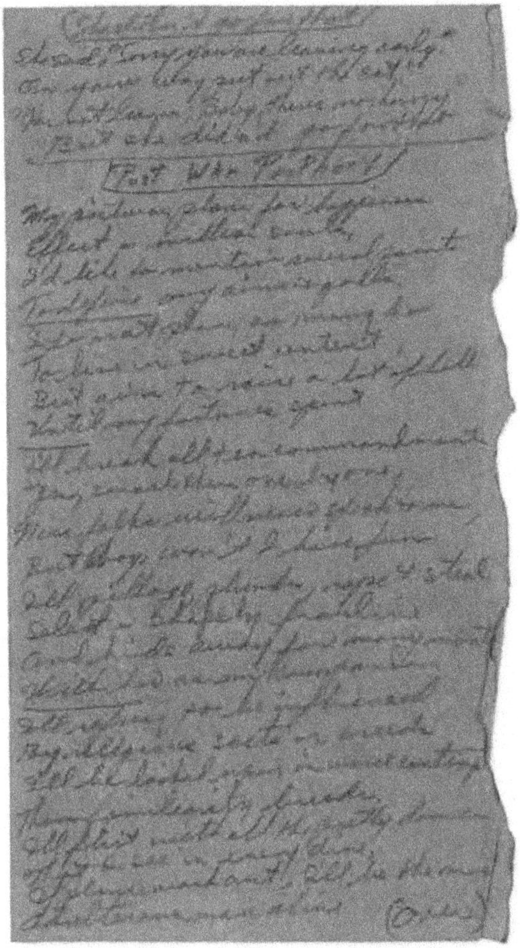

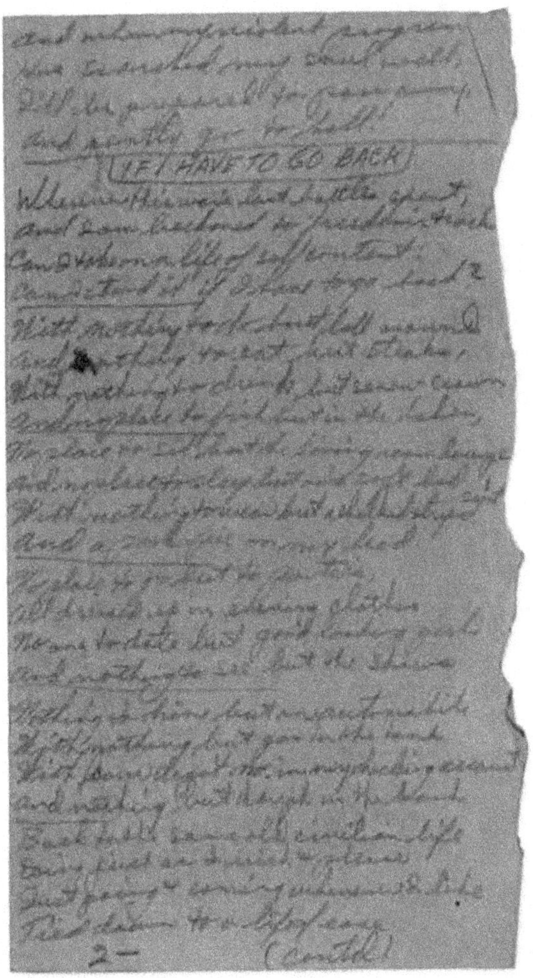
IF I HAVE TO GO BACK
2 —
(Cont'd)

Its Communal

Just a note to you Kriegies who dropped
in late. On connecting your life to the communal state.
You'll find before long 'ere you selected to stay
That the best way of life is the communal way.
We have communal pots and communal pan
Com. shows and com. cans...
Our paper is com. and so's our pen
There's even com. coal in a com. bin.
There's com. brushes and communal brooms
We've a communal school in a communal room.
Com classes and com books...
And even the teachers wear com looks.
There's a com news room with com news
And two com papers from which you can choose.
There are com docks with com drugs
We've even got pants with com bugs
There's a com playground with com sports
And com privies we call the "aborts"
But the one thing is lacking and brighter this life...
And that's com shacking with a communal wife.

HEART THAT FAILED

A plane 4 a pilot with silver wings
Up in the ocean of heavens blue
Swinging high above where the swallow sings
O'er ascending the rainbows hill.

The pilot, possessor of hand and brain
Guides the craft in its eager climb
While the motored heart, with throbbing strains
Beats a cadence of metered rhyme.

The brain was trained to guide the hand
& the hand, to guide the plane.
& the motored heart was built to stand
The trials of stress and strain.

But if the throbbing heart should fail
& the pilot should leave his plane,
With brain & hand & chute to bail
Out in the depth of space

Deserting craft with stilling heart
He exploits to extol
Then think ye heavens gates would past
For the crafts undying soul.

2 - cont'd) If I have to go back

[illegible] to [illegible] [illegible] [illegible], that
[illegible] [illegible] [illegible] [illegible]
[illegible] [illegible] [illegible] it
If I have to go back

Tis Communal

Just a note to youth [illegible], who [illegible]
in hate.
On connecting your life to the communal
You'll find before long once you [illegible] [illegible]
that the best range of life is the communal way.
We have com[illegible] & com. [illegible]
Com. Showers & com. [illegible]
[illegible] in com. & [illegible]
There's a com. [illegible] in a com. [illegible]
There is com. [illegible] & com. [illegible]
There's a com. salad with com. [illegible]
Com. [illegible] & [illegible]
And even the [illegible] com. [illegible]
There's a com. [illegible] & a com. that
[illegible] [illegible] com., [illegible]
There's com. [illegible] with com. [illegible]
& two com. [illegible] from which you [illegible]
there's com. [illegible] with com. [illegible]
There's com. [illegible] with com. [illegible]
There's a com. playground with com. sports
(OVER)

and com. [illegible] we call the "shorts"
But the one thing is lacking & [illegible]
this life
and that's [illegible] sleeping with [illegible]
[illegible] [illegible].

HEART THAT FAILED

A [illegible] silver [illegible]
[illegible] in the [illegible] of [illegible]
Swinging high above [illegible] the [illegible]
O'er [illegible] the [illegible]
The spirit, possessor of hand & brain
Guided the craft with [illegible] hand,
While the [illegible] heart [illegible]
Beats a [illegible] of [illegible].
The brain was [illegible] to guide the hand
& the hand to [illegible] the [illegible]
& the [illegible] heart [illegible] & [illegible]
The [illegible] of [illegible] & strain
But if the [illegible] heart should fail
& the [illegible] leave his [illegible],
[illegible] brain & hand [illegible]
[illegible] the depths of space
[illegible] craft [illegible] [illegible]
[illegible] to [illegible]
[illegible] [illegible] wait
For the craft's [illegible]

Times That Try Kriegies Souls

Kriegies wrote to wife requesting her to send chocolate and Sugar. The dutiful spouse answered, "such commodities are scarce over here. "Don't you know there's a war going on?"

Kriegie received a pair of socks from the S and in the toe of one was the name and address of the donor. The grateful Kriegie wrote the lady and thanked her from the bottom of his heart. She replied to his letter: "I'm glad you liked them but I really knit them for fighting men and not comrades in prison camps."

Kriegie received a letter from his mother containing some sound advice: "Lt. Frieds' crew went down so you are lucky; I bet you are meeting some fine people in Germany, so don't ever try to escape. I'm sure the Germans will treat you nicely." She added, "Take care of colds and call the doctor when you are ill. I wish I could send you some candy but I am imagine the X takes care of that. Do you get enough money for show, candy, etc? (Try the Berlin Casino, dancing nightly)"

Kriegie received an anxiously awaited letter from his everloving sweetheart and seeking to put his mind at ease and to point out that she was being true she said, "I met the most handsome flying instructor and he has the most beautiful convertible. He has been trying for months to get overseas, but they just won't let him....his experience is invaluable."

Kriegie received letter from wife..."I'll still love you dear, even if you are a coward."

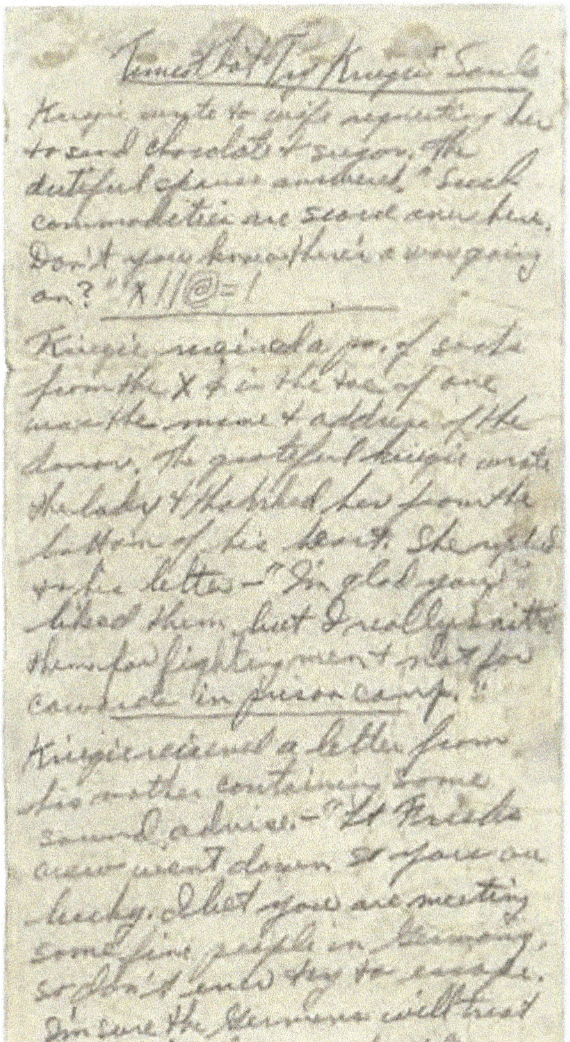
[illegible] of Kriegie [illegible]

Kriegie wrote to wife requesting her to send chocolate & sugar. The dutiful spouse answered, "Such commodities are scarce over here. Don't you know there's a war going on?" X!!@=!

Kriegie received a pr. of socks from the X & in the toe of one was the name & address of the donor. The grateful kriegie wrote the lady & thanked her from the bottom of his heart. She replied to his letter—"I'm glad you liked them, but I really knitted them for fighting men & not for cowards in prison camp."

Kriegie received a letter from his mother containing some sound advice.—"Lt Brooks crew went down so you are lucky. I bet you are meeting some fine people in Germany, so don't ever try to escape. I'm sure the Germans will treat you nicely (cont'd)

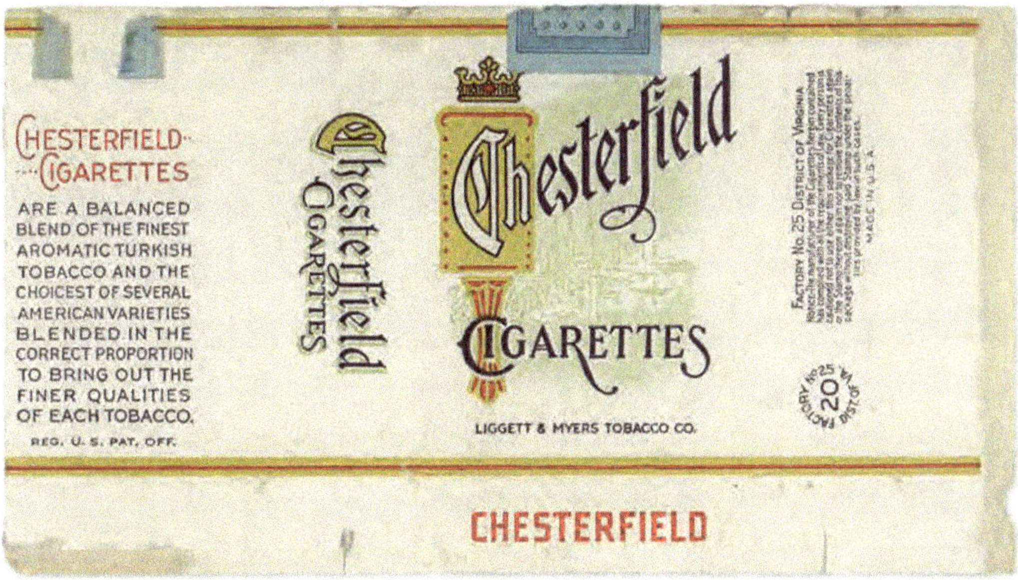

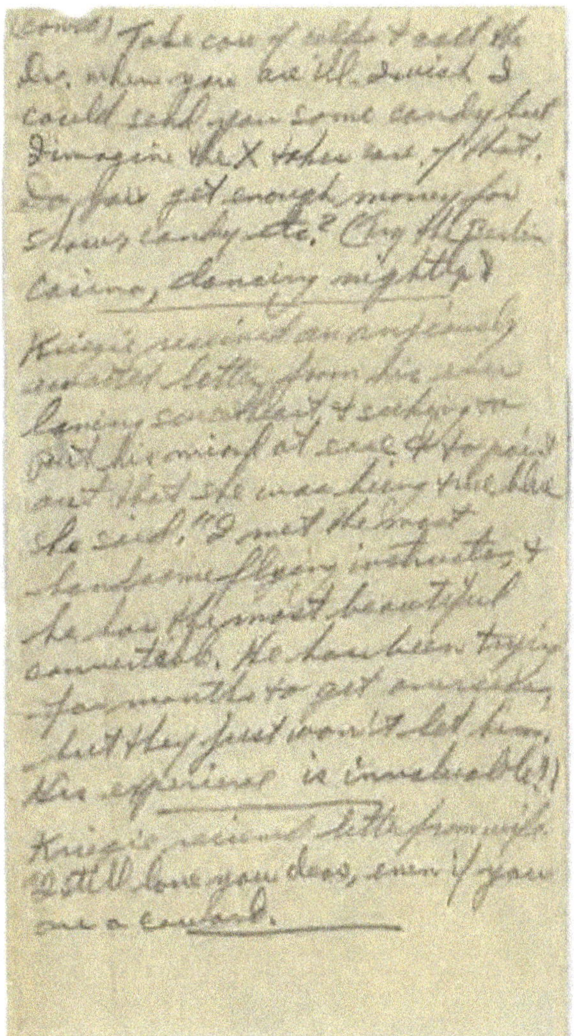
(cont.) Take care of colds & call the Dr. when you are ill. I wish I could send you some candy but I imagine the X takes care of that. Do you get enough money for shows, candy etc.? (Try the Garden Casino, dancing nightly.)

Krieger received an exceedingly exciting letter from his ever loving sweetheart, & asking him to put his mind at ease & to point out that she was living the life. She said, "I met the longest handsome flying instructor & he has the most beautiful convertible. He has been trying for months to get me a ride, but they just won't let him, his experience is invaluable(!!)"

Krieger received letter from wife. "I still love you dear, even if you are a coward."

Heaven Help the 2nd Louie

And when the combat target's Berlin
The second louey draws the mission
But if it's a snap like Bust or Calais
The brass will shine in lead position
So God be good and peace protect him
A special place in heaven devote him
Free from army regulations that haunt him
And one thing more, God, please promote him.

We Thank Thee Oh God

We thank thee, Oh God, for our mighty land
That thou hast created with thine own hands.
We thank thee for each mountain and plain
Each valley and hill of waving grain
We pray, oh Lord, the same humble way
As on the first Thanksgiving Day...
When the Pilgrims gave their thanks to thee
For a bountiful harvest and a nation to be
Now after years of thy preservation
And guidance, its grown to a mighty nation
But after each year of toil and strain
That self-same prayer we say again
And above all, oh God, we ask of thee
That it will remain the "Land of the Free".

MR. VON SCHLEPPEN – FEDDER FODDER
(given in dialect at labor day show)
By Harold A Fedder

Gentlemen
I am here this evening to discuss a
subject dear to the hears of all Kriegies...
a subj that has been discussed many times...
a subj ever more dear than women...a subj
to please every Kriegies' Palate...FOOD!
It is my privilege to represent a co. that
is proud of its product. A product which
looks like steak, feels like steak, &
smells like steak.
The flavor is unmistakable...need I say more...Ja Das ist
Richtig...Blood sausage. As a rep.
of the Limberdick Blood Sausage Co....
makers of the meat you can't beat...
Tis my intention to shove up the sales...
The Pres. Of the Co. said...shove the sales up!
Can't you picture a blood sausage
loaf made with delicious brown
bead. It ain't only nutrient –
nictrictch – good for you, but it
instantly, if not sooner, puts
lead in your pencil, even if you
ain't got nobody to write to.
Here in Germany where man is dying,
they don't call the a doctor, they call
a rep of the L.D.B.S.Co and give him
a meat injection. This is no laughing
matter gentlemen, blood sausage is not to be
pfffted on. Think of what would happen
if you refused to use the product of the
L.D.B.S.Co. Think of the unhappiness of the
girls whose hand made the meat you can't beat.
Think of me...how that Uncle Joe is about to
foreclose the mortgage. How could I buy war
bonds so that we could rid the world of these
American Lft Gangsters. Gentlemen, please
buy my meat...it can't be beat.

A PILOT'S PILOT

I've flown on high on silvery wings
Far far above all earthly things
Beyond the reach of the storm swept earth
Above all clouds of sadness girth.
Up where I'm free from all binding chances
High above the billowing clouds
I've played with the dancing sunbeams there
And lived through the dazzling moonlit air
Thus I've flown through the peaceful sky
So near to God on this throne on high
And when I bid my friends adieu
I was the pilot of the plane I flew
But the sky was destined as the earth below
One day red with blood to flow.
So instead of the peaceful wild blue space
It became an aerial warrior's place
The silver wings flit about no more
But pointed for battle have gone to war
Now the heavens are ripped asunder
Torn and rocked by battle thunder
Of vast armadas of warring wings
Where often death in triumph sings
Where once the cool breeze smote my face
But still I fly to heights unknown
Even nearer to God on his heavenly throne
For as I fly through this treacherous sky
He is the pilot of the plane, not I.

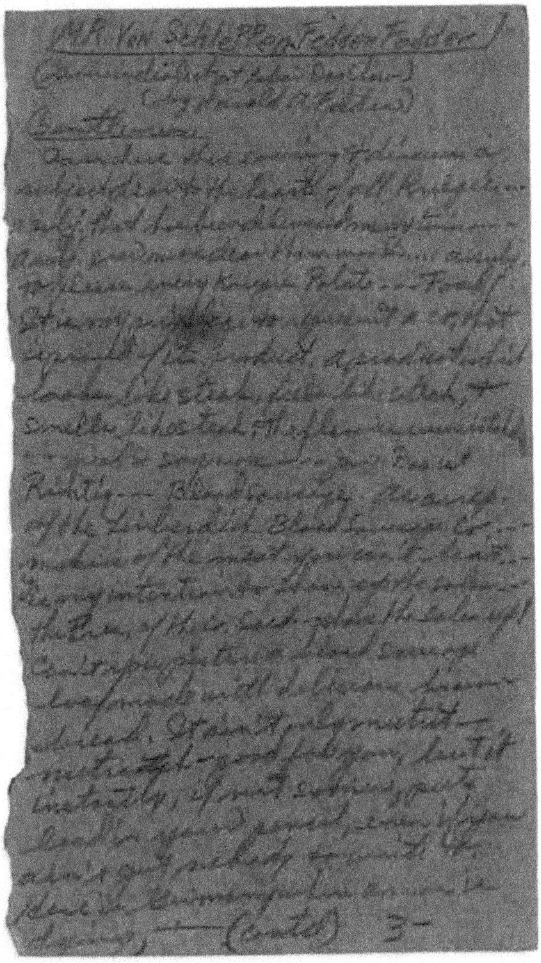

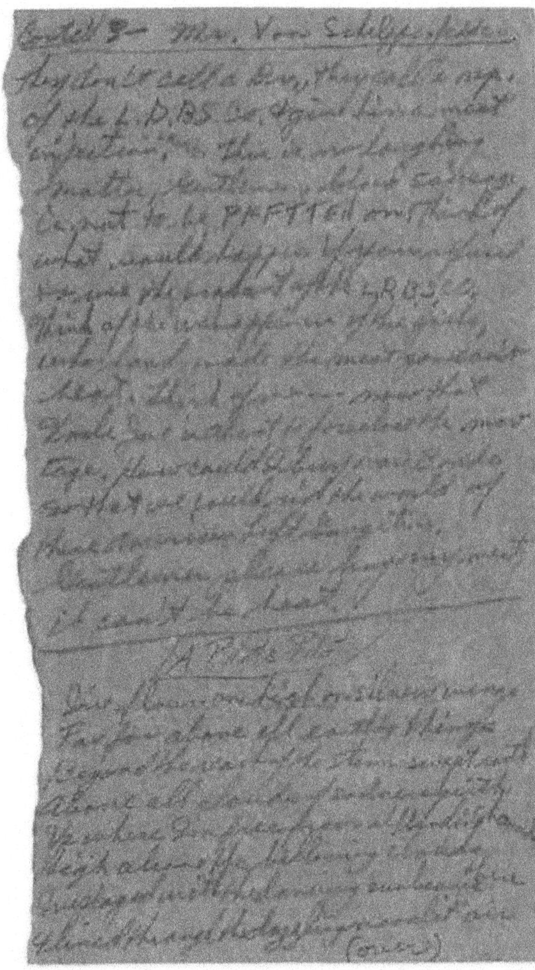

GONE AND FORGOTTEN

Just a small wooden cross, somewhere in France.
At the head of a mound, where poppies prance
The mark the grave of a forgotten flyer
Who fought and died in the bloody mire
That covered the earth and filled the air
Of a war-torn world cast deep in despair.

MELLOW MEMORIES

When my thoughts return to places in the USA
When the thought of flying as the fun of the day
I realize we didn't know
Just how far our luck would go.
How we'd moan when we had to fly
Those practice missions, way up high,
Then we'd fly all over the "flower state..."
We didn't soar long the E.T.O.
But dropped right into the hands of the POW
Where we sit and wait for this mess to end
Till the day we return to family and friends
When we get back to the land of the free
We'll have a few brews with the treat on me
And we'll have a sight and shed a tear
As we recall our sojourn over here.

TALL DARK AND FLAT-FOOTED

Poor unhappy puke 4-F
Wine and women are all that's left
Medals, ribbons, combat fame
High blood-pressure, pulse too low,
He's almost dead, he'll have you know.
Falling arches, can't see much
Diagnosis: Just no guts!

Here the flowers hang [illegible]
[illegible] on her throne so high,
[illegible]
[illegible]
[illegible]
[illegible]
[illegible]
[illegible]
[illegible]
[illegible]
Now the [illegible]
[illegible]
[illegible]
[illegible]
[illegible]
[illegible]
But still fly to heights unknown
[illegible] thundering [illegible]
[illegible] through the [illegible] sky
He is the [illegible] of flying [illegible]

[illegible] + Together

Just a small wooden cross, [illegible]
At the head of [illegible] poppies [illegible]
That marks the grave of [illegible]
Who fought + died in the bloody mud
That covered the earth [illegible]
[illegible] would [illegible]
(4 - contd)

[illegible]

[illegible] my thoughts [illegible]
[illegible] of flying [illegible]
Is really a [illegible]
Just how far [illegible]
How we'll [illegible] to fly
[illegible] way up high
[illegible] fly [illegible]
[illegible]
[illegible] in the R.F.T.C.
[illegible]
[illegible]
[illegible]
[illegible]
[illegible]
[illegible] + shed a tear
[illegible]

[illegible] + Flat-Footed

Poor, unhappy [illegible]
[illegible]
[illegible]
All [illegible]
[illegible]
He's [illegible]
Falling [illegible] can't be [illegible]
[illegible] - Just no [illegible]

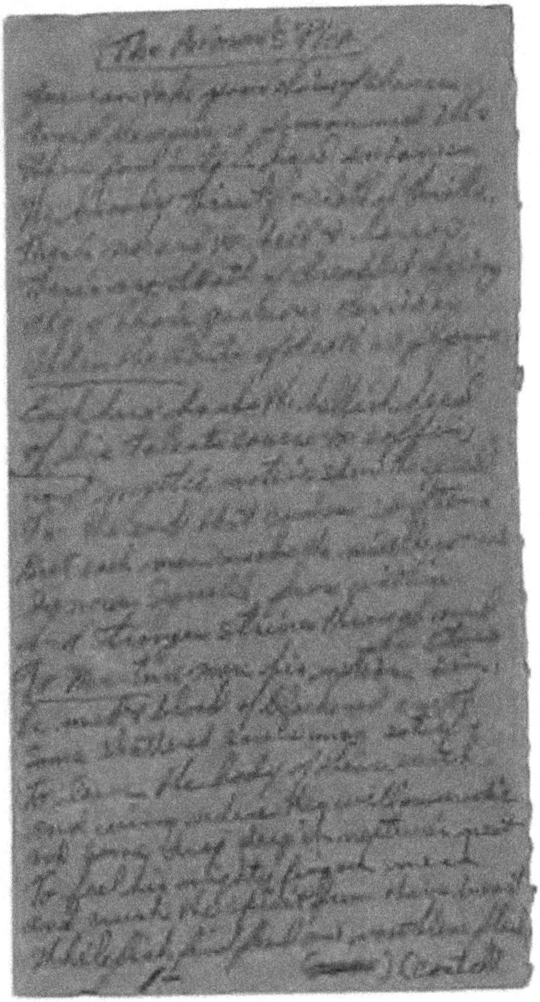
The Airman's Plea

THE AIRMAN'S PLEA

You can take your choice of chances
Avoid the source of man-made ills
Where foul Satan's hand enhances
The bloody thirst for lethal thrills
There's no end to hell & horror
There's no death of dreadful dying
Along Thor's gruesome corridor
When the darts of death are flying.
Each hero has the hellish heed
of his talents course to coffin,
and mystic motives spur the speed
to the end that comes so often.
But each man mocks the mirthless mars
Ignores Ignoble from within
And stronger strives through mud or stars
To Muster more his nations sin
The mud and blood of blackened earth
Some shattered souls may satisfy
To leave the body of their earth,
and wing where they will never die
and some drop deep in Neptune's nest
to feel his mighty fingers mesh
and crush the spirit from their breast
while fish find feed on worthless flesh.

Come on & join the Air Corp or
You too can be an aviation cadet

Come on & join the Air Corps
It's a great life they say
You never do no work at all
Just fly around all day
While others work & study hard
And grow old & blind
We take the air without a care
And you will never mind
You take her up & spin her
And with an awful tear
The wings come off, the ship folds up
But you will never care
For in about two seconds
Another pair you'll find
You'll dance with Pete and the angels sweet
But you will never mind
A thousand miles away from land
You hear your engines spit
You see the props come to a stop
The damned old engine quit
Now you can't swim, the ship won't float
And shore is miles behind
(cont'd)
But oh what a dish for the crabs & fish
But you will never mind,
Now if you meet a zero
He shoots you down in flames
Don't waste your time. Bite him
And call that bastard names
Just push your stick to the wall
& pretty soon you'll find
There ain't no hell, & all is well
And you will never mind.
We're just a bunch of heathens
We do not give a crap.
About the groundlings point of view
And all that sort of crap
We want about ten million planes
Of every other kind
And then of course our own air force
And we will never mind.
Come on & get promoted
As high as you desire
You're riding on a gravy train
When you're on an army flier
Now just when you're about to be
A General you will find
Your wings come off, your ship folds up
But you will never mind.

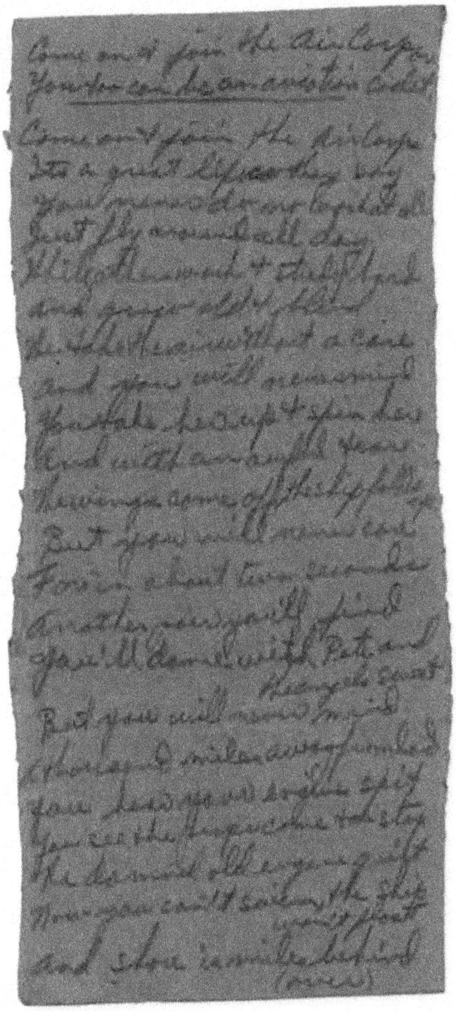

Come on & join the Air Corps
You too can be an aviation cadet

Come on & join the Air Corps
Its a great life so they say
You'll never do any work at all
Just fly around all day
[illegible]
and [illegible]
the [illegible] without a care
And you will never mind
You take her up & spin her
[illegible] with an awful [illegible]
The wings come off the ship folds up
But you will never care
For in about two seconds
Another world you'll find
You'll dance with Pete and the angels' court
But you will never mind
A thousand miles away from land
You hear your engine spit
You see the prop come to a stop
The damned old engine quit
Now you can't swim, the ship won't float
And shore is miles behind
(over)

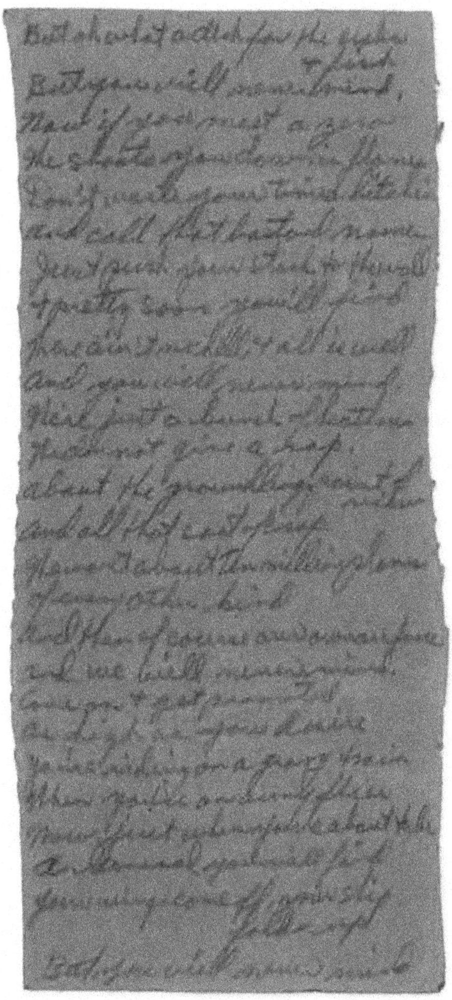

But oh what a dish for the fishes + fins
But you will never mind,
Now if you meet a zero
He shoots you down in flame
Don't waste your time bitchin
And call that bastard names
Just push your stick to the wall
& pretty soon you'll find
there ain't no hell, & all is well
And you will never mind
We're just a bunch of hot air
Who do not give a heap
About the grumbling [illegible]
And all that sort of crap
We aren't about [illegible]
Of any other kind
And then of course our own air force
and we will never mind.
Come on & get promoted
As high as you desire
You're riding on a gravy train
When you're on a [illegible]
Then just when you think about the
[illegible] you will find
Your wings come off your ship
folds up
But you will never mind

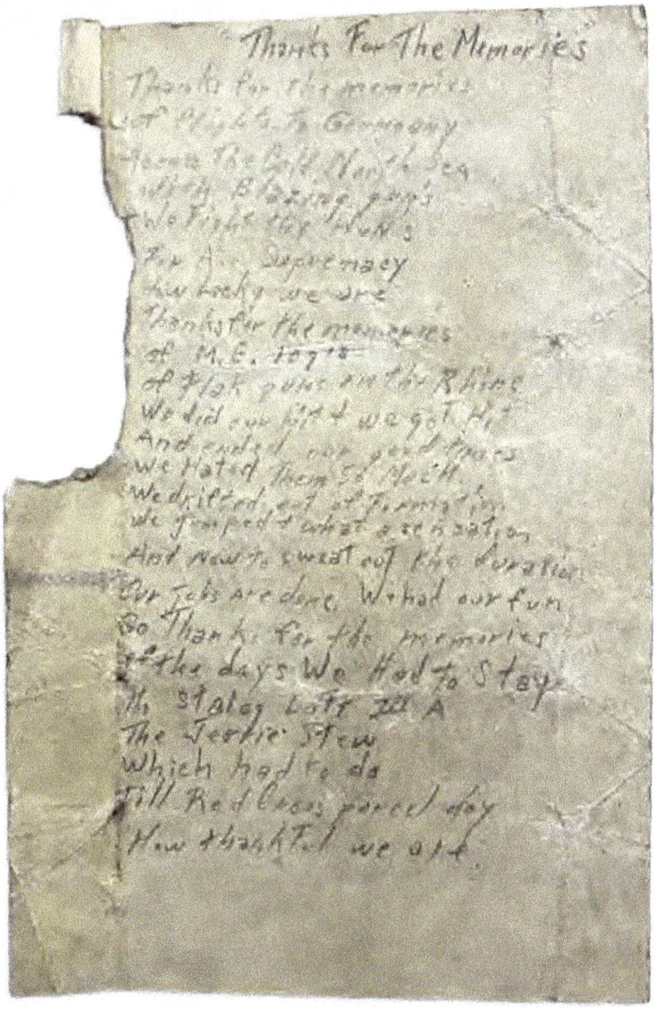

Thanks For the Memories

Thanks for the memories
of flights to Germany
Across The Cold North Sea
With Blazing gun's
We Fight the Hun's
For Air Supremacy
How Lucky we are
Thanks for the memories
Of M.E. 107's
Of Flak guns on the Rhine
We did our bit & we got Hit
And ended our good times
We hated them So Much
We drifted out of formation
We jumped & what a sensation
And now to sweat out the duration
Our Jobs are done. We had our fun
So Thanks for the memories
Of the days We Hold To Stay
In Stalag Loft III A
The Jerrie Stew
Which had to do
Till Red cross parcel day
How thankful we are.

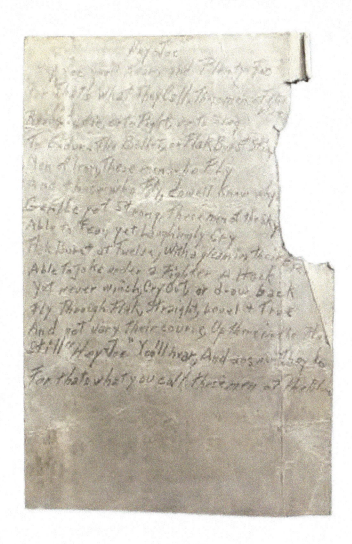

Hey Joe

Hey Joe

Hey Joe you'll hear, and Plenty Too
For That's What They Call. These men of the Blue
Ready to die, or to Fight, or to sing
To Endure The Bullet, or Flak Burst Sting
Men of Iron, These men who Fly
And those who Fly, do well know why
Gentle yet Strong, These men of the Sky
Able to Fear, yet Laughingly Cry
Flak Burst at Twelve, with a gleam in their eye.
Able To joke under a Fighter Attack
Yet never winch, Cry out, or draw back
Fly Through Flak, Straight, Level & True
And not vary their course, Up there in the Blue
Still "Hey Joe" You'll hear, And answer they do,
For tats what you call these men of the Blue.

The Bee Dash Two Four

The Bee Dash Two Four

Down in flak valley where black smoke mushrooms grow
Where the fighters escort & big bombers go
Where engines are feathered & parachutes bloom
Where messerschmitts play tricks with a zoom
That Bee dash two four, oh, the 4 engine whore
The lads that fly in her are sure to be sore
At fifty five inches she can't even cruise
Oh, that Bee dash two four

We're briefed in the morning they say there's no flak
We fly down the valley & never come back
They say that the weather is CAVU
You can't see the ground from 100 feet true

The secondary was [illegible] in the sea
Circle & wander where our escort may be
Then off to the target without an escort
Down in that damn valley where a brave man [illegible],

We hit the I.P. at eleven o nine,
Bomb bays are open & all is so fine,
Then all of a sudden from out of the blue
A 190 burst knocks out number two

We feather up & continue our run
Bombs are away, & our job is all done
We head out for home & all is so swell
Then number three catches on fire & starts burning like hell

The flak gets thicker, we lose number four
The flying old crate ain't a plane no more
With chutes all buckled, we head for the deck
We're glad to be clear of that flaming old wreck

Instead of those four engines churning away
We sit here in Germany day after day
Doin nothing but cursing that [illegible]
That old flying coffin, that Bee dash two four

The Bee Dash Two Four

Down in flask valley were black mushrooms grow
Where the fighters escort & big bombers go
Where engines are feathered & parachutes bloom
Where messerschmitts play & ride by with a zoom

That Bee dash two four; oh, that 4 engine whore
The lads that fly in her are sure to loose
At fifty five inches she won't even cruise
Oh, that Bee dash two four

We're briefed in the morning, they say there's no flok
We fly down the valley & never come back
We say that the weather is CAVU
You can't see the ground from 100 feet trees

The rendezvous over an isle in the sea.
Circle & wonder where our escort may be
Then off to the target without an escort
Toward that damn valley where brave men abort.

We hit the I.P. at eleven-o-nine,
Bombays are open & all is so fine,
Then all of a sudden from out of the blue
A 190 burst knocks out number two

We feather up & continue our run
Bombs are away, & our job is all done
We head out for home & all is so swell
Then she catches on fire & starts burning like Hell

The flack gets thicker, we loose number four
The flying old crate ain't a plane no more
With chutes all buckled, we head for the deck
We're glad to be clear of that flaming old wreck.

Instead of those four engines burning away

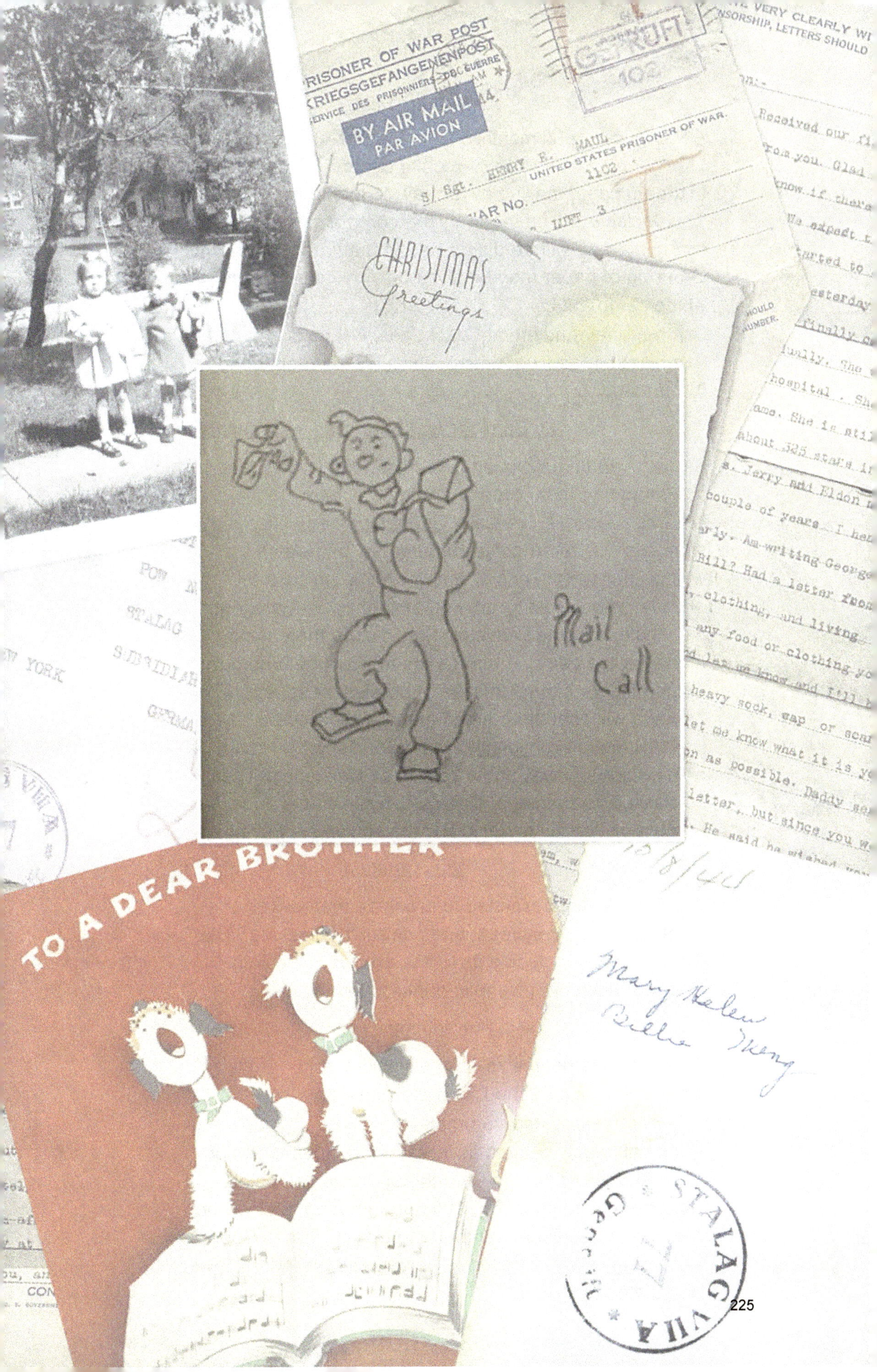
PRISONER OF WAR POST
KRIEGSGEFANGENENPOST
BY AIR MAIL
PAR AVION
UNITED STATES PRISONER OF WAR.
CHRISTMAS
Greetings
Mail Call
TO A DEAR BROTHER
STALAG VIIA

VI. Mail.

1). A.P.O.W can send monthly: 2 letters and
4 cards
2). In urgent case, mailing by airmail, or telegrams, is possible. The decision will be made by the commander.
3). Incoming mail will be distributed immediately after arrival.
4). Ordering of paper may be done only by intermedium of the camp- officer.
5. Camp-money and private packages, will be distributed after examination, on fixed times, which will be mentioned at formation.

VII. Barracks and Barracks - equipments.

1). Barracks and barracks equipments of the P.O.W. are to be handled In an orderly and official way.
2). He, who damages, or steals, German property (stores, store latches, Store-gates, bed-frames, bed-slates, window panes etc.) has to answer for it. In case the offender is not able to answer or cannot be found out, the whole camp will have to pay In case there is no money in the camp, it can be taken from the fund out of the officers-camp. In case of carelessness, the damage will cost three times the original amount. Damage done intentionally, can be punished by court, or in disciplinary way under special circumstances it can be classed as sabotage. The barracks leader is responsible for his barrack, and the equipment therein.

VIII. Canteen

1). The P.O.W. are permitted to organize their own canteen which they lead, and control themselves. The commander will decide as to the articles to be sold.
2). The production of alcoholic drinks is forbidden.

IV. Punishments.

1). Offences against the military discipline, and orders, will be punished, and a disciplinary manner by the camp-commander.
2). Punishable action, such as threatening, possession of arms and munition, out- and thrust-arms, pamphlets, destroying with intention, sabotage, muting, etc. will be traced, and punished by the resp.United States Court, according to Military articles of war, civilian federal laws, and state laws.

VI. M a i l.

1). A P.o.W. can send monthly : 2 letters and 4 cards
on the forms supplied by the camp-authorities.
The letters are gathered, by the camp-leader, and handed over to the camp authorities, who will care for further mailing.

2). In urgent cases, mailing by air-mail, or telegrams, is possible. The decision will be made by the commander.

3) Incoming mail will be distributed immediatly after arrival.

5). Ordering of papers may be done only by intermedium of the camp-officer.

5). Camp-money and private packages, will be distributed after examination, on fixed times, which will be mentioned at formation.

VII. Barracks and Barracks-equipments.

1). Barracks and barracks-equipments of the P.o.W. are to be handled in an orderly and careful way.

2). He, who damages, or steals, German property (stores, storelatches, store-gates, bedframes, bed-slates, window-panes etc.) has to answer for it. In case the offender is not able to answer or cannot be found out, the whole camp will have to pay. In case there is no money in the camp, it can be taken from the fund out of the officers-camp. In case of carelessness, the damage will cost three times the original amount.
Damage done intentionally, can be punished by court, or in disciplinary way. Under special circumstances it can be classed as sabotage. The barracksleader is responsible for his barrack, and the equipments therein.

VIII. C a n t e e n.

1). The P.o.W. are permitted to organize their own canteen which they lead, and control themselves. The commander will decide as to the articles to be sold.

2). The production of alcoholic drinks is forbidden.

IX. Punishments.

1). Offences against the military discipline, and orders, will be punished, in a disciplinary manner, by the camp-commander.

2). Punishable actions, such as threatening, possession of arms and munition, cut- and thrust-arms, pamphlets, festroying with intention, sabotage, mutiny, etc. will be traced, and punished by the resp. United Srvice Court according to military articles of war, civilian federal laws, or state laws.

Night mares – Prison Camp Blues – Prisoner Dreams

1. Veal cutlets & Boston Baked Beans – sliced tomatoes & French Fries – a Bowl of summer vegetables – ½ chocolate cream pie with vanilla ice cream, white bread & butter – chocolate malted milk.

2. T-Bone-Steak with French Fries – sweet milk & coffee – bread & butter – Apple Pie with ice cream & strawberry short cake.

3. Hot cakes – Link sausage – Butter & maple syrup – coffee.

4. Sandwich cookies & Toll house cookies Broken into a Bowl of milk.

5. Hot dogs with Chili Con Carney – Milk Shake – Banana Split.

6. Hot Biscuits – with Butter and honey – coffee

7. Chocolate Hot Fudge Sundae with Angel Food cake. Heavy on whip cream.

8. Barbecued Beef sandwich with milk shake with whip cream.

9. Potato Pan cakes with Bacon & eggs with syrup. Cereal & Coffee.

10. Hamburger loaf with Trimmings – Milk & Coffee – Pudding with whip cream.

11. Lemon merenge pie with milk.

12. Spaghetti with meat balls – Heavy on the gravy.

13. Veal cutlets with spaghetti gravy – French Fries – French Break Double chocolate Sundae - coffee

14. Ravioli – chickin – sweet potatoes – cranberry sauce and all The trimmings. Butterscotch pudding with whip cream.

15. Hershey Pie – make pie crust – melt with butter with 10 Hersey cho. Bars. Mix 20 marshmellows – while cooling add 6 egg whites – nuts – Fruit salad Bananas and Topp off with merenge.

16. Hershey Layer Cake – make Layer Cake – Between each layer add bananas & Melted milk chocolate. For Icing melt milk cho & marshmellows – make thick icing – serve cold.

17. 2 Plain Hershey Bars with Filling of Peanut Butter

18. Regular corn meal Pan cakes with 2 sppons of cocoa

19. Corn Fritters – Donut Dough – whole kernel corn minus Juice – Fry as donuts Serve with syrup or honey.

20. sliced candy oranges – chopped marshmellows – sliced bananas – mix it all with whipp cream * sugar – serve as salad.

21. ½ ice-cream – ½ melted marchmellows – 1 cup of cream – 20 marchmellows – box of ice-cream powder – mix and freeze in ice box.

22. Poor Boy Sandwich – loaf of French Bread – spit in the middle all different kinds of cold cuts and sauces. – malted milk with whipp cream.

23. hot cakes with bacon and eggs – coffee and toast.

24. Glazed Donuts and milk – use plenty of butter.

25. Plenty of Good Italian Food with Italian Pastry.

Nightmares [illegible] Prison Camp Blues – [illegible] Dreams

1. Veal cutlets & Boston bake beans – sliced Tomatoes & French Fries – a Bowl of summer vegetables – ½ chocolate cream pie with vanilla Ice Cream – white Bread & butter – Chocolate malted milk.
2. T-Bone-steak with French Fries – sweet milk & coffee – Bread & butter – Apple Pie with Ice-cream & strawberry short cake.
3. Hot cakes – link sausage – butter & maple syrup – coffee.
4. Sandwich cookies & Toll house cookies Broken into a bowl of milk.
5. Hot Dogs with chilli con carney – milk shake – Banana split.
6. Hot Biscuits – with butter and honey – coffee
7. Chocolate Hot Fudge Sundae with Angle Food cake. Heavy on whip cream
8. Barbacued Beef sandwich with milk shake with whip cream.
9. Potato Pan cakes with Bacon & eggs with syrup – Cereal & coffee.
10. Hamburger loaf with Trimmings – milk & coffee – Pudding with whip cream
11. Lemon merange Pie with milk
12. Spaggetti with meat Balls – Heavy on the gravy.
13. Veal cutlets with spaggetti gravy – French Fries – French Bread – Double chocolate Sundae – coffee
14. Ravaoli – chicken – sweet Potatoes – cranberry sauce and all the trimmings – [illegible] pudding with whip cream
15. Hershey Pie – make pie crust – melt [illegible] with butter with 10 hershey choc. bars. mix 20 marshmallows – while cooling add 6 egg whites – nuts – Fruit salad Bannanas and Topp off with merange.
16. Hershey Layer cake – make layer cake – Between each layer add bananas & melted milk chocolate. For icing melt milk cho & marshmallows – make Thick icing – serve cold.
17. 2 Plain hershey Bars with Filling of Peanut Butter
18. Regular corn meal Pan cakes with 2 spoons of cocoa
19. Corn Fritters – Do nut Dough – whole kernel corn minus Juice – Fry as Donuts serve with syrup or honey.
20. sliced canty oranges – chopped marshmallows – sliced [illegible] [illegible] all with whipp cream & sugar – serve as salad.
21. ½ ice cream – ½ melted marshmallows – 1 cup of cream – 20 marshmallows – box of ice-cream powder – mix and Freeze in [illegible].
22. Poor Boy sandwich – loaf of French bread – cut in middle and all different kinds of cold cuts and sauces – malted milk with whipp cream.
23. Hot cakes with bacon and eggs – coffee and Toast.
24. Glazed Do[illegible] and milk – use plenty of butter.
25. Plenty of Good Italian Food with Italian pastry.

Who's Who…

Mary J was Mary Jane, Dad's little sister.
Mary Jane Maul Painter Hinton
December 13, 1931 – November 2017

Grandma was Dad's mom's mother.
Johanna (Joannae) Katherine Schmiz
October 28, 1877 – August 27, 1953

Meng's were Dad's mother's twin sister and her husband.
Helen C. Schneider Meng
October 4, 1901
February 23, 1990

Walter George Meng
December 13, 1898
June 22, 1986

Service Flags
A service flag is a flag family members of those serving in the United States Armed Forces can display. The flag is officially defined as a white field with a red border, with a blue star for each family member serving in the Armed Forces of the United States during any period of war or hostilities. Gold stars represented those who lost their lives.

I believe my grandparents had a star for each person they knew serving in the United States Armed Forces versus family members serving.

George Bischoff was part of dad's crew and a Bombardier.

Billy (William) Lloyd was a part of dad's crew and a Tail Gunner.

How is the food and clothing question? If prisoners actually answered this question correctly, it would have been redacted by the censors. The prisoners were freezing in the winters, not proper clothing, shoes, and they were starving at not even 2,000 calories a day. Also, by the time my dad received this letter it was a new season… winter, when my dad, his crew, and thousands of POW's were marching in the dead of Germany's winter.

Snookie was Kathleen Marie Graef Schneider. She was Dad's first cousin and the sister of Dad's life-long best friend, Uncle Bern Snyder.
February 27, 1919 – March 10, 2007

Sis was Virginia Maul Munger, also called Ginny, was my dad's sister.
April 1928 – 1982

Letter prior to this of April 5th was prior to my dad's capture May 8th.

WRITE VERY CLEARLY WITHIN THE LINES. IN ORDER TO EXPEDITE CENSORSHIP, LETTERS SHOULD BE TYPED OR PRINTED IN BLOCK CAPITALS.

Dear Son:- Alton, Ill. 9/6/44

Received our first word from you yesterday. So happy to hear from you. Glad to know you are O.K. We are all fine. Let us know if there is anything you would like for us to send you. We expect to hear from you regularly now since your mail has started to come through. Sis and Mary J. started back to school yesterday. Sis is a Senior, and Mary J. is in 8th grade. Mary J. finally came out of her sick spell O.K. She has gained gradually. She weighed only 50 lbs. when she came home from the hospital . She finally got up to 72 lbs. Grandma is about the same. She in still living with the Meng's. We now have about 325 stars in our service flag. Have only 3 gold ones. Jerry and Eldon met three weeks ago. The first time in a couple of years. I hear from your crew members folks regularly. Am writing George's mother today. Have you heard from Bill? Had a letter from his wife last week. How is the food, clothing, and living conditions in the camp? If there is any food or clothing you need and it is permissable to send let me know and I'll be glad to send it. If you should need heavy sock, cap or scarf or the like for the winter months, let me know what it is you want and I'll get it to you as soon as possible. Daddy sent the shoes you asked for in your last letter, but since you were taken prisoner, they were returned. He said he wished you had had them instead of him. If you need them, and it is permissable to send them, we will send you another pair. Snookie was married about two months ago. We have had quite a lot of weddings lately. There is so much news I would like to tell you, but I'm afraid it won't pass the censor. See Johnson occasionally at church. He has gained weight. All your friends ask about you, and want you to know they haven't forgotten you.

CONTINUE ON TOP PANEL OVERLEAF

☆ U. S. GOVERNMENT PRINTING OFFICE: 1944 16—30013-1

TOP PANEL
What kind of work are you doing? Dad has been kept pretty busy at the store, especially with the opening of school. Sis worked all last week. I talk to Ras nearly every day. She is writing you today. Please write as often as you can. I will write regularly, and hope you will receive it. Your card received yesterday was the first word we had from you since your letter of April 5th. Since we now have your address the future looks brighter, We shall continue to pray. Good luck and God bless you, Love Mother
FROM (SENDER'S FULL NAME AND ADDRESS)
MRS. BERTHA M. MAUL
710 FRANKLIN ST.,
ALTON, ILLINOIS
PRISONER OF WAR POST
KRIEGSGEFANGENENPOST
SERVICE DES PRISONNIERS DE GUERRE
BY AIR MAIL
PAR AVION
GEPRÜFT
RANK AND NAME (CAPITAL LETTERS) STAFF SGT. HENRY E. MAUL
UNITED STATES PRISONER OF WAR.
PRISONER OF WAR No. (SEE NOTE ON FLAP) NOT ALLOTTED
CAMP NAME AND No. STALAG LUFT 3
SUBSIDIARY CAMP No.
COUNTRY GERMANY
CENSOR
VIA NEW YORK, N. Y.
IMPORTANT: FOR PRISONERS IN GERMAN HANDS THE PRISONER OF WAR NUMBER SHOULD BE CLEARLY INDICATED IF KNOWN. IT MUST NOT BE CONFUSED WITH THE ARMY SERIAL NUMBER.
W. D., P. M. G. Form No. 111
April 1944

To: Staff Sgt. Henry E. Maul Prisoner of War No: Not Allotted Camp Name and No: Stalag Luft 3 Country: Germany

From: Mrs. Henry C. Maul
710 Franklin St.
Alton, Illinois

Mailed: 9/6/1944

Dear Son: - Alton, Ill. 9/6/44

Received our first word from you yesterday. So Happy to hear from you. Glad to know you are O.K. We are all fine. Let us know if there is anything you would like for us to send to you. We expect to hear from you regularly now since your mail has started to come through. Sis and Mary J. started back to school yesterday. Sis is a Senior, and Mary J. is in 8th grade. Mary J. finally came out of her sick spell O.K. She has gained gradually. She weighed 50 lbs when she came home from the hospital. She finally got up to 72 lbs Grandma is about the same. She is still living with the Meng's. We now have about 325 stars in our service flag. Have only 3 gold ones. Jerry and Eldon met three weeks ago. The first time in a couple of years. I hear from your crew members folks regularly. Am writing George's mother today. Have you heard from Bill? Had a letter from his wife last week. How is the food, clothing, and living conditions in the camp? If there is any food or clothing you need and it is permissible to send let me know and I'll be glad to send it. If you should need heavy sock, cap or scarf or the like for the winter months, let me know what it is you want and I'll get it to you as soon as possible. Daddy sent the shoes you asked for in your last letter, but since you were taken prisoner, they were returned. He said he wished you had had them instead of him. If you need them, and it is permissible to send them, we will send you another pair. Snookie was married about two months ago. We have had quite a lot of weddings lately. There is so much news I would like to tell you, but I'm afraid it won't pass the censor. See Johnson occasionally at church. He has gained weight. All your friends talk about you, and want you to know they haven't forgotten you. What kind of work are you doing? Dad has been kept Pretty busy at the store, especially with the opening of School. Sis worked all last week. I talk to Rae nearly every day. She is writing you today. Please write as often as you can. I will write regularly, and hope you will receive it. Your card received yesterday was the first word we had from you since your letter of April 5th. Since we now have your address the future looks brighter, We Shall continue to pray. Good luck and God bless you, Love Mother

Who's who...

Dad's plane was shot down and he was taken POW May 8th. Parents received his letter mailed May 30th on September 17th.

Dad broke his ribs after landing in a tree from when his plane went down, but I suspect the POW's were not allowed to talk about these issues or want to worry their family.

Dad was raised in the Catholic Church and, as many POW's did, prayed a lot to help them through the troubling times.

Grandma was Dad's mom's mother.
Johanna (Joannae) Katherine Schmiz
October 28, 1877 -August 27, 1953

Aunt Rose was Rosa J. Schneider the daughter of Johanna (Joannae) Katherine Schmiz and William (Gulielmi) Schneider

Johanna (Joannae) Katherine Schmiz
October 28, 1877 -August 27, 1953

and William (Gulielmi) Schneider
October 10, 1861 - February 28, 1915

George Bischoff was part of dad's crew and a Bombardier.

Jim was part of dad's crew and co-pilot of the plane.

Boschert was Paul Boschert that served in the 106th Infantry Division And captured at the Battle of the Bulge.

Mary J was Mary Jane, Dad's little sister.
Mary Jane Maul Painter Hinton
December 13, 1931 - November 2017

Sis was Virginia Maul Munger, also called Ginny, was my dad's sister.
April 1928 - 1982

Mr. Bingenheimer was John Bingenheimer
1867-1949

Dad received this letter January 10th, far after Christmas when he was in a different POW camp.

WRITE VERY CLEARLY WITHIN THE LINES. IN ORDER TO EXPEDITE CENSORSHIP, LETTERS SHOULD BE TYPED OR PRINTED IN BLOCK CAPITALS.

Dear Son:- Monday. Sept 18, 1944.

Just received our first letter from you dated May 30.
We are glad to hear you are OK & hope you have not been
wounded. I'm so glad you have not forgotten your prayers
I will send you a rosary & prayerbook as soon as I can.
Read your letter to grandma White. She gave me a rosary
that belonged to Aunt Rose which she wants me to send you.
She said to tell you she was OK. You might drop her a card
Her address is 1719 Warden. Aunt Nellie hasn't received her
card yet, but said she will be looking for it. You will
probably hear from Bill Johnson, he got your address from
daddy. I had a letter from George's mother today. He seems to
have the same address [illegible] have. Do you see him? Had
a letter from Jim's wife Friday last. He writes he is working
in a vegetable garden & taking a course in Spanish, algebra, and
that he is fine. Have you heard from or about Bill as yet?
Lucker was home on furlough last week (Roger). I think Bo-
chut is still in Indiana. Bob Eggemann is leaving next week
for service. He is in his last year at Acton High. Mary
Jane is in 8th grade. She's getting along fine now. We have all
been well. All your friends inquire about you. Daddy & I
are still making novenas for you. Mrs. Ireland brought me
a crucifix & statue of St Jude & also enrolled you in the St Jude
Apostolate. I will send these to you in my package. Do you
have plenty of warm clothing, socks, underwear, handkerchiefs? If
not I'll send you some. Better give me your size. Fr. Beume
always asks about you. He sent a 25 word letter off to you
from us as soon as we had your first card. Hope you
have it by now. We had our back porch enclosed with
glass for winter & screens for summer. Just had the house
painted. Sis & Mary Jane have been keeping the present

CONTINUE ON TOP PANEL OVERLEAF

☆ U. S. GOVERNMENT PRINTING OFFICE 1944 16—[illegible]

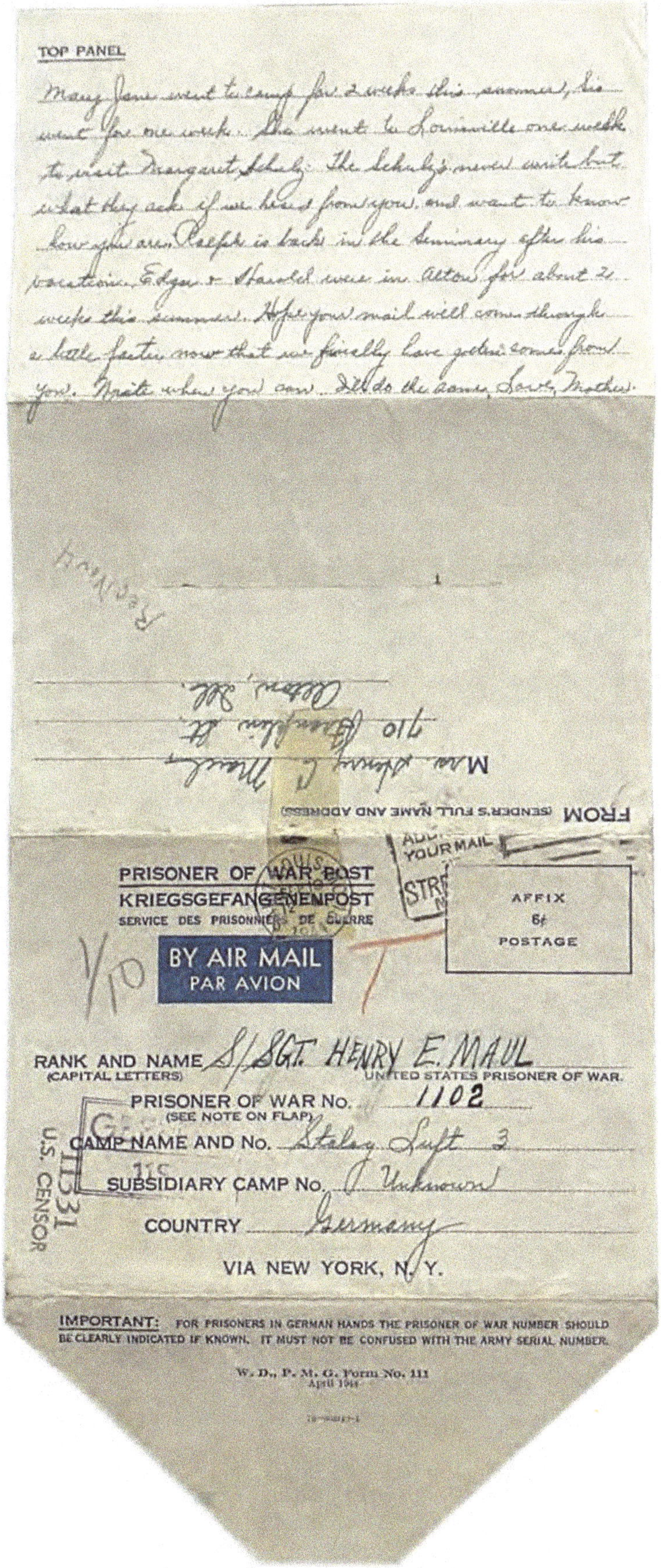
TOP PANEL

Mary Jane went to camp for 2 weeks this summer, Sis went for one week. She went to Louisville one week to visit Margaret Schulz. The Schulz's never write but what they ask if we heard from you and want to know how you are. Ralph is back in the Seminary after his vacation. Edgar & Harold were in Alton for about 2 weeks this summer. Hope your mail will come through a little faster now that we finally have gotten some from you. Write when you can. I'll do the same, Love, Mother.

FROM (SENDER'S FULL NAME AND ADDRESS)
Mrs. Henry E. Maul
710 Franklin St.
Alton, Ill.

PRISONER OF WAR POST
KRIEGSGEFANGENENPOST
SERVICE DES PRISONNIERS DE GUERRE

BY AIR MAIL
PAR AVION

AFFIX 6¢ POSTAGE

RANK AND NAME (CAPITAL LETTERS) S/SGT. HENRY E. MAUL
UNITED STATES PRISONER OF WAR.
PRISONER OF WAR No. (SEE NOTE ON FLAP) 1102
CAMP NAME AND No. Stalag Luft 3
SUBSIDIARY CAMP No. ? Unknown
COUNTRY Germany

VIA NEW YORK, N. Y.

U.S. CENSOR 11331

IMPORTANT: FOR PRISONERS IN GERMAN HANDS THE PRISONER OF WAR NUMBER SHOULD BE CLEARLY INDICATED IF KNOWN. IT MUST NOT BE CONFUSED WITH THE ARMY SERIAL NUMBER.

W. D., P. M. G. Form No. 111
April 1944

To: S/Sgt. Henry E. Maul
Prisoner of War No: 1102
Camp Name and No: Stalag Luft 3
Country: Germany

From:
Mrs. Henry C. Maul
71O Franklin St
Alton, Ill.

Mailed: 9/18/1944
Received: 11/4/1944

Monday, Sept 18, 1944

Dear Son:-
Just received our first letter from you dated May 30. We are glad to hear you are OK. Hope you have not been Wounded. I'm so glad you have not forgotten your prayers. I will send you a rosary & prayerbook as soon as I can. Read your letter to grandma tonite. She gave me a rosary that belonged to Aunt Rose which she wants me to send you. She said to tell you she was OK. You might drop her a card. Her address is 1719 Worden. Aunt Nellie hasn't received her Card yet, but she said she will be looking for it. You will probably hear from Bill Johnson. He got your address from daddy & had a letter from George's mother today. He seems to have the same address you have. Do you see him? I had a letter from Jim's wife Friday last. He writes he is working in a vegetable garden & taking a course in Spanish, algebra and that he is fine. Have you heard from or about Bill as yet? Lucker was home on furlough last week (Roger). I think Boo-cherts is still in Indiana. Bob Eggesnamm is leaving next week for service – his is in her last year at Alton High. Mary Jane is in 8th grade. She's getting along fine now. We have all Been well. All your friends inquired about you. Daddy & I are still making novenso for you. Mrs. Ireland brought me a crucifix & statue of St. Jude & also enrolled you in the St. Jude Apostolate. I will send these to you in my package. Do you have plenty of warm clothing socks, underwear, handkerchiefs? If not I'll send you some. Better give me our size. Fr. Brume always asks about you. He sent a 25 word letter off to you from us as soon as we had your first card. Hope you have it by now. We had our backporch enclosed with glass for winter screens for summer. Just had the house painted. Sis & Mary Jane have been keeping the grass cut. Mary Jane went to camp for 2 weeks this summer, Sis went for one week. She went to Louisville one week to visit Margaret Schulz. The Schulz's never write but what they ask if we heard from you and want to know how you are. Ralph is back in the Seminary after his vacation. Edgar & Harold were in Alton for about 2 weeks this summer. Hope your mail will come through a little faster now that we finally have gotten some from you. Write when you can. I'll do the same, Love, Mother

Who's who...

From Leona, Dad's first cousin. Leona was Dad's dad's sister. Leona and her husband Bill Todd owned a bakery in St. Louis.

Ted was Theodore Todd, Leona and Bill's son.
January 13, 1930- May 7, 2019

Grandma and Grandpa are Herman and Grace Theresa Maul Baumeister. Grace was dad's great or grand aunt.
Grace Theresa Maul Baumeister
January 3, 1883 - April 5, 1973

Herman Baumeister
June 22, 1876 - June 4, 1955

Rec Nov. 4

St. Louis, Mo Sept. 20. 1944

Dear Sonny,

Your parents were here in town yesterday and had supper with us, then we took in the ball game, Browns played the Washington Senators but our Brownies lost in 11 th inning, Your mom and I were wishing you and Billy could have been with us, as there were a lot of service men enjoying it. I read your letter your ma received last week, and we were mighty glad to know you are O.K. I don't know if you knew, [redacted]

Your sisters are getting big, as our Ted is too, Bill will hardly

know him when he gets home.

Grandma & Grandpa Baumeister said to tell you they are thinking of you a lot and wish you luck and send their love too.

We are busy making pastries these days, your mom took a lot home with her as they like sweets.

Be seein you soon I hope

Love – Your Cousin Leona

WM. V. Todd Bakery
2841 N. Union Blvd.
St. Louis, Mo.

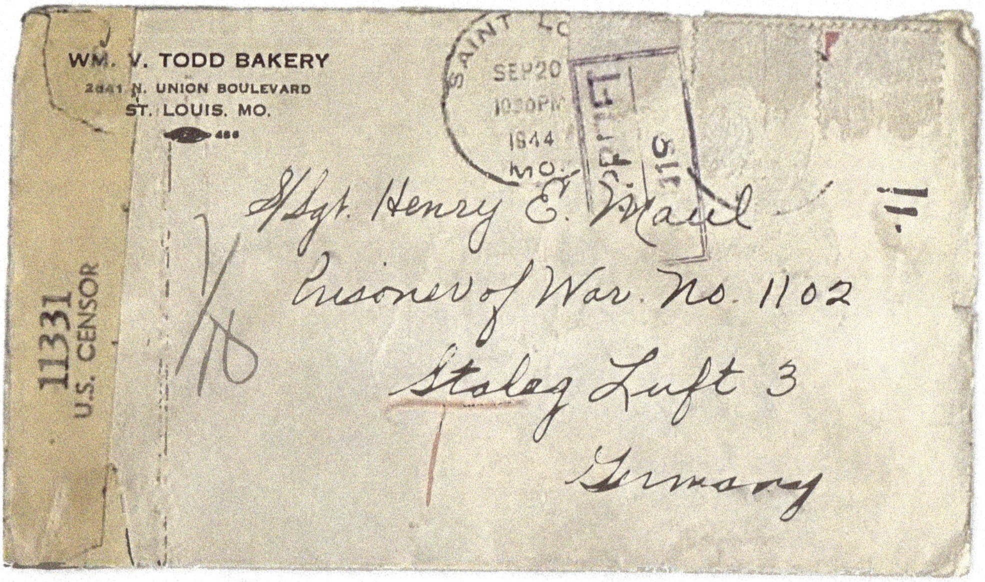

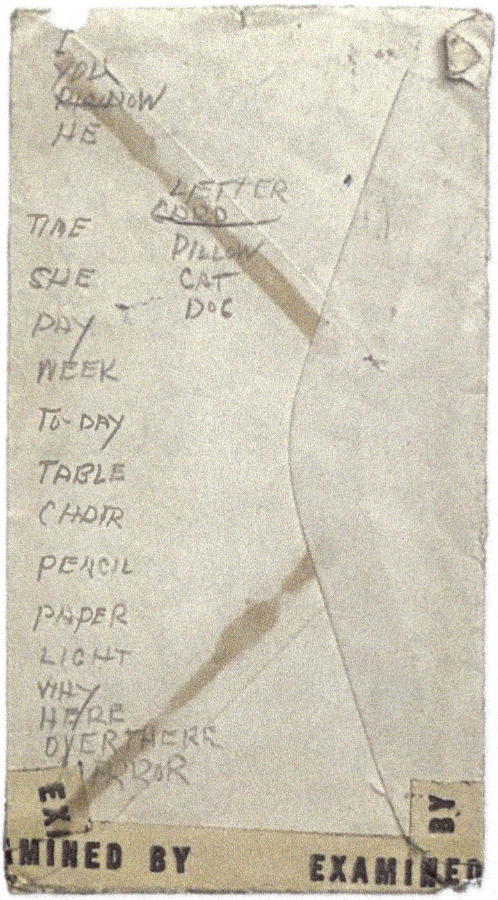

To: S/Sgt. Henry E. Maul
Prisoner of War No: 1102
Camp Name and No: Stalag Luft 3
Country: Germany

Mailed: 9/20/1944
Received: 11/4/1944

St. Louis, Mo. Sept 20, 1944

Dear Sonny,

Your parents were here in town yesterday and had supper with us, then we took in the ball game, Browns played the Washington Senators but our Browns lost in the 11th inning. Your mom and I were wishing you and Billy could have been with us, as there were a lot of service men enjoying it. I read your letter your ma received last week, and we were mighty glad to know you are O.K. I don't know if you knew,
(REDACTED)
Your sisters are getting big, as our Ted is too. Bill will hardly know him when he gets home. Grandma & Grandpa (Baumeister) said to tell you they are thinking of you a lot and wish you luck and send their love too.

We are busy making pastries these days, your mom took a lot home with her as they like sweets.

Be seein you soon I hope
Love – Your Cousin Leona

WRITE VERY CLEARLY WITHIN THE LINES. IN ORDER TO EXPEDITE CENSORSHIP, LETTERS SHOULD BE TYPED OR PRINTED IN BLOCK CAPITALS.

Rec. Nov 4

Alton, Ill's

Dear Son, 9-25-44

Thought it about time for me to write to let you know we do think of you everyday, hoping these few lines do you find you well and O.K.

The weather today is much colder 65 we have our furnace going all the time now, I guess next week I will have to take all our screen's down, and get set for a long winter, last week we got our coal bin filled up, I think it last for a long time.

Mary-Jane is getting bigger everyday, she often speak's of you, she don't think that you will know her, the way she is growing, corky is still the same dog, he is just a good pal, sis went horse-back riding yesterday afternoon, and last-night she complaint of her leg's acking, today she is O.K. Mother is feeling pretty good now, and is putting on just a little weight, and I am just holding my own, Bill Johnson stop's in the Store often, and alway's ask about you, son if you can mail him a card he surely is a nice boy. Last night the Eggemann's came out, we played pinochle, Mr Eggemann

CONTINUE ON TOP PANEL OVERLEAF

☆ U. S. GOVERNMENT PRINTING OFFICE : 1944 16-30042-1

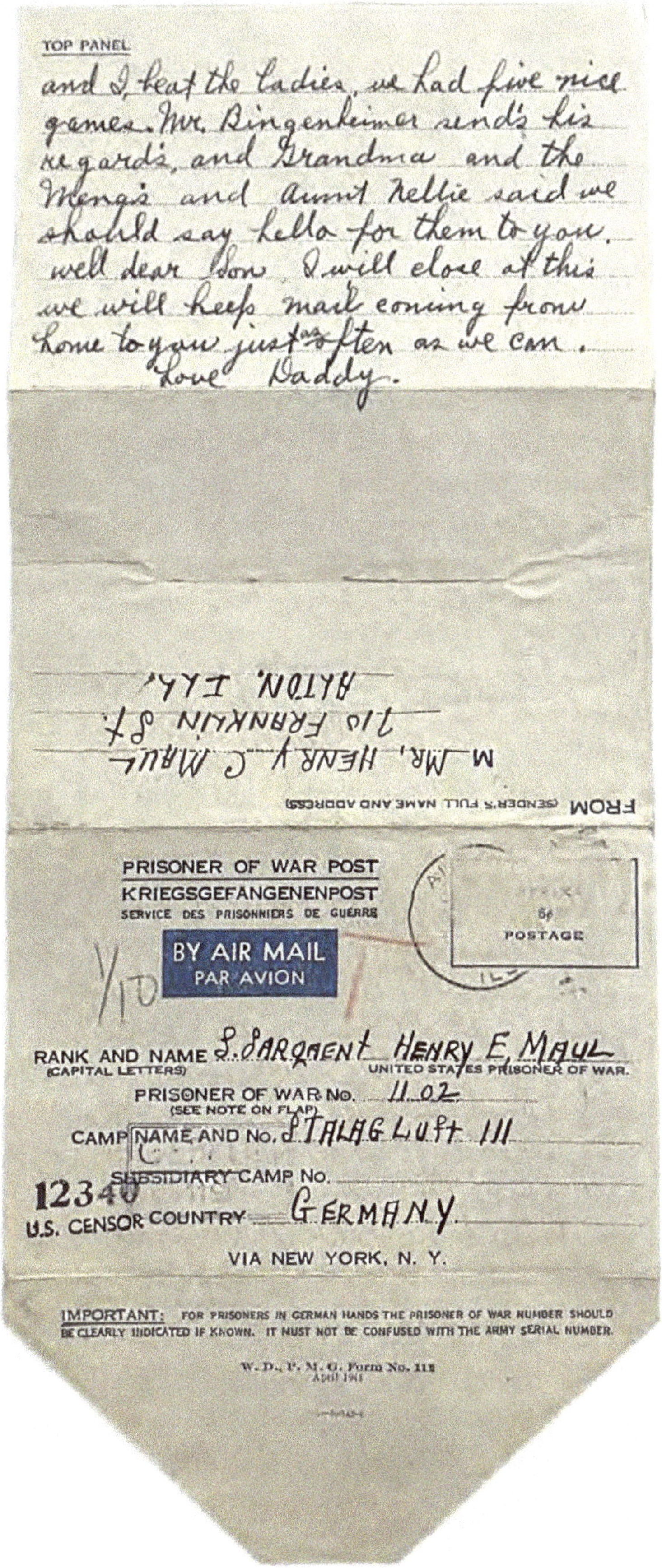
TOP PANEL

and I beat the ladies, we had five nice games. Mr. Bingenheimer send's his regard's, and Grandma and the Meng's and Aunt Nellie said we should say hello for them to you. well dear Son I will close at this we will keep mail coming from home to you just as often as we can.
Love Daddy.

FROM (SENDER'S FULL NAME AND ADDRESS)
M. MR. HENRY C. MAUL
710 FRANKLIN ST.
ALTON, ILL.

PRISONER OF WAR POST
KRIEGSGEFANGENENPOST
SERVICE DES PRISONNIERS DE GUERRE

BY AIR MAIL
PAR AVION

6¢
POSTAGE

RANK AND NAME S. SARGENT HENRY E. MAUL
(CAPITAL LETTERS) UNITED STATES PRISONER OF WAR.

PRISONER OF WAR No. 1102
(SEE NOTE ON FLAP)

CAMP NAME AND No. STALAG LUFT III

SUBSIDIARY CAMP No.

12340
U.S. CENSOR COUNTRY GERMANY

VIA NEW YORK, N. Y.

IMPORTANT: FOR PRISONERS IN GERMAN HANDS THE PRISONER OF WAR NUMBER SHOULD BE CLEARLY INDICATED IF KNOWN. IT MUST NOT BE CONFUSED WITH THE ARMY SERIAL NUMBER.

W. D., P. M. G. Form No. 111
April 1944

To: S. Sargaent Henry E. Maul
Prisoner of War No: 1102
Camp Name and No: Stalag Luft 3
Country: Germany

From: Mr. Henry C. Maul
710 Franklin St.
Alton, Ill.

Mailed: 9/25/1944
Received: 11/4/1945

Alton, Ill's
9-24-44

Dear Son,

Thought it about time for me to write to let you know we do think of you everyday, hoping these few lines do you find you well and O.K.

The weather today is much colder 65 we have our furnace going all the time now, I guess next week I will have to take all our screens down, and get set for a long winter last week we got our coal bin filled up, I think it last for a long time.

Mary-Jane is getting bigger everyday. she often speak's of you, she don't think that you will know her the way she is growing, corky is still the same dog, he is just a good pal, Sis went horse-back riding yesterday afternoon, and last-night she complaint of her leg's acking, today she is O.K. Mother is feeling pretty good now, and is putting on just a little weight, and I am just holding my won, Bill Johnson stop's in the Store often, and always's ask about you, Son if you can mail him a card he surely is a nice boy. Last night the Eggemann's came out, we played pinochle, Mr Eggemann and I beat the ladies, we had five nice games. Mr. Bingenheimer send's his regard's, and Grandma and the Meng's and Aunt Nellie said we Should say hello for them to you. well dear Son, I will close at this we will keep mail coming from home to you just as often as we can.

Love Daddy.

WRITE VERY CLEARLY WITHIN THE LINES. IN ORDER TO EXPEDITE CENSORSHIP, LETTERS SHOULD BE TYPED OR PRINTED IN BLOCK CAPITALS.

Dear Son:- (4) October 2, 1944.

At this time I have received 3 cards and 1 letter from you. The cards were dated June 3, June 16, July 14, and the letter, which was received last was dated May 30th. I feel sure there are more cards and letters on the way. I received your letter on Sept. 18th. This is the fourth letter we have written you, as you will notice I have numbered it on top. We are glad to know you are well, and hope you will do your best to stay that way. It gave me great pleasure to hear you say you had been doing a lot of praying. I know if you keep this up you will be able to bear your burden easier, and some day we can all have a happy reunion. [redacted]

If you do not receive our mail regularly, you will know it is on it's way. I got another prayerbook for you from Fr. Brune. He sends his regards. He took your address, so you may be hearing from him soon. Mrs. Boschert was in the store last week and inquired about you. Paul is stationed in Indiana, and comes home every week end. Are any of your crew with you? George has the same address you do. Everett is at Stalag XI B [redacted] I'm going to write to George as soon as his mother sends me his complete address. I have a picture of the crew which was taken shortly before you went down. Geo. sent it home to his mother. I hear from her quite often. Jim's wife asked me for your address. You should be hearing from her soon. I took some pictures yesterday, which I will send in your package. The girls are getting so tall. Virginia is taller than dad. Mary Jane has almost caught up to me. She is coming along fine now, and what a big relief. Daddy and I

CONTINUE ON TOP PANEL OVERLEAF

U. S. GOVERNMENT PRINTING OFFICE: 1944 16—35065-1

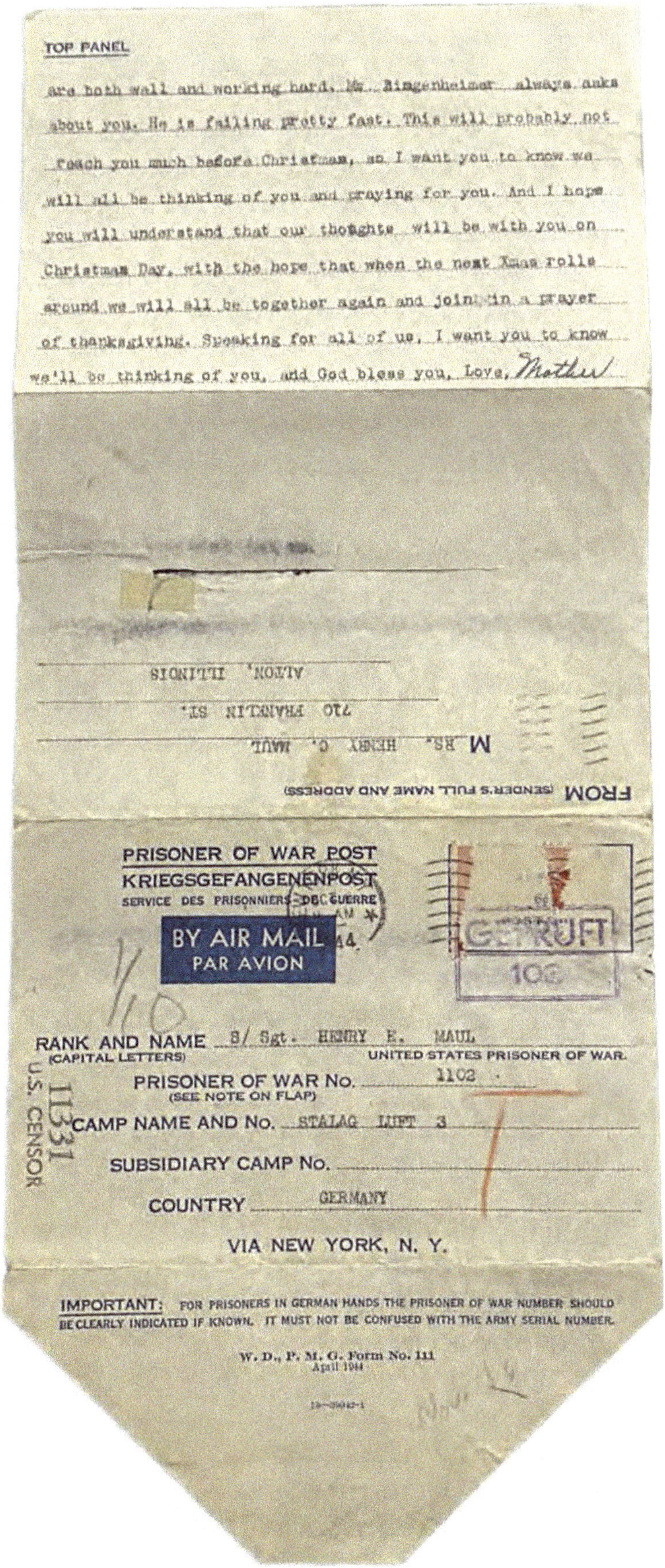

TOP PANEL

are both well and working hard. Mr. Bingenheimer always asks about you. He is failing pretty fast. This will probably not reach you much before Christmas, so I want you to know we will all be thinking of you and praying for you. And I hope you will understand that our thoughts will be with you on Christmas Day, with the hope that when the next Xmas rolls around we will all be together again and join in a prayer of thanksgiving. Speaking for all of us, I want you to know we'll be thinking of you, and God bless you, Love, *Mother*

FROM (SENDER'S FULL NAME AND ADDRESS)

MRS. HENRY C. MAUL
710 FRANKLIN ST.
ALTON, ILLINOIS

PRISONER OF WAR POST
KRIEGSGEFANGENENPOST
SERVICE DES PRISONNIERS DE GUERRE

BY AIR MAIL
PAR AVION

RANK AND NAME (CAPITAL LETTERS) S/ Sgt. HENRY E. MAUL
UNITED STATES PRISONER OF WAR.

PRISONER OF WAR No. (SEE NOTE ON FLAP) 1102

CAMP NAME AND No. STALAG LUFT 3

SUBSIDIARY CAMP No.

COUNTRY GERMANY

VIA NEW YORK, N. Y.

U.S. CENSOR 11331

IMPORTANT: FOR PRISONERS IN GERMAN HANDS THE PRISONER OF WAR NUMBER SHOULD BE CLEARLY INDICATED IF KNOWN. IT MUST NOT BE CONFUSED WITH THE ARMY SERIAL NUMBER.

W. D., P. M. G. Form No. 111
April 1944

To: S/ Sgt. HENRY E. MAUL
Prisoner of War No: 1102
Camp Name and No: STALAG LUFT 3
Country: GERMANY

From: MRS. HENRY C. MAUL
710 FRANKLIN ST.
ALTON, ILLINOIS

Mailed: 10/2/1944
Received: 11/16/1945

Dear Son: - (4) October 2, 1944.

At this time I have received 3 cards and 1 letter from you. The cards were dated June 3, June 16, July 14, and the letter, which was received last was dated May 30th. I feel sure there are more cards and letters on the way. I received your letter on Sept. 18th. This is the fourth letter we have written you, as you will notice I have numbered it on top. We are glad to know you are well, and hope you will do your best to stay that way. It gave me great pleasure to hear you say you had been doing a lot of praying. I know if you keep this up you will be able to bear your burden easier, and some day we can all have a happy reunion. (REDACTED)
If you do not receive our mail regularly, you will know it is on it's way. I got another prayerbook for you from Fr. Bruna. He sends his regards. He took your address, so you may be Hearing from him soon. Mrs. Boschert was in the store last week and inquired about you. Paul is stationed in Indiana, and comes home every week end. Are any of your crew with you? George has the same address you do. Everett is in Stalag X1 B (REDACTED) I'm going to write to George as soon as his mother sends me his complete address. I have a picture of the crew which was taken shortly before you went down. Geo. sent it home to his mother. I hear from her quite often. Jim's wife asked me for your address. You should be hearing From her soon. I took some pictures yesterday, which I will send in your package. The girls are getting so tall. Virginia is taller than dad. Mary Jane has almost caught up to me. She is coming along fine now, and what a big relief. Daddy and I are both well and working hard. Mr. Bingenheimer always asks about you. He is failing pretty fast. This will probably not reach you much before Christmas, so I want you to know we will all be thinking of you and praying for you. And I hope you will understand that our thoughts will be with you on Christmas Day. with the hope that when the next Xmas rolls around we will all be together again and join in a prayer of thanksgiving. Speaking for all of us, I want you to know we'll be thinking of you, and God bless you. Mother

Mary Helen Meng
William Meng
(Dad's First Cousins)

Photo sent from
Helen & Walter Menge
(Helen was Dad's mom's
twin sister).

Note photograph was
sent to Stalag VII.
Received October 8,1944

Who's who...

The Browns were an American League St. Louis baseball team. They played in Sportsman's Park until 1953 when they moved to Baltimore, Maryland and changed their name to the Baltimore Orioles.

The Cardinals are a National League St. Louis baseball team. They also played in Sportsman's Park at the same time as the Browns.

Sis was Virginia Maul Munger, also called Ginny, was my dad's sister.
April 1928 - 1982

Mary J was Mary Jane, Dad's little sister.
Mary Jane Maul Painter Hinton
December 13, 1931 - November 2017

"The store" was the popular Maui's Shoes on Third Street in Downtown Alton. My grandfather owned it until the mid-1950's.

Paul Boschert served in the 106th Infantry Division and captured at the Battle of the Bulge.

Mr. Wilkerson and Mr. Jun were family friends.

Fr. Brune was the priest at St. Mary's Church.

WRITE VERY CLEARLY WITHIN THE LINES. IN ORDER TO EXPEDITE CENSORSHIP, LETTERS SHOULD BE TYPED OR PRINTED IN BLOCK CAPITALS.

10-23-44
Alton, Ill's.

Dear Son,

Today is Monday and the weather is beautiful, the last couple of week's just cool in the morning and during the day it moderate to about 65 to 70, a nice fall this year, hope you are enjoying the same. we finally got our house finished in painting on the outside it sure stand's out and look's mighty nice. The Brown's lost out of the Serious they ~~won~~ win the pennant in the American League, but the Cardinals beat them four out of six games, and they sure were good games. We took some pictures and mailed them last week, I hope you have them by now, I myself really didn't take a very good picture, I hope you really can see Lois Sis & Mary-Jane have growin. We still stay good and busy at the store, we are getting more shoes right along, they all want the best. Paul Boeckert's Mother was in the store today, and she said that Paul is in New, York. she always ask us about you and Paul send's his best regards. Yesterday afternoon Mr. Wilkinson & Mr. Jim and I went fishing, I was the only that caught any just one, such luck, well

CONTINUE ON TOP PANEL OVERLEAF

☆ U. S. GOVERNMENT PRINTING OFFICE: 1944 16-35043-1

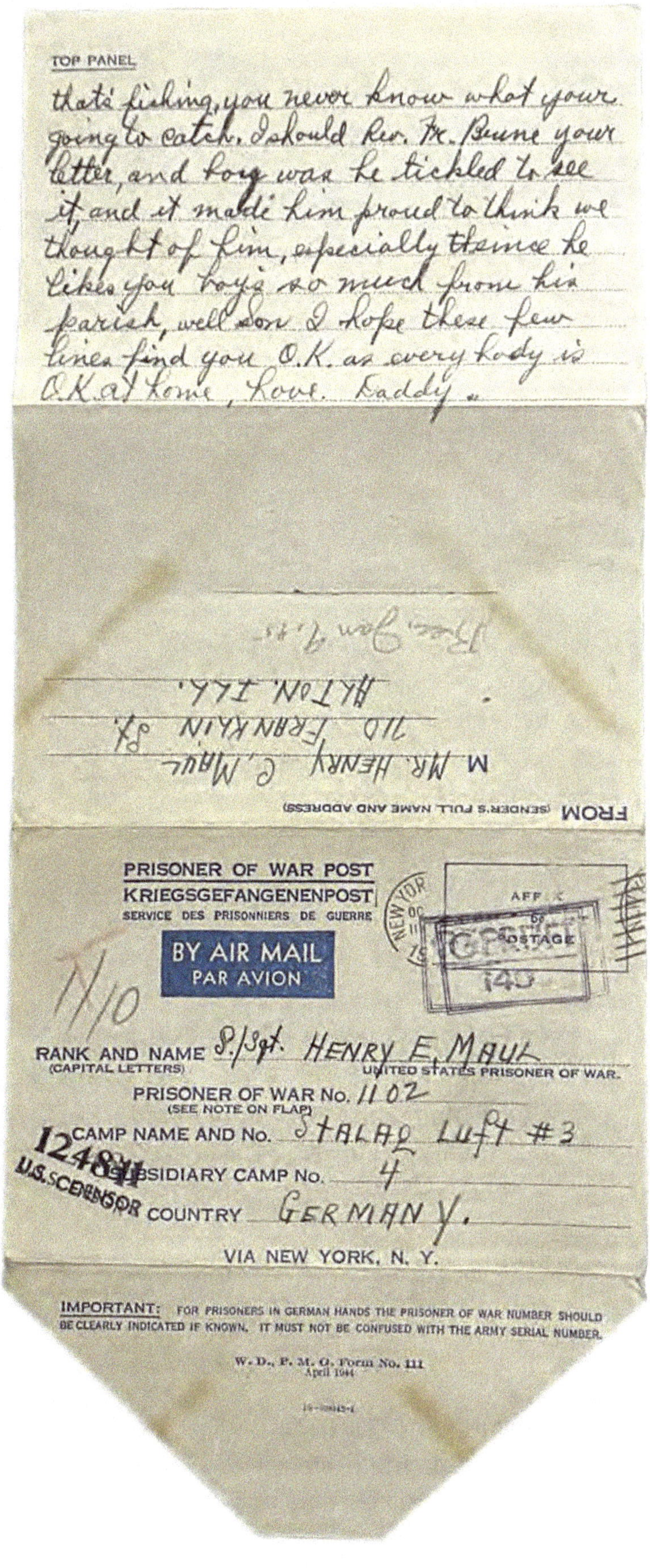
TOP PANEL

thats fishing, you never know what your going to catch. I should Rev. Mr. Beune your letter, and boy was he tickled to see it, and it made him proud to think we thought of him, especially since he likes you boys so much from his parish, well Son I hope these few lines find you O.K. as every body is O.K. at home, Love. Daddy.

Rec. Jan 9, '45

FROM (SENDER'S FULL NAME AND ADDRESS)
M MR. HENRY E. MAUL
710 FRANKLIN ST.
ALTON, ILL.

PRISONER OF WAR POST
KRIEGSGEFANGENENPOST
SERVICE DES PRISONNIERS DE GUERRE

BY AIR MAIL
PAR AVION

11/10

AFFIX 6¢ POSTAGE

NEW YORK

RANK AND NAME (CAPITAL LETTERS) S/Sgt. HENRY E. MAUL
UNITED STATES PRISONER OF WAR.
PRISONER OF WAR No. 1102 (SEE NOTE ON FLAP)
CAMP NAME AND No. STALAG LUFT #3
SUBSIDIARY CAMP No. 4
COUNTRY GERMANY.
VIA NEW YORK, N. Y.

124811
U.S. CENSOR

IMPORTANT: FOR PRISONERS IN GERMAN HANDS THE PRISONER OF WAR NUMBER SHOULD BE CLEARLY INDICATED IF KNOWN. IT MUST NOT BE CONFUSED WITH THE ARMY SERIAL NUMBER.

W. D., P. M. G. Form No. 111
April 1944

To: S./Sgt. Henry E. Maul Prisoner of War No: 1102
Camp Name and No: Stalag Luft 3
Subsidiary Camp No: 4
Country: Germany

From: Mrs. Henry C. Maul
710 Franklin St.
Alton, ILL.

Mailed: 10/23/1944
Received: 1/9/1945

10-23-44

Dear Son, Alton, Ill's.

Today is Monday and the weather
is beautiful, the last couple of week's
just cool in the morning and during
the nice day it moderate to about 65 to 70, a
nice fall this year, hope you are enjoying the same. we finally got our house
finished in painting on the outside it sure
stand's out and look's mighty nice.
The Brown's lost out of the Serious they
~~when~~ win the pennant in the American
League, but the Cardinals beat them four
out of six games, and they sure were good
games. We took some pictures and mailed
them last week, I hope you have them by
now, I myself really didn't take a very
good picture, I hope you really can see how
sis & Mary-Jane have growin. We still
stay good and busy at the store, we are
getting more shoes right along, they all
want the best. Paul Boschert's Mother was in
the store today, and she said that Paul is
in New, York. she alway's asks us about
you and Paul send's his best regards.
Yesterday afternoon Mr. Wilkinson & Mr. Jun
and I went fishing, I was the only that
caught any just one, such luck, well
that's fishing, you never know what your
going to catch. I should Rev. Fr. Brune your
letter, and boy was he tickled to see
it, and it made him proud to think we
thought of him, especially ~~th~~ since he
likes you boy's so much from his
parish, well Son I hope these few
lines find you O.K. as everybody is
O.K. at home, Love. Daddy.

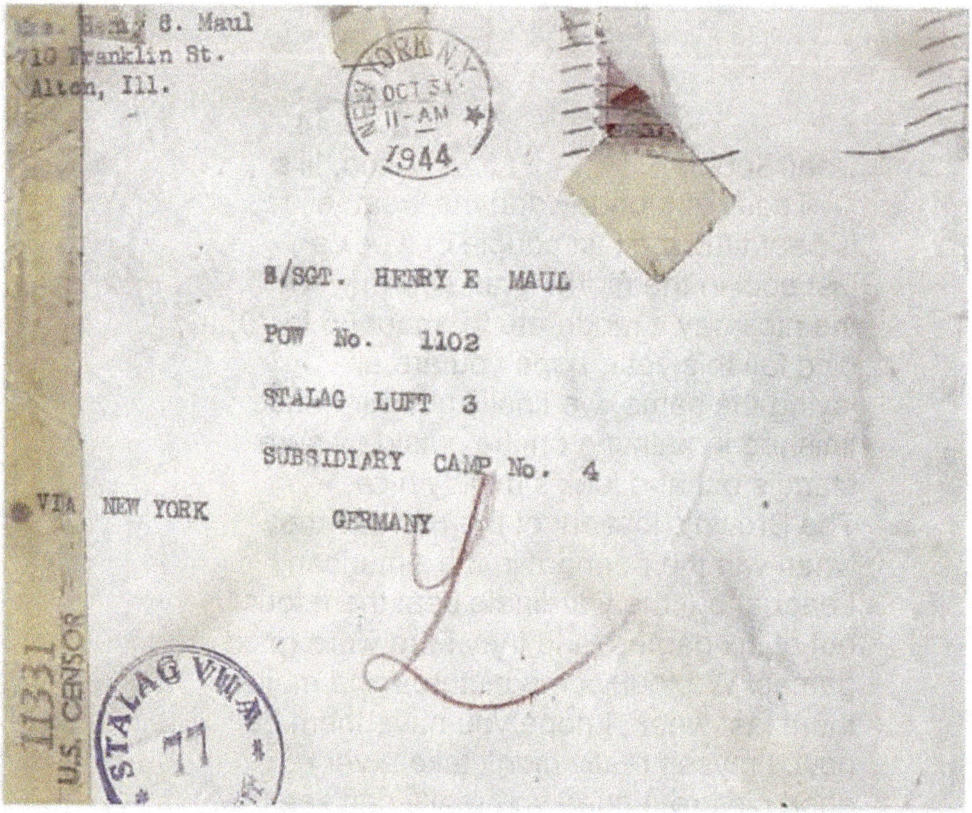
6. Maul
Franklin St.
Alton, Ill.
NEW YORK N.Y.
OCT 31
11-AM
1944
S/SGT. HENRY E MAUL
POW No. 1102
STALAG LUFT 3
SUBSIDIARY CAMP No. 4
VIA NEW YORK
GERMANY
11331
U.S. CENSOR
STALAG
77

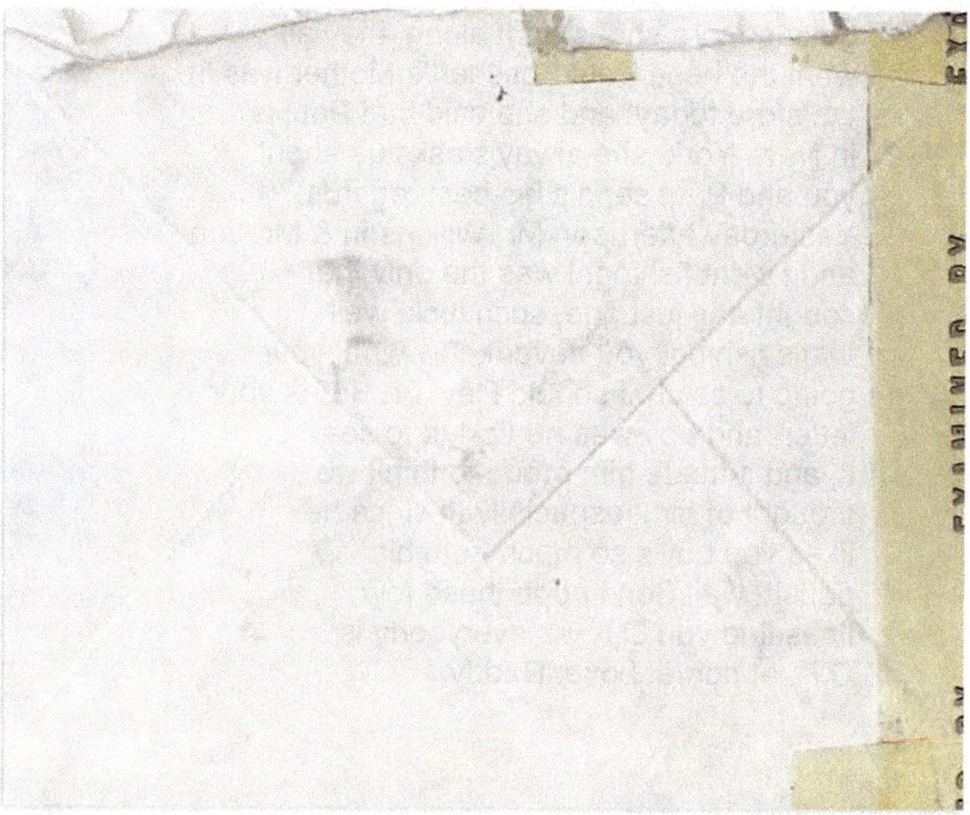

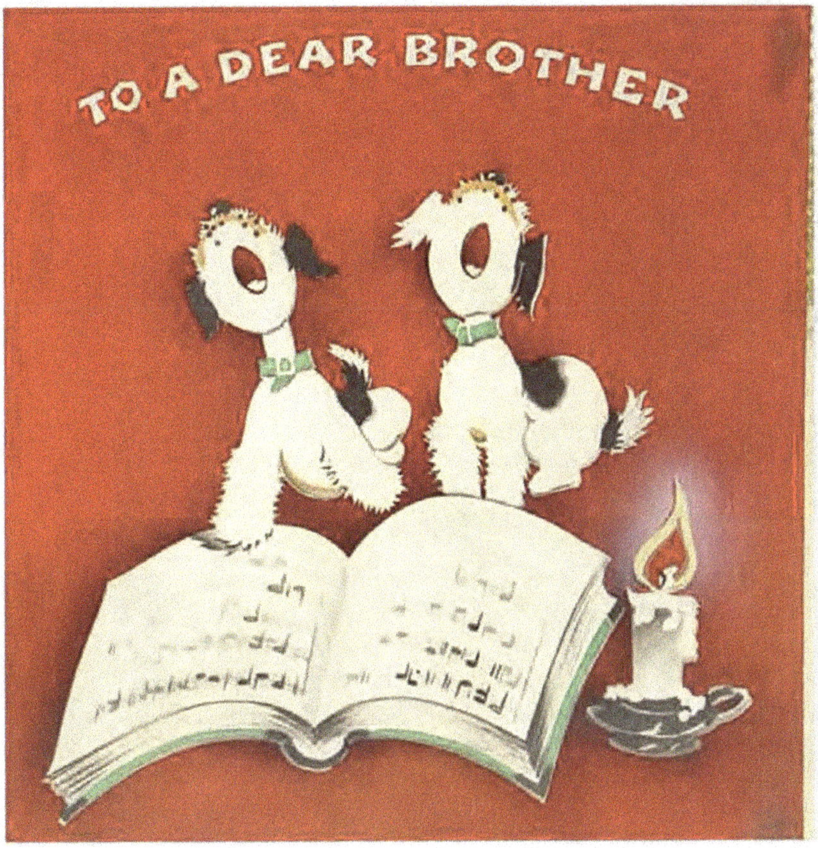

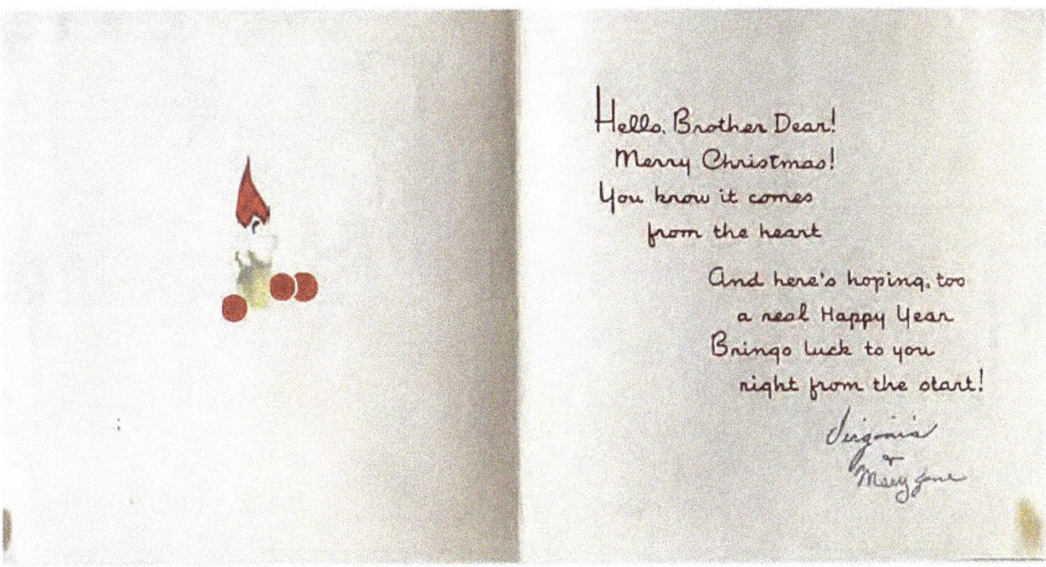

Virginia and Mary Jane were Dad's younger sisters.

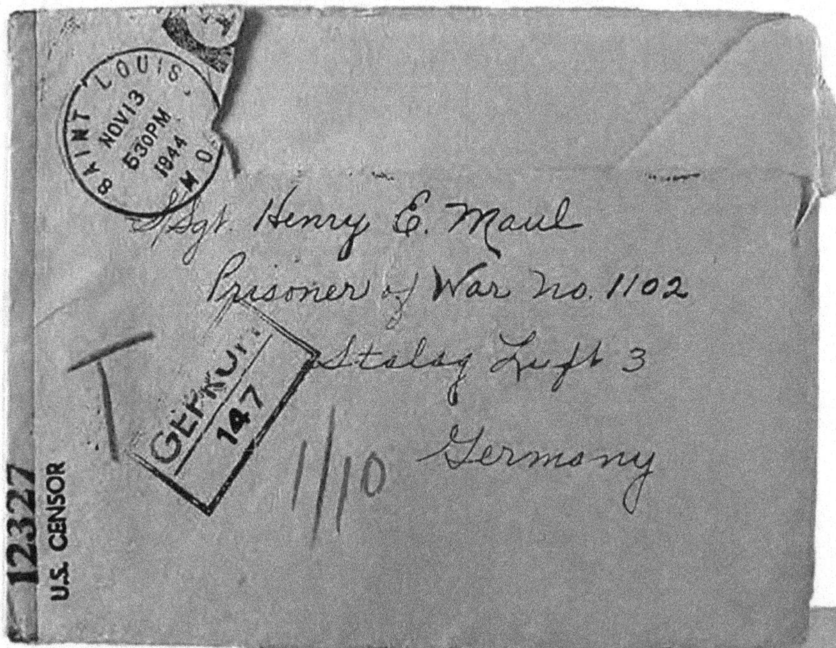

ENVELOPE

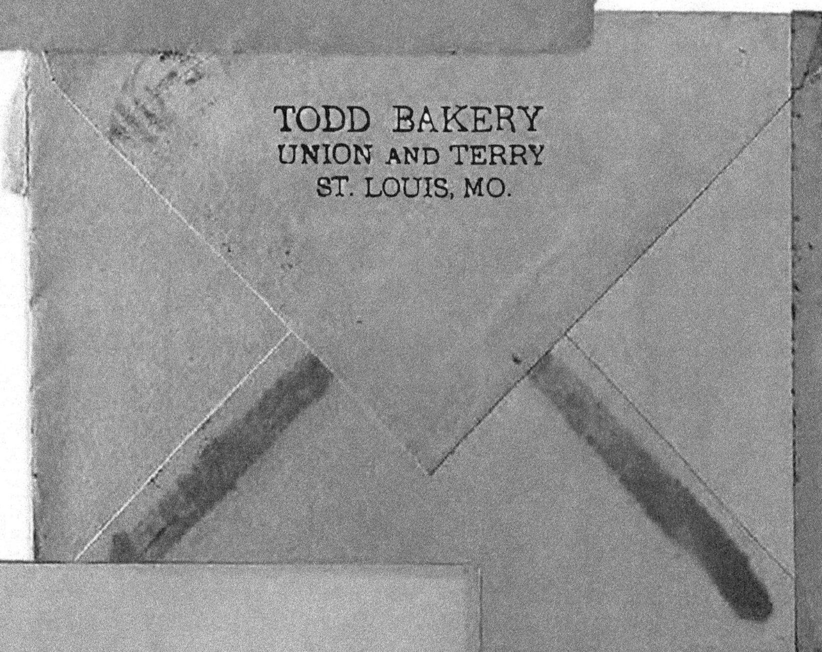

Date Mailed:
Nov 13, 1944

Date Received:
Jan 10, 1945

Back of card

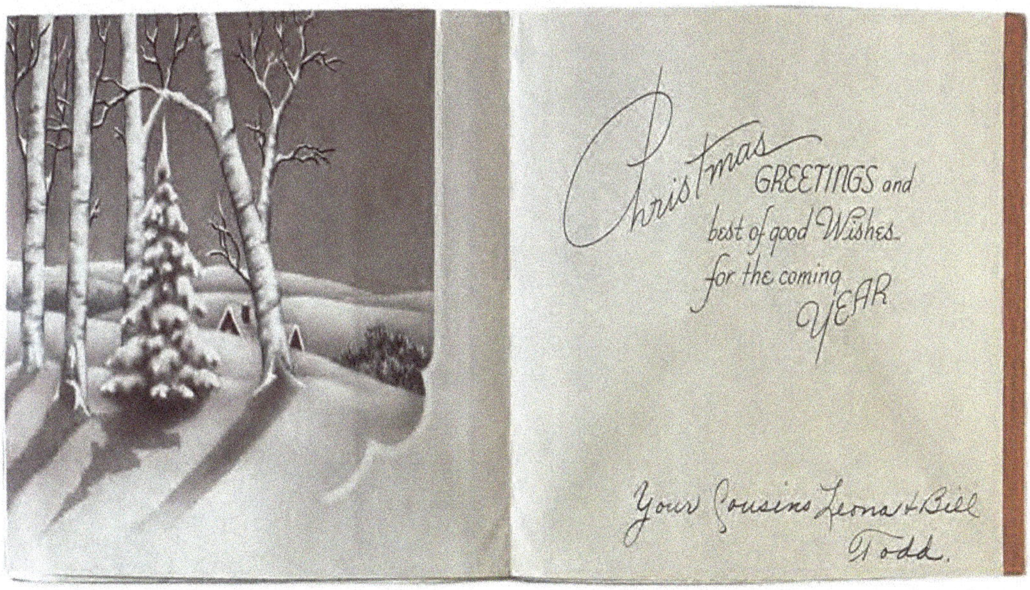

Leona Baumeister Todd
Dad's 1st Cousin
Henry C. Maul's Sister

Card from Red Cross 1944 Christmas

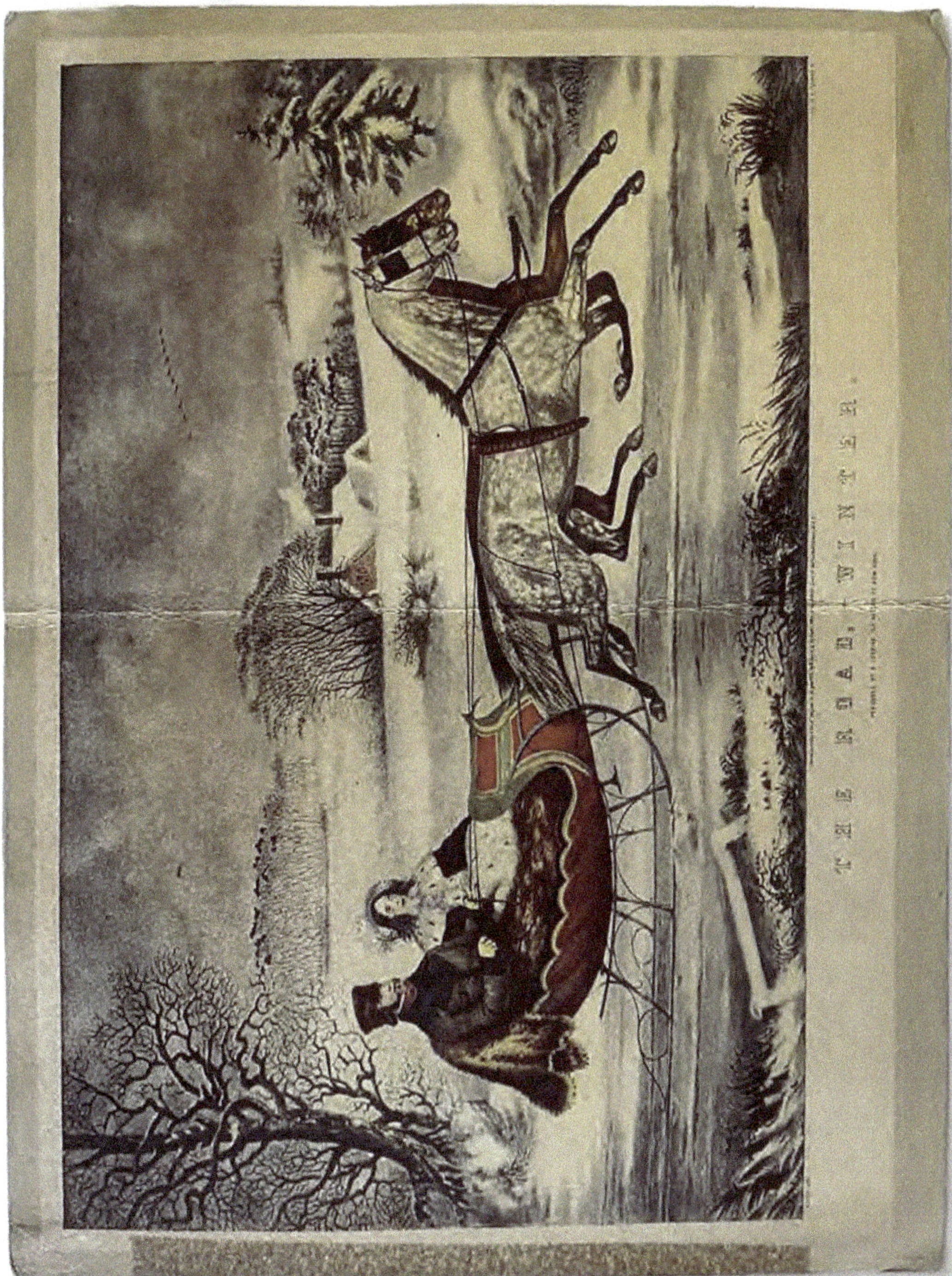

Christmas Card from the Red Cross

- 1944 -

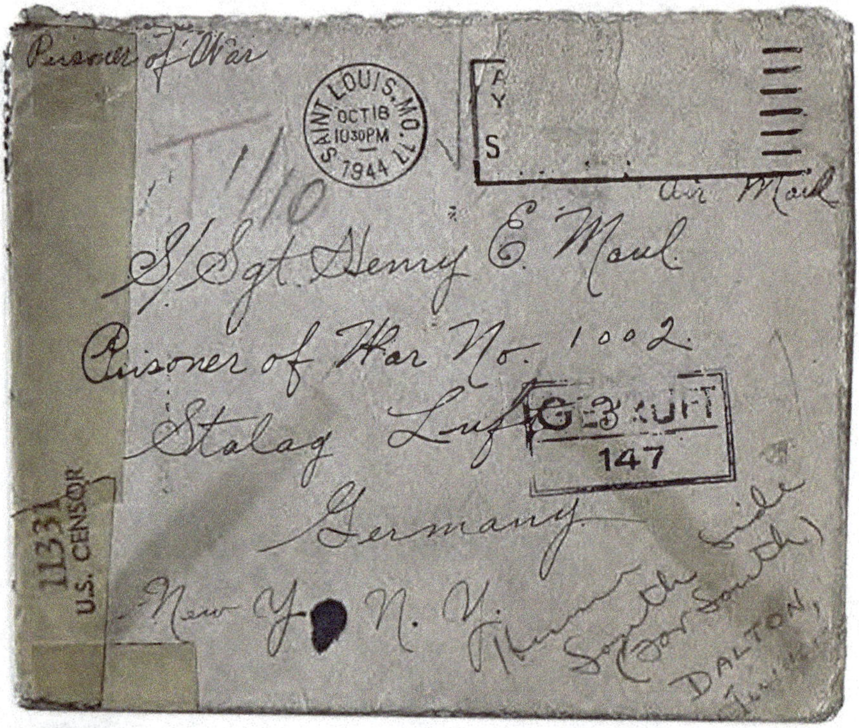

Date Mailed: Oct 18, 1944

Date Received: Jan 10, 1945

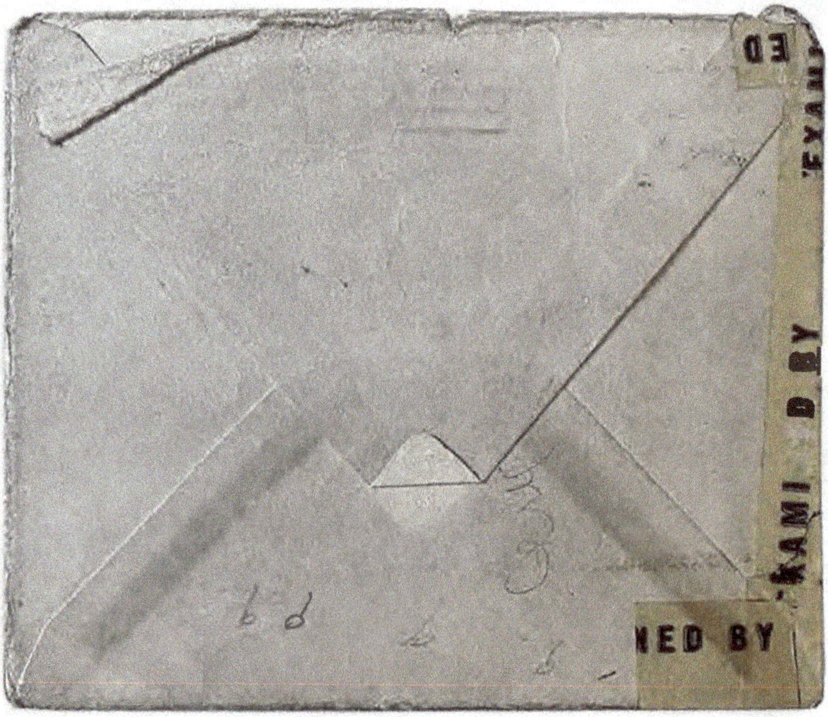

Back of Envelope

Grace Theresa Maul Baumeister Sherman

Dad's 1st Cousin

Henry C. Maul's Sister

Sadly, my dad's parents (my grandparents) did not hear from their son after November 1944. I do not have any letters or cards written to my dad after the October letters and November Christmas cards.

It was not until after Dad was liberated May 12, 1945, that his parents would hear from him again.

It must have been a glorious day!

The *Life*

of a

Waist Gunner

Boeing School of Aeronautics

Army Class 26-42

Graduation Date August 8, 1942

(Dad is front row, very right)

96th Bomb Group

The 96th Bomb Group flew B-17 Flying Fortresses to targets across occupied Europe from May 1943 until April 1945.

B-17 Flying Fortress (Dad's plane)

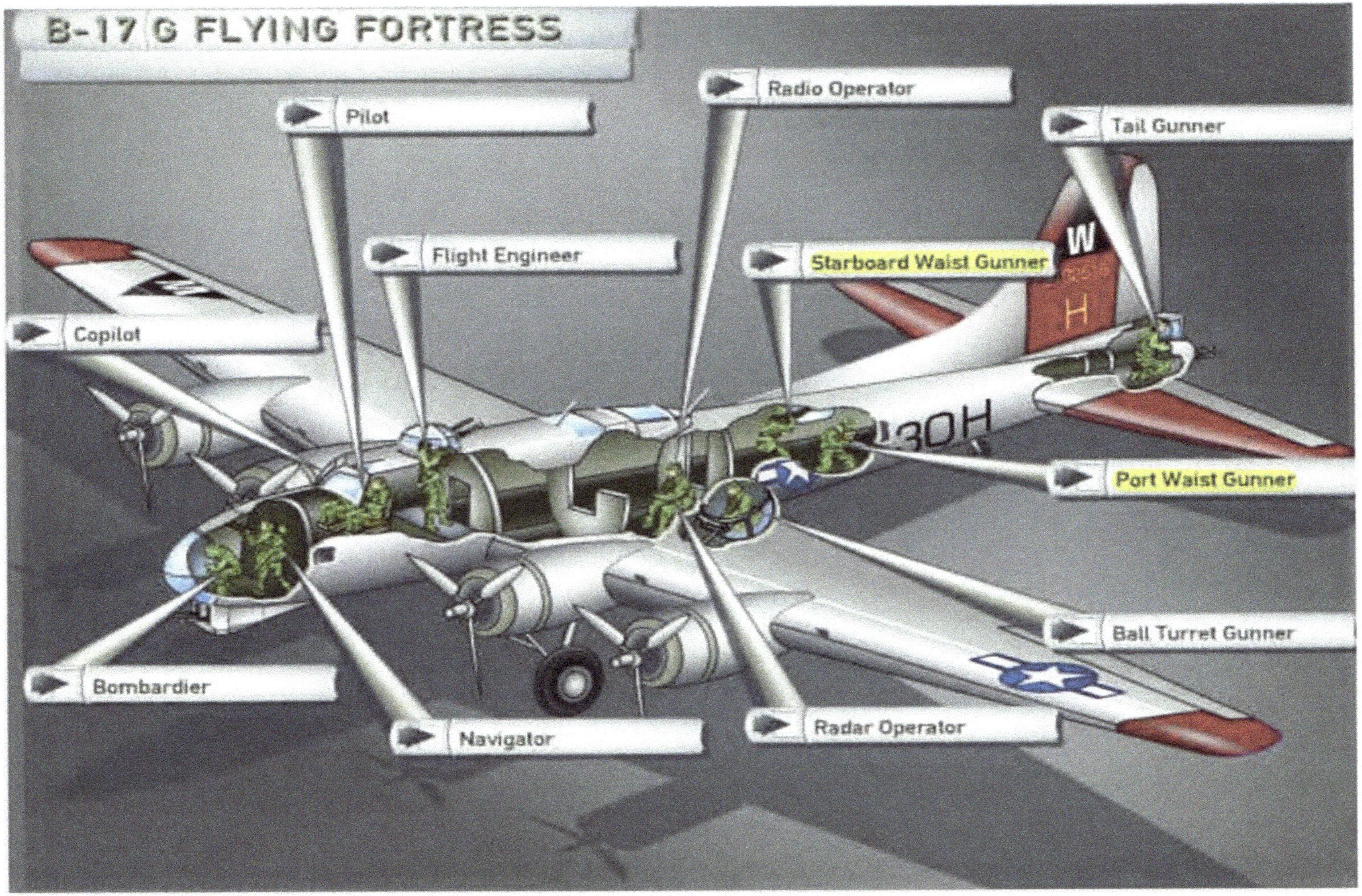

B-17 Flying Fortress Crew Locations

Starboard and Port Waist Gunner Positions

Each of the panels that look like windows is where 2 waist gunners stood totally exposed to the weather...and enemy fire.

Managing the waist guns was uncomfortable and hazardous. Operating at altitudes up to 25,000 feet in an unpressurized cabin, temperatures often plunged to -60° F. Frostbite, hypoxia, and the challenge of operating in bulky flight gear and flak jackets made aiming and firing the guns a constant challenge.

Waist Gunners wore flak helmets, flak suits, oxygen masks, and an armor plate contoured to the curve of the fuselage below the windows. The armor plate was the waist gunner's only protection from the flak and bullets.

Standing at their guns, the gunner's body filled a larger target area than was the case for the rest of the crew, who were sitting or kneeling. Waist gunners incurred the largest number of casualties of all the Flying Fortress crew positions.

B-17 Flying Fortress

Waist Gunner

Dad's job as a Waist Gunner on the 'Laura Jane'

Dad's Patches & Medals
(not all medals were available)

Prisoner of War Medal

(awarded posthumously)

Staff Sargeant Stripes

Curtiss Wright, an airplane manufacturer in St. Louis
(Dad was able to work for Curtiss Wright before his training)

Army Engineering

Good Conduct

Army Air Corp

Purple Heart

KCommandant of Stalag Luft III

Oberst Friedrich Wihelm von Lindeiner-Wildau

Dad's POW Life in Stalag Luft III

Since a few months of my dad's POW time was spent at Stalag Luft III, this is information about his life there. He was eventually moved to Stalag IV (which I have learned was beyond inhumane), Stalag VI, and Stalag II. The differences in each POW camp are in the last now-declassified document of this book.

Stalag Luft III was a Luftwaffe-run (aerial-warfare) POW camp during World War II, which held captured Western Allied Air Force personnel.

History

Stalag Luft III was established in March 1942 near Sagan, Lower Silesia, in what was then Germany (now Żagań, Poland), 100 miles south-east of Berlin. The site was selected because of its sandy soil making it difficult for POW's to build tunnels to escape.

The German military made each branch of their military responsible for the POW's of the same branch. Therefore, the Luftwaffe were responsible for any Allied aircrew taken prisoner. That included captured naval aviators, like members of the British Fleet Air Arm.

The first compound of Luft III (the East Compound) was opened in March 1942. The first POW's to Luft III, or kriegies, as they called themselves, were British, but by the end of 1942, they housed USAAF personnel. The North Compound for British airmen, (where the "Great Escape" later occurred) opened in March 1943. A South Compound for Americans was opened in September 1943. USAAF prisoners began arriving at the camp in significant numbers and the West Compound was opened in July 1944 for US officers. Each compound consisted of fifteen

single-story huts. Each was a 10-by-12-foot bunkroom that slept twenty-two men in five triple-deck bunks. Eventually the camp grew to a total of more than 10,000 POW's.

Building Stalag Luft III

The builders of the Stalag Luft III planned ahead creating several design features that made escape extremely difficult. The digging of escape tunnels was made difficult by several factors: the barracks were raised 24 inches off the ground to make it easier for guards to detect tunneling; the camp had been constructed on land that had a very sandy subsoil; the surface soil was dark grey, so it could easily be detected if anyone dumped the brighter, yellow sand found beneath it above ground, or even just had some of it on their clothing. The loose, collapsible sand also meant the structural integrity of any tunnel would be very poor. A third defense against tunnelling was the placement of seismograph microphones around the perimeter of the camp, which were expected to detect any sounds of digging.

POW Activities

There was a substantial library with schooling facilities available, where many POW's earned degrees such as languages, engineering, or law. The exams were supplied by the Red Cross and supervised by academics who were also POW's in Luft 111. The prisoners also built a theater and put on quality bi-weekly performances. The prisoners used the camp amplifier to broadcast a news and music radio station they named Station KRGY, short for Kriegsgefangener (POW's) and published two newspapers, the Circuit and the Kriegie Times, which were issued four times a week.

Newcomers

POW's operated a system where newcomers to the camp were vetted to prevent German agents from infiltrating their ranks. Any POW who could not be vouched for by two POW's who knew the prisoner by sight was severely interrogated and afterwards

escorted continually by other prisoners, until he was deemed to be a genuine Allied POW. Several infiltrators were discovered by this method, and none are known to have escaped detection in Luft III.

GOONS

German guards were referred to as "goons" and, unaware of the Allied meaning, willingly accepted the nickname after being told it stood for "**G**erman **O**fficer **O**r **N**on-Com". German guards were followed everywhere they went by prisoners, who used an elaborate system of signals to warn others of their location. The guards' movements were then carefully recorded in a logbook kept by officers. Unable to stop what the prisoners called the "Duty Pilot" system, the Germans allowed it to continue and on one occasion the book was used by Kommandant von Lindeiner to bring charges against two guards who had slunk away from duty several hours early.

The 800 Luftwaffe guards were either too old for combat duty or young men convalescing after long tours of duty or from wounds. Because the guards were Luftwaffe personnel, the prisoners were accorded far better treatment than that granted to other POW's in Germany.

Food

Food was an ongoing matter of concern for the POW's. The recommended dietary intake for a normal healthy inactive adult male is 2,150 calories. Luft III issued "Non-working" German civilian rations which allowed 1,928 calories per day, with the balance made up from American, Canadian, and British Red Cross parcels and items sent to the POW's by their families. As was customary at most camps, Red Cross and individual parcels were pooled and distributed to the men equally. The camp also had an official internal bartering system called a *Foodacco* – POW's marketed surplus goods for "points" that could be "spent"

on other items. The Germans paid captured officers the equivalent of their pay in internal camp currency, lagergeld, which was used to buy what goods were made available by the German administration. Every three months, weak beer was made available in the canteen for sale. As Non-commissioned officers did not receive any "pay" it was the usual practice in camps for the officers to provide one-third for their use but at Luft III all lagergeld was pooled for communal purchases. As British government policy was to deduct camp pay from the prisoners' military pay, the communal pool avoided the practice in other camps whereby American officers contributed to British canteen purchases.

Recreational Program

Stalag Luft III had the best-organized recreational program of any POW camp in Germany. Each compound had athletic fields and volleyball courts. The prisoners participated in basketball, softball, boxing, touch football, volleyball, table tennis and fencing, with leagues organized for most. A 20 ft × 22 ft × 5 ft pool used for storing water for firefighting, and “occasionally” available for swimming.

Mail

POW’s could send 2 letters and 4 cards monthly. If mail was deemed urgent, airmail or telegrams were possible. Incoming mail was distributed immediately.

Hygiene

POW’s were allowed one 2-minute cold shower every two months. They had the latrine located between barracks 3 and 4 where they could use the water basins to “wash-up” in between showers…if you could stomach the odor, rats, lice, and fleas.

History Speaks Through Photographs

Imagine spending several/many nights looking through hundreds of World War II and Prisoner of War photographs trying to grasp the subject matter and your father's time as a POW. Then, imagine coming across a photograph with someone you recognize in it...your very own father, at the young age of 20! ...then finding a second!

On the next page are the two photographs of my dad while he was a Prisoner of War.

My father was a POW in at several different camps before he was forced into "The Marches" were 257,000 prisoners of war between January and April 1945 walked in the dead of winter, no food except for what they could "catch" (mice, chickens), poorly clothed, and in poor health.

Dad was first assigned to Stalag Luft III, as he indicates on one of the first pages of his diary. While in Stalag Luft III he received 2 bricks of coal to stay warm and cook his food, one cold shower every two months...for two minutes, and six slats for his bed (no mattress, no board...just slats (try turning over at night)).

Many of the following photographs were taken by prison guards with cameras stolen from prisoner's care packages. Many photographs taken by the guards are all staged showing the prisoners looking their best, but these were not true depictions of life as a prisoner of war.

Imagine 200-250 men in each building, not enough beds (stacked 3 high), six slats for each bunk (no mattress or pillow), many men having to sleep on the floor.

The care and food my dad received while at Stalag Luft III was "adequate" at best. However, once he was moved to Stalag Luft IV, and future camps, his care changed drastically. There were no showers at Stalag Luft IV and the food left the men starving. Not only where the men starving, they seldom received their care packages that they so counted on to keep their spirits up and stay connected to family back home. This accounts for my dad telling my mom to spend $30 a month at the grocery story, whether they needed food or not. He never wanted to go hungry again. And, hungry, my sisters and I never were. My parents always had huge cabinets of dry goods and a double freezer full of meats and more.

In the following pages you will see photographs of Stalag – Luft III, the Kommandant, the showers, and, last but not least, the dreaded German 88mm Gun Flak that brought down my dad's plane. This weapon could take out any plane in one, maybe two, shots...and it was dead accurate.

22 Men Slept Here

(Dad is very top row, very right)

Latrine or bathroom. Note round wash basins

Men were allowed 1 cold shower

every 2 months for 2 minutes.

(Dad is second from right)

Prisoners coming into the Vorlager (outside perimeter)

"Roll Call"

After Roll Call

Stalag Luft III

Prisoners playing a baseball game.
(only at Stalag Luft III)

Back of
Barracks 1, 2, 3

Barracks (aka Huts)
5, 4, then latrine
then, Barracks
3, 2, 1

POW Showers
One every 2 months
2 minutes long
Cold water only

Scenes of Stalag Luft III

The Dreaded German 88mm Gun Flak

The weapon that took down my dad's plane in one shot.

German

POW Camps

Location of German Camps and Hospitals Where American Prisoners of War and Civilian Internees Are Held (Based on information received to December 31, 1944).

PRISONER OF WAR CAMPS

CAMP	NEAREST TOWN	MAP SQUARE
Stalag II A	Neubrandenburg	B 2
Stalag II B	Hammerstein	C 1-2
Stalag III A	Luckenwalde	B 2
Stalag III B	Fürstenburg/Oder	C 2
Stalag III C	Altdrewitz	C 2
Stalag III D	Berlin-Steglitz	B 2
Stalag IV A	Hohnstein	B-C 3
Stalag IV B	Mühlberg	B 2
Stalag IV C	Wistritz	B 3
Stalag IV D	Torgau	B 2
Stalag IV D/Z	Annaburg	B 2
Stalag IV F	Hartmannsdorf	B 3
Stalag IV G	Oschatz	B 2
Stalag V A	Ludwigsburg	A-B 3
Stalag V B	Villingen	A 4
Stalag VI G	Bergisch-Neustadt	A 2
Stalag VI J	Krefeld	A 2
Stalag VII A	Moosburg	B 3
Stalag VII B	Memmingen	B 4
Stalag VIII B	Teschen	D 3
Stalag 344	Lamsdorf	C 3
Stalag VIII C	Sagan	C 2
Stalag IX B	Bad Orb	A-B 3
Stalag IX C	Bad Sulza	B 2
Stalag X B	Bremervörde	A-B 2
Stalag X C	Nienburg	A 2
Stalag XI A	Altengrabow	B 2
Stalag XI B	Fallingbostel	B 2
Stalag XII A	Limburg	A 3
Stalag XII D	Wahbreitbach	A 3
Stalag XII F	Freinsheim	A 3
Stalag XIII C	Hammelburg	B 3
Stalag XIII D	Nürnberg-Langwasser	B 3
Stalag 383	Hohenfels	B 3
Stalag XVII A	Kaisersteinbruch	C 4
Stalag 398	Pupping	B-C 4
Stalag XVIII A	Wolfsberg	C 4
Stalag XVIII C(317)	Markt-Pongau	B-C 4
Stalag 357	Oerbke	A 2
Stalag XX A	Torun	D 2
Stalag XX B	Marienburg	D 1
WK 8—BAB 21	Blechhammer	D 3

CAMPS FOR AIRMEN

Luft I	Barth	B 1
Luft III	Sagan	C 2
Luft IV	Grosstychow	C 1
Luft VII	Bankau	C-D 2
Stalag XVII B	Krems/Gneixendorf	C 3
Dulag Luft	Wetzlar	A 3

NAVAL AND MERCHANT MARINE CAMPS

Marlag-Milag	Tarmstedt	A-B 2

GROUND FORCE OFFICERS' CAMPS

Oflag IV C	Colditz	B 2
Oflag VII B	Eichstätt	B 3
Oflag IX A/H	Spangenburg	B 2
Oflag IX A/Z	Rotenburg	B 2-3
Oflag X B	Nienburg	A 2
Oflag XI (79)	Brunswick	B 2
Oflag 64	Altburgund	C 2

LAZARETTS (Hospitals)

	NEAREST TOWN	MAP SQUARE
IV A	Res. Laz. Elsterhorst (Hohnstein)	C 3
IV G	Leipzig	B 2
V B	Rottenmunster	A 4
VI C	Res. Laz. Lingen	A 2
VI G	Res. Laz. Gerresheim	A 2
VII A	Freising	B 2-3
IX B	Bad Soden/Salmünster	A 3
IX C	Obermassfeld	B 2-3
IX C	Meiningen	B 3
IX C	Hildburghausen	B 3
X A	Res. Laz. II, Schleswig	B 1
X B	Sandbostel	A-B 2
XIII D	Nürnberg-Langwasser	B 3
XVIII A/Z	Spittal/Drau	B-C 4
Marine Lazarett Cuxhaven		A 1
Luftwaffen Lazarett 4/11 Wismar		B 1
Res. Laz. II Vienna		C 3-4
Res. Laz. Graz		C 4
Res. Laz. Bilin		B-C 3
Res. Laz. Wollstein		C 2
Res. Laz. II Stargard		C 2
Res. Laz. Schmorkau		C 2
Res. Laz. Königswartha		C 2
Res. Laz. Ebelsbach		B 3

CIVILIAN INTERNEE CAMPS

Ilag Biberach	B 4
Ilag Liebenau	B 4
Ilag VII/H Laufen	B 4

Key

- Prisoner of War Camps
- Camps for Airmen
- Officer's Camps
- Civilian Internee Camps
- Hospitals (Lazaretts)
- Marlag and Milag

Scale: 72 miles per inch.

Published by
THE AMERICAN
NATIONAL RED CROSS

"The March"

The March

"The March" has been called: "The Great March West", "The Long March", "The Long Walk", "The Long Trek", "The Black March", "The Bread March", and "Death March Across Germany", but most survivors just called it "The March". Dad referred to it as "The Marches" because he endured more than one and commented it was the worst part of the entire ordeal of being a prisoner of war...the below zero temperatures, the starvation (scavenging for rodents, wild chickens…so much worse than the camps), the endless walking going "nowhere".

"The March" refers to a forced marches during the final stages of World War II in Europe. There were 257,000 Prisoners of War held in German military prison camps, of which more than 80,000 POW's were forced to march west across Germany, Poland, and Czechoslovakia in one of the coldest winters in history, over between January and April 1945.

German authorities could see the Soviet Army advancing on the Eastern Front, so they decided to evacuate POW camps hoping to delay the liberation of the prisoners. At the same time, hundreds of thousands of German civilian refugees, most of them women and children, as well as civilians of other nationalities, were also making their way westward on foot.

Some of the POW camps were:

- From Stalag Luft IV at Gross Tychow in Pomerania the prisoners faced a 500 mile march in blizzard conditions across Germany
- Stalag VIII-B, had what became known as the "Lamsdorf Death March"
- Stalag Luft III in Silesia to Bavaria

(My dad was a part of all three of these camps, Stalag III, Stalag IV, and Stalag XIII-D). ugh!

<u>Motive</u>

Adolf Hitler issued an order on 19 July 1944 "concerning preparations for the defense of the Reich". The German civilian population were issued instructions for preparations for

evacuations of "foreign labor" (slave labor) and civilians away from the advancing Soviet Army in the east. Their goal was to make "preparations for moving prisoners of war to the rear" which prolonged the war for hundreds of thousands of Allied personnel, as well as causing them severe hardship, starvation, injuries and/or death. May POW's died during the marches, only to be left behind.

There were great concerns among POW's over the motives for moving them westward. Many different and conflicting rumors abounded, including suggestions that:

- They were being moved toward concentration camps to be killed.
- POW's would be force-marched until their deaths from exhaustion).
- They would be held hostage to leverage peace deals.

Evacuation Routes

There were three main POW evacuation routes west:

- The "northern route", included POW's from Stalag XX-B, Stalag XX-A and Stalag Luft IV. It is estimated that 100,000 POW's took the northern route. It went from Stalag Luft IV at Gross Tychow, Pomerania, to Stettin to Stalag XI-B and Stalag 357 at Fallingbostel. Some prisoners were marched from here at the end of the war towards Lübeck, however, for most, Fallingbostel was their final destination. The route involved crossing the River Oder and the Elbe. Various groups of POW's were distributed across an area of more than 500 square miles, with some still far behind on roads to the west of Danzig (Gdansk): so the reality was much less organized than it might first appear.
- A "central route", started at Stalag Luft 7 at Bankau, near Kreuzburg in Silesia (now Poland), via Stalag 344 (formerly and usually known as Stalag VIII-B) at Lamsdorf, to Stalag VIII-A at Görlitz, then ending at Stalag III-A at Luckenwalde, 19 mi south of Berlin.
- The "southern route", from Stalag VIII-B (formerly Stalag VIII-D) at Teschen (not far from Auschwitz) which was led

through Czechoslovakia, towards Stalag XIII-D at Nürnberg and then onto Stalag VII-A at Moosburg in Bavaria.

The direction of travel was not consistent. An individual group would sometimes travel in circles and end up at a previous stopping point; it often zig-zagged. It is estimated the distance covered as 990 miles.

The forced march of thousands of western Allied POW's from Stalag Luft VI at Heydekrug beginning in July 1944 was the first of the series of marches known as the Long March. My dad was not a part of this march, thank goodness! The POW's were marched either to Stalag Luft IV at Gross Tychow (a journey which also involved a 60-hour journey by ship to Swinemünde), or to Stalag XX-A at Thorn in Poland (with part of the distance covered by cattle train).

The Marches

January and February 1945 were among the coldest winter months of the 20th century in Europe, with blizzards and temperatures as low as -13 °F, and until the middle of March, temperatures were well below 32 °F. Most POW's were ill-prepared for the evacuation, having suffered years of poor rations and wearing clothing ill-suited to the appalling winter conditions.

In most camps, the POW's were broken up in groups of 250 to 300 men and because of the inadequate roads and the flow of battle, not all the prisoners followed the same route. The groups would march up to 25 miles a day - resting in factories, churches, barns and even in open fields. Long processions of POW's were wandering over the northern part of Germany with little or nothing in the way of food, clothing, shelter, or medical care.

Experiences

Prisoners from different camps had different experiences: sometimes the Germans provided farm wagons for those unable to walk. There seldom were horses available, so teams

of POW's pulled the wagons through the snow. Sometimes the guards and prisoners became dependent on each other, other times the guards became increasingly hostile. Passing through some villages, the residents would throw bricks and stones, and in others, the residents would share their last food. Some groups of prisoners were joined by German civilians who were also fleeing from the Russians. Some who tried to escape or could not go on were shot by guards.

Those with intact boots had the dilemma of whether to remove them at night - if they left them on, trench foot could result; if they removed them, they may not get their swollen feet back into their boots in the morning or get frostbite. Worse still, the boots may freeze or, more likely, be stolen.
With so little food they were reduced to scavenging to survive. Some were reduced to eating dogs and cats — and even rats and grass—anything they could obtain. My dad did not talk much about the war, but he did talk about having only grass to eat as his meals. Already underweight from years of prison rations, some were at half their pre-war body weight by the end.

Because of the unsanitary conditions and a near starvation diet, hundreds of POW's died of disease along the way and many more were ill.

Dysentery was common: 80% of the POW's on the northern line of march were suffering from dysentery. Sufferers had the indignity of soiling themselves and having to continue to march, and being further weakened by the debilitating effects of illness. Dysentery was easily spread from one group to another when they followed the same route and rested in the same places.

Frostbite was also very common which could lead to gangrene. Typhus, spread by body lice, was always a risk for POW's, but was now increased by using overnight shelters previously occupied by infected groups. Some men simply froze to death in their sleep.

On top of these issues, the POW's were constantly under air attack by Allied forces mistaking the POW's for retreating German troops.

As winter came to an end, some of the German guards became less harsh in their treatment of POW's. As the columns reached the western side of Germany they ran into the advancing western Allied armies. For some, this brought liberation. Others were not so lucky. They were marched towards the Baltic Sea, where Nazis were rumored to be using POW's as human shields and hostages. It was later estimated that a large number of POW's had marched over 500 miles by the time they were liberated, and some had walked nearly 930 miles.

New Zealander Norman Jardine explained how, once liberated, his group of POW's were given a revolver by a U.S. Army officer and told to shoot any guards who had treated them unfairly. He stated that "We did!"

On 4 May 1945 RAF Bomber Command implemented Operation Exodus, and the first prisoners of war were repatriated by air. Bomber Command flew 2,900 sorties over the next 23 days, carrying 72,500 prisoners of war.

Operation EXODUS

After the end of hostilities in Europe, orders were received May 2,1945 that 300 repatriated POW's were arriving by air at 1100. All arrangements were made for their reception, and the provision of refreshments laid on in the Social Club.
Seven Douglas Dakotas landed with repatriated POW's on the following day and more throughout the month, until by the end of May, 72 Dakotas had brought 1,787 POW's.

Operation EXODUS was in full swing and May 1945 was even busier with 443 Avro Lancasters, 103 Dakotas, 51 Handley Page Halifaxes, 31 Consolidated Liberators, 3 Short Stirlings, 3 Lockheed Hudsons, and 2 Boeing Fortresses bringing 15,088 personnel.

The Aftermath

The total number of US POW's in Germany was in the region of 93,000-94,000 and official sources claim that 1,121 died. The British Commonwealth total was close to 180,000 and while no accurate records exist, if a similar casualty rate is assumed, the number who died would be around 2,200. According to a report by the US Department of Veterans Affairs, almost 3,500 US and Commonwealth POW's died as a result of the marches. It is possible that some of these deaths occurred before the death marches, but the marches would have claimed the vast majority.

It is guessed that between 2,500 and 3,500 American, British and Commonwealth POW deaths on the marches.

Former POW's preparing to board an Avro Lancaster B Mark I in Lubeck, Germany for Repatriation.

March Timeline

- 13 July 1944 – evacuation of Stalag Luft VI at Šilutė (Heydekrug) in Lithuania begins, to Stalag Luft IV at Gross Tychow involving a force march and 60hr journey by ship to Swinemünde, or by force march and cattle train to Stalag XX-A at Thorn in Poland.
- 17 December 1944 – The SS shot seventy-one captured American POW's in the Malmedy massacre.
- 24 December 1944 – POW work camps near Königsberg (now Kaliningrad) are evacuated.
- 27 December 1944 to April 1945 – POW's at Stalag VIII-B (formerly Stalag VIII-D) at Teschen began their forced march through Czechoslovakia, towards Dresden, then towards Stalag XIII-D at Nürnberg and finally on to Stalag VII-A at Moosburg in Bavaria.
- 12 January 1945 – Red Army launched offensive in Poland and East Prussia.
- 19 January 1945 – evacuation from Stalag Luft 7 at Bankau, near Kreuzberg, Poland, begins in blizzard conditions – 1,500 prisoners were force marched then loaded onto cattle trucks and taken to Stalag III-A at Luckenwalde, south of Berlin. Evacuation of work party 344 at (Piaski), part of Stalag VIIB, prisoners commenced march on foot.
- 20 January 1945 – Stalag XX-A at Thorn, Poland started evacuation.
- 22 January 1945 – Stalag 344 at Lamsdorf, Silesia was evacuated.
- 23 January 1945 – Evacuation began at Stalag XX-B at Marienburg, Danzig.
- 27 January 1945 to February 1945 – evacuation *Dad Marched* began at Stalag Luft III, Sagan, to either Stalag III-A at Luckenwalde, 30 km south of Berlin, or to Marlag und Milag Nord, near Bremen, or to Stalag XIII-D,

near Nürnberg, then onto Stalag VII-A near Moosburg, Bavaria.

- 29 January 1945 - Stalag IID Stargard (now Stargard Szczeciński, Poland) was evacuated. Almost a thousand men struggled into formation. There were about five-hundred Russians, two-hundred Frenchmen, one-hundred Americans and twenty-five Canadians in the march. The POW's were put on a forced march along a northern route in blizzard conditions via Settin (Szczecin) to arrive at Stalag II-A, Neubrandenburg on February 7, 1945.
- 6 February 1945 to March 1945 – Evacuation from Stalag Luft IV at Gross Tychow, Pomerania began an eighty-six-day forced march to Stalag XI-B and Stalag 357 at Fallingbostel. Many prisoners were then marched from here at the end of the war towards Lübeck.
- 8 February 1945 – Stalag VIII-C at Sagan was evacuated. The POW's marched across Germany to Stalag IX-B near Bad Orb, and arrive there 16 March.
- 10 February 1945 – Stalag VIII-A at Görlitz was evacuated.
- 14 February 1945 – Commonwealth and US bomber squadrons attacked Dresden.
- 19 March 1945 – Hitler issued the Nero Decree.
- 3 April 1945 – Stalag XIII-D at Nürnberg was evacuated. *Dad Marched*
- 6 April 1945 – Stalag XI-B and Stalag 357 at Fallingbostel were evacuated.
- 16 April 1945 – Oflag IV-C, (Colditz Castle), was liberated.
- 16 April 1945 – POW's left behind at Fallingbostel were liberated by the British Second Army.
- 17 April 1945 – Bergen-Belsen concentration camp was liberated.
- 19 April 1945 – POW column was attacked by allied aircraft at Gresse resulting in 60 fatalities.
- 22 April 1945 – Stalag III-A at Luckenwalde was liberated by Soviet forces.

- 27 April 1945 – US and Soviet forces met at the River Elbe.
- 29 April 1945 – Stalag VII-A at Moosburg was liberated by Patton's Third United States Army.
- 30 April 1945 – Berlin falls to the Red Army and Hitler commits suicide.
- 4 May 1945 – German forces surrendered on Lüneburg Heath.
- 10 May 1945 – The last POW's evacuated from Stalag 357 / Stalag XI-B at Fallingbostel are liberated.
- 12 May 1945 – The Red Army releases Commonwealth and US POW's at Stalag III-A, Luckenwalde.

The March To Moosburg

With 80,000 other POW's, my dad left Stalag Luft IV in Kiefheide January 31, 1945 and marched until February 7th to Nurnberg during one of the colest winters on record.

At Midnight, April 4th, they left Nurnberg and marched until April 16th. This march ended in Moosburg with hot showers for everyone. (see dad's notes on this march)

Dad's notes from his 2nd march from Nürnberg, April 4, 1945 to Moosburg, April 16, 1945.

Wed. April 4. 45

Left Nurnberg 12:00 AM

OCHENBRUCK - 4:30 P.M. 18 K. S of NURNBERG About 3 P.M. P47s straffed to our rear & dive bombed

Arrived at Polling at 11: P.M.

Thurs. APR. 5.

Polling 3½ K. N. of Newmarkt slept in barn

Left at 10 AM Arrived in NEWMARKT About noon. - Horrible Night - slept outdoors in Pine Grove in RAIN

1 K. S. of Polling we watched Heavies bomb Nur.

Fri. 8:30 A.M. APR. 6

MUHLHAUSEN - 12 K. S. of Newmarkt

PFARR dorf -

Berching

2 men to English Red X Parcel

Beilengries

walked up steep mt. in rain to -

SAT. APR. 7.

Paulshofen

Town on Plateau atop mt.

Leave Sun. Morning at 5 AM.

SUN. APR. 8

Prnsdorf

Two Hr rest at noon in orchard with semi-stockade Fence

MENDELSTETTEN - 6. P.M.

Leave Town Mon. Morning & cross DANUBE River at 11: AM.

MON. APRIL 9

NEUSTADT on the DANUBE, walked right through town BY 11:35 AM

Tues. Apr. 10

siegenburg! 2 men to belgian R.C. parcel

GROSRAMMELSDORF. slept Here & received A Belgium R.C parcel for 7 men on leaving town

wed APR 11

HOLZHAUSEN - 2 DAYS & 3 Nights

FRI. APR. 13

HOLZHAUSEN. LEAVE AT 9 AM. 2 MEN to No. 10 R.C. PARCEL. TAPS for our LATE great PRES FDR. ARRIVE AT farm outside of GAMMELSDORF. 2 men to French R.C. parcel

SAT. APR. 14.

GAMMELSDORF (outskirts 1K.)

2 days & 3 Nights

SUN. Apr. 15.

went to A Real church in town.

MON APR 16. Left GAMMELSDORF 10:30 AM

Arrive Moosburg 4:30 PM

Received Hot shower

300 MEN to A TENT.

OCHENBRUCK
Polling
MUHLHAUSEN
PFARR DORF
STADT BERCHING
Beilengries
PAULUSHOFEN
AMTMANNSDORF
PON DORF
SCHAMHAUPTEN

Sandersdorf
MENDELSTETTEN
ForcHeim
MARCHING
NEUSTADT
MUHLHAUSEN
siegenBurg
GROSRUMMELSDORF
PFEFFENHAUSEN
HOLZHAUSEN
GAMMELSDORF
MOOSBURG

Operation EXODUS

Wed. April 4. 45
Left Nurnberg 12:00 AM
OCHENBRUCK – 4:30 P.M. 18K. S of
NURNBERG about 3 P.M. P.47s
Strafford to our rear & dive bombed
ARRIVED AT Polling at 11: P.M.

Thurs. APR. 5.
Polling 3 ½ K.N. of Newmarkt slept in barn
Left at 10 AM. Arrived in Newmarkt about
Noon. – Horrible Night – Slept outdoors in Pine
Grove in Rain
1 K.S. of Polling we watched Heavies bomb Norris

Fri. 8:30 A.M. APF. 6
MUHLHAUSEN – 12 K.S. of Newmarkt
PFAARRDORF –
Berching
2 men to English Red X Parcel
Beilengries
Walked up steep mt. in rain to-

Sat. Apr 7.
Paulshofen
Town on Plateau a top mt.
Leave sun. morning at 8. A.M.

Sun. Apr. 8
Pensdorf
Two Hr. rest at noon in orchard with
semi-stockade Fence
Mendglstetten – 6. P.M.
Leave Town Mon. Morning & Cross
Danube River at 11.A.M.

Mon. April 9
Neostadt on the Danube, walked
Right through town by 11:25 A.M.

Tues. Apr. 10
Siegenburg! 2 men to belgion R.C. parcel
Grossammeisdorf. Slept Here & received a
Belgium R.C. parcel for 7 men on leaving town

Wed Apr 11
Holzhausen – 2 days & 3 nights

FRI. APR. 13
HOLZHADSEN. Leave at 8A.M. 2 men to NO. 10
R.C. PARCEL. TAPS for or Late great Pres
F.D.R. Arrive at farm outside of
Gammelsdorf. 2 men to French R.C. parcel

SAT. Apr. 14.
Gammelsdorf Coutskirts 1K.
2 days & 3 nights

SUN. Apr. 15.
Went to a real church in town.

MON APR 16. Left Cammelsdorf 10:30AM
Arrive Moosburg 4:30 P.M.
Received Hot shower
300 men to a tent.

OCHENBRUCK	SANDERSORF
POLLING	MEDELSTETTEN
MUHLHAUSEN	FORCHEIN
PLARR DORF	MARCHING
STADT BEREHING	NEUSTADT
BEILENGRIES	MUHSHAUSEN
PAULOSHOTEN	SLEGENBURG
AMTMANNSDORF	GROSRUMMELSDORF
PONDORF	PFCFTEN HAUSEN
SCHAMAAUPTEN	HOLZHAUSEN
	GAMMELSDORF
	MOOSBURG

USAF Memorial at Stalag Luft IV

Remembering The March...

POW Currency

Nowhere to spend it

Kriegsgefangenen=Lagergeld 6·1728777
Gutschein über 1 Reichsmark
Dieser Gutschein gilt nur als Zahlungsmittel für Kriegsgefangene und darf von ihnen nur innerhalb der Kriegsgefangenenlager oder bei Arbeitskommandos in den ausdrücklich hierfür bezeichneten Verkaufsstellen verausgabt und entgegengenommen werden.
Der Umtausch dieses Gutscheines in gesetzliche Zahlungsmittel darf nur bei der zuständigen Kasse der Lagerverwaltung erfolgen.
Zuwiderhandlungen, Nachahmungen und Fälschungen werden bestraft.
Der Chef des Oberkommandos der Wehrmacht
Im Auftrage:

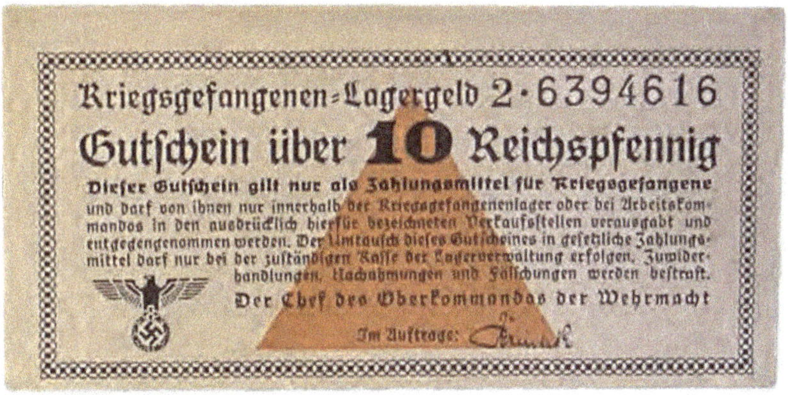
Kriegsgefangenen=Lagergeld 2·6394616
Gutschein über 10 Reichspfennig
Dieser Gutschein gilt nur als Zahlungsmittel für Kriegsgefangene und darf von ihnen nur innerhalb der Kriegsgefangenenlager oder bei Arbeitskommandos in den ausdrücklich hierfür bezeichneten Verkaufsstellen verausgabt und entgegengenommen werden. Der Umtausch dieses Gutscheines in gesetzliche Zahlungsmittel darf nur bei der zuständigen Kasse der Lagerverwaltung erfolgen. Zuwiderhandlungen, Nachahmungen und Fälschungen werden bestraft.
Der Chef des Oberkommandos der Wehrmacht
Im Auftrage:

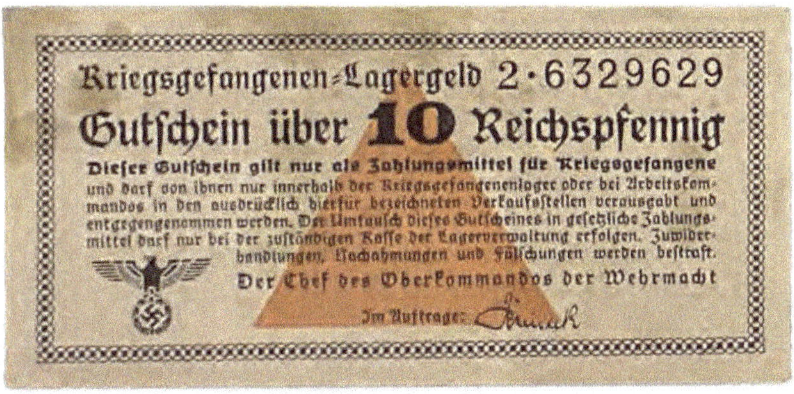
Kriegsgefangenen=Lagergeld 2·6329629
Gutschein über 10 Reichspfennig
Dieser Gutschein gilt nur als Zahlungsmittel für Kriegsgefangene und darf von ihnen nur innerhalb der Kriegsgefangenenlager oder bei Arbeitskommandos in den ausdrücklich hierfür bezeichneten Verkaufsstellen verausgabt und entgegengenommen werden. Der Umtausch dieses Gutscheines in gesetzliche Zahlungsmittel darf nur bei der zuständigen Kasse der Lagerverwaltung erfolgen. Zuwiderhandlungen, Nachahmungen und Fälschungen werden bestraft.
Der Chef des Oberkommandos der Wehrmacht
Im Auftrage:

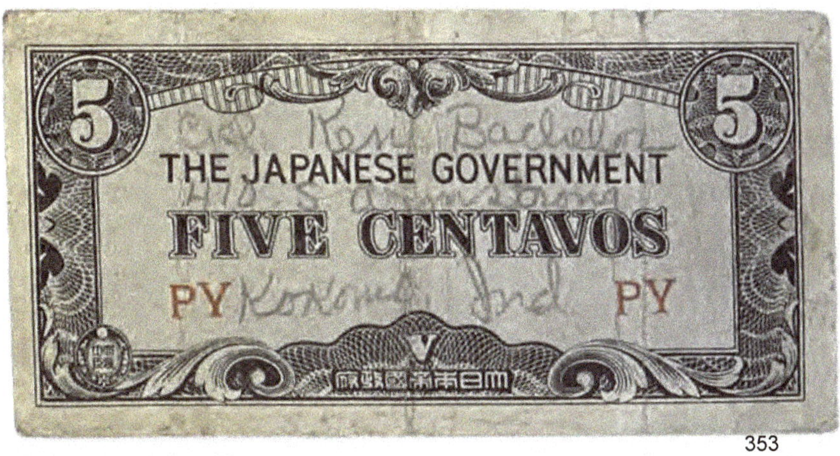
5
5
THE JAPANESE GOVERNMENT
FIVE CENTAVOS
PY
PY

Paper Currency

Dad received after liberation

100
BANQUE DE FRANCE
100

100
957
BANQUE DE FRANCE
S.14669
100
CENT
FRANCS
NE. 22-8-1940. NE.
LE CAISSIER GÉNÉRAL
LE SECRÉTAIRE GÉNÉRAL
S.14669
957

50
BANQUE DE FRANCE
50
302
J.9918
CINQUANTE
FRANCS
247933302
LE CAISSIER GÉNÉRAL
LE SECRÉTAINE GÉNÉRAL
EF.9-3-1939.EF.
J.9918
302

ÉMIS EN
FRANCE
SÉRIE DE 1944
69510492
DEUX
SÉRIE DE 1944
2
FRANCS

D·92514487
1
Rentenbankschein
Eine Rentenmark
Ausgegeben auf Grund der
Verordnung vom 15. Oktober 1923 (R.-G.-Bl. I S. 963)
BERLIN, den 30. Januar 1937.
Deutsche Rentenbank
Präsident und Vorstand:
1
1
1

50
BANQUE DE FRANCE
50

50
BANQUE DE FRANCE
50
302
J.9918
CINQUANTE
FRANCS
LE CAISSIER GÉNÉRAL
LE SECRÉTAIRE GÉNÉRAL
J.9918
EF.9-3-1939.EF.
302

Reichsmark
10
10
Reichsbanknote
K·19167452

K·19167452
Reichsbanknote
Zehn
Reichsmark
Ausgegeben auf Grund des Bankgesetzes vom 30. August 1924.
Berlin, den 22. Januar 1929
Reichsbankdirektorium
10
10
10

It is interesting that my dad saved so many wrappers from candy, chocolate, cheesecake, bathroom tissue, and other items.

Red Cross Parcels

Chocolate Wrappers

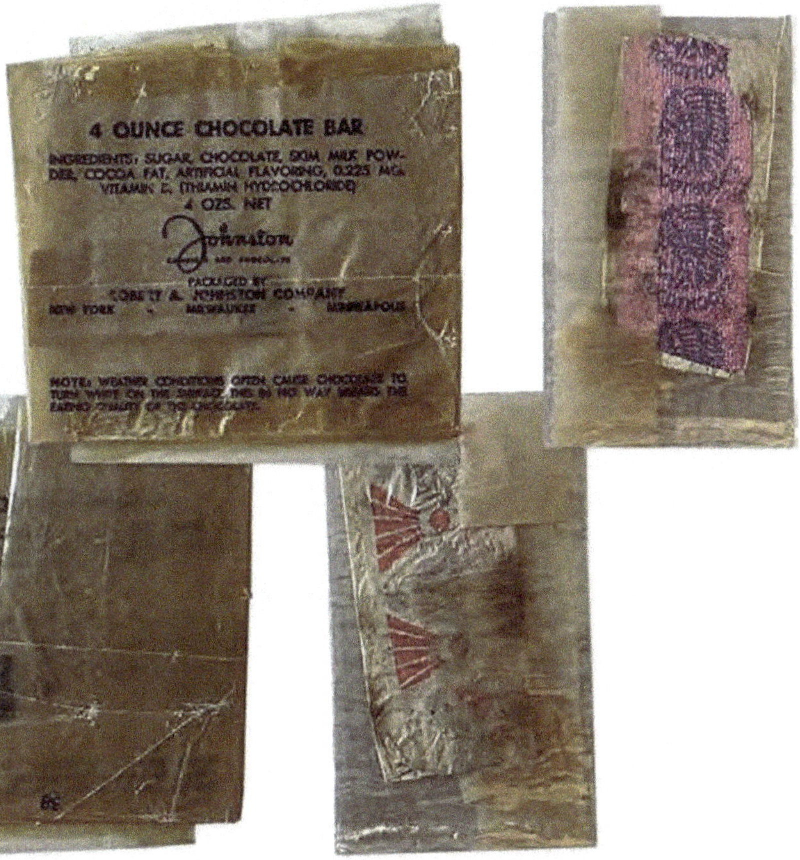
4 OUNCE CHOCOLATE BAR
INGREDIENTS: SUGAR, CHOCOLATE, SKIM MILK POWDER, COCOA FAT, ARTIFICIAL FLAVORING, 0.225 MG. VITAMIN B1 (THIAMIN HYDROCHLORIDE)
4 OZS. NET
Johnston
PACKAGED BY
ROBERT A. JOHNSTON COMPANY
NEW YORK - MILWAUKEE - MINNEAPOLIS
NOTE: WEATHER CONDITIONS OFTEN CAUSE CHOCOLATE TO TURN WHITE ON THE SURFACE. THIS IN NO WAY INJURES THE EATING QUALITY OF THE CHOCOLATE.

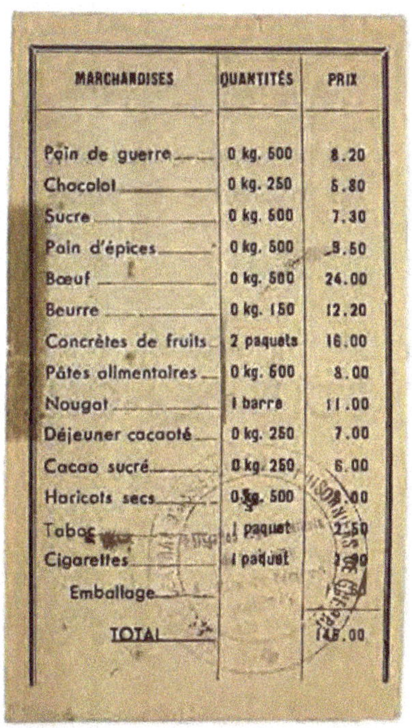

MARCHANDISES	QUANTITÉS	PRIX
Pain de guerre	0 kg. 500	8.20
Chocolat	0 kg. 250	5.80
Sucre	0 kg. 500	7.30
Pain d'épices	0 kg. 500	9.50
Bœuf	0 kg. 500	24.00
Beurre	0 kg. 150	12.20
Concrètes de fruits	2 paquets	16.00
Pâtes alimentaires	0 kg. 500	3.00
Nougat	1 barre	11.00
Déjeuner cacaoté	0 kg. 250	7.00
Cacao sucré	0 kg. 250	6.00
Haricots secs	0 kg. 500	[illegible]
Taba[illegible]	1 paquet	2.50
Cigarettes	1 paquet	[illegible]
Emballage		
TOTAL		[illegible]

CROIX ROUGE FRANÇAISE

COMITÉ CENTRAL D'ASSISTANCE AUX PRISONNIERS DE GUERRE

Délégation de la Somme

COLIS DE NOËL

Contents of French Red Cross parcel

Red Cross Parcels

German
Cheese Cake

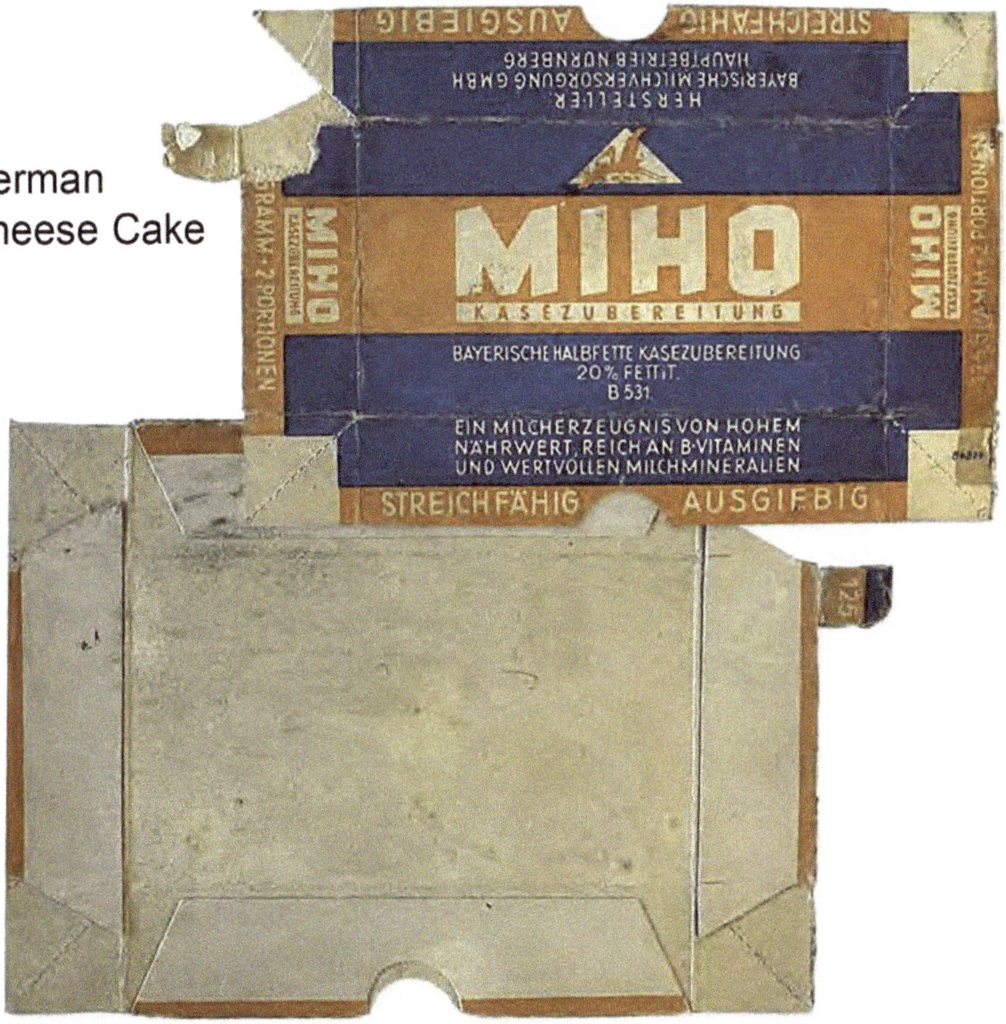

Bathroom
Tissue

Red Cross Parcels

Chocolate Bar

Red Cross Parcels

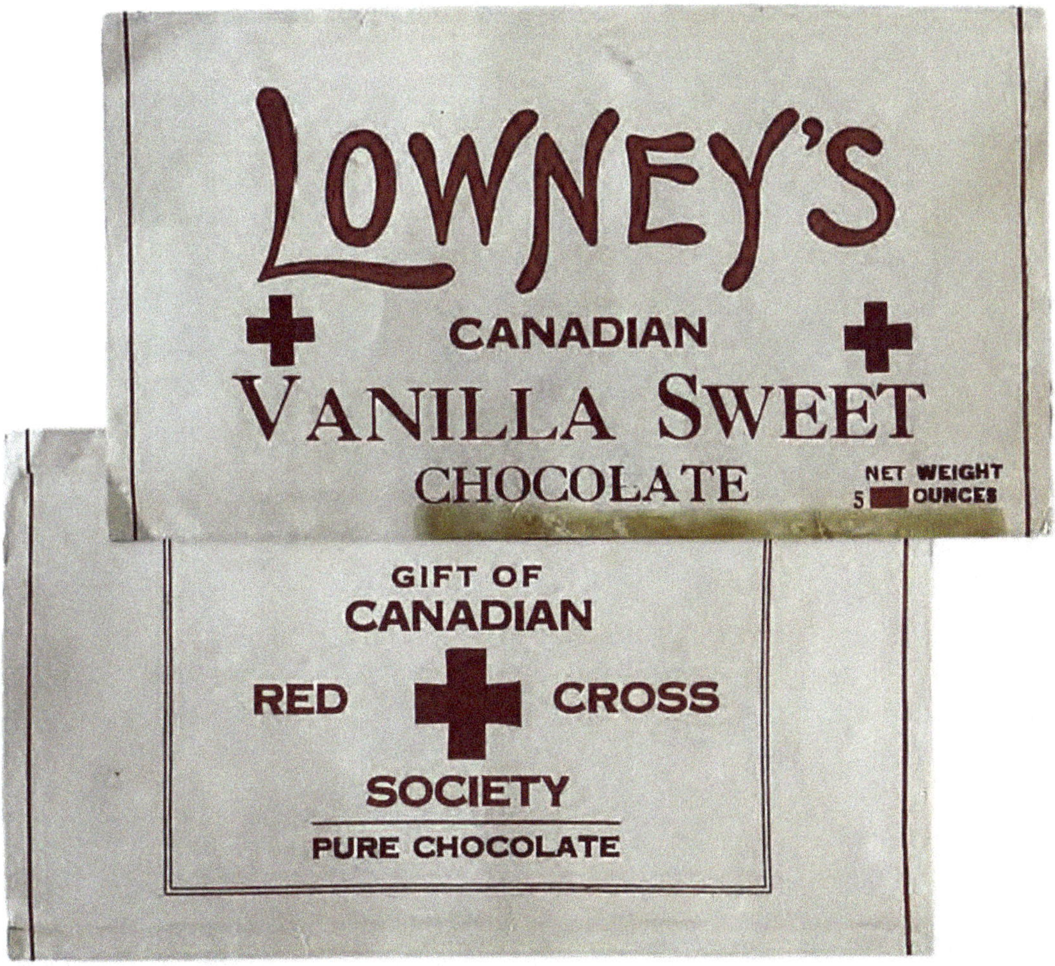

Chocolate Bar

US Propoganda

Token Items Saved

Matches Box

Match Box Cover

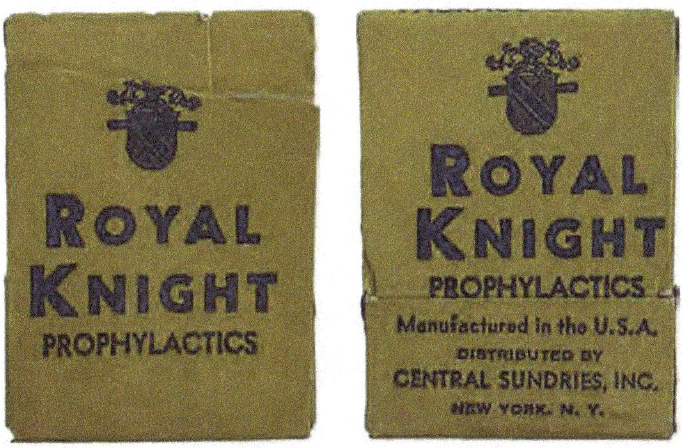

Prophylactics

The following Nazi items were confiscated from the enemy by my dad after Liberation.

Eagle Hat Medallion
Polish Military Officer

Shoulder Board
Panzer Tank
Division 512

Ornamental
Metal Head of
Swagger Stick
German

German Nazi Items

German Trench Fighting Knife
Parade Dagger K98 Bayo CUT DOWN *"cot* 44"

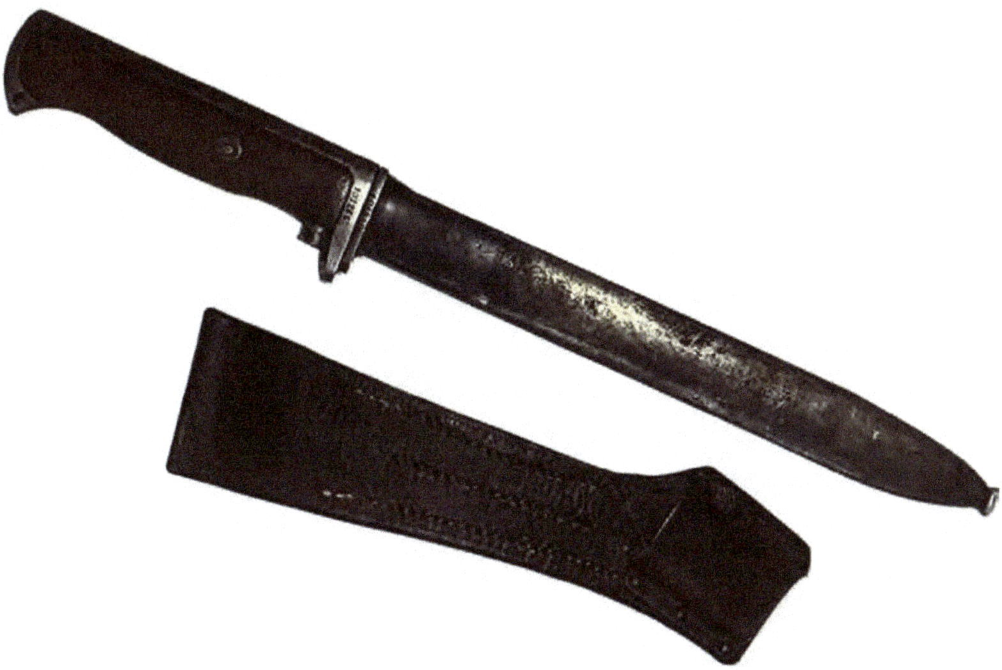

German Nazi Items

Belt Buckles

Items taken from Germans on POWs way to liberation.

German Nazi Items

German Kriegsmarine Armband

German State Service Armband

German Aircraft Clock

German Nazi Items

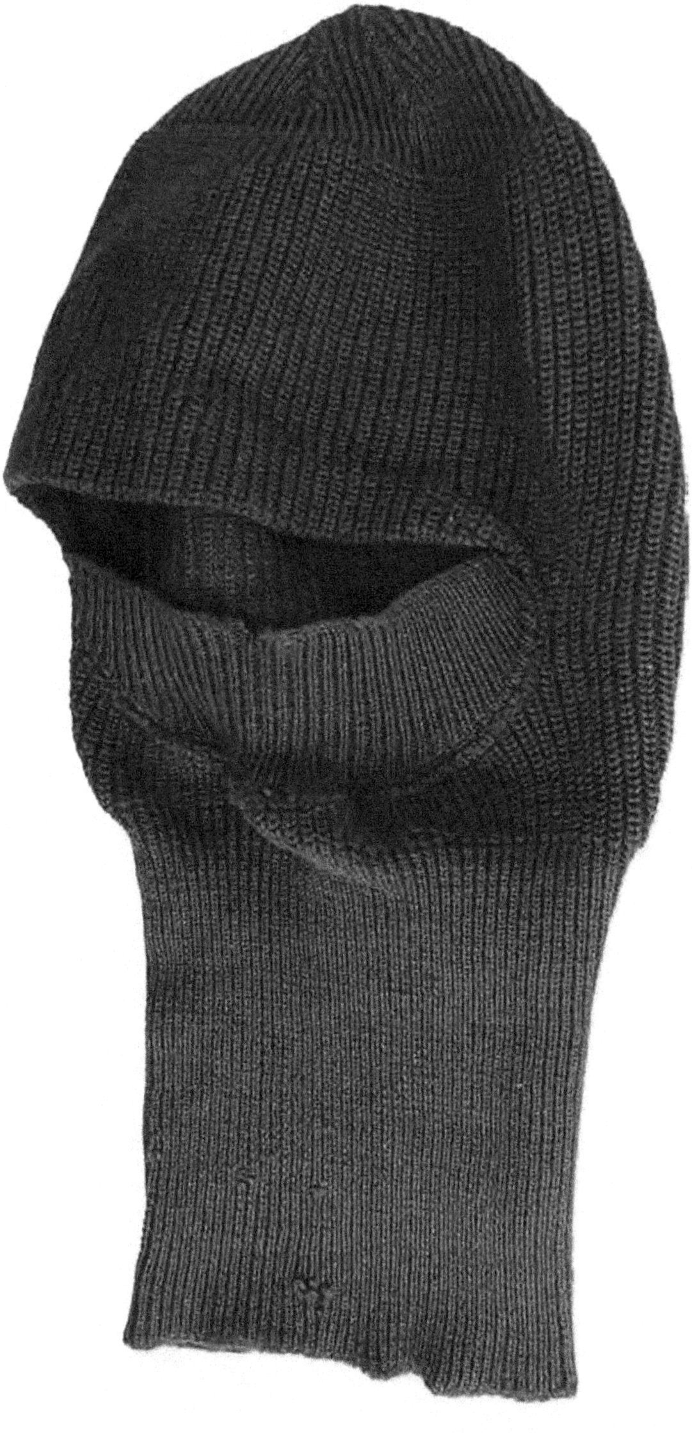

Winter Face Mask

M35 ET64 German Kriegsmarine Helmet

German Nazi Items

M35 ET64 German Kriegsmarine Helmet

German Nazi Items

M35 ET64 German Kriegsmarine Helmet

…ir Medal For Sgt. Henry Maul Given to Mother

The Air Medal, awarded to Staff Sgt. Henry E. Maul, a prisoner of war in Germany, was presented to his mother, Mrs. Henry C. Maul, during a ceremony Friday evening at the home of his parents, 710 Franklin. Major Donald J. H. Roberts, air forces, stationed at Scott Field, assisted by Capt. Donet C. Smith, East St. Louis, made the presentation.

Citation for the medal read, "For meritorious achievement while participating in heavy bombardment missions over enemy occupied continental Europe. The courage, coolness and skill displayed by this enlisted man upon these occasions reflect great credit upon himself and the armed forces of the United States.

Sgt. Maul, whose plane was forced down during a bombing raid over Germany on May 8, is at Stalag Luft III.

Sgt. Henry Maul Freed … Year

Almost a y… his capture … S/Sgt. Hen… of war of … 1944, was … May 12, … Henry C… have be… from th…

The … definit… his pa… been a pris…

An aerial engi… Forces, member of the … B-17, S/Sgt. Maul had been listed missing after a mission over Germany. About a month later, on June 15, his parents were informed by the War Department that he was a prisoner. Last autumn came a card from him in … German prison camp, then a …ng period with no word at all. An Air Medal awarded Sgt. Maul …ter he was made prisoner was …esented early last April to his …other in a ceremony at Scott …eld

GULFPORT FIELD, Mi… (…cial)—Private First Class … Maul, son of Mr. and Mrs. … C. Maul, 710 Franklin avenu… …ton, Ill., has been graduated … the army Air Forces Tech… Training Command school … Pfc. Maul, an airplane mecha… in civilian life at Curtiss-Wrig… Corp., St. Louis, Mo., has bee… trained in maintenance of carg… and transport type airplanes.

Sgt. H. E. Maul, Engineer on a B-17, Missing

Was in Action Over Germany — In Service 14 Months

Staff Sergt. Henry E. Maul, 20, an aerial engineer on an army air forces B-17, has been reported missing in action since May 8 over Germany, according to a War Department message received late Sunday night by his parents, Mr. and Mrs. Henry C. Maul, 710 Franklin.

Arriving in the European Theater of Operations on Easter Sunday, April 9, Sergt. Maul already has flown on missions over six European countries, Germany, France, Belgium, Holland, Switzerland and Norway, he wrote his parents. His last letter, dated May 3, was postmarked May 8, the day he was reported missing. He was based in England.

Sergt. Maul's father operates Maul's Brown-Bilt Shoe store at …

…RGEANT HENRY MAUL, son of Mr. and Mrs. Henry Maul, 710 Franklin street, who is going to advanced gunnery school at Salt Lake City. He received training at La… Vegas, Nev., al…

… Maul He… …n 60-Day Fu…

…/Sgt. Henry E. Maul, …neer on a B-17 Flying … who was held prisoner by … mans for almost a year, … home Wednesday evening to … a 60-day furlough with hi… …ents, Mr. and Mrs. Henry C. … 710 Franklin.

Sent overseas early in … 1944, Sgt. Maul had complete… missions over Europe before … plane was forced down over G… many May 8, 1944. He ente… service in March, 1943.

Alton Evening Telegraph
Newspaper Clippings
1943

Mrs. Henry C. Maul is visiting her son, Henry Eugene, who is stationed at the Army Air Corps base, Gulfport, Miss. Mrs. Maul left for the south Tuesday, accompanied by her daughter, Virginia, and mother, Mrs. Rose Schneider.

June 8, 1943

GULFPORT FIELD, Miss. (Special)—Private First Class Henry E. Maul, son of Mr. and Mrs. Henry C. Maul, 710 Franklin avenue, Alton, Ill., has been graduated from the army Air Forces Technical Training Command school here. Pfc. Maul, an airplane mechanic in civilian life at Curtiss-Wright Corp., St. Louis, Mo., has been trained in maintenance of cargo and transport type airplanes.

October 13, 1943

Sergeant Henry E. Maul arrived Friday evening to visit his parents, Mr. and Mrs. H. C. Maul, of 710 Franklin avenue, and will remain for 17 days. He recently completed a course in a flexible gunnery school at Las Vegas, Nev., and is enjoying a delay in route stay in Alton while on his way to Salt Lake City. This is Maul's first visit home since entering service eight months ago.

November 20, 1943

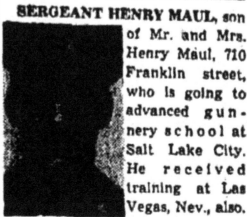

SERGEANT HENRY MAUL, son of Mr. and Mrs. Henry Maul, 710 Franklin street, who is going to advanced gunnery school at Salt Lake City. He received training at Las Vegas, Nev., also.

November 29, 1943

Alton Evening Telegraph
Newspaper Clippings
1944

Mr. and Mrs. L. E. Hunt of 1106 State street have received word of the safe arrival of their son, Lieutenant Lawreance W. Hunt, in England. Before entering service Lieutenant Hunt practiced law in Alton, with offices on West Third street.

Mrs. M. A. Crivello of 1000 Alby street is receiving medical attention at St. Anthony's Infirmary.

Henry C. Maul is visiting his son, Sergeant Henry C. Maul, stationed at Dyersburg Air Base, Dyersburg, Tenn.

February 22, 1944

Sgt. H. E. Maul, Engineer on a B-17, Missing

Was in Action Over Germany —In Service 14 Months

Staff Sergt. Henry E. Maul, 20, an aerial engineer on an army air forces B-17, has been reported missing in action since May 8 over Germany, according to a War Department message received late Sunday night by his parents, Mr. and Mrs. Henry C. Maul, 710 Franklin.

Arriving in the European Theater of Operations on Easter Sunday, April 9, Sergt. Maul already has flown on missions over six European countries, Germany, France, Belgium, Holland, Switzerland and Norway, he wrote his parents. His last letter, dated May 3, was postmarked May 8, the day he was reported missing. He was based in England.

Sergt. Maul's father operates Maul's Brown-Bilt Shoe store at 121 West Third.

A graduate of Marquette High school, Sergt. Maul was employed at Curtiss-Wright Corp., plant in St. Louis before entering service in March, 1943. He took combat training at Dyersburg, Tenn., and joined his Flying Fortress crew at Kearney, Neb.

May 22, 1944

Sgt. Henry Maul Nazis' Prisoner

Staff Sgt. Henry E. Maul, son of Mr. and Mrs. H. C. Maul, 710 Franklin, is a prisoner of war of the German government, according to a telegram received by Mr. and Mrs. Maul from the United States government Thursday night.

Sergeant Maul, in service since March 22, 1943, was reported missing in action May 8, after a raid on Germany.

June 16, 1944

Alton Evening Telegraph
Newspaper Clippings
1945

Air Medal For Sgt. Henry Maul Given to Mother

The Air Medal, awarded to Staff Sgt. Henry E. Maul, a prisoner of war in Germany, was presented to his mother, Mrs. Henry C. Maul, during a ceremony Friday evening at the home of his parents, 710 Franklin. Major Donald J. H. Roberts, air forces, stationed at Scott Field, assisted by Capt. Donet C. Smith, East St. Louis, made the presentation.

Citation for the medal read, "For meritorious achievement while participating in heavy bombardment missions over enemy occupied continental Europe. The courage, coolness and skill displayed by this enlisted man upon these occasions reflect great credit upon himself and the armed forces of the United States.

Sgt. Maul, whose plane was forced down during a bombing raid over Germany on May 8, is at Stalag Luft III.

April 16, 1945

Sgt. Henry Maul Freed After Year

Almost a year to the day after his capture in a bombing mission, S./Sgt. Henry E. Maul, a prisoner of war of Germany since May 8, 1944, was liberated last Saturday, May 12, his parents, Mr. and Mrs. Henry C. Maul of 710 Franklin, have been informed in a message from the Red Cross.

The message today was the first definite word about him to reach his parents in six months. He had been a prisoner in Stalag IV.

An aerial engineer of the Air Forces, member of the crew of a B-17, S/Sgt. Maul had been first listed missing after a mission over Germany. About a month later, on June 15, his parents were informed by the War Department that he was a prisoner. Last autumn came a card from him in a German prison camp, then a long period with no word at all.

An Air Medal awarded Sgt. Maul after he was made prisoner was presented early last April to his mother in a ceremony at Scott Field

May 17, 1945

Sgt. Henry Maul Home On 60-Day Furlough

S/Sgt. Henry E. Maul, an engineer on a B-17 Flying Fortress who was held prisoner by the Germans for almost a year, arrived home Wednesday evening to spend a 60-day furlough with his parents, Mr. and Mrs. Henry C. Maul, 710 Franklin.

Sent overseas early in April, 1944, Sgt. Maul had completed six missions over Europe before his plane was forced down over Germany May 8, 1944. He entered service in March, 1943.

June 14, 1945

Alton Evening Telegraph
Newspaper Clippings
1945

Arrive at San Antonio

SAN ANTONIO, Tex., (Special) —First Lt. Donald E. Jackson, 825 Langdon, and S/Sgt. Henry E. Maul, 1408 Liberty, of Alton and S/Sgt. Ned R. Lewis, 615 Bowman, East Alton, have arrived here at the army air forces redistribution center. Lt. Jackson, husband of the former Miss Marilyn Stanton and son of Mr. and Mrs. Alfred Jackson of Alton, wears the Purple Heart, the Air Medal with four Oak Leaf clusters and the Distinguished Flying Cross, which he won during 18 months of service as a bombardier in the European theater. S/Sgt. Maul and S/Sgt. Lewis formerly were German prisoners of war. A gunner, S/Sgt. Maul, served in the European theater for 14 months. S/Sgt. Maul, son of Mr. and Mrs. Henry C. Maul of Alton, holds the Air Medal. S/Sgt Lewis, son of Mr. and Mrs. William R. Lewis of East Alton, won the Air Medal while serving as a radio operator-gunner. He was in the European theater six months.

September 24, 1945

Sgt. Henry E. Maul Discharged, Home

T/Sgt. Henry E. Maul has been discharged from service and has returned home. The son of Mr. and Mrs. H. C. Maul, 1408 Liberty, he was in service 2¼ years, and was overseas more than a year. An engineer on a B-17, he was forced down and taken prisoner by the Germans, May 8, 1944, and was liberated a year later.

October 30, 1945

POW Newspaper

(this was the only copy my dad received)

...e-
...age
...e of
...d 20
...High
...e and
...defeat-
...more of
...aign 52-
...wn.

...rth gym.
Wildcats.
...bina sows
...er. Posey
... 49 piglets.
...superin-
...polis Union
...s the city's
...se defeated
...nstate high-
...Fire de-
...ation grade-
...artsville and
...feed eleva-
...t Vincennes,
...Gilmor issued
...marry Ruth
...Indianapolis
...president of
...years. Emil
...New York
...sed the 500-
...rmerly used
...by Ringling

...d its new
...ster County
...o prisoners
...wrestled a

Saturday night blues

by Lt. Leonard E. Hamaker, Stalagluft III, Germany

covering Bowling Green, Louisville, Lexington, Covington, Owensboro and Paducah. Wallace Jones ...ints for Harlan High as ...tate high-school ... Day-

69, Bangor dentist. Rockland's former mayor Richardson was named police chief. New mayors: George Doyle, Democrat, defeated Russell Squire at Waterville; Belfast's Mayor Hanson and Bath's Mayor Rogers were reelected un-...osed; Alderman Law... Dol-

German Newspaper

Wochenblatt

der Landesbauernschaft
BAYREUTH

Amtliches Organ des Reichsnährstandes

Folge 8 — 7. Jahrgang

Bayreuth, 24. Februar 1945

DIE MERKTAFEL

Der Kartoffelanbau ist vor allem in den mittel- und großbäuerlichen Betrieben der Hauptverbrauchergebiete beträchtlich auszuweiten. Hochertragreiche Speisesorten verdienen den Vorzug.

Für die Entwicklung eines Kalbes ist es ohne Bedeutung, ob es in den ersten Lebenswochen fettarme oder fettreiche Milch erhält, darum sollten Kälber grundsätzlich nur die Milch von fettärmeren Kühen erhalten oder beim gebrochenen Melken den fettarmen ersten Teil des Gemelks.

Wehrmacht und Wirtschaft benötigen dringend Heu und Stroh. Darum müssen die den einzelnen Betrieben auferlegten Heu- und Strohkontingente schnellstens erfüllt werden.

Wie ich zu hoher Milchleistung und -ablieferung kam

Von Bauer Hermann Büchner, Dörfles bei Coburg
(Ausgezeichnet mit dem 1. Preis unseres Preisausschreibens)

Nachdem ich in den letzten drei Jahren mit unter den Siegern im Milchleistungswettbewerb des Milchhofes Coburg war, glaube ich mich an dem Preisausschreiben des Wochenblattes mit obigem Thema beteiligen zu können.

Mein kleiner Betrieb umfaßt 12,30 ha landwirtschaftlich genützte Fläche, davon sind 3,30 ha Pachtland. Bodenart: sandiger Lehm, teilweise mit Kies untermischt; Wiesen zur Hälfte gute Niederungswiesen, die zweite Hälfte (Pachtland) trocken, etwas anmoorig. Höhenlage: 300 m über dem Meeresspiegel. Hauptkulturarten: Getreide 3 ha, Oelfrüchte 0,50 ha, Kartoffeln 1 ha, Futterrüben 0,50 ha, Wicken-Hafer-Bohnengemenge (Zwischenfrucht) 0,25 ha, Futtermais 0,25 ha, Luzerne und Klee 0,75 ha, Gemüseanbau im Vor- und Nachbau 3 ha. Viehbestand: 2 Pferde, 5 Milchkühe, 3 Jungrinder, 4 Schweine. Arbeitskräfte: Betriebsführer, Ehefrau, Tochter, 1 Kriegsgefangener, 1 Landjahrmädchen; da intensiver Gemüsebau im Sommer 5 Frauen im Tagelohn.

Die Milchleistung meines Betriebes stellt sich wie folgt dar:

	Stalldurchschnitt	Fettgehalt	Anzahl der Kühe
1937	2300 kg	3,9 v. H.	5
1940	3024 kg	3,8 v. H.	4
1941	3551 kg	3,7 v. H.	4
1942	3018 kg	3,7 v. H.	4
1943	3154 kg	3,7 v. H.	5

Nach einem Jahr Pflichtmilchkontrolle im Jahre 1937 war der Fettgehalt mit 3,9 v. H. als gut anzusehen, dagegen genügte mir jedoch die Milchleistung nicht. Der erste Schritt zur Steigerung des Milchertrages, der getan werden mußte, war die Ausmerzung der Tiere, die bei gleicher Fütterung stärker abfeiten. Nachdem ich nach dem Abmelken meinen Viehbestand um 2 Kühe verringert hatte, kam das anfallende Futter den übrigen Tieren zugute und die Milchleistung stieg. Hierbei ist zu berücksichtigen, daß in den ersten Kriegsjahren noch etwas Kraftfutter gegeben werden konnte. Es wurden Brauereiabfälle gefüttert. Von den in den Jahren 1938 bis einschließlich 1942 vorhandenen Kühen trat in ihrer Leistung besonders eine hervor, die mit 4000 kg und 3,7 v. H. Fettgehalt weit über dem Durchschnitt lag. Auf diese Leistungskuh wurde die weitere Nachzucht aufgebaut.

In der Erkenntnis, daß auch das Vatertier hinsichtlich des Milchertrags bei der Vererbung eine wichtige Rolle spielt, war von der zuständigen Zuchtbullengenossenschaft auf meine Einwirkung hin ein mit dem ersten Milchleistungspreis (Abstammung) ausgezeichneter Jungbulle angekauft worden, so daß die Nachzucht väterlicher- sowie mütterlicherseits in bezug auf Milch und Fett zu den besten Hoffnungen berechtigte. Daß der Stalldurchschnitt im Jahre 1942 etwas zurückgegangen war, ist darauf zurückzuführen, daß die beste Kuh notgeschlachtet werden mußte und zwei Jungkühe noch nicht im vollen Milchertrag standen.

Auf die eigene Futtergrundlage, die in den beiden letzten Jahren nach dem Fehlen von Kraftfutter allein maßgebend wurde,

> Sommer-Oelfruchtanbau weitmöglichst ausdehnen! Ueberall, wo es nicht möglich war, das Oelfruchtanbausoll durch den Anbau von Winterölfrüchten zu erfüllen oder wo die Winterölfrüchte ausgewintert sind, müssen [illegible] Sommerölfrüchte zusätzlich bestellt werden. Das Anbausoll muß unbedingt erreicht werden.

wurde größter Wert gelegt. Da der Betrieb zu stark parzelliert ist (20 Teilstücke), konnte kein Weidebetrieb eingerichtet werden. Neben dem Herbstaustrieb kam nur die Stallfütterung in Frage.

Mein Prinzip ist, so bald und so lang wie möglich Grünfutter zu füttern. Da Rübsen alljährlich als erstes Grünfutter anfällt, wurden jedes Jahr 25 a Rübsen mit etwas Winterwicken untermischt angebaut. Ueber dieses erste Grünfutter verfügt man schon Anfang bis Mitte April. Der erste Schnitt Luzerne folgt sodann und darauf der erste Schnitt Klee. Durch den starken Frühgemüsebau fällt nebenbei auch noch genügend Grünfutter an, das zur Viehfütterung Verwendung findet. Dann kommen in der Reihenfolge die zweiten Schnitte von Luzerne und Klee (mit Kunstdünger oder Jauche nachgeholfen), Futtermais als Nachfrucht frühräumender Gemüsearten (Salat, Spinat und Kohlrabi) und in der Zwischenzeit wieder genügend Abfälle von Gemüse. Im Juli nach der Ernte der vorgekeimten Frühkartoffeln oder der Pflückerbsen wird sofort ein Wicken-Bohnen-Hafer-Gemenge ausgesät, das im Herbst neben den sauber geernteten Rübenblättern anfällt und wie diese restlos verfüttert wird. Zur Ausfüllung von kleinen Lükken dienen der 2. Grasschnitt und der 3. Schnitt Luzerne. Inzwischen kommt das Vieh bereits auf die Herbstweide, wo es in manchen Jahren bis Ende November belassen wird.

Bei der Winterfütterung wird Heu und Grummet (für Milchkühe das beste) verabreicht. Die volle Sättigung erziele ich durch Beifütterung von Haferstroh und eine Zugabe von Gehaltsrüben, die zur Verhütung von Durchfall gut mit Kalk vermischt werden. Weiter erhalten die Kühe genügend Wasser und zeitweise Salz. Den frischgekalbten Kühen verabreiche ich die anfallende Kleie und die Oelfruchtschrot-Rücklieferung. Ein Silo ist leider noch nicht vorhanden.

Zur Hebung der Milcherträge wird weiter in meinem Betrieb auf ein richtiges, trockenes Melken (Ausmelken, Nachmelken und Massieren des Euters) gesehen. Auf die Aufzucht der Jungtiere wird großer Wert gelegt (Tummelplatz mit Graswuchs, Licht und Sonne). Damit die Tiere beim ersten Grünfutter wieder frischmelkend werden, wird die Abkalbzeit nach Möglichkeit auf den Winter und das zeitige Frühjahr verlegt. Auf gutes Putzen, tägliche Einstreu und auf Klauenpflege wird streng geachtet. Der helle, luftige Stall wird öfter gekalkt.

Die Erzeugung jedoch allein tut es nicht, wenn die Ablieferung nicht Schritt mit ihr hält. Zu meinem Haushalt zählen 11 Personen, darunter drei Kinder. Im Jahre 1942 wurden von der erzeugten Milch 92 v. H. und im Jahre 1943 90,4 v. H. abgeliefert. Es blieben jährlich für den Haushalt und die Aufzucht von drei Jungkälbern im ganzen 1552 kg Milch.

Im Haushalt wird äußerst an Vollmilch gespart und viel Magermilch verwendet. Die Aufzuchtkälber erhalten nur bis zur 4. Woche Vollmilch, in der 4. bis 6. Woche werden sie allmählich auf Magermilch unter Zusatz von Kälbermehl, Lein und Kleie umgestellt. Es wird sofort aus dem Eimer getränkt. Schlachtkälber werden nach 14 Tagen abgestoßen. Im Schweinestall wird keine Vollmilch verwendet.

Wenn auch die Milcherzeugung und -ablieferung in meinem Betrieb noch keine Spitzenleistungen sind, so bin ich doch bestrebt, sie ständig noch zu steigern.

> „Der Tod wartet auf alle Überlebenden eines verlorenen Krieges, auf die Männer, auf die Kinder, auf die Frauen und auf die Ungeborenen, auf Arbeiter, Bauern, Bürger und Soldaten, auf Nazis und solche, die dann vorgeben würden, es nie gewesen zu sein, auf Preußen und Ostmärker, auf Bayern und Westfalen, auf Evangelische und Katholische gleichermaßen wie auf die Gottgläubigen."

German Newspaper

Bauerntöchter, stellt euch dem Melkunterricht zur Verfügung!
Sicherstellung der Brotversorgung
Holz ist kriegsentscheidender Rohstoff!
Der Reichsbauernführer
I. A.: gez. Zschirnt
1. Februar und März sind die Monate des Holzeinschlages. Jeder beeile sich, seine Holzumlage zu erfüllen!
Flaschen-Sammlung
am 24. u. 25. Februar
Abholung durch die Wehrmacht
Der Reichsbeauftragte der NSDAP für Altmaterialerfassung

German Newspaper

Schweineweide im Fichtelgebirge

Von Hans Geyer, [illegible] bei Wunsiedel

Meine Erfahrungen gehen dahin, daß das Grünland von Schweinen durch ein planmäßigem Abweiden der Grasnarbe genau so gut ausgenutzt wird wie vom Rind, ja, daß das Schwein das Rind sogar hinsichtlich der Ausnutzung der Weide übertrifft. Durch eine Schweineweide macht sich der Bauer mehr oder weniger während des Sommers vom sonstigen Futter vollkommen unabhängig. Hinzu kommt aber noch daß derjenige Bauer die gesündesten Schweine hat, der sie vom Frühjahr bis zum Herbst auf die Weide treiben kann.

Meine Erfahrungen in dieser Hinsicht stützen sich nun auf 6 Jahre. Im Jahre 1935 kam mir der Gedanke, mich mit der Schweinezucht zu befassen, da ich der Auffassung war, daß auch im Fichtelgebirge systematische Schweinezucht möglich, ja sogar eine Notwendigkeit sei. Im Jahre 1938 hatte ich bereits 7 Muttersauen. Mein Zuchtmaterial war gut und meine Zucht wurde anerkannt. Ich hatte selbstverständlich in der Zwischenzeit auch meine Stallanlagen dementsprechend geändert, so daß auch in dieser Richtung alles in Ordnung war.

Nur eines fehlte noch auf meinem Betrieb, und das war die Weide. Im Frühjahr 1939 wurde nach den Plänen der Landwirtschaftsstelle Wunsiedel eine Fläche von 2 Tgw., die im Jahre 1938 mit einer Weidemischung angesät war, eingekoppelt und am 20. April 1939 wurden die Schweine zum erstenmal auf die Weide ausgetrieben.

Die gesamte Fläche von 2 Tgw. ist in 7 Koppeln eingeteilt. In der Mitte der Fläche ist der Triebweg, so daß sich die Koppeln rechts und links vom Triebweg befinden. Am Eingang der Weide errichtete ich eine [illegible] Schutzhütte, die besonders in der heißen Jahreszeit von den Tieren sehr gerne aufgesucht wird.

Alljährlich sobald der Frühling ins Land zieht, wird ausgetrieben, und die Schweine bleiben auf der Weide bis in den Spätherbst. Wenn der erste Schnee fällt, wird abgetrieben.

Auf der Fläche von 2 Tgw. halte ich 8 bis 10 Muttersauen, die bei ganz geringer Beifütterung sich den ganzen Sommer über auf der Weide ernähren. Mehrmals ist es sogar schon vorgekommen, daß die eine oder andere Muttersau auf der Weide ferkelte, ohne daß irgendwelche Schäden bei den Tieren aufgetreten sind.

Die Schweineweide hat 2 große Vorteile: 1. eine wesentliche Arbeitserleichterung, 2. eine außerordentliche Futtereinsparung. Es wäre mir heute im 6. Kriegsjahr überhaupt nicht möglich, 10 Muttersauen mit dem wirtschaftseigenen Futter ernähren zu können, da doch Getreide fast nicht mehr zur Verfügung steht. Die Tiere fühlen sich auf der Weide außerordentlich wohl; selbst strömender Gewitterregen macht den Sauen gar nichts aus. Die Sauen gehen höchstens bei sehr großer Hitze in die Hütte und nützen die kühle Nacht zum Weiden aus.

Betonen möchte ich noch, daß sich mein Betrieb und insbesondere die Weide 600 m über dem Meeresspiegel in einer rauhen Gebirgslage befindet. Die Weide ist scharfen Winden von allen Seiten ausgesetzt, und trotz dieser Verhältnisse sind Krankheiten in meinem Schweinebestand, solange ich die Schweine auf die Weide treibe, noch nicht vorgekommen. Die Tiere werden ungeheuer abgehärtet. Diese Abhärtung bewährt sich hervorragend und der beste Beweis für meinen Erfolg ist der alljährliche günstige Absatz von Zuchttieren (Eber und trächtigen Sauen) nach allen Gauen Deutschlands. Es ist selbstverständlich, daß die Tiere auf der Weide das Gras am liebsten in ganz jungem Zustand nehmen, denn in diesem Zustand ist es ja auch am nährstoffreichsten.

Aufn.: Privat

Schweineweide im Fichtelgebirge

Alle Tiere bleiben 4 bis 6 Wochen in einer Koppel, dann werden die Koppeln gewechselt. Wenn der Koppelwechsel durchgeführt wird, ist es selbstverständlich, daß die Koppel gereinigt werden muß. Die Koppel selbst wird dann mit etwas Kalkmergel bestreut und verschlossen. So geht der Umtrieb vom Frühjahr bis zum Herbst. Im Mai, wenn der Graswuchs am stärksten ist, werden einige Koppeln zu Heu gemäht, da ja sonst das Gras überständig wird.

Die Weide kam in den letzten 2 Jahren voll zur Entfaltung, was darauf zurückzuführen ist, daß der Boden im Laufe der Jahre erst von den Tieren richtig festgetreten wurde, wodurch dann die Grasnarbe sich verdichtete und damit verbesserte. In den ersten Weidejahren war deshalb der Ertrag lange nicht so gut wie heute.

Die Erfahrung auf meinem Betrieb hat gezeigt, daß Schweinezucht ohne den gesundheitsfördernden Weidegang unmöglich ist. Weidegang senkt ohne Zweifel die Ferkelsterblichkeit und verlängert die Zuchtfähigkeit der Sauen. Die Weideschweine bekommen festen Rücken und vor allen Dingen eine korrekte Beinstellung.

Zusammenfassend kann ich nur jedem Bauern und Landwirt, auch wenn er nur Gebrauchszucht treibt, dringend raten, sich eine Schweineweide anzulegen, da doch fast auf jedem Betrieb in der Nähe des Hofes bestimmt eine Fläche ist, die sich hierfür eignet. Durch eine Schweineweide wird die Sommerfutterfrage ohne weiteres gelöst. Die Haltung der Schweine auf der Weide bringt eine wesentliche Arbeitserleichterung und die Schweinebestände bleiben viel gesünder als im Stall.

Obstbaum-Winterspritzung durchführen!

Die ausschlaggebende Bedeutung der Obstbaumspritzung auf Höhe und Güte des Ertrages steht außer jedem Zweifel. [illegible] Verfügung. Gelbspritzmittel oder Dinitrokresolpräparate werden in Pastenform („Beerolin D", „Dinitan", „Hercynia", „Selinon-Neu" u. a.) oder in Pulverform („Detal", „Hercynia-Gelb" u. a.) geliefert. Es empfiehlt sich, in Abänderung der [illegible] die Pasten 1,5 v. H. (= 1,5 kg auf 100 Liter Wasser) und die Pulverpräparate 0,75 v. H. zu verwenden. In dieser Brühenstärke sind die Gelbspritzmittel den Obstbaumkarbolineen überlegen, wobei die Wirkung vom Zeitpunkt der Anwendung unabhängig ist. Es kann im Gegensatz zu den Karbolineen im Februar-März, wie auch kurz vor dem Schwellen der Knospen, mit dem gleichen Erfolg gespritzt werden. Bei Spätspritzungen auf die schwellenden oder den Aufbrechen nahen Knospen sind die Verbrennungsgefahren im Vergleich zu den Karbolineen geringer. Obstbaumkarbolineum emulgiert ist bei Kernobst [illegible] prozentig, bei Steinobst 6–8 prozentig [illegible]. Bei Spätspritzungen auf die [illegible] Knospen geht man in der Konzentration um 1–2 v. H. oder 3 v. H. bis [illegible] v. H. zurück, um Verbrennungsgefahren vorzubeugen. Steinobst ist besonders empfindlich. Zu späte Spritzungen zeigen in ihrer Wirkung gegen die Schädlinge als weniger sicher. Obstbaumkarbolineum aus Schweröl ist bei Kernobst [illegible] prozentig und bei Steinobst [illegible] prozentig anzuwenden. Die Verbrennungsgefahren sind größer als bei den zwei vorgenannten Präparaten. Bezugsmöglichkeiten gibt das Pflanzenschutzamt Bayreuth auf Anfrage bekannt.

In allen Fällen müssen die Bäume bei der Winterspritzung mit großer Spritzflüssigkeit [illegible] gespritzt werden und dabei die Zweigenden besonders sorgfältig behandelt werden.

Wenn auch nach erfolgter Winterspritzung, noch Apfelblütenstecherkäfer zuwandern — Kontrolle mit Fanggürteln, unter denen sich die 4 mm langen, graubraunen mit hellgrüner Querbinde gezeichneten Käfer sammeln —, so wird man nach Knospenaufbruch nochmals mit einem Berührungsmittel, z. B. mit einem Pyrethrumpräparat oder dem neuen Spritzgesarol, spritzen.

In Niederbayern hat im letzten Jahr die Schrotschußkrankheit die Kirschenernte fast völlig zunichte gemacht, die Zwetschgenernte schwer geschädigt und die Blätter vorzeitig abfallen lassen. Wo diese Krankheit auftritt, empfiehlt es sich, die Winterspritzung mit einer Kupferspritzung zu kombinieren und möglichst erst kurz vor dem Schwellen der Knospen vorzunehmen, also z. B. 1,5 v. H. Gelbspritzmittelpaste und 1,5 v. H. Kupferspritzmittel oder 6 v. H. Obstbaumkarbolineum emulgiert und 1,5 v. H. Kupferspritzmittel. (Oft ist jedoch eine weitere Nachblütenspritzung mit Schwefelkalkbrühe [illegible] und Bleiarsenatpulver 0,4prozentig nicht zu umgehen.) Die Mischbarkeit der Gelbspritzmittelbrühe mit einer Kupferspritzmittelbrühe ist noch umstritten, doch liegen aus der Praxis gute Erfahrungen vor.

Der Winterspritzung unserer Obstbäume kommt jetzt insofern eine erhöhte Bedeutung zu, als infolge des Fehlens von Nikotin und anderen Blattlausmitteln nur auf diese Weise einem katastrophalen Blattlausauftreten begegnet werden kann. Da im letzten Jahr die Beerensträucher von den Läusen ebenfalls stark befallen waren, ist auch hier die Winterspritzung am Platze; sie erfolgt am zweckmäßigsten mit einer Mischbrühe aus Gelbspritzmittel oder Obstbaumkarbolineum emulgiert mit

38

German Newspaper

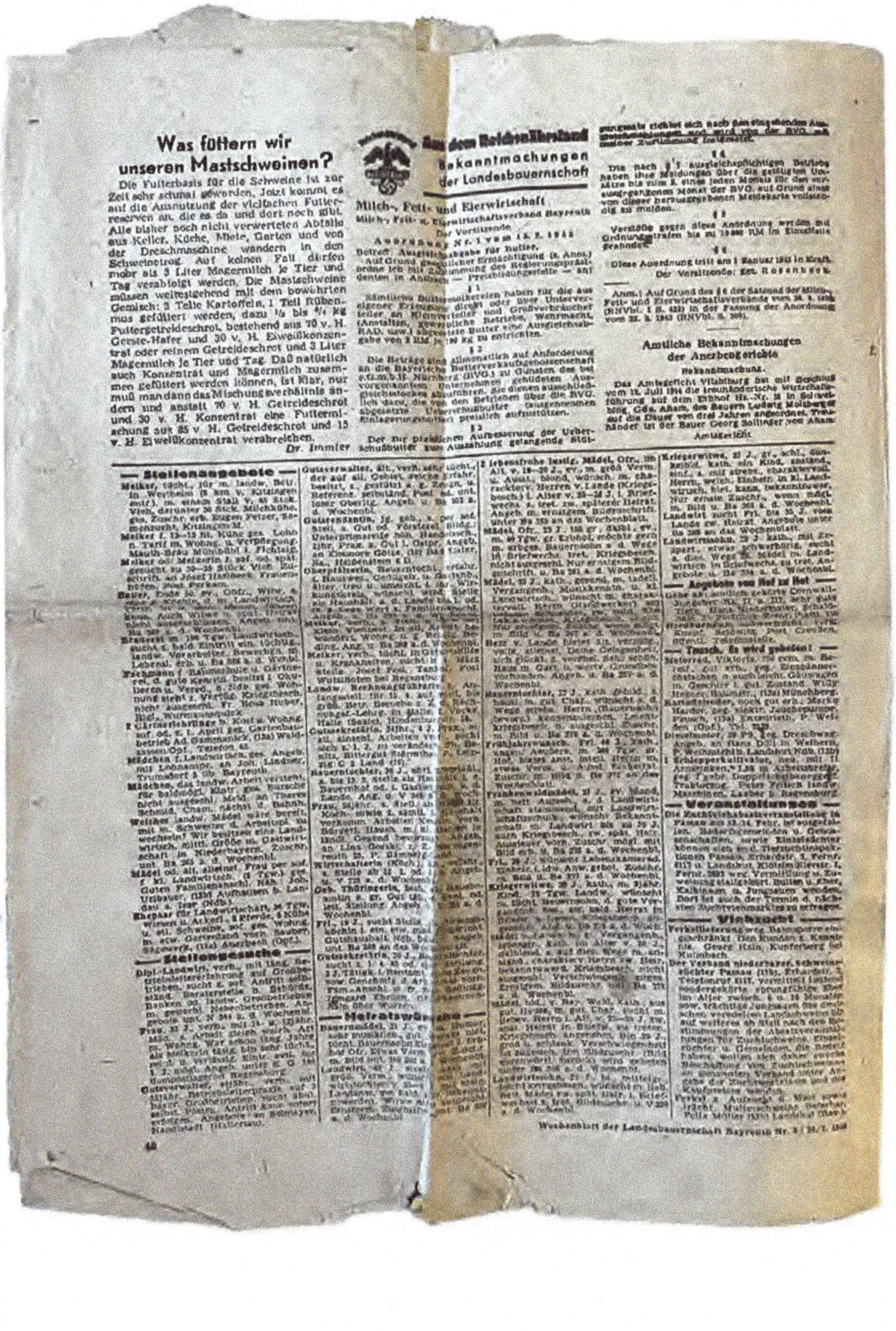

Was füttern wir unseren Mastschweinen?

Die Futterbasis für die Schweine ist zur Zeit sehr schmal geworden. Jetzt kommt es auf die Ausnutzung der vielfachen Futterreserven an, die es da und dort noch gibt. Alle bisher noch nicht verwerteten Abfälle aus Keller, Küche, Miete, Garten und von der Dreschmaschine wandern in den Schweinetrog. Auf keinen Fall dürfen mehr als 3 Liter Magermilch je Tier und Tag verabfolgt werden. Die Mastschweine müssen weitestgehend mit dem bewährten Gemisch: 3 Teile Kartoffeln, 1 Teil Rübenmus gefüttert werden, dazu ½ bis ¾ kg Futtergetreideschrot, bestehend aus 70 v. H. Gerste-Hafer und 30 v. H. Eiweißkonzentrat oder reinem Getreideschrot und 3 Liter Magermilch je Tier und Tag. Daß natürlich auch Konzentrat und Magermilch zusammen gefüttert werden können, ist klar, nur muß man dann das Mischungsverhältnis ändern und anstatt 70 v. H. Getreideschrot und 30 v. H. Konzentrat eine Futtermischung aus 85 v. H. Getreideschrot und 15 v. H. Eiweißkonzentrat verabreichen.

Dr. Immler

Bekanntmachungen der Landesbauernschaft

Milch-, Fett- und Eierwirtschaft

Milch-, Fett- u. Eierwirtschaftsverband Bayreuth

Der Vorsitzende

Anordnung Nr. 1 vom 15. 2. 1943

Betreff: Ausgleichsabgabe für Butter.

Diese Anordnung tritt am 1. Januar 1943 in Kraft.

Der Vorsitzende: gez. Rosenbeck.

Amtliche Bekanntmachungen der Anerbengerichte

Bekanntmachung.

Amtsgericht

— Stellenangebote —

— Stellengesuche —

— Heiratswünsche —

— Angebote von Hof zu Hof —

— Tausch. Es wird geboten: —

— Veranstaltungen —

— Viehmarkt —

40

Wochenblatt der Landesbauernschaft Bayreuth

Red Cross Prisoner of War Bulletin

(Dad's mom received this bulletin monthly)

PRISONERS OF WAR BULLETIN

Published by the American National Red Cross for the Relatives of American Prisoners of War and Civilian Internees

VOL. 3, NO. 6 WASHINGTON, D. C. JUNE 1945

Liberated Prisoners of War from Germany

By Col. George F. Herbert, AGD Chief, Casualty Branch

As the Allied forces swept victoriously through Germany and the lands occupied by its forces, many thousands of prisoners of war were freed from German camps. American soldiers, jubilant with freedom, knew that Uncle Sam would be well prepared to care for them. The War Department and the theater commanders recognized this fact long before the camps were liberated, and made provisions for the welfare of these men who had been prisoners of war.

Almost immediately after being liberated, many were flown to large camps in the European Theater of Operations especially set up to receive them. At these assembly centers a thorough physical examination is given and the best food the Army has to offer is served them. New uniforms are distributed and partial payments are made from the pay which has accumulated while they have been prisoners of war. Recreation is provided while they await return to the United States. But they do not wait long, for these men have *priority* in returning to the United States over all other military personnel with the exception of the sick and wounded. In fact, many of them are returned by air whenever air transportation is available.

In the meantime, the families at home are passing around the telegram received from the Adjutant General informing them of their son's or husband's return to military control. These telegrams are dispatched to families immediately upon receipt of such information in the War Department, and a second telegram is sent giving the news of expected arrival in the United States as soon as it is learned that certain groups of men are returning. The men themselves are given an opportunity, through the Red Cross, to send a message home prior to their departure from overseas, wherever communication facilities permit.

The Journey Home

Aboard ship these men are served the best of meals. When the ship arrives at its destination in the United States the liberated prisoners are immediately debarked and transported to the staging area connected with the port of debarkation. The commander of the port welcomes the men personally on behalf of the Chief of Staff of the Army, Gen. George C. Marshall, and shortly thereafter dispatches a safe-arrival message to the next of kin of the men who arrived. A band usually strikes up a military air. At a recent docking, the strains of "God Bless America" brought accompanying words from the men, sung with a fervor and heartfelt emphasis that would be hard to match. After termination of the welcoming ceremonies the men are given a physical screening examination and assigned barracks in which freshly made beds await them.

(Continued on page 12)

Liberated American prisoners, after receiving release kits at an assembly center in France, tell their experiences to a Red Cross worker. Names as given, left to right: Pvt. Wallace Butterfield, Pfc. William M. Smith, Pvt. Blair A. Colby, Pfc. Aubrey Rogers, Pfc. Harry R. Shaw, Jr., and Miss Rosanne Coyle.

Red Cross Prisoner of War Bulletin

A Welcome and a Report to Our Liberated Prisoners

To you who have been liberated from German prison camps and are now headed home, this is a word of welcome. We know these last months of the war have been hard ones; that home and the niceties of home will mean a great deal against the primitive background from which you have emerged. After you have had time to settle down, we hope that you will go over the family file of issues of PRISONERS OF WAR BULLETIN. For two years the BULLETIN has striven to give the facts accurately and still hold out some hope to your families of your eventual safe return. Some of you have already seen copies of the BULLETIN in the prison camps in Germany, but, when we were obliged to describe the gradually worsening conditions from last fall onwards, it was banned by the Germans.

Detailed reports which have reached Washington in recent months from the Protecting Power (the government of Switzerland), the International Committee of the Red Cross, and liberated American prisoners of war have all told of the disintegration and chaos inside Germany that were the inevitable prelude to the end of the war. In the midst of this chaos, some of our American and other Allied war prisoners driving the several hundred Allied relief trucks inside Germany, and Swiss nationals convoying the solid trains to strategic points in Germany, have been killed or seriously wounded by the Allied planes which swarmed over the country. To these men who fought to get supplies to the prisoners up to the last day, we render tribute.

In fulfillment of its responsibility, the American Red Cross—with the help of the International Red Cross and the Swiss and Swedish authorities—used every available facility in meeting last winter's emergency caused by the manner in which Germany moved hundreds of thousands of American and other Allied prisoners in forced marches over long distances. As you best know, the German government did not make adequate provision to feed or shelter them or even to care for the sick. At the time the mass evacuations began, practically all the camps where there were large numbers of Americans were stocked with food packages and other supplies, which, in large part, had to be abandoned.

We know you have not all received equal Red Cross service, particularly the men who were captured in the December bulge and in part not even reported by the disintegrating German government as prisoners of war until they were liberated to tell the story. If supplies failed to reach you, they were always on Germany's doorstep. Sometimes it was lack of German cooperation and coordination (though some Germans who did help to get goods through will eventually be recognized); more often, in recent months, it was the paralyzing of German transport by our planes; and sometimes, in spite of diligent effort, it was the human error of our own calculations.

Meeting the Emergency

Even before the disintegration of Germany had become apparent, steps were taken, with the fullest cooperation of the American authorities, the Allied high command, and the Swiss, to secure freight cars and motor trucks outside Germany in order to get supplies in and then to distribute them to the men on the roads and in the camps. Within a few weeks, several hundred motor trucks operated by Swiss drivers and Allied prisoners of war were delivering these urgently needed supplies far and wide inside Germany.

During the last six months, goods have moved steadily from the United States, through Sweden, to the port of Lübeck, and thence by rail, by canal barges, and by heavy auto trucks to camps and marching columns in northern Germany. Simultaneously, solid trains and truck convoys have gone from Switzerland to railheads and distribution centers in southern Germany. At the end of April, International Red Cross warehouses in Switzerland, Sweden, and inside Germany held over 100,000 tons of relief supplies from all Red Cross societies for Allied prisoners.

It was impossible in the developing chaos to organize these delivery services on a fully satisfactory basis. Risks had to be taken, and there is no doubt that some of the supplies intended for American and other Allied prisoners have fallen into enemy hands. With German citizens looting their own railroad trains in search of food and clothing, it was inevitable, in the confusion and destruction caused by incessant Allied bombing of roads and railroads, that some relief goods intended for Allied prisoners would go astray.

Concentration Camps

The disclosures recently made of conditions which existed for years in German political concentration camps have outraged civilized opinion throughout the world. Whatever shortcomings the Geneva Convention may have, it at least helped to place our prisoners of war and civilian internees on a different footing from political prisoners and slave laborers, who perished by thousands in camps which neutral inspectors were never permitted to visit.

Outside of normal human mortality for the long years or months you spent in Germany, over 99 percent of our American prisoners will return to their families in this country. Some of you will return with scars of barbed-wire confinement; all of you will have undergone hardships. However imperfectly the application of this Treaty may have affected you individually, it did help many of our American prisoners. You may not be aware of the fact that the State Department, working closely with the War Department, sent scores of cable protests based on information from the reports of Swiss inspectors, which helped, if only modestly, to alleviate your condition. You who were part of 2,000,000 Allied prisoners being shuffled from point to point in Germany may also not be aware of the fact that our own Army, with millions of German prisoners taken in a few months, is now meeting a supreme test to carry out the Treaty of Geneva in providing for these German prisoners in Europe.

Swiss and Swedish Help

The government of Switzerland and the International Red Cross Committee have always honestly reported the conditions in prisoner of war camps, whether good or bad. However, neither the Protecting Power nor an organization like the IRCC can bring about improvements in bad conditions without the full cooperation of the Detaining Power. The Protecting Power and the IRCC, like us, endeavored by all possible means to make your lot easier, and to deliver to you the supplies we knew you needed. Conditions in Ger-

Red Cross Prisoner of War Bulletin

Moving Supplies into Germany

Reserve supplies of gasoline, shipped from the United States, were carried in trailers.

Convoy with Swiss drivers, and accompanied by a representative of the International Red Cross, ready to leave Switzerland.

American trucks were loaded with food packages at International Red Cross warehouse in Geneva, Switzerland.

Trucks entered Germany in daily convoys to deliver food and medicines to Allied prisoners of war in camps and on the road.

many did not always permit us to accomplish what we attempted to do. Yet during the period of war they moved to you and other Allied prisoners in German-occupied countries over 300,000 tons of relief supplies—the equivalent of a solid European freight train 150 miles long. All European railroads, including those of France, Switzerland, Sweden, Germany, Poland, Denmark, Norway, Hungary, and Rumania, moved these goods free of charge. And thousands of Swiss worked as volunteers in this action. Nor do we omit Sweden, whose sailors made many crossings of the Baltic in small ships from Göteborg to Lübeck with relief supplies, at constant risk of Allied mines and Allied bombing, up to the very moment of the British occupation of Lübeck.

If sometimes you received British or Canadian Red Cross packages, or borrowed American Red Cross packages from French or Belgian or other Allied camp spokesmen, we do not want you to think that your own government or Red Cross was not alert to this. These were all the results of outside reciprocal arrangements, where we planned that our own Allied prisoners in Germany would pull together just as the Allied governments and Allied Red Cross societies have worked in unison. And where you have benefited from the kindness of an Allied prisoner in one camp, we have tried to return this—or more—through the International Red Cross to an Allied prisoner in another camp.

MAURICE PATE, *Director*
Relief to Prisoners of War
American Red Cross

Naval Personnel Reported Missing in Action

By Capt. Albert C. Jacobs, USNR
Director, Dependents Welfare Division, Bureau of Naval Personnel

Casualties are the heavy price the nation is paying, and must continue to pay, for victory. As never before, the impact of increasing casualty lists is being felt by the poor and the rich, by the humble and the great. Officers and men representing every section of our country man the mightiest battle fleet the world has ever known. Many of their families have borne with fortitude the news that loved ones are "missing in action." Unfortunately, before final victory is won, many other navy families will have received a "missing in action" telegram.

The fortitude of such families is the more commendable because the great majority of our officers and men now fighting were, not so long ago, civilians following peaceful occupations, with no thought of war. Unexpectedly catapulted into the fray, they have become the most efficient fighters in history. Only a small percentage were trained for war and schooled to the vicissitudes thereof.

Every family to whom the sad word is sent that a husband, a son, a father, or a brother is "missing in action" will naturally want to know what this term means; what the chances are that he will be found alive and well, that he will be a prisoner of war, or that he has lost his life. The family will also be eager to know how soon more information may be expected.

"Missing in action" means simply that the officer or man cannot be accounted for after combat with the enemy. As yet no information is available to indicate his fate. So far as is known, he has not been found. There is no evidence that he has survived or that he has been taken prisoner, nor is there proof that he has given his life for his country.

So far as naval personnel are concerned, the term "missing in action" has distinctive significance. Due to the nature of naval warfare it is oftentimes extremely difficult to determine accurately what has happened to officers and men following an engagement. The oceans swallow up so rapidly all evidence of engagements fought upon them.

"Missing in action," it is easy to see, is a very broad and general term. It includes, unfortunately, many who are probably dead, but concerning whom proof of death is lacking. It also includes personnel unaccounted for after combat, but who happily will prove to be survivors. To illustrate: A ship is lost during the black of a Pacific night—the fate of some of our officers and men is unknown—they must be listed as "missing in action." A submarine on a combat mission is long overdue—what has happened to it is unknown—the officers and men can only be placed in the status of "missing in action." A plane from one of our carriers does not return after a combat mission—the pilot may be safe on some isolated atoll; he may have been captured by the Japanese; he may have crashed and died at sea—there is nothing to do but place him in the status of "missing in action."

A question frequently asked is how long will an officer or man be carried in the "missing" status. The answer is dependent on many factors. In the absence of a report that he is a survivor or a prisoner of war, or of clear evidence that he is dead, he will be carried in such status for at least 12 months. During the year all available evidence concerning his status will be considered to determine whether it definitely establishes his death.

An officer or man will be continued in the status of "missing" beyond the year when the circumstances indicate that he may be an unreported prisoner of war, or alive in some isolated community. Such a decision, which is communicated to the next of kin by the Bureau of Naval Personnel, means that on the basis of all available evidence the Navy still has some doubt as to his status.

Experience has proved that in many cases 12 months are not sufficient to clarify the status of "missing" naval personnel. We have learned to our sorrow that the Japanese have been neither prompt nor accurate in releasing the names of prisoners of war to the International Committee of the Red Cross. The reports concerning approximately 44 percent of the naval prisoners held by the Japanese have been received more than 12 months after their "missing" status began. Two years and more have not infrequently elapsed before word has been initially received that "missing" persons are prisoners of war in the hands of the Japanese. An enlisted man "missing" from the *USS Houston* during the battle of the Java Sea (February 28 to March 1, 1942) was first reported a prisoner of war on February 17, 1945. For nearly three years his family had received no word from him. Some naval personnel have even been rescued and have returned who have never been reported as prisoners of war.

Not only have the Japanese been slow in releasing the names of prisoners of war, but they frequently have failed to report deaths occurring in their camps. Families have been notified that a report has just been received that their loved ones are prisoners of war; it has then been the sad duty of the Navy to inform the families of a subsequent report that death occurred many months before the announcement that they were prisoners of war.

The decision that naval personnel be continued as "missing" after 12 months has frequently been based simply on the possibility that they may be unreported prisoners of war of the Japanese. The officers and men of an overdue submarine have often been continued in the "missing" status after 12 months because *of the complete lack of data* concerning the submarine.

The Germans, on the other hand, have reported prisoners of war with reasonable promptness. Experience has established that naval personnel "missing" as a result of action with the Germans, and concerning whom no word is received for 12 months, are in fact dead.

In Guam and the Philippines some navy personnel hid from the enemy and were never captured. They were helped by natives and often organized guerrilla bands. The story of Radio Electrician George R. Tweed, U. S. Navy, is known by the entire country. He had been carried as "missing in action" from December

10, 1941, to the summer of 1944.

Presumption of Death

A finding of death is made when a survey of all the available sources indicates beyond doubt that the presumption of continuance of life has been overcome. There is no chance of his being an unreported prisoner of war or being alive in some isolated place. If a finding of death is made, his pay accounts are closed as of the presumptive date of death, that is, the day following the expiration of the 12 months' absence, and the various benefits, such as the six months' death gratuity, become payable.

A finding of presumptive death concerning an officer or man of the Navy means simply that as of the date thereof *he is for the purpose of naval administration no longer alive. It does not mean that death occurred on that or on any other certain date.* For purposes other than naval administration, the law does not make these findings binding or conclusive. But commercial insurance companies have, almost without exception, accepted them as evidence of the fact of death, and have paid insurance claims on the basis thereof. Their understanding settlement of claims based on the deaths of naval personnel has been most praiseworthy.

Through March 31, 1945, 5,867 officers and men of the Navy had been continued in a "missing" status beyond the 12 months' period, while findings of presumptive death had been made in regard to 8,132 officers and men. In 5,867 cases the Navy could not, on the basis of the evidence available, make findings of death and request the payment of death benefits.

Findings of presumptive death are *never made when the* "missing" status has not continued for at least 12 months. If a person's status is changed from "missing" to "dead" prior to the expiration of 12 months, it is only on the basis of clear and unmistakable evidence of death. Whenever, subsequent to the expiration of the 12 months, cumulative or other evidence establishes beyond doubt that a "missing" person is no longer alive, a prompt finding of presumptive death will be made. Also, there will be such a finding whenever justified by lapse of time without specific information being received. It has been the policy of the Navy to review, at the end of the second 12 months, the cases of all personnel continued "missing" at the end of 12 months when no new evidence has been received in the interim.

Because of the peculiar circumstances involved, 4,220 officers and men of the Navy have been continued in a "missing" status beyond 24 months. Most of these were "missing" following the battle of the Java Sea, the loss of Wake, and the loss of the Philippines. Their fate being unknown—they could have been captured, could have escaped, could have died—it has been necessary to continue their "missing" status. On the basis of available information such status could not be terminated.

Dependency Support

During this period of uncertainty—and the Navy fully appreciates the heartaches caused by the "missing" telegrams it must send—when families are suffering deep anguish and sorrow, provision must be made for the support of dependents of "missing" naval personnel. The various benefits contingent on death, such as pensions, insurance, and the death gratuity, cannot be paid during the "missing" status. The law, however, provides that the total pay and allowances of the "missing" person will be credited to his account during the continuance of such status. The law further provides that allotments from his pay made by the "missing" person will continue to be paid therefrom, particularly those for the support of dependents and for the payment of insurance premiums. These allotments may be increased or new ones registered by the director of the Dependents' Welfare Division of the Bureau of Naval Personnel upon proof of the need therefor. It is not the practice to allot 100 percent of a "missing" person's pay, because it is deemed advisable to leave some on the books for the officer or man to draw upon his return. Also, family allowance benefits are available for the eligible dependents of "missing" enlisted personnel.

Once a person is placed in a "missing" status, pay and allowances continue to be credited to his account until evidence of death is received in the Navy Department, or until, after an absence of 12 or more months, a finding of presumptive death is made. If his status is changed to deceased, his heirs become entitled to the accumulated pay and allowances.

The Navy's Growth

It is a matter of common knowledge that since the early days of the war our Navy has grown tremendously. Many ships of all sizes are now available for an engagement. For this reason, personnel not actually killed in an action have a much greater chance of rescue than in the days of the Java Sea, the Coral Sea, Midway, or Guadalcanal. Because of the size and strength of our fleet, units can be left behind to search for "missing" personnel even though the action is of a continuing nature. In the early days of the war, our ships had of necessity to leave battle areas without delay in order to utilize to the utmost our slim and diminished naval power and to protect the ships still afloat. Even under such conditions, when our weakened fleet performed miracles against great odds, the rescue operations, implemented by such ingenious inventions as the inflated rubber boat, and so forth, are now a matter of record. In July of 1943, when our fleet was growing stronger, several weeks elapsed before a complete survivor list of the *USS Helena* could be sent from the South Pacific, and during this period 167 officers and men were rescued from two islands under Japanese domination. Outstanding also were the rescues of our aviation personnel shot down in the actions against the Jap stronghold at Truk. In short, the chances of rescue at the outset have become greater, but there is also, unfortunately, an increased likelihood that those not rescued in the early days of an operation have made the supreme sacrifice.

There has again been a definite trend on the part of commanding officers to report personnel as "killed" much oftener *than was the case in the early days of the war. If the* evidence clearly establishes death, officers and men are so listed in the initial report, even though their bodies may not have been recovered. In other cases, even though originally listed in the initial report as "missing," where the evidence is unmistakable, commanding officers will in amplifying reports change the status to "dead." In this respect commanding officers were often overcautious in the early days of the war; on the basis of experience they now treat such cases more realistically. If no hope for survival remains, the initial report is of death.

It has, furthermore, become the practice to order the commanding officer or the senior surviving officer of a ship that has been lost to the Bureau of Naval Personnel in order

to clarify the casualty status of the ship's company. On the basis of such first-hand factual information the status of many "missing" personnel has been changed to "dead," but only where the evidence is clear.

Aviation Personnel

Changes have taken place also in regard to "missing" aviation personnel. It was factually demonstrated during recent operations in the Philippines that many of our fliers who were shot down, or otherwise forced down, landed in the islands and were befriended by the guerrillas. In many instances they ultimately returned to naval jurisdiction. In other cases reports have been received from guerrilla forces that our fliers were captured or killed by the Japanese after landing. In short, when air action takes place over enemy-occupied territory in which there are also friendly forces, factual information concerning "missing" personnel has been received much more quickly than in the past. Because of this factor the "missing" status has often been clarified within the year.

There have been many instances of "missing" naval personnel returning under the most extraordinary circumstances. The day of miracles is not past. The stories of adventure, of hardship, of ingenuity, of miraculous stamina exhibited by the survivors of sunken ships and plane crashes make fiction pale into insignificance.

Miraculous Escapes

Going through the records, one is surprised to note the number of "missing" officers and men who have been eventually located and returned to safety. From the hundreds of tiny islands and atolls in the Pacific, where natives often rescue them and assist them in the return to their bases, and from the frozen wastes of Greenland and the Aleutians, where our ships carry on a tireless search, "missing" persons have returned under miraculous circumstances. Sometimes, long after reasonable hope has gone, they have found their way back through the jungles of the vast area of the Pacific, or from the treacherous, creviced glaciers of the far north. Unfortunately, however, such miraculous rescues are the exception rather than the rule.

On July 2, 1944, 600 miles from Columbo, Ceylon, the *SS Jean Nicolet* was torpedoed by a Japanese submarine. The officers and men, the

(Continued on page 15)

Wounded Americans liberated from a German Lazarett. Names as given, left to right: S/Sgt. Paul O. Bergman, T/Sgt. Don V. Sage, Sgt. John L. Donalson, S/Sgt. John M. Holzermer, Pvt. Ralph Ford, Sgt. James E. Coalter, and Pvt. George W. Mandeville. Note Red Cross cartons stuffed in broken windows.

Letter from France

The following letter from an American prisoner of war from Stalag XII A at Limburg was written from an assembly center for recovered American military personnel in France on April 19 to his wife in Pittsfield, Massachusetts.

Darling:

I hardly know where to begin, and my mind is spinning with things to tell you. But, first, I'm very safe and quite well and supremely happy to be free again. I'm dying to see you, dearest, and Wendy and all, but it is wisest to follow the Army's orders and take hospitalization until I am in perfect health again.

I hope that you were promptly notified that I was a P.W., and that you did not have to sweat out the "missing in action" telegram long. I worried about that.

Right now, I am in a field hospital with a mild touch of dysentery and malnutrition. It is nothing serious. I am up and about all day, in the best of spirits, and so glad to be back in the arms of the U. S. Army and the Red Cross that tears come to my eyes when I think of it, and how lucky we are. We are getting the best of treatment and food. I'm on a regular diet, so you see my malnutrition isn't too serious.

You'd hardly know me right now. My face is O.K., a little pale, I guess, but still the "laughing gray eyes," etc. My head has been shorn, clipped but not shaved, because we found some lice eggs in it yesterday. Lice! Lord, yes, I was quite lousy for awhile—we all were. And we tried to keep it down as best we could, but it was impossible, sleeping in barns as we had been for six weeks. I'm very thin and have lost about 25 or 30 pounds, I guess, chiefly in the arms and legs, but it won't take long to regain most of it here and soon. We lost the weight on the march—15 to 20 kilometres a day on very little food—a not very nourishing soup for breakfast, and a cup of weak "coffee" and a fifth of a loaf of bread with a *bit* of "butter" or cheese or meat for supper. That diet was varied *somewhat*—sometimes a *bit* more, more usually less—for all of my four months' captivity, and, darling, that was a lot more than some P.W.'s got in other parts of hell's corners, that is geographically called Germany.

For about a total of 8 weeks, however, Red Cross No. 10 food parcels, or small portions of them, were available, and they were a Godsend—believe me! I doubt if as many of us would have survived were it not for what little Red Cross the Germans would let us get. They withheld it from us, or we were never at the proper place for us to receive it. When I say "us" I refer chiefly to P.W.'s who were taken in recent months, as I was, for whom the boche

had no suitable facilities or time or men to devote the proper care or treatment. At the same time, I was lucky to be with a group that got as good treatment as I did—which was pretty poor at best—so that I have suffered very little as compared to others who were taken at the same time, but who went various and diverse ways. Darling, as for the details of the four months, wait until we can talk—save this letter and we'll go over it and I can give you a full account of P.W. life. For the rest of the letter, I'll try to account for the past week with reference to the past, present, and future, so hold on.

A week ago today, at about this time in the afternoon, I had the unique experience of watching the 9th Army spearhead assault a town less than a mile distant from us. We had been ordered to march from a small village, where we had been lying in a barn for ten days, to another town seven kilometres distant. As we approached the town we could hear the German 88's firing from its outskirts on a ridge some distance to our right. When we were within a mile of the town (let's call it "W"), a squadron of USAAF's P-47s came over, so we had to disperse into the field and lie down in case they strafed us. They floated around awhile and finally located the 88's position and the show began. First the heavy bomb that each plane carries—dive-bombing—and the ack-ack opened up, but it was meager and way off its mark. Then each plane released its rockets in turn at the targets. After that, they strafed the town and, thank God, not us. When the squadron got through, another repeated the performance. You can't imagine how it *felt to have the Yanks so close*. When the planes were done, artillery and tanks from the ridge across the way opened up on the town and, although we couldn't spot them, we could sure get a good look at their fire—and what it was doing. Since the planes had gone, the German noncom in charge of us (a decent guy as Krauts go) turned us around and marched us back. We were sweating out the tanks—hoping they wouldn't fire at us, because we were on a ridge ourselves—over three hundred P.W.'s. They must have spotted us for what we were, because they fired at a motorcycle five hundred yards distant just after our column turned off the road away from the scene of action. I felt like crying when we had to march away from the Yanks—so near and yet so far. We marched 'til way after dark but didn't cover much ground, because we walked in circles. Some managed to escape, and those that tried and failed had rifle butt bruises to prove it. We were put in a barn that night and were so surprised to find that we could sleep till late in the morning, so we knew something was up. It seems most of the guards had taken off in the night. This was Friday, the 13th, and a day that I'll never forget, although there were lots of older P.W.'s who had dreamed of this day for longer than I. The old German noncom told us that we would be liberated that day—the Yanks were way past us by then—and he and a handful of guards stayed there to maintain order. Sure enough, along about 3 P.M., a lieutenant colonel and a small column that were out looking for us rode into the village and we were free men again.

You'll never know what a kick that was. I didn't think the Colonel would appreciate an embrace, so I kissed his jeep instead. That evening we had our first G. I. food—K rations—and no Christmas dinner ever tasted better.

We were billeted in another German town for the night—the civilians were chased out of their homes—and on the 14th we were taken by quartermaster trucks back to a supply and evacuation base, where I lived until the 17th—when planes carried us back to this camp in France. Believe me, there is nothing so highly organized and so well organized as the good old U. S. Army—that it can evacuate its recaptured personnel at the rate it is doing. The morning of the 18th I was sent to the hospital and tomorrow I move to the convalescent hospital across the road, where I hope to be for just a short time.

That, in a nutshell, is what I've done in the past week. Yesterday, I had my first hot shower since December 6—my birthday—and I hated to get out of it. Today, I got a new clothing issue and a PX ration of cigarettes, gum, fruit juice, etc., plus a Red Cross ditty bag with cigarettes, toilet articles, cards, a book and gum—little stuff that means so much to us now. But the most important item I've spent very little time on—food. That's all a P.W. thinks and talks about—and, for the most part, lives for. He dreams of it, and discusses it daily and by the hour—varied dishes, and ways of cooking different foods. The chief trouble is that since we've been repatriated we've been fed so well on such good food that it has taken the edge off all our appetites for the food we discussed as P.W.'s. One thing I know, though—I'm never going to be hungry again. In the hospital here, I've eaten more in one meal than I usually eat in three. At the evacuation base, the Red Cross served coffee and doughnuts—nectar and ambrosia. I've had fresh oranges and apples at the airport mess when we arrived in France—and bread pudding—pancakes, French toast and oatmeal this morning, and eggnog. Wonderful steak for dinner. Peanut butter and jelly and *white* bread galore. I never dreamed a G. I. kitchen could serve so much good food, and I'm afraid I'm gorging myself on it. Also, I'm getting plenty of vitamin pills and paregoric between meals—which speaks for itself.

Well, darling, I'm sure I've written more than anyone wants to censor, but then I haven't imposed that job on anyone for a long time. I'll write tomorrow. It's funny writing to you again—but I hope I won't be writing for long.

LIBERATED AMERICANS TO GUARD GERMAN PRISONERS

It was announced on April 29 that American officers and enlisted men who have been liberated from enemy prison camps will be assigned to guard camps for German prisoners. The announcement stated that these men, "who have experienced captivity and detention by the enemy, are considered to be eminently qualified for these duties."

It is planned to use returned Americans both in administrative capacities and as guards.

The announcement was made by Maj. Gen. Thomas A. Terry, commanding general of the Army Second Service Command, whose headquarters are on Governors Island, New York.

For officers, administrative duties would include command of camps and command staff work, such as arranging menus for prisoners, it was stated. Enlisted men would perform office routine, checking prisoners in and out, supervision of prisoners in work camps, preparing job lists, and similar functions.

Red Cross Prisoner of War Bulletin

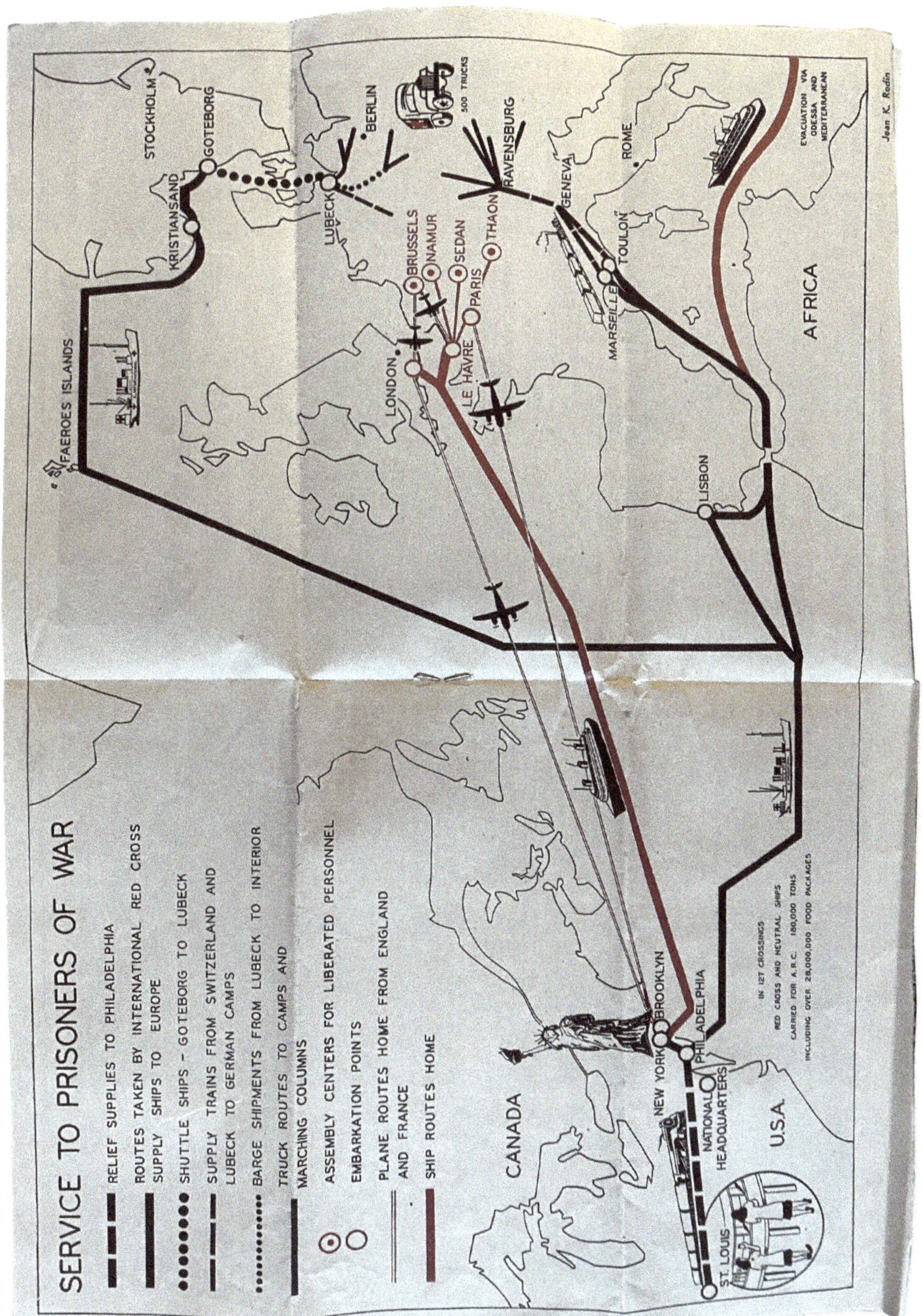

Red Cross Prisoner of War Bulletin

Far East Letters

Shanghai War Prisoners' Camp
April 11, 1944

Dearest Mother:

Again I am kindly permitted by the Japanese authorities to write you. I have received almost 110 letters from you. How I thank God for them, and treasure them. About 15 from Uncle Ayer and others. I am well, have sufficient to eat, and ample to wear. I look forward to your package. Mrs. L. Baer, 75 Route Mayen, Shanghai, sends me a few things occasionally. She is a Swiss Christian Scientist, but her funds are low, and she cannot afford to send me very much . . . but does as best she can. I am well and busy in my library. Almost 6,000 fine books. The room is attractive. I keep flowers in it. Here we hold services, etc. When books wear out I send them to Shanghai, and have them beautifully rebound. Of course, I love this room and am proud of it and receive many compliments. We have fine dentists, surgeons, and have just received many Red Cross medical supplies and food packages from the States, additional blankets, shoes, coats, sweaters, etc.

Osaka
Undated

Dear Family:

What luck! Just getting this written (July 25) when your letters arrived. Received your package of August 20, 1943, on May 28, 1944. You can imagine my boost in morale. Expecting more in near future. As you encourage, I am in there pitching. Bill Anson died in Philippines. The first bombing took care of my trombone. Thoughts of all of you keep me going. Say hello to everyone. Pictures wonderful. With hope and lots of love.

Camp Hoten
Undated

Dear Mother and Father:

Hoping all is well. I'm O. K. and in good health. Give my best regards to friends and loved ones. I would be pleased to receive many pictures and letters. Tell Mr. Graham who works at Jasper High School that his son Roy was O. K. October 8, 1942, when I left the Philippines. We have received a library from the Red Cross. Now I am spending much time reading.

Tokyo, No. 5 Camp
Undated

Dear Mom:

Writing again to let you know that I am still O. K. How are things going back there in Newark? Please try to get in touch with me. I hope things end soon as 5 years is a long time to be away from home. Best of health till then.

Osaka, No. 263
Undated

Dearest Mother:

I am beginning to wonder if everyone I used to know has become illiterate. Every opportunity that I have been afforded I have written, but alas, all in vain, as I have received no letters. Many of the fellows have received 50 and 60 letters.

When I return, I am sure you will want to hear some of the tall yarns that I have to spin, but, if I have received no letters, I will get a divorce, settle in California, and buy a map that doesn't show Georgia.

American prisoners of war at Zentsuji. Names as given, left to right: 2nd Lt. A. H. Chestnut, 2nd Lt. James I. Mallette, 1st Lt. Ben W. Riall, 1st Lt. Harold A. Arnold, 1st Lt. Bruce Walcher, and 1st Lt. Ralph W. Yoder.

Fukuoka
July 1944

Dear Family:

Received your letter and pictures, and had the thrill of a lifetime. Send more. I'm still a picture of health, and in a good frame of mind.

Tokyo
March 24, 1944

Dearest Mother:

I have written a card and a radiogram since my arrival in Japan in December. Wish I could hear from you soon. Sorry I was shot down before any Christmas parcels arrived for me.

My health is still good. Have had an earache the past few days, but over now. Am working in the Tokyo area POW post office here in camp. Sorting letters. You'll find my taste increase in food, soup and fish, and in enjoyment. I have learned to really appreciate the good things of life. My experiences have taught me much. F. E. Cowart, San Benito, and T. A. Cressner, drugstore, Wesleco, are in this camp.

Osaka, No. 152
Undated

Dear Sister:

Everything is about the same here as it was the last time I wrote to you. I am working 13 days out of 14. As yet I have only received the one box, but I am sure I will get another one before long. I would give anything for a Stateside candy bar. I sure miss all of you, and hope it won't be long till I see you again. Hoping to hear from you soon.

(Readers are again reminded that, in their letters and in the messages from them broadcast by the Japanese, prisoners of war are not allowed to speak freely. The letters, moreover, show a keen anxiety to avoid adding to the families' worries.—Editor.)

MEDICAL CARE AT SHANGHAI

According to a recent report by cable from the International Red Cross Delegate in Shanghai, medical attention is given the internees in the Shanghai Civil Assembly Centers by Drs. T. C. Borthwick, M. K. Garnick, and J. H. L. Patterson, assisted by five qualified nurses. Dental service is not available in the camp, but internees requiring treatment are permitted to visit the dentist in the Chapei Civil Assembly Center once a week.

The canteen in the Shanghai Civil Assembly Center, according to the Delegate's report, is open twice a week, during which time fresh eggs, peanut butter, cigarettes, matches, thermos bottles, canned fish, and other items are sold.

The internees brought to the camp ample supplies of clothing and bedclothes of their own. Kitchen equipment, which had been short, is gradually being improved through donations by the Swiss consulate.

Each internee is permitted to send, each month, one local and one foreign message, but there is no restriction on the number of 25-word foreign messages which internees may receive.

Religious services are conducted for Protestant, Catholic, and Jewish internees.

MESSAGE FROM GENERAL WAINWRIGHT

The following message from Lt. Gen. Jonathan M. Wainwright was broadcast from Tokyo in the middle of April:

I am well and comfortably housed. Please inform all the family and Jimmy. Wire Mrs. S. M. Ausbun of Paris, Texas, that her brother is well.

This was the first word received by Mrs. Wainwright from her husband since last August. The "Jimmy" referred to is Adjt. Gen. James A. Ulio, who was associated with General Wainwright in the Philippines. The brother of Mrs. Ausbun is Sergeant Carroll, the general's orderly.

General Wainwright was transferred from Taiwan (Formosa) to Camp Hoten, in Manchuria, late in 1944.

Red Cross Prisoner of War Bulletin

AMERICANS LIBERATED AT RANGOON

Early in May the War Department was informed that 73 American prisoners of war had been liberated in the capture of Rangoon, Burma, by British forces. Most of the men had never been reported as prisoners, and were still listed by the War Department as missing in action. The Japanese had never even reported this as a camp where American prisoners were detained, and, therefore, no Red Cross supplies could be sent there.

The War Department stated at the time of the announcement that as soon as a complete list of the names of the liberated prisoners was available their next of kin would be notified.

NOTIFYING FAMILIES OF LIBERATED PRISONERS

An agreement made early in May between the War Department and the American Red Cross provided that the Red Cross may notify families of liberated American prisoners of war of their liberation, when the men request this service. The responsibility of caring for liberated prisoners and arranging transportation home for them, together with the many other military duties, made it difficult for the Army to notify next of kin as promptly as they would have liked of the liberation of prisoners.

Cabled and telegraphed lists of names of liberated prisoners are now being sent by Red Cross field directors overseas to national headquarters in Washington. From here they are sent with all dispatch to local chapters, whose representatives personally deliver the news to the next of kin.

In addition to this service the Red Cross will, if the situation warrants it, send a cable inquiring about a liberated prisoner's family, when it is apparent that the prisoner expects to be in Europe long enough to receive the reply. A similar service is planned for liberated Allied prisoners of war who have relatives in the United States.

Prisoners of War Bulletin invites reprinting of its articles in whole or in part. Its contents are not copyrighted.

PACKAGING CENTERS

With stock piles in Europe, or en route thereto, totaling about 10,000,000 American Red Cross standard food packages, production in the Philadelphia, New York, St. Louis, and Brooklyn Packaging Centers was reduced early in April to about 200,000 a week. By the end of May, by which time 28,000,000 packages had been shipped abroad, operations were discontinued.

Besides supplying, throughout April and May, food packages to all American and other Allied prisoners of war who could be reached anywhere in Germany, large numbers were furnished to liberated American prisoners on their homeward journey through assembly centers and evacuation points, in addition to the supplies they received from the U. S. Army. Arrangements were made some time ago whereby, on the cessation of hostilities in Europe, all stock piles of American Red Cross food packages would be placed at the disposal of SHAEF, and these reserves filled a very vital need.

A substantial supply of special Far Eastern packages has been built up and is being held in the United States for possible future shipment to American and other Allied prisoners still in Japanese hands.

The women volunteers who so faithfully manned the packaging center assembly lines since this operation began in March 1943 have made a most important contribution to the national effort. Their readiness at all times and under all sorts of conditions to perform this service has earned the heartfelt gratitude of all prisoners of war who have received packages.

FAR EAST RELIEF SUPPLIES

A Russian ship carrying additional relief supplies for American and Allied prisoners in the Far East left a West Coast port in the latter part of April for Vladivostok.

This latest shipment, consisting of 1,500 tons, included 115,000 American Red Cross food packages, 112,000 Canadian Red Cross food packages, 3,000 Indian food packages packed by the Canadian Red Cross, 184 tons of medical supplies, and 15 tons of YMCA and National Catholic Welfare Conference goods.

At the time of this shipment there were still in Vladivostok about 700 tons of relief supplies, and negotiations were in progress with the Japanese to pick up the supplies for distribution to Allied prisoners and civilian internees in the Far East.

IRCC WHITE BOOK

Mr. Carl J. Burckhardt, President of the International Red Cross Committee, recently announced in Geneva that a white book would soon be published containing correspondence exchanged with the Germans on the matter of atrocities in *concentration* camps.

Mr. Burckhardt also disclosed that, but for the persistent efforts of the IRCC, the Germans would have denounced the Geneva Convention at the end of 1943. This, he stated, would have left millions of Allied prisoners virtually unprotected.

Swedish trucks leaving Goteborg for Lübeck, Germany. These trucks, plainly marked in German, International Committee of the Red Cross, were used for delivering relief supplies to camps and marching columns in northern Germany.

Red Cross Prisoner of War Bulletin

Stalag III B "Pirates." Picture taken at Fürstenburg/Oder in June 1944. Names as given, left to right: (sitting) Cronin, Bennett, Terris, Workman, Harmon; (standing) Taylor, Easterbrook, Vincich, Gaskin, Bosse, Ray, and Denton.

Exchanges of Prisoners in France

Last October 16, an American Red Cross field director, Andrew G. Hodges, attached to the 94th Infantry Division in France, was given an unusual assignment. He was asked by the Chief of Staff of the 94th to see what could be done for 53 Americans known to be prisoners on the Isle of Groix in the Bay of Biscay. The Americans were in dire need of food, clothing, and medical supplies.

Hodges wrote to the German commander of the garrison on the Isle of Groix and, while awaiting a reply, journeyed to Rennes to pick up supplies. In the meantime 25 more Americans were taken prisoner.

After days of negotiation, Hodges finally received word on October 28 that the German officials were waiting to see him on the German side of the Etel River. Hodges crossed the Etel on an auxiliary sailboat manned by French civilians and was received by two German officers, who told him that it would not be possible for him to distribute the supplies personally. The Germans, however, gave their word that the supplies would go to the Americans, and set October 30 as the date for Hodges to return with supplies.

When Hodges brought the supplies he remarked jokingly that it would be easier to return the Americans to their own lines to feed them. The German officer immediately stated that his side would be willing to exchange men. The American Red Cross field director asked whether the Germans would abide by the Geneva Convention in such an exchange. The Germans agreed and Hodges returned to the American lines, after arranging for frequent trips to the German lines to bring supplies to the Americans.

Feeling that events had gone beyond his authority, Hodges went to Paris to discuss arrangements with International Red Cross representatives. The International Red Cross favored the exchange, provided the stipulations of the Geneva Convention were adhered to. Hodges returned to the 94th Division headquarters and found that the Chief of Staff had obtained permission from his superior, Maj. Gen. Harry I. Maloney, for the exchange on a man for man basis.

Two more trips to the German lines completed arrangements, and the exchange, set for November 15, came off with a maximum of efficiency. Seventy-five Americans were exchanged for a like number of Germans.

Pleased at the smooth conduct of the exchange, the Division Chief of Staff requested the Red Cross field director to see about an exchange in the St. Nazaire sector.

Hodges, without any advance notice to the Germans that he was coming, got into his jeep and drove to the German lines. His daring got him through. The Germans blindfolded him for the three-hour journey into their lines, part of it by torpedo boat across the Loire River.

The arrangements were made, and Hodges completed his second exchange near Pornic, across the river from St. Nazaire, on November 29.

By Christmas, Hodges arranged for a third exchange in the Lorient sector, where the first exchange was made.

On January 1 the 94th Division Chief of Staff paid tribute to Hodges for his 13 trips into the German lines by awarding him the Bronze Star.

AMERICAN PRISONERS IN THE CHANNEL ISLANDS

Camp Jersey, in the Channel Islands, was visited on February 15, 1945, by a Delegate of the International Red Cross. At that time there were 19 American prisoners of war in the camp, of whom 3 were officers, but the number has since risen to 36. The American representative was Colonel Reybold.

The prisoners lived in heated, well-ventilated barracks, according to the report, and had beds with mattresses and sufficient blankets. Medical attention and rations were satisfactory. The prisoners had books and a sports ground, and were permitted walks outside of camp.

In February and March the SS *Vega* made two trips from Lisbon to the Channel Islands with supplies of Red Cross food packages, which were distributed under the control of British Red Cross representatives who frequently visited Camp Jersey. A further shipment of food packages and clothing was made in April.

FAR EASTERN LETTERS AND PICTURES

Readers are urged to send to the Editor, Prisoners of War Bulletin, American Red Cross, Washington 13, D. C., copies of letters and pictures received from American prisoners of war and civilian internees held by Japan. They will then be used, as far as possible, in the Far Eastern edition of the Bulletin, the first issue of which will appear in August.

Red Cross Prisoner of War Bulletin

After Germany's Collapse

All American prisoners of war held by Germany have been liberated and are now home or on their way. Throughout April and May a steady stream of liberated men reached American shores, and the military authorities are returning the men to their homes as expeditiously as the seriously disorganized condition of Europe permits.

Since the American Red Cross began publishing PRISONERS OF WAR BULLETIN in June 1943, one of our main objectives has been to let our prisoners of war tell their own story of conditions, Red Cross services, and general camp activities through its columns—in letters from the prisoners themselves, in interviews with repatriates, in reproductions from camp newssheets, and in factual reports from neutral inspectors who had visited the camps and talked with the men.

We have had several opportunities recently to talk with returned prisoners, some of whom were frank enough to state that, while in Germany, they had the feeling that their relatives at home were being given a distorted picture of life in German prisoner of war camps, but that when they had carefully read a complete file of PRISONERS OF WAR BULLETIN after their return they were satisfied the American Red Cross had given their families a fair and balanced picture in words that avoided adding to the heavy load of anxiety which the relatives of the men had borne so patiently. Among 100,000 men there must inevitably be some who will feel that we have erred on the side of giving the families too much comfort and consolation, and perhaps as many others who will consider that we have unnecessarily disturbed their relatives by reporting that conditions in a certain camp were bad at the same time that the men there were writing home "everything here is fine, so don't worry about me."

This will be the last issue of PRISONERS OF WAR BULLETIN devoted mainly to activities in Europe, but beginning in August, the American Red Cross will publish a bulletin devoted entirely to the Far East, where some 15,000 American prisoners of war and civilian internees are still held by Japan.

All next of kin of prisoners of war in the Far East, whose names are carried on the rolls of the Office of the Provost Marshal General, will automatically receive copies of the Far Eastern edition as they are published from time to time, just as they have received their copies of PRISONERS OF WAR BULLETIN. Other readers who are interested in the Far East and who desire to receive the Far Eastern edition are requested to fill out the blank form on page 15 of this issue and return it to the Editor, PRISONERS OF WAR BULLETIN, American Red Cross, Washington 13, D. C. Their names will then be added to a special Far Eastern mailing list which will be prepared by the Red Cross and will be independent of the next-of-kin list maintained by the Office of the Provost Marshal General.

The American Red Cross staff, and especially those concerned with the publication and distribution of PRISONERS OF WAR BULLETIN, have regarded it as a high privilege to render this service to the families and friends of our prisoners of war and civilian internees. To the many hundreds who have written us about the help and guidance which the BULLETIN has brought to them in their anxious days of waiting, our sincere thanks are now expressed.

GILBERT REDFERN
Editor

Letter to the Editor

748 Page Street
San Francisco 17, California

Dear Sir:

I have just returned from the Philippines after 1,135 days' interument under the Japs. They took care of us in Camp John Hay and Camp Holmes (Baguio), and also at Bilibid prison in Manila.

It's wonderful to be home again and I wish to express my sincere thanks to the American Red Cross for all you have done for myself and other Americans interned in the Philippines during these past three nightmarish years.

One of my most wonderful remembrances is that of December 25, 1943—Christmas Day!—when we in the Baguio camp received the wonderful food packages and medical supplies. Needless to say, it was really a grand Christmas and one I will always remember.

The Red Cross has assisted us immeasurably since our liberation also, and—well—I just can't tell you how thankful I am.

We are all looking forward to the liberation of Americans in other war areas, particularly those in Hong Kong and Singapore.

Many, many thanks again, and you may rest assured that the American Red Cross will always hold a warm spot in my heart.

Most sincerely,
WALTER M. MOORE

April 1945

Questions and Answers

Q. *Do all wounded AAF prisoners repatriated during the war get disability discharges from the Army?*

A. Every effort is made to reassign a repatriated AAF member (in a noncombatant capacity) unless he specificially indicates his desire for a certificate of disability for discharge.

Q. *What becomes of the personal effects of a flier reported missing in action?*

A. Before preparing them for shipment, it is customary for a commanding officer in an overseas theater to retain the personal effects of an individual for a "holding period," which may extend over some months after he has been reported missing in action, on the chance that the individual will find his way back to his base. After the "holding period" has elapsed, the effects are made ready for shipping and are brought back to this country when transportation is available, and, in the case of an army flier, delivered to the Effects Quartermaster, Army Effects Bureau, Kansas City Quartermaster Depot, Kansas City, Missouri. Personal effects of navy fliers are forwarded to next of kin in the Pacific Area from Personal Effects Distribution Center, U. S. Naval Supply Depot, Clearfield, Utah, and to those in the Atlantic Area from Personal Effects Distribution Center, U. S. Naval Supply Depot, Scotia, New York.

The effects of Marine Corps personnel are handled *from the same centers as those of navy personnel.*

Coast Guard personnel's effects are distributed from U. S. Coast Guard Headquarters, Military Morale Division, Washington, D. C.

There is no way of determining the length of time that may elapse between the report of missing in action and the receipt by the next of kin of these effects, but it usually requires at least six months and may take as much as a year.

Red Cross Prisoner of War Bulletin

will be more difficult, more spectacular, but they will still be made.

Chances of Survival

What are the chances that a "missing" person will prove to be a survivor? A general answer is impossible because the circumstances vary in every case. It is unfortunately true that of the naval personnel reported "missing" since Pearl Harbor considerably more have been determined to be dead than have proved to be alive. This is likely to continue. When a man loses his life on land, his sacrifice is usually disclosed rather rapidly by the finding of his body. At sea, however, a man may lose his life and leave no evidence of that fact. Therefore, many naval personnel, in fact dead, must be listed as "missing." Nearly 17,000 officers and men of the Navy carried at one time as "missing" are now listed as "killed."

From the standpoint of percentages it is expected that fewer naval personnel will be placed in the "missing" status than formerly, because of basic factors already discussed.

Machines, the marvels of modern inventive ingenuity, cannot take the place of human beings. In the final analysis, manpower will win the war, and, for victory, precious personnel will continue to be lost. The Navy is keenly aware of the fact that nothing can compensate for the loss of those dear to us. The countless billions the war is costing in materiel seem infinitesimal when we learn of a loved one's death. The American people are facing the sacrifices war entails with bravery and fortitude.

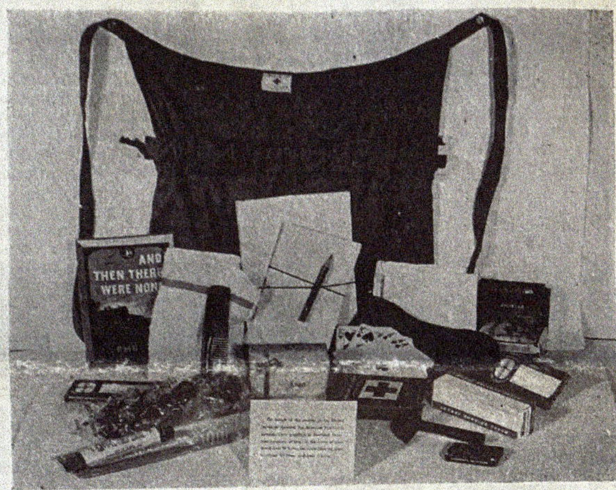

For use on the journey home, these Red Cross release kits are distributed to American prisoners.

Release Kits for Liberated Americans

An urgent request for an additional 50,000 release kits came by cable late in April from Henry W. Dunning, the American Red Cross representative at SHAEF. The cable stated that "the kits are filling a great need." They are distributed to liberated American prisoners of war when they reach the assembly centers preparatory to repatriation, or at ports of call on the journey home.

About 100,000 release kits, packed by women volunteers at the New York Packaging Center, were shipped from the United States in February and March. Of this total, 71,400 were shipped to France, 10,000 to the Soviet Union, 9,500 to Italy and 5,000 to Egypt for American prisoners returning via Russia, and 4,000 to the Philippines. The additional 50,000 requested by cable were put into production immediately.

Prisoners of War Bulletin
JUNE 1945
Published by
The American National Red Cross
Washington 13, D. C.

Return Postage Guaranteed

U. S. POSTAGE
1½c PAID
Philadelphia, Pa.
Permit No. 1513

MRS. BERTHA W. NAUL,
710 FRANKLIN STREET,
ALTON, ILLINOIS.

Postmaster—If addressee has removed and new address is known, notify sender on FORM 3547, postage for which is guaranteed.

A 1944 Christmas in Stalag Luft III

by John Rowan,
105 Ellsworth Place, Cary, NC 27511

It was the best of times, it was the worst of times; it was the season of Light, it was the season of Darkness; it was the spring of hope, it was the winter of despair; we had everything before us, we had nothing before us.

Charles Dickens was writing of another time, of another place. But his words could not have been more apt in describing the Christmas season for those of us who were prisoners of war in a Luftwaffe camp in northern Germany.

It was the best of Christmases, it was the worst of Christmases.

I was an unwilling inhabitant of Block 46 in the Center Compound of Stalag Luft III, close to the Polish border, about ninety miles southeast of Berlin. The camp was designed for flying officers — both Americans and those from various countries of the British Commonwealth.

The circumstances of my being there had been irrevocably determined by the attempt of our B-17G trying to occupy a few cubic feet of air at the same time a burst of German flak decided to stake its claim to the same chunk of sky.

And so I, the lead navigator — along with pilot Tony Zotollo, co-pilot Bob Lawson, bombardier Joe Loiacano, and assistant lead navigator Wayne Livesay — found ourselves distributed among the various blocks throughout the Center Compound.

We were an experienced lead crew. I was flying what was to have been my 30th and next-to-last mission on August 9th when it ended over the Scheldt Estuary of Holland. Probably not more than five missions stood between any of the officers or enlisted men and the end of their tours.

Center Compound was a thriving concern when we arrived. By that I mean military organization prevailed. Senior American Officer Col. Delmar T. Spivey made most of the difference. His West Point training, eighteen years of active service in the Regular Army and Army Air Forces and command experience insured a discipline that worked for the benefit of all. Whatever little we had, each one of us got a just, equitable share of that little.

Food was short. German rations were meager and iffy and a now-and-then thing. The latrines were stinking messes. Washing facilities were laughable. Medical care almost nonexistent. Cooking facilities barely more so. And the smells, noise, primitive living conditions of hundreds of unwashed men crowded together in sealed barracks in the early winter of 1944 is something that will never leave my memory.

And yet, and yet.

By November, we thought the end was in sight. A certain generosity with our hoards seemed appropriate. We began to plan for Christmas. Our planning centered on that very good thing in a very small package — the Red Cross parcel.

The Red Cross parcel was a marvel of planning, a marvel of thoughtfulness. Within its corrugated confines was home — meat, cheese, soap, milk, raisins, sugar. Cigarettes, too. the smells, tastes and textures of a life 3,000 miles away. One of these per week per man was heaven.

The one-third to one-half parcel we were issued during this time was close enough to heaven. Tight belts can always be tightened even more. A stingier hand with the schmear of Sell's liver pate on the slice of German army bread which made up breakfast meant a more lavish hand at Christmas. Weaker coffee today promised a richer brew tomorrow. A thinner slice of Spam on a K-Ration cracker today meant the feast of tomorrow for our combine.

A combine — about twelve men — was the basic block unit. Our triple decker beds surrounded our communal living space, a small table and a couple of benches. The combine lived, slept, cooked, and messed together. And a week before Christmas, we learned that we would receive a special issue of a special Red Cross parcel. One per man. Unheard of delights! Canned turkey. Condensed honey. A Crosse

ı 1944 CHRISTMAS, cont'd...

ẓ Blackwell plum pudding. A pipe and tobacco, playing ards, checkers, salted nuts, a wash cloth. One per man! And vhat we had saved besides.

And so, when Christmas Day dawned, we bashed the ;ash all day. In kriegie terms, "gash" is anything extra, sur- ılus, over-and-above. To "bash" it is to use it up with no hought for the future.

Unheard of surplus! And the luxury of being able to give. Ve prepared Kriegie Bread/Fruit Cake with Butterscotch cing and offered tiny pieces to our visitors — crew mem- ıers scattered in other blocks, other friends. And to Col. ;pivey and his staff who visited to judge the combine deco- ating contest.

I carved a Virgin Mary and an Infant out of Red Cross vory soap. The Christ Child lay in a crib of wood shavings plenty of that from our "mattresses") and was illuminated ıy a shaft of light from the overhead 40-watt or so naked ıulb, coming through the craftily-placed hole on the manger's oof of cardboard.

But the most vivid memory, the one that is an present to ne fifty years later as yesterday's, was Christmas Eve. We ıll gave our parole. And so I was able to attend Midnight Vlass in the theater/church in Block 45. Some German guards ıttended, in their best uniforms. They did not seem out of ılace to me on that night. It was a bitter night. The frozen ;now popped and snapped under our feet on the way back to 3lock 46. The moon painted the surrounding pines on the ıright sky. And I stopped to hear "Silent Night" rising to the ;ky from one of the barracks. There was a dead silence as ;veryone paused to listen to this beautiful traditional Christ- nas carol.

And so, I wish a "Merry Christmas" once again to my ;ombine as I did fifty years ago. To Oliver Joplin of Texas, Roy Eggman of Indiana, Harry Hillman of New Hampshire, Delbert Little of Ohio, Frank Irizarry of Long Island, Ed Brazis of New York, George McFall of Wisconsin, Kyle

EX-POW BULLETIN, DECEMBER 1994

Gilliam of Tennessee, and especially to Eldon (Sig) Sigurdson of Minnesota, my bunkmate, trailmate, and helpmate during the terrible times that came after we were marched out of Stalag Luft III.

Photo courtesy of U.S. Air Force Academy Library

"I count myself in nothing else so happy,

as in a soul remembering good friends."

Shakespeare

Happy Holidays

Ann Landers Newspaper Clipping

THE TELEGRAPH Mon., Nov. 28, 1988 B-5

ENTERTAINMENT

Stalag VII-A letter unleashes a flood of memories

DEAR ANN LANDERS: I was thrilled to see the letter in your column by Retired Lt. Col. B. McD. Jr. He recounted the events that took place Sunday morning, April 29, 1945, at Stalag VII-A in Moosburg, Germany, where he was a prisoner of war, along with 30,000 others.

The writer described his feelings when the first tank poked its nose over the hill and Gen. Patton's Third Army tanks made their way to the main gate of that prison camp. A huge roar went up from all of us who knew we were free at last!

I was the American security officer at the front gate when that skinny GI shinnied up the flagpole, tore down the ugly German swastika and replaced it with the beautiful Stars and Stripes.

Capt. Dynamite Dunn commanded the tank company that took the camp. He was a fraternity brother (Kappa Alpha) from the University of Maryland, as were two other fellow officers, Lt. William A. MacGregor and Lt. Page B. Pratt. We were taken to headquarters and given royal treatment. What a day!

Thanks, Ann, for bringing back some memories of that fateful day 43 years ago. — Robert L. Hartman, Charleston, W.Va.

DEAR ROBERT HARTMAN: One of the most rewarding aspects of writing this column is providing the thread of humanity that binds us one to the other. I never know, when I print a letter, how many lives I will touch. When I receive feedback, such as the letter you wrote, it gives me a feeling of enormous satisfaction.

Space does not permit the printing of all the letters from "Moosburgers" who were on hand when Gen. Patton's Third Army came in and liberated the POWs, but here are two more.

DEAR ANN LANDERS: When that great letter appeared from the lieutenant colonel from Irving, Tex., a whole host of memories flooded my mind.

I was 19 years old, a ball gunner on a B-17. We had been shot down just two months before, over Berlin, and considered ourselves darned lucky to be alive.

I was at Moosburg, Germany, on April 29, 1945, when Gen. Patton and his men came rolling down the road. I will never forget the smiles on the faces of his courageous men as they rode into our camp. What a fabulous-looking guy Patton was with his ivory-handled pistols gleaming in the sun!

ANN LANDERS

Thank you, Ann, for the best column ever. — Robert L. Copelin (Lubbock, Tex.)

DEAR ANN LANDERS: My husband was a POW at Stalag VII in Moosburg, Germany. Unfortunately, he didn't live to see Gen. Patton's Third Army come thundering down the road. My beloved husband died of tuberculosis just three months before. He wrote some wonderful letters that were sent to me, along with his medals and personal belongings after he died.

In one of his letters he said, "I hope to God this is the last war we will ever fight. It is such a cruel and senseless way to settle differences. I will never forget the face of a German lad I killed last week. He was handsome and young, somebody's son and maybe a husband and father — like me. War is hell." — Nameless Please in Northern California.

Time Magazine

May 29, 2000

Somewhere in France
October 6, 1918

Dear Winifred,

Sitting on head of cot, map case on knee and head ducked beneath canvass leanto against side of company officer's wagon, smoldering fire and dirty dishes in immediate front with orderly (likewise dirty) prowling around in imitation of a working man. Lt. DeLessquaur's tent beyond fire with nothing but his feet sticking out, and an occasional drizzle—Picture this and you have the ideal gypsy outfit which we resemble.

I got back to the company and for a solid day read five week's accumulated mail—about fifty letters with six or seven from you. I never received so much mail at one time before in my life. It certainly was a red-letter day and make no mistake.

I discovered this was Sunday by bumping into an open air Mass conducted by our chaplain, a prince of a fellow and as sincere and straightforward a priest as they make them . . .

The war news continues to be the best ever. We have just received word of Germany, Austria and Turkey asking for an armistice to discuss peace on basis of President Wilson's fourteen proposals. I don't believe they will get an armistice any more than Bulgaria did, tho the Allies may allow them to discuss the question. All this will be history when you receive this letter.

At any rate we're licking the tar out of the Germans and I'm a live part of it. Still that's not saying much because things are lively everywhere now. The spirit of the boys is great and they are brimming over with confidence. On the other hand I believe the morale of the enemy to be lower than at any previous stage of the war. These are stirring times and regardless of my personal outcome I'm glad to be here . . .

I'm feeling fine and fit to fight—one reason being that I've had a bath three weeks later than any one else in the company. Note I'm not mentioning when! Pardon the allusion. We reckon history from one of them to another!

Sincerely, Bob

Time Magazine

May 29, 2000

lection edited by Carroll will be published as a book next May by Scribner's), the correspondence included here suggests a larger historical pattern: soldiers enlisted in the two World Wars are generally upbeat and optimistic, brimming with good-natured confidence. By contrast the G.I.s of the cold war, fighting in Korea and Vietnam, write letters of doubt and confusion, unsure whether dying in a Chosin Reservoir crater or Mekong Delta rice paddy for Old Glory made practical sense. Fear of death, however, permeates them all, no matter in which bloodstained decade they were composed.

BUT IT WOULD BE A DISSERVICE TO their authors to dwell only on the sad finality of these letters full of playful language and good cheer, even under the most harrowing circumstances. After all, most were responses written in the glow of morale boosted by receiving news from home that life was still normal there, that Dad was still priding himself on the tomatoes bursting ripe in the vegetable garden, that Little Brother had just smacked his first stand-up double or that Sis had been accepted at the local university. The mundane details of life in the U.S.—the score of Friday night's football game, the pattern of a soft cotton dress bought special on Main Street—have always been the rare joy of American soldiers far from home. For every Dear John letter serving notice that a soldier had been dumped by his best girl, a thousand others served warm reminders of Mom's cooking for a holiday picnic under the oak tree in the backyard. And it was in this home-and-hearth spirit that the doughboys, G.I.s and grunts wrote back.

It's important too to remember the restrictions on servicemen's correspondence. Whereas in the Civil War soldiers could wax poetic in detailed epistles about the topography around battlefields, the long rock gullies of the Maryland countryside or the paltry food rations at Vicksburg, 20th century U.S. troops were censored from describing their surroundings for fear of tipping off the enemy to military movements. As a result their letters home are far more personal, more expressive of the gripping fears and hopeful longings of young men with no illusions left. Each one of these introspective letters sounds the distant and disturbing echo of a lone bugle blowing taps. ■

Brinkley is professor of history and director of the Eisenhower Center of American Studies at the University of New Orleans

Photocopies or typed transcripts of letters from any of America's wars, on any subject, may be sent to the Legacy Project, Attn.: Andrew Carroll, Box 53250, Washington, D.C. 20009 (include phone no.)

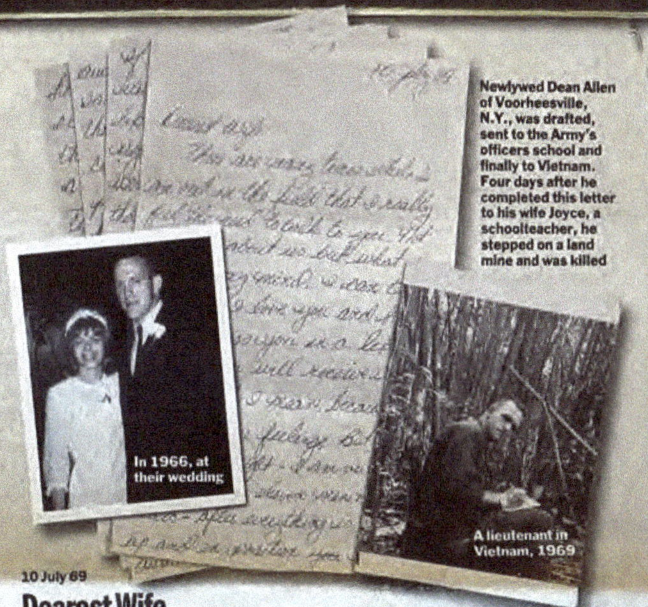

Newlywed Dean Allen of Voorheesville, N.Y., was drafted, sent to the Army's officers school and finally to Vietnam. Four days after he completed this letter to his wife Joyce, a schoolteacher, he stepped on a land mine and was killed

In 1966, at their wedding

A lieutenant in Vietnam, 1969

10 July 69

Dearest Wife

There are many times while I am out in the field that I really feel the need to talk to you. Not so much about us but what I have on my mind. I can tell you that I love you and how much I miss you in a letter and I know you will receive it and know what I mean, because you have the same feelings. But many times like tonight—I am out on ambush with eleven men and a medic—after everything is set up and in position I have nothing to do but lay there and think—why I am here as well as all the men in my platoon? . . . why I have to watch a man die or get wounded—why I have to be the one to tell someone to do something that may get him blown away—have I done everything I can do to make sure we can't get hit by surprise?—are we really covered from all directions? How many men should I let sleep at a time—1/4, 50% or what? . . .

Being a good platoon leader is a lonely job. I don't want to really get to know anybody over here because it would be bad enough to lose a man—I damn sure don't want to lose a friend. I haven't even had one of my men wounded yet let alone killed but that is too much to even hope for to go like that. But as hard as I try not to get involved with my men, I still can't help liking them and getting close to a few. I get to know their wives' names or their girls and kids if they have any. They come up and say, "Hey, 26"—they all call me 26 because that is my call sign on the radio—"Do you want to see a picture of my wife/girl?" or "Look at what my wife or girl wrote." . . .

If I had prayed before or was religious enough to feel like I should—or had the right to pray now—I probably would say one every night that I will see the sun again the next morning & will get back home to you. Sometimes I really wonder how I will make it. My luck is running way too good right now. I just hope it lasts.

I have already written things I had never planned to write because I don't want you to worry about me anyway. Don't worry about what I have said; these are just things I think about sometimes. I am so healthy I can't get a day out of the field, and you know I'm too damn mean to die.

Hon, I better close for now and try to catch a few z's. It will be another long night.

Sorry I haven't written more but the weather is against me. You can't write out here when it rains hour after hour. I love you with all my heart.

All my love always, Dean

Joyce today remembers

The following documents were classified, but are now declassified. Some are illuminating, some are long, all are interesting. Each helped to put the pieces of the puzzle of Dad's journey together.

Some of the following pages have the number: 4566. This is the Missing Air Crew Report Number.

MACR - Missing Aircraft Crew Report

MACR 4566

BISCHOFF, GEORGE A.	0707831	POW	15 JUN	168065
BRADEEN, EVERETT O. JR.	11,118,525	POW	18 MAY	141108
GUILLORY, LOUIS D.	38,379,036	POW	9 JUN	162093
JENSEN, CURTIS S.	39,290,207	POW	9 JUN	162093
KAPISCHKE, ELMER FRED	36,636,493	POW	18 MAY	141108
KING, FRANK L. JR.	0809966	POW	18 MAY (mes.013032 12 Jan.45 tentatively selected for repatriation)	141106
LLOYD, WILLIAM N.	18,217,669	POW	9 Jun	162093
MAUL, HENRY E.	36,478,234	POW	9 JUN	162093
SMITH, JAMES C.	0818964	POW	1 JUN	154062

Additional Plane Crash Information

From information later received, upon crash-landing the pilot and radio operator were thrown clear of the aircraft, the former suffering a broken leg as a result. A short while later the aircraft apparently blew up. Also, further information received indicates that the tail gunner died somewhere in Germany while being moved from one prison camp to another. Further details are doubtless available from other enlisted members of the crew.

Pilot - F.J.King
Co-pilot J.C.Smith
Bomb. - W.W.Reade
Eng. - L.Guillory
R.Waist- H.Maul
L.Waist- E.Kapischke
Ball G.- C.Jensen
Tail G.- W.Lloyd
Radio - E.Bradeen

Report of Capture of Prisoner of the Army Air Forces

REPORT ON CAPTURE OF [illegible] OF THE [illegible] AIR FORCES

POST:	Headquarters, Airbase A 21/XI Airfield - Command Fassberg
PLACE:	F a s s b e r g
DATE:	9 May 1944
REGARDING:	Downing of a Fortress
AT:	unknown
ON:	unknown
NAME:	M A U L
FIRST NAME:	E Henry
RANK:	Sgt
ASN:	36478234 T 43 - 43 A
RESULT:	captured, will be transferred to Oberursel on 9 May 1944
PLACE AND TIME OF CAPTURE:	8 May 1944, 1600 h

N a m e illegible
1st Sgt

cut on flat

EUS

AGPO-CR 201 (Maul, E Henry 36 478 234)

file in 10 PRP [illegible]
Flynn 18 July 47
Cas Sect
58743

123129

American Information on Captured Plane

[redacted]

4566

1. AAF STA 138 — 8TH AF
96TH — 338TH — NONE
2. AAF STA 138 — SEE OTHER SIDE
BERLIN, GERMANY — COMBAT
3. 10/10 STRATOCUMULUS TOPS ESTIMATED 8000 FT. VIS. 15 MILES PLUS
4. 8/3/44 — 1000 — 5140N 1106E
MAY
(X)
5. (X)
6. B-17G — 42-38082
7. R-1820-97 — 3W002079
SW-002869 — SW 41-55033 — SW-003163
8. NUMBERS OF 50 GUNS ON THIS SHIP WERE NOT TAKEN AND NOT
NOT KNOWN.
9. X
10. 10 — 0
Total 10

1.	PILOT	P	KING, JR., FRANK L.	2/LT	0-809966
2.	CO-PILOT	P	SMITH, JAMES C.	2/LT	0-818464
3.	NAVIGATOR	P	BISCHOFF, GEORGE A.	2/LT.	0-707831
4.	BOMBARDIER		TEADE, WILLIAM H.	2/LT	0-757560
5.	ENGINEER TT	P	GUILLORY, LOUIS D.	T/SGT.	38379038
6.	RADIO OPER - RG	P	BRABEEN, JR., EVERETT O.	T/SGT	11116525
7.	ASST. ENGINEER RW	P	KAPISCHKE, ELMER FRED	S/SGT.	36838483
8.	ASST. RADIO OPER	P	ST. JENSEN, CURTIS S.	39290207	S/SGT
9.	ARMORER, TG		LLOYD, WILLIAM H.	S/SGT.	18217869
10.	ASST ARMORER	P	LW. MACE, HENRY E.	S/SGT.	38478234

BAXTER, MORRELL J. — 2/LT — 0-756152 — X
MILES, ROBERT A K — 2/LT — 0-819139 — X

SEE #14

NONE AVAILABLE

SEE OTHER SIDE

NONE MADE

9 MAY, 1944

CAPT. MARVIN K. PETERSON, CAPT., AIR CORPS

[redacted]

Prisoner ID's

Identification markings (Tags)

George A. Bischoff, 0 707831

Louis L. Guillory, 38379036

Elmer F. Kapischke, 365384092

Curtis E. Jensen, 39290207

Henry E. Maul, 36478234

James C. Smith, 0 818964

Everett O. Bradsen, 11118525

EU 1754

Prisoner Capture Status

8.May.1944. 1000
Ostenholz
S. of Fallingbostel
Type: Fortress 230062
338 NB Squadr.
96 Group
Arifield Snetterton

17.May. KU 1754

T/Sgt.	BRADRUM	Everett Osmrn 11118525 Lz.Fallingbostel	capt
1st.Lt.	KING	Frank L. Jr 0-809966	capt
2nd.Lt.	SMYTH	James 0-818964	capt.
2nd.Lt.	BISCHOFF	George Arthur 0-797831 Hosp. Fassberg	capt
2nd.Lt.	READE	William	dead
T/Sgt.	GUILLORY	Louis Daniel 38379036	capt.
S/Sgt.	MAUL	Henry Eugene 36478234	capt
S/Sgt.	KAPISCHKE	Elmer Fred 366 38453	capt
S/Sgt.	LLOYD	William Nordell 18217669	capt
S/Sgt.	JENSEN	Curtis Sh. 39290207	capt
	THOMAS	Howard M. 39568802	

Mack
4566

Prisoner Internment Location

Dulag Luft were Prisoner of War transit camps for German-captured members of the Air Force during World War II. Their main purpose was to act as collection and interrogation centres for newly captured aircrew, before they were transferred in batches to the permanent camps.

DATE AND TIME AIRCRAFT WAS SHOT DOWN: 8 May 1944 - Time 10.00 CASUALTY NO. KU 1754

PLACE OF CRASH: Ostenholz near Fallingbostel

TYPE OF AIRCRAFT: Fortress

REPORTING OFFICE: Flying Field Celle

NAME	RANK	SERIAL NUMBER	CAPT'D WOUNDED DEAD	PLACE OF INTERNMENT
SMITH, James 17 October 1920 - Bayonne, N.J.	2nd/Lt.	0-818964	Captured	Dulag Luft
JENSEN, Curtis Sherald	S/Sgt.	39290207	Captured	Dulag Luft
[redacted] GUILLORY, Louis Daniel	T/Sgt.	38379036	Captured	Dulag Luft
LLOYD, William Kendall 7 November 1924 - Tex.	S/Sgt.	18219669	Captured	Dulag Luft
MAUL, Henry Eugene 1924	S/Sgt.	36478234	Captured	Dulag Luft
KING, Frank L.	2nd/Lt.	0-809966	Wounded	Hospital Fallingbostel (2 June Dulag)
BRADEEN, Everett	T/Sgt.	- . -	Wounded	Hospital Fallingbostel (2 June Dulag)

Downing Number KU 1754 1st. Follow up Report from 1 June 1944
BISCHOFF, George Arthur 2nd/Lt. 0-707631 Captured Dulag Luft
7. June 1918 - USA

Downing Number KU 1754 2nd. Follow up Report from 13 June 1944
KAPISCHKE, Elmer Fred S/Sgt. 36638493 Captured Dulag Luft

REMARKS:

Dulag Luft, 20 May 1944 / No.

4566

Captured Personnel Report

Report Concerning Captured Air Forces Personnel

Hdq: Airbase Command A 21/XI, Airfield Command Fasberg

Place and Time: Fassberg, 8 May 1944

Subject: Fortress, place unknown, date unknown

Name: Bischoff, A George, Lt., 0 707631

Disposition: Captured, (wounded) in Fassberg

Date and Time of Capture: 8 May 44, at 1600 hours

Name: Maul, E. Henry Sgt., 36478234

Disposition: Captured, will be sent to Oberursel 9 May 44

Place and Time of Capture: 8 May 44, at 1600 hours

KU 1754

Casualty Questionnaire

AFPPA-12 4566

CASUALTY QUESTIONNAIRE

1. Your name George A. Bischoff Rank 1st Lt. Serial No. 0-707831

. Organization 96 HB Gp Commander Travis (full name) Rank Col. Sqn CO R.B.Good (full name) Rank Major

3. What year 1944 month May day 8 did you go down?

4. What was the mission, Berlin, target, ________, target time, 1100, altitude, 20,000 feet route scheduled, ________, route flown ________

5. Where were you when you left formation? About 5 miles south of Bremen (Verden, Germany)

6. Did you bail out? Yes

7. Did other members of crew bail out? Yes

8. Tell all you know about when, where, how each person in your aircraft for whom no individual questionnaire is attached bailed out. A crew list is attached. Please give facts. If you don't know, say: "No Knowledge". Co-pilot, Waist Gunners, Tail Gunner, Ball Turret Operator, Engineer bailed out. Approximately in same place. Pilot & Radio Operator crashlanded airplane due to lack of workable parachutes. Bombardier was killed in the airplane.

9. Where did your aircraft strike the ground? Within ten (10) mile radius of Verden

10. What members of your crew were in the aircraft when it struck the ground? (Should cross check with 8 above and individual questionnaires) Pilot - Radio Operator - Bombardier (dead)

11. Where were they in aircraft? Pilot in cockpit - Radio Operator in Radio room Bombardier in Nose.

12. What was their condition? Radio Operator badly shot up and injured. Bombardier dead. Pilot ok

13. When, where, and in what condition did you last see any members not already described above? ________

14. Please give any similar information on personnel of any other crew of which you have knowledge. Indicate source of information. ________

(Any additional information may be written on the back)

(over)

6-3862, AF

Dad's German Capture Information

(Translated)

Anlage 2.

For Official Use Only

Nur für den Dienstgebrauch!

Information about enemy captures

Angaben über Gefangennahme von feindlichen Luftwaffenangehörigen.

Air Force Member

Distributor

Verteiler:

Kdo.Fl.H.Bereich

Luftgaukommando

Dulag Luft

Agency

Dienststelle: Fliegerhorstkommandantur A 21/XI Platzkommando Fassberg . . . . . .

Place , Time

Ort , Zeit : Fassberg, 9.5.1944 . . . .

Plane

Abschuß

Betr.: Emergency Landing einer Fortress . . . .

Notlandung

bei: 1) unbekannt . . . .

am : . unbekannt . . . .

Name

Name , Vornamen: M a u l, E. Henry . . . .

Rank

Dienstrang: . . . Sgt. . . . . Nr.d.Erk.Marke: 364 782 34 / T.43-43.A

Whereabouts

Verbleib: 2) . . . . gefangen . , wird am 9.5.44 nach Oberursel überführt

Date of Capture

Ort und Zeit d. Gefangennahme: . 8.5.44 . . . - 16.oo Uhr- . . . .

Name of Hospital

Bezeichnung des Lazarettes: . . . .

Place and time of burial

Ort und Zeit der Beisetzung: . . . .
(Grablage evtl.nachmelden)

1) Genaue Angabe des Aufschlagortes und dessen Lage zu größerem Bezugsort, bei Großstädten Angabe des Vorortes, Stadtteiles oder der Straße.

2) Ob gefangen, verwundet, vermißt, flüchtig oder tot geborgen.

Hauptmann

~~Formblatt~~ Anlage 2.

Nur für den Dienstgebrauch!

Angaben über Gefangennahme von feindlichen Luftwaffenangehörigen.

Verteiler:
Kdo.Fl.H.Bereich
Luftgaukommando
Dulag Luft

Dienststelle: Fliegerhorstkommandantur A 21/XI Platzkommando Faßberg . . . . . .

Ort , Zeit : Faßberg, 9.5.1944 . . . .

19.MAI 1944

Betr.: Abschuß / Notlandung einer . . Fortress . . . .

bei: 1) unbekannt . . . .

am : unbekannt . . . .

Name , Vornamen: . M a u l, E. Henry . . . .

Dienstrang: . . . . Sgt. . . . Nr.d.Erk.Marke: 364 782 34 ✓ .T.43-43.A

Verbleib: 2) . . . . gefangen . , wird am 9.5.44 nach Oberursel überführt

Ort und Zeit d.Gefangennahme: . 8.5.44 . . . - 16.oo Uhr- . . . .

Bezeichnung des Lazarettes: . . . .

Ort und Zeit der Beisetzung: . . . .
(Grablage evtl.nachmelden)

---

1) Genaue Angabe des Aufschlagortes und dessen Lage zu größerem Bezugsort, bei Großstädten Angabe des Vorortes, Stadtteiles oder der Straße.

2) Ob gefangen, verwundet, vermißt, flüchtig oder tot geborgen.

Hauptm. [signature]

Next of Kin Contact Person

4566

1st Lt. Frank L. King, Jr.	Mrs. Agda G. King (Mother) Post Office Box 469, El Dorado, Arkansas.
2nd Lt. James C. Smith	Mrs. Jane M. Smith, (Wife) 633 Salem Avenue, Elizabeth, New Jersey,
2nd Lt. George A. Bischoff	Mrs. Susan Biscoff, (Mother) 2363 24th Street, Long Island City (5), New York.
2nd Lt. William W. Reade	Mrs. William W. Reade, (Wife) 2534 Dellwood Drive, Atlanta, Georgia.
T/Sgt. Louis D. Guillory	Mrs. Alvie Guillory, (Wife) 709 South Claiborne Avenue, New Orleans, Louisiana.
T/Sgt. Everett O. Bradeen, Jr.	Mrs. Gladys E. Bradeen, (Mother) 15 Jefferson Street, Old Town, Maine.
S/Sgt. Elmer F. Kapischke	Mr. Rein Kapischke, (Father) 2955 Archer Avenue, Chicago, Illinois.
S/Sgt. Curtis S. Jensen	Mrs. Anna . Jensen, (Mother) 5267 Everts Lane, San Diego, California.
S/Sgt. William N. Lloyd	Mr. William H. Lloyd, (Father) Route Two, Blanket, Texas.
S/Sgt. Henry E. Maul	Mrs. Bertha M. Maul, (Mother) 710 Franklin Street, Alton, Illinois.

The following 110-page study was performed by the Military Intelligence Service War Department of the different Prisoner of War camps where American Allied men were imprisoned by German forces. The study looks at everything the POW's enjoyed, endured, and were a part of, from the amount of drinking water they had available, to how often they were allowed to bathe...or not. They also included information on the POW's marches.

If you look at the newspaper clippings from 1945 you will see that when my dad was returned to the United States after his imprisonment, he was only furloughed for 60 days, not released from service. At the end of the 60-day furlough, my dad returned to service and went to San Antonio, Texas, where I believe he was de-briefed. He and the other POW's gave their input that contributed to this report.

If you are even a little interested in World War II history, this is the document to read...and re-read.

Many thanks to the more than 92,000 men and women that contributed to this informative report.

Examination

of

American Prisoners of War

in

Germany

November 1, 1945

Restricted Classification
Removed Per
Executive Order 10501
per AGAR-S (71058)

RESTRICTED

AMERICAN PRISONERS OF WAR

IN

GERMANY

Prepared by
MILITARY INTELLIGENCE SERVICE
WAR DEPARTMENT

1 November 1945

Restricted Classification
Removed Per
Executive Order 10501
per AGAR-S (71058)

Restricted Classification
Removed Per
Executive Order 10501

RESTRICTED

AMERICAN PRISONERS OF WAR
in
GERMANY

Introduction

Conditions in German prisoners of war camps holding Americans varied to such an extent that only by examination of individual camps can a clear picture be drawn. This report contains summaries of 12 typical German installations ranging from Stalag Luft 3, a well organized camp for Air Force officers, through Stalag 2B, an average Ground Force enlisted men's camp, to chaotic Stalag 9B, established for enlisted men captured during the Von Rundstedt offensive of December 1944.

Germany held a total of 92,965* American prisoners of war in these categories:

Air Forces - 32,730
Ground Forces - 60,235

In contrast to the number of Ground Force officers who formed only some 10% of the Ground Force prisoners of war, almost 50% of the Air Force personnel falling into enemy hands were officers. Figures for both branches soared during the 10 months after 6 June 1944 when totals were:

Air Forces - 15,093
Ground Forces - 9,274

Total - 24,367

For army prisoners of war, Germany had three principal types of camp. OFLAG, a contraction of Offizier Lager (officers' camp), as its title denotes held officers. STALAG, a contraction of Stamm Lager (main camp) held enlisted men. DULAG, a contraction of Durchgangs Lager (entrance camp) was a transit camp but in the minds of airmen became synonymous with interrogation center. LUFT (air) appended to a name indicated that the camp held flying personnel. Generally, camps housing airmen were under the jurisdiction of the Luftwaffe, and camps housing ground troops under the jurisdiction of the Wehrmacht.

Prisoners of war (PW) formed camps within camps and had their own organizations. In officers' camps they were headed by the Senior American Officer (SAO) who was just what his name implied. In enlisted men's stalags, the Man of Confidence (MOC) was usually an NCO elected by his fellow PW, but sometimes he was appointed by the Germans.

Source material for this report consisted of interrogations of former prisoners of war made by CPM Branch, Military Intelligence Service, and reports of the Protecting Power and International Red Cross received by the State Department (Special War Problems Division).

- X X X -

* 1 Nov. 45 Records.

RESTRICTED

CONTENTS

RESTRICTED

DULAG LUFT

Introduction Dulag Luft, through which practically all air force personnel captured in German-occupied Europe passed, was composed of three installations: the interrogation center at Oberursel, the hospital at Hohemark and the transit camp ultimately at Wetzlar.

INTERROGATION CENTRE

Location Auswertestelle West (Evaluation Center West) was situated 300 yards north of the main Frankfurt-Homburg road and near the trolley stop of Kupferhammer - the third stop after Oberursel (50°12' N. - 8°34" E.). Oberursel is 13 kilometers northwest of Frankfurt-on-Main.

Strength The number of PW handled rose from 1000 a month in late 1943 to an average monthly intake of 2000 in 1944. The peak month was July 1944 when over 3000 Allied airmen and paratroopers passed through Auswertestelle West. Since solitary confinement was the rule, the capacity of the camp was supposedly limited to 200 men, although in rush periods as many as five PW were placed in one cell. Strength on any given day averaged 250.

Description The main part of the camp consisted of four large wooden barracks two of which, connected by a passage and known to PW as the "cooler," contained some 200 cells. These cells, eight feet high, five feet wide and 12 feet long held a cot, a table, a chair and an electric bell for PW to call the guard. The third barrack contained administrative headquarters. The fourth building, a large "L" shaped structure, housed the interrogating offices, files and records. Senior officers lived on the post; junior officers outside in a hotel. The commandant lived on a nearby farm. The entire camp was surrounded by a barbed-wire fence but was equipped with neither perimeter floodlights nor watchtowers.

U.S. Personnel Since PW were held in solitary confinement, and only for limited periods of time, no U.S. staff existed.

German Personnel German personnel - all Luftwaffe - was divided into two main branches: Administrative and Intelligence. Under Intelligence came officers and interpreter NCOs actually taking part in the interrogations and other intelligence work of the unit. The total strength of this branch was 50 officers and 100 enlisted men. Administrative personnel consisted of one guard company and one Luftwaffe construction company, each consisting of 120 men. Some members of the staff were:

Oberstleutnant Erich Killinger: Commandant
Major Junge : Chief of Interrogation

Major Boehringer	: Executive Officer
Captain Schmeidewindt	: Record Section Chief
Leutnant Böninghaus	: Political Interrogator

Later there were attached to the staff representatives of the General Luftzeugmeister's department, the General der Kampfflieger's section, the Navy and the S.S. Occasionally members of the Gestapo at Frankfurt were permitted to interrogate PW.

Treatment

The interrogation of Allied PW at the hands of Auswertestelle West personnel was "korrect" as far as physical violence was concerned. An occasional interrogator, exasperated by polite refusals to give more than name, rank, serial number or, more occasionally, perhaps by an exceptionally "fresh" PW, may have lost his temper and struck a PW. It is not believed that this ever went beyond a slap on the face dealt in the heat of anger - certainly physical violence was not employed as a policy. On the other hand, no amount of calculated mental depression, privation and psychological blackmail was considered excessive.

Upon arrival, PW were stripped, searched, and sometimes issued German coveralls. At other times they retained the clothing in which they were shot down. All were shut up in solitary confinement cells and denied cigarettes, toilet articles and Red Cross food. Usually the period of confinement lasted four or five days, but occasionally a surly PW would be held in the "cooler" for the full 30 days permitted by the Geneva Convention as a punitive measure, and Captain William N. Schwartz was imprisoned 45 days. Interrogators often used threats and violent language, calling PW "murderers of children" and threatening them with indefinitely prolongued solitary confinement on starvation rations unless they would talk. PW were threatened with death as spies unless they identified themselves as airmen by revealing technical information on some such subject as radar or air combat tactics. Confinement in an unbearably overheated cell and pretended shootings of "buddies" were resorted to in the early days. Intimidation yielded inferior results and the friendly approach was considered best by the Germans.

Food

Rations were two slices of black bread and jam with ersatz coffee in the morning, watery soup at midday, two slices of bread at night. No Red Cross parcels were issued. PW could obtain drinking water from the guards.

Health

As a rule, men seriously needing medical treatment were sent to Hohemark hospital. Those suffering from the shock of being shot down and captured received no medical attention, nor did the 50% suffering from minor wounds. Some PW arrived at permanent camps still wearing dirty bandages which had not been changed at Oberursel even though their stay had been of two weeks' duration. Upon several occasions PW were denied

the ministration of either a doctor or medical orderly and there is at least one instance where a flyer with a broken leg was refused treatment of any sort until he had answered some of the interrogator's questions four days after his arrival.

Clothing — PW received no Red Cross clothing. Instead they wore German fatigues or the uniforms in which they had been captured - minus leather jackets which were customarily confiscated.

Work — None

Pay — None

Mail — None

Morale — There is little doubt that the living conditions were expressly designed to lower morale and to produce mental depression of the most acute kind. Still, due partially to briefings which acquainted them with Oberursel and partially to their innate sense of loyalty, most PW successfully withstood the harsh treatment and yielded no important military information other than name, rank and serial number.

Welfare — Neither the Protecting Power, which was refused admission for a long time, nor the Red Cross nor the YMCA could do anything to ameliorate the condition of PW in the interrogation center.

Religion — None

Recreation — None

Liberation — On 25 April 1945 American troops overran Oberursel. They found Auswertestelle West no longer a going concern. Some 10 days earlier, its departments already widely dispersed over what remained of Germany, the installation had ceased to exist even as a headquarters of the German Air Interrogation service. Its records had been burnt or evacuated and its leading personalities, taking with them what remained of their organization, had fled to a new site at Nurnberg-Buchenbuhl. The new Dulag headquarters at Nurnberg did not survive the parent unit by many days. It was not long before Oberstleutnant Erich Killinger, the commandant, was discovered by Allied interrogators in an army cage. With the former roles of captive and interrogator now so completely reversed, it was a slightly apprehensive but stubborn Killinger who accompanied his captors back to the scene of his former triumphs at Oberursel.

HOHEMARK HOSPITAL

As soon as the Luftwaffe took over the Oberursel installation in December 1939 it became obvious that a high percentage of PW would be in need of medical

attention. To meet this, the camp authorities requisitioned part of Hohemark hospital one mile west of the interrogation center. This hospital had been used since World War I as a health resort and clinic for all types of brain injuries and contained a large number of German soldiers wounded in this war.

The wards for PW were on the second floor and comprised one single room, two double rooms and several rooms with four beds, totaling 65. Discipline was very mild. The doors of the wards were not always locked at night, and the only guards were the German medical orderlies. German medical treatment was excellent, as was the food, which came from Red Cross special invalid parcels and from the hospital kitchen. Walking cases were frequently allowed to meet and take meals together. Other ambulatory cases, as soon as their condition permitted, were allowed parole walks through the surrounding grounds and countryside.

Wounded men were sometimes interrogated directly during their stay at the hospital. At other times, they were not interrogated until after their convalescence when they were sent to Oberursel. The comparatively luxurious single and double rooms were set aside as places where high-ranking Allied PW could be interrogated in circumstances which the Germans considered appropriate to their rank. These PW did not have to be wounded to gain admission to Hohemark.

Several British and American orderlies formed part of the hospital complement. They were headed by an Edward Stafford, an American who was captured while flying in the RAF Ferry Command and called himself "Captain." His assistant was Captain Kenneth Smith, who was receiving treatment for facial burns during his stay. Inmates of Hohemark received the normal allotment of outgoing letters, but only the permanent staff received incoming letters. PW's only religious activity was listening to the Bible readings of a Hauptmann Offerman.

Hohemark was liberated simultaneously with Oberursel.

TRANSIT CAMP

Location

On 10 September 1943 the Dulag Luft transit camp, where PW who had been interrogated awaited shipment to permanent stalags, was moved from Oberursel to Frankfurt-am-Main. Here it was situated in the Palm Gardens only 1430 yards northwest of the main railroad station - a location which was a target area and therefore endangered the lives of PW.

On 15 November 1943 the Swiss stated, "This visit (to the camp) leaves a bad impression because of the new situation of the Dulag, so exposed to attacks from the air, which is not in conformity with Article 9 of the (Geneva) Convention."

Thus the following Swiss announcement in the spring of 1944 came as no surprise: "Dulag Luft, Wetzlar, is succeeding Dulag Luft, Frankfurt, which was destroyed in course of one of the latest (24 March) air raids on Frankfurt. The camp is situated on a slightly elevated position approximately three to four kilometers west north west from Wetzlar, a town some 50 kilometers north of Frankfurt-on-Main and is a former German army camp (Flak troops)."

Strength

During the first nine months of 1943, 1000 PW a month passed through the transit camp. This increased to 1500 a month, half British and half American, in the last three months of the year. Statistics for October 1944 follow:

Incoming Personnel Total	1963
Daily Average	63
Total American	1312
Officers	155
NCOs	739
Total British	651
Officers	155
NCOs	496

Camp strength fluctuated from day to day. On the Swiss visit of 10 November 1944 it was 311; on 13 March 1945 it was 526. Except for the permanent staff of 30, PW seldom stayed more than eight days.

Description

During May and June 1944, inmates lived in 18 tents pitched on the eastern side of the camp area. On 13 July 1944, they moved to the newly-constructed buildings: five barracks and one large bungalow which held the messes and the store rooms. Capacity of the camp was 784, with tents available in case of a sudden influx. Two of the sleeping barracks were reserved for officers, two for NCOs, and the remaining one accommodated the permanent camp staff, sick rooms and medical inspection room. The mess had space for 300 men in the main room. The camp staff, the officers and the enlisted men ate separately.

Each room in the barracks held six to eight triple-decker bunks - 18 to 24 men. Each bed had a mattress filled with wood shavings and one pillow. All barracks had special wash rooms with built-in basins and running cold water.

Unoccupied space within the barbed wire was somewhat limited after the erection of the last two barracks and the laying out of vegetable gardens cultivated for and by the PW. The area gave a neat appearance, however with tidy paths and well-tended lawns.

U.S. Personnel

Senior Allied Officer at Wetzlar was Colonel Charles W. Stark who enjoyed exceptionally friendly terms with

the Germans and drew many concessions from them. Members of his staff were:

1st Lt. Gerald G. Gille	: Adjutant
2nd Lt. Arthur C. Jeros	: Adjutant
2nd Lt. Herbert Schubert	: Mess Officer

In addition, the staff comprised:

1 Chaplain
5 Kitchen orderlies
4 Mess orderlies
5 Store orderlies
4 Barracks chiefs
3 Medical orderlies
4 Barracks orderlies
1 Gardener
1 Carpenter

A previous Senior American Officer was 1st Lt. John C. Winant.

German Personnel

The housekeeping organization consisted of:

Oberstleutnant Becker	: Commandant
Major Riess	: Camp Officer
Major Selzer	: Camp Officer
Major Heyden	: Camp Officer
Dr. Thomai	: Medical Officer
Dr. Wenger	: Medical Officer
Hauptmann Schmid	: Security Officer

In November 1944 there was reported the existence at the camp of an interrogation center. According to Colonel Stark, treatment was good and correct in every way. Some PW arriving from Oberursel were in solitary and asked purely "political" questions for two or three days. Then they were admitted to the transit camp. Chief of this interrogation section was Major Ernst Dornseifer.

Treatment

Treatment was better here than at any other American PW camp in Germany. German and American staffs seemed to cooperate with each other, resulting in favorable living conditions to both parties. The Senior Allied Officer operated Wetzlar as a rest camp where PW suffering from the harsh treatment at Oberursel might regain their strength and morale before traveling to permanent camps. As a result neither Germans nor Americans provoked any untoward incidents.

Food

No food shortage existed at Wetzlar, even though the Germans repeatedly cut their ration until the daily issue per man was officially announced in March 1945 as:

Meat	35 grams
Potatoes	320 "
Margarine	31 "

Butter	25 grams
Sugar	25 "
Bread	75 "
Salt	20 "
Coffee (ersatz)	5 "

For three days:

Barley	10 grams
Millet	21 "
Hulsenfruchte	53 "
Cheese	14 "
White Cheese	14 "

The difference between this sub-sustenance diet and the good meals actually eaten by PW was made up by Red Cross food. One parcel per PW was drawn each week and 90% of all Red Cross food was given to the kitchen to improve German rations. Usually the stock on hand consisted of four months' supply. Even in September 1944 when the order was given to cut food reserves to a very minimum, Wetzlar authorities allowed PW to keep four weeks' supply on hand. In March 1945, anticipating a possible evacuation from Wetzlar to the interior of the Reich, the [illegible] authorized the issue of two Red Cross food parcels per man per week, both to strengthen PW for the march to come and to prevent the loss of food which would be abandoned in the event of a sudden move.

The kitchen - staffed by Americans - was well equipped with two large cooking ranges, three boilers, a dish-washing room, a potato-peeling room, a tin-opening room and an adjacent storeroom.

<u>Health</u>

The sick bays were able to accommodate 40 men in beds, two of which were in a separate room reserved for contagious diseases. The medical inspection room was described as adequate and all necessary medicines and instruments were made available either from Red Cross sources or - to a lesser extent - from the Germans. Good medical treatment was received from the German staff doctor who cooperated first with Lt. Anthony S. Barling, RAMC, and then with Captain Peter Griffin during their brief stays in camp.

Each man received a hot shower upon his entrance to the compound and was subsequently permitted to take one each week. Although the barracks washroom taps ran only cold water, hot water could usually be drawn elsewhere some hours during the day. A 10-seat outdoor latrine was supplemented by satisfactory toilets of the modern flush type.

Although many men arriving from Oberursel were wounded and exhausted the general state of health was considered good.

Clothing

Large numbers of PW arrived without outer uniforms, and sometimes without underclothing or shoes. Each new arrival was equipped with at least the following articles - all of which were supplied not by the Germans but by the Red Cross:

1 shirt
1 pr. drawers
1 undershirt
1 pr. socks
1 necktie
1 pr. trousers
1 blouse
1 pr. shoes
1 set toilet articles

Initially, the shortage of American stocks necessitated the drawing of British clothing. Later, however, most of the clothing issued was of American origin, and eventually it was possible to keep adequate stocks of British and American items separately. In March 1945 it was no longer possible to provide PW with neatly packed "captive cases" a sort of suitcase containing the articles listed above, for the supply was exhausted.

Work

Since air force personnel consisted solely of commissioned and non-commissioned officers, no work beyond some of their own housekeeping chores were required of them.

Pay

PW received no pay, but when the camp opened in the summer of 1944, the finance committee of Stalag Luft 3, Sagan, sent the permanent staff a fund of over 4000 reichmarks.

Mail

Transients were allowed to send their first letter or a postcard form informing next-of-kin of their status and address, but received no incoming mail. The permanent staff drew the usual allotment of letter forms and received incoming mail as well. Some air mail from the United States was received within three weeks. Average time for both air and surface mail was four months. As with all Luftwaffe camps, letters were censored at Sagan.

Morale

The Senior Allied Officer agreed with statements of the Swiss Delegates and German camp authorities that Wetzlar was an excellent camp and that "such favorable conditions are hardly to be found elsewhere in Germany." Morale of men leaving Oberursel was usually at its lowest ebb, and it is small wonder after receiving food, clothing and mingling in comparative freedom with their fellow Americans, that their spirits soared back to a level approaching normality. Most of them left Wetzlar prepared to face the difficulties of their new lives as PW.

Welfare The Protecting Power visited Wetzlar in May, July, November 1944 and March 1945 - each time forwarding the complaints of the Senior Allied Officer and making a complete report on camp conditions.

The Red Cross supplied PW with practically all their food, clothing and medical supplies but made no visit until January 1945, when they wrote a report of their inspection.

From the YMCA, the camp received most of its library, which eventually totaled 1500 books, and equipment for indoor games and outdoor sports.

Religion For some months the only religious activity was the regular Sunday service conducted by Warrant Officer Hooton, RAF, a Methodist. Early in 1945 Captain Daniel McGowan, a Catholic priest, conducted both Catholic and Protestant services every Sunday.

Recreation New arrivals were usually in such condition as not to want strenuous exercise. Games, therefore, were as a rule limited to milder sports such as deck tennis. Once a week some PW were permitted walks outside the camp. The most popular indoor pastimes were reading, playing cards, discussing the new experience of being a PW and playing some of the table games provided by the YMCA.

Evacuation & Liberation The Wetzlar camp log from 27 through 30 March follows:

27 March 1945

0530 German order to evacuate all those able to walk with the exception of few permanent staff, who should remain to run the place. 143 remained including Col. Stark, Lt. Jeros, Lt. Comdr. Jennings, Capt. Griffin, Lt. Gills and Capt. Rev. McGowan. German personnel left were 107 men, 34 women, including Maj. Dornseifer, Lt. Weyrich, and Mr. Rickmers.

0730 Transport left (82 men)

0830 We hear gun fire and sounds of approaching vehicles. Germans from across the road move into our shelters.

0945 Hear our troops are 4 kms west of us. Heavy gun fire all around.

1030 Heavy firing continues all around us. German guards are voluntarily laying down their arms.

1230 Col. Stark calls Mr. Rickmers and Lt. Weyrich into office and states that all guards turn in weapons and a system of joint sentry duty be posted. They agree and he is now in command - Maj. Dornseifer cooperating fully in this.

1430 Activity has been heavy all around us all afternoon.

1700 Fairly quiet for the moment. Col. ordered two privates to be put in the guard house cells as they are obviously drunk. German guards brought liquor into camp. He has issued orders for no drinking including the Germans.

2030 Col. sent F/Lt. Lyons, Sgt. Hanson and Mr. Rickmers to try contacting our forces in the west and report our location.

2300 Still very active all around us - M.G. fire and artillery.

2400 Still a good deal of firing. Most of the personnel sleep in shelters.

28 March 1945

0630 Fairly constant gun fire and activity all night.

1000 Dr. Griffin takes wounded Pfc. into Wetzlar for operation. Armored column passing to east of us.

1200 Lt. Valentine arrives in jeep. Boy, are we happy to see a Yank!

1500 Col. Stark and Capt. Griffin are off to Staff HQ with Lt. Valentine.

1700 Sgt. Hanson and Mr. Rickmers return. There has been heavy firing around us all day.

1800 6 German paratroopers walk into camp and surrender. They are locked up.

1830 Col. Stark returns with 3 War News Correspondents including Belden.

2400 Things are fairly quiet.

29 March 1945

0940 Spot cub plane landed on play field.

0945 Dogs were shot.

1000 Lt. Col. Grant of 7th Armored Division (?) arrived in jeep advising us of 750 PWs he had picked up. Limburg PWs are lousy and half starved. We have sent for them and will put them up here.

1200 Four Piper Cubs landed.

1300 Maj. McDougall (?), Medical Officer, arrived and will stay the afternoon in order to help with Limburg PWs.

1400 Col. Stark and party go out to recc'y some German motor equipment.

1415 Maj. Dornseifer gave Col. Stark a list of his people who he is anxious to have out of camp as they have strong party sympathies and might make trouble. Col. Stark turns them over to an Infantry Patrol. They include the following: Sgt. Lohmann, Sgt. Hickmann, Cpl. Busch, Cpl. Stoeckel and Cpl. Schaaf.

1420 First lot of distressed PWs arrived and are deloused, bathed and clothed.

1530 Maj. Tesse, PWX-SHAEF executive, arrives with load of PWs.

1745 We are to be loaded with PWs. They have been arriving all PM.

2130 Finished feeding for night. 400 odd still to be deloused.

30 March 1945

Work continues thru the day, delousing and feeding PWs arriving in camp. Maj. Tesse returns and advises us to expect 320 PWs from Hadamar in the morning. This lot will include 14 General officers and 79 Field Grade officers. Seven PWs return from our last transport, including W/Comdr. Carling-Kelly. Today the remaining German personnel was officially put to work in the office, on kitchen detail, policing camp, etc. They are dealt with thru Maj. Dornseifer, Mr. Rickmers and Sgt. Keller.

Work is going on to prepare for the maximum number this camp will hold. Medical officers have arrived and are organizing their departments. They hope to start evacuating the worst cases shortly. The Hadamar contingent started arriving at 1100.

With the arrival of British officers who outranked him, Col. Stark was no longer Senior Allied Officer present. Major Tesse of PWX-SHAEF, suggested that the staff remain and help in processing PW expected to arrive within the next two weeks. A stay of such length did not seem necessary to Col. Stark and at 0515 in the morning of 31 March he drove away in a German car with Comdr. Jennings, USNR, and S/Sgt. Leo Hughes, AAF, leaving a note for Lt. Gills. He proceeded by motor and air transport to Paris, arriving 3 April 1945.

-XXX-

STALAG LUFT 1

(Air Force Officers)

Location Stalag Luft 1 was situated at Barth, Germany, (54°22' N - 12°42' 30" E), a small town on the Baltic Sea 23 kilometers northwest of Stralsund.

Strength Stalag Luft 1 was opened in October 1942 as a British camp, but when the Red Cross visited the camp in February 1943, two American non-commissioned officers had already arrived. By January 1944, 507 American air force officers were detained there. The strength of the camp grew rapidly from this date until April 1944 when the Red Cross reported 3,463 inmates. New compounds were opened and quickly filled. Nearly 6,000 PW were crowded into the camp in September 1944, and at the time of the liberation of the camp 7,717 Americans and 1,427 Britons were returned to military control.

Description Early in 1944 the camp consisted of two compounds designated as South and West Compounds, containing a total of seven barracks in which American officers and British officers and enlisted men were housed. A new compound was opened the last of February 1944 and was assigned to the American officers who were rapidly increasing in number. This compound became North 1, and the opening of North 2 Compound on 9 September 1944 and North 3 Compound on 9 December 1944 completed the camp as it remained until 15 May 1945. The South Compound was always unsatisfactory due to the complete lack of adequate cooking, washing, and toilet facilities. The West Compound, however, provided inside latrines and running water in the barracks. North 1 Compound formerly housed personnel of the Hitler Youth, and because of its communal messhall, inside latrines, and running water taps, it was considered by far the best compound. North 2 and North 3 Compounds were constructed on the same design as the South Compound, and were as unsatisfactory.

The completion of the last two compounds gave the camp an L-shape appearance, which followed the natural contours of the bay on which the camp was situated. Guard towers were placed at strategic intervals, and although the compounds were intercommunicating the gates were closed at all times after the Spring of 1944. Prior to that, gates were kept open during the day.

Each barrack contained triple-tiered wooden beds equipped with mattresses filled with wood chips. A communal day-room was set aside in almost every barrack, but equipment was negligible. Lighting was inadequate throughout the camp, and since the

Detaining Power required the shutters to remain closed from 2100 to 0600, ventilation was entirely insufficient.

In addition to the buildings for housing, North 1 and West Compounds contained 1 kitchen-barrack, 1 theater room, 1 church room, 1 library, and 1 study room each. These were used by all compounds because no other facilities were available. Maintenance of the buildings was completely lacking in spite of the fact that the officers volunteered to take care of many of the repairs if furnished the necessary equipment.

Stoves for heating and cooking varied in each compound except that facilities in all compounds were inadequate. Many of the buildings were not weather proof, and the extremely cold climate of northern Germany made living conditions more difficult for the PW.

U.S. Personnel

Major Wilson P. Todd was the Senior American Officer until 19 January 1944 when Colonel William A. Hatcher arrived and replaced him. Colonel Jean R. Byerly acted as his Executive Officer until the opening of the North 1 Compound of which he became SAO. Toward the last of February however, Colonel Hatcher protested so strongly to the Detaining Power over the poor conditions in the camp that he was suddenly transferred to Stalag Luft 3 leaving Colonel Byerly as the SAO. At that time the compounds had been run as separate camps with little coordination between the compounds. After meeting with the Senior officers of all barracks, it was agreed that the British and Americans would be administered seperately but with very close liaison, and that all Americans would be administered under a Provisional Wing Headquarters composed of four American groups. This organization was established on 6 April 1944 and remained somewhat the same until the liberation. Upon the arrival of Colonel Hubert Zemke, the Provisional Wing was turned over to his command.

Several changes were made as the camp enlarged, but for the most part the camp administration was carried out on a military basis similar to the operation of an air base. At the time Colonel Byerly turned over the command to Colonel Zemke, his staff was as follows:

Captain M. W. Zahn	Adjutant
Colonel C. R. Greening	CO, GP. 1
Colonel E. A. Malmstrom	CO, Gp. 2
Lt. Col. G. Wilson	CO, Gp. 5
Lt. Col. F. S. Gabreski	CO, Gp. 6

(Groups 3 and 4 were British Groups).

Because the advance of the Russians indicated an early liberation, Colonel Zemke changed the organization to an inter-Allied wing, nominating Group Captain C. T.

Weir as chief of staff of the organization called Provisional Wing X. Group commanders were retained and continued to be responsible for the administration, security, discipline and welfare of their own groups, but more emphasis was directed toward staff operations in the event of liberation. For this work, the following staff was appointed and served until the entire camp was evacuated:

Captain C. T. Weir	Chief of Staff
Captain H. W. Zahn	Adjutant
Lt. Col. C. F. McKenna	A-1
Lt. Col. L. C. McCollom	A-2
Lt. Col. J. V. G. Wilson	A-3
Lt. Col. Luther Richmond	A-4
Lt. Col. B. E. McKenzie	Provost Marshall
Major J. J. Fischer	Judge Advocate
1st Lt. J. S. Durakov	Russian Interpreter
2d Lt. T. L. Simmons	Finance Officer

Each staff officer had several assistants to aid him in the performance of his duties. There also existed a Security organization.

German Personnel

The German personnel changed frequently during the existence of the camp. The officers, their positions, and the dates that they served are listed below.

Commandant:	Oberst Sherer	Sep. 43 to Jan. 45
	Oberst Warnstedt	Jan. 45 to Apr. 45
Adjutant:	Hauptmann Tems	Sep. 43 to Mar. 44
	Hauptmann Erbsloh	Mar. 44 to June 44
	Major Buchard	June 44 to Apr. 45
Lager Officer W.	Hauptmann Eilers	Sep. 43 to Feb. 44
	Hauptmann Wolf	Feb. 44 to June 44
	Hauptmann von Beck	Feb. 44 to Oct. 44
	Hauptmann Luckt	Oct. 44 to Jan. 45
	Major Opperman	Jan. 45 to Apr. 45
Lager Officer N.1	Hauptmann Erbsloh	Feb. 44 to June 44
	Major Schroeder	June 44 to July 44
	Haupt. von Stradiot	Jul. 44 to Oct. 44
	Hauptmann Probst	Oct. 44 to Dec. 44
	Major Steinhower	Dec. 44 to Apr. 45
Lager Officer N.2	Major Sprotte	Sep. 44 to Oct. 44
	Major Steinhower	Oct. 44 to Dec. 44
	Hauptmann Bloom	Dec. 44 to Apr. 45
Lager Officer N.3	Hauptmann Probst	Dec. 44 to Apr. 45

Of the above listed German officers, Major Opperman was the local Nazi leader and instructed the lager personnel and guards on all Nazi policies. The other outstanding members of the Nazi party were Oberst Sherer, Major Sprotte, Major von Miller, Major Schroeder, Hauptmann Erbsloh and Hauptmann Tems.

Following the Normandy invasion the ardent Nazis tried to discuss the Nazi policy with the senior officers and to sway them to the German viewpoint of the war against the Russians. The Americans, nevertheless, did not enter into any discussions.

Treatment

Prior to April 1944 treatment was considered fairly good. Following the April meeting of the Protecting Power, however, the German attitude towards PW became more severe. New orders regarding air raids were issued by the Germans. These required all personnel to be inside when the "immediate warning" siren was blown. As a result, three cases of German patrol guards shooting at men inside the camp occurred during May. At the same time the Commandant issued regulations authorizing guards to use firearms to avenge what they termed "insults to German honor". The German interpretation of this order was extremely liberal, and more shooting developed. Oberst Scherer also became more severe in confining PW to the arrest-lock for minor infractions of German disciplinary regulations. He further denied all Red Cross foods and personal parcels as well as tobacco to PW undergoing confinement in the arrest-lock. This restriction was protested to the Protecting Power without results because the Commandant refused to forward the correspondence to Switzerland. A visit by the Protecting Power in July gave the SAO the opportunity of bringing these facts to the representatives' attention. Even though the commandant was spoken to severely about his most recent violations of the Geneva Convention, it was not until the Protecting Power informed the German Foreign Office which in turn wrote to Oberst Scherer directly that Red Cross and personal parcels were allowed PW in the arrest-lock.

After Oberst Warnstedt became commandant conditions became even worse. Instructions to the guards on the use of fire arms were liberalized, and on 18 March 1945, 2d Lieutenant E. F. Wyman was killed and a British officer was wounded during an air raid warning that was not heard by 95% of the men in the same area. The defective system and the "shoot to kill" order were responsible for this incident.

Both Oberst Warnstadt and Oberst Scherer were inclined to inflict mass punishment by restricting an entire barrack for one person's infraction of a rule, and several protests to the Protecting Power had to be made about these occurrences. However, little satisfaction was gained from these protests, and mass punishments continued to be the general policy.

Food

Food was handled through a central warehouse for Red Cross parcels with all German food being prepared in separate kitchens in each compound. The German food was prepared by personnel hired by the German authorities or by Czechs who had been captured while serving with the Allied forces. Red Cross parcels, when available, were issued at the rate of one per person per week. The distribution of this food was made by the barrack blocks, each barrack receiving one-third of its total weekly

parcels three days a week. All food with the exception of the German ration was prepared by individuals in their own rooms. Only North 1 Compound used their communal kitchen to combine the German ration and the Red Cross parcel items to supply complete meals.

The German food ration up until 1 October 1944 consisted of 1800 to 1200 calories daily per man. The ration was gradually cut until it contained only 800 calories. In September, October and November 1944, Red Cross supplies became so low that they, too, had to be cut. During this period men were put on half-parcels each week. A shipment was received in November and PW then drew the normal parcel each week during December in addition to a Christmas parcel. In January the parcel supply again took a drop, and the men received one-half parcel per week and in February only one-quarter parcel per week. From 3 March 1945 until the last of the month no parcels were distributed, and the German ration deteriorated to an extent that toward the end of the month, men became so weak that many would fall down when attempting to get from their beds. American "MP's" were placed around garbage cans to prevent the starving PW from eating out of the cans and becoming sick. About 1 April 1945 a shipment was received from Lubeck via Sweden, and from that time until the evacuation the men obtained sufficient food.

Until this "starvation" period, the normal daily menu would consist of about six potatoes, one-fifth of a loaf of bread, margarine, marmalade, a small piece of meat (usually horsemeat), two vegetables (cabbage, parsnips, beets or turnips) tea and coffee, and a small amount of sugar. In addition, a thin barley soup was frequently served.

Health

In January 1944 a medical record on every man in camp was established, and as new PW arrived, they were required to make out a similar record. The form consisted of recording any injuries or illnesses incurred since MIA, the nature of these, and the medical treatment needed by those not fully recovered while in camp. Illnesses and injuries incurred at camp were also included.

Originally the camp contained only a small infirmary which could accommodate thirty bed patients and provide two rooms for daily sick call. In September 1944 another large barrack was built adjoining the infirmary and provided adequate facilities for hospitalization. When the infirmary was enlarged, the Protecting Power made arrangements with the IRCC to send additional supplies which included surgical instruments. Although serious cases were sent to Stalag 2-A at Neubrandenburg, the hospital staff at the camp was able to care for most of the ill and injured men.

The most serious detriment to the health of PW at this camp was the very poor sanitation. One bath-house containing 10 shower-heads represented the only facilities for over 4,000 officers to bathe, and it was also used as a delousing plant for new arrivals or for any outbreaks of body-crawling insects. Early in 1945 an additional bathhouse was completed which contained 20 shower-heads. Insufficient quantities of wash basins and soap made laundering difficult, and no arrangements were made to care for the men's laundry outside of the camp. Bed linen was theoretically changed once a month, but this period was greatly extended with the influx of new PW. No facilities existed for the disposal of garbage not cared for by incinerators, and latrine and wash drains were so unsatisfactory that the areas around the barracks were frequently flooded.

The climate in the region was extremely cold, and both the number of stoves and the amount of fuel issued were insufficient to maintain good health. Upper respiratory diseases were a source of concern to the medical staff, and this became a great danger when the Germans required the shutters to remain closed during the night. Small ventilators were allowed open but offered insufficient air under the crowded conditions.

The medical staff of two British doctors and six orderlies was too small, and although additional doctors were requested, it was not until 1 March 1945 that an American doctor, Captain Wilbur E. McKee arrived. The staff was considered very capable and cooperative at all times, but was hampered by the lack of medical supplies and facilities to handle such a large number of patients.

Clothing

The Germans issued no clothing to the PW at this camp except 30 sets of German coveralls and 30 pairs of wooden shoes for the kitchen help; these were obtained only after repeated protests. The Red Cross supplied quantities of uniforms and blankets, but the camp expanded so rapidly that supplies were always inadequate until the summer of 1944 when a very large shipment was received enabling each man in camp to have two complete uniforms and two blankets. However, in February 1945 many of the uniforms had become threadbare and a redistribution of uniforms was made.

The Germans also confiscated many articles of clothing under the claim that these items of American uniforms too closely resembled civilian clothes, thus violating the security regulations of the camp.

Work

All PW at the camp were either officers or non-commissioned officers, and although many of the NCO's came to the camp as volunteers for work in a "supervisory" capacity, they refused to work upon arriving

at the camp and learning that the work was actually orderly duty. British and American privates were promised for these duties but never arrived.

Pay — The rate of pay was RM 7.50 for the officers. Money was turned over to the Finance Officer who in turn made available to each officer sufficient amounts to take care of postage and toilet articles. The unused portion was made a part of the communal fund for the enlisted men.

Mail — All incoming mail at Stalag Luft 1 was censored at Stalag Luft 3 until January 1945. Some pieces of mail received at the camp had been in transit six and seven months, and normally men would be in the camp seven months before receiving their first news from home. The average time in transit from the United States was 19 weeks. Toward the end of the war, the transit time was longer due to the transportation tie-up.

Great difficulty was experienced in getting letter and card forms in sufficient quantities to have the normal ration issued each month. On several occasions none was available even though the commandant was informed that stocks were low and that additional supplies should be requisitioned.

Officers were permitted to send three letters and four postcards per month, while the enlisted men were allowed to send two letters and four postcards per month.

Morale — The morale of men was particularly good after the Allied invasion of the continent, and remained high until the starvation period during which time there was a definite decline. Normally speaking, however, the morale was at all times good.

Welfare — Representatives of the International Red Cross visited the camp approximately every four months, sometimes at the same time that the representative of the Protecting Power made inspection trips. Every attempt was made by these representatives to keep ample supplies of food parcels and clothing issues flowing into the camp, and the shortages of supplies were blamed on lack of cooperation of the Commandant of the camp or the bogging down of transportation facilities. The Protecting Power representatives did not seem to bring sufficient pressure to bear on the German officials to improve the camp conditions in the earlier stages, but after the Spring of 1944 improvements would be noted after these visits. The Protecting Power delegates promptly turned over to the IRCC and the YMCA all of the requisitions for supplies and equipment. These agencies were equally prompt in filling the orders. The YMCA representative went to the camp every 3 to 4 months and arranged for supplies of athletic equipment, books, musical

instruments, theatrical supplies as well as telegrams to the next of kin. His visits were considered very valuable as morale builders.

<u>Religion</u>

Protestant services were held from the time the camp was opened, but it was eight months before a Catholic priest was obtained for men of that faith. As the strength of the camp increased the Germans obtained additional clergymen until there were three Catholic and three Protestant chaplains. Unfortunately only two of the compounds offered satisfactory facilities for holding church services, and requests for other compounds to use the communal mess hall in North 1 compound were refused. Outdoor services were held when weather permitted.

<u>Recreation</u>

Outdoor recreation was hampered through lack of sufficient sportsgrounds. Only West and North 1 Compounds were there full-sized football and baseball fields, and although teams from other compounds were permitted to use this field for competitive sports, spectators were excluded. Excellent sports equipment was available throughout the camp, however, and the men in the other compounds managed to improvise games suitable to the limited space.

The two bands formed at the camp offered extremely good entertainment and provided music for theatrical productions which were frequently given. A radio was received through the YMCA, but the extra loudspeakers were not permitted in barracks by the Detaining Power.

An educational program was started early in 1944. When the camp became overcrowded, and communal rooms had to be sacrificed for living quarters, group study was no longer possible. Technical books of all kinds were available in the well-stocked libraries for individual study.

Many of the men with artistic talent spent their time in creative work, such as wood-carving, painting, drawing, and constructing models. The Recreation Officer collected all of these items for a post-war exhibit since an unusual amount of talent was apparent in the results.

<u>Liberation</u>

On 30 April 1945 the SAO had several conferences with the Commandant, who had orders to move the camp to prevent it from falling into the hands of the Russians. The SAO stated PW would not move unless force was used, and the commandant finally agreed to avoid bloodshed. At about 2200 that evening, the guards turned out the perimeter and street lights. A few moments later these same guards were observed marching out of the camp leaving the gate unlocked. As soon as this news was conveyed to the SAO, he formally took over the camp. The following morning the PW military police of the camp were put in charge of all guard stations

to see that the men remained orderly and stayed in the camp. Another organization was formed to serve as exterior guards to prevent wandering parties of Germans from coming into the camp. On 1 May 1945 contact parties were sent out to make contact with Russian advance troops. After two or three days of having Russian commanders of scouting parties visit the camp, the Russian commander of the area was finally reached, and arrangements were made to provide food for the PW.

Evacuation Although the actual liberation was performed by the Russians, no effort was made by them to evacuate the PW from the area. On 6 May 1945, Colonel Byerly, the former SAO left camp with two officers of a British airborne division and flew to England the following day. After reporting to 8th Air Force headquarters on the conditions at the camp, arrangements were made to evacuate the liberated PW by air. This operation was completed on 15 May 1945.

- X X X -

STALAG LUFT 3

(Air Force Officers)

<u>Location</u>

Until 27 January 1945, Stalag Luft 3 was situated in the Province of Silesia, 90 miles southeast of Berlin, in a stand of fir trees south of Sagan (51°35' North latitude - 15°19'30" East longitude).

In the January exodus, the South Compound and Center Compound moved to Stalag 7A, Moosburg (48°27' North latitude - 11°57' East longitude). The West Compound and North Compound moved to Stalag 13D, Nurnberg-Langwasser (49°27' North latitude - 11°50' East longitude) and then proceeded to Moosburg, arriving 20 April 1945.

<u>Strength</u>

On 14 April 1942 Lt. (j.g.) John E. Dunn, O-6548, U. S. Navy, was shot down by the Germans and subsequently became the first American flyer to be confined in Stalag Luft 3, then solely a prison camp for officer PW of the Royal Air Force. By 15 June 1944, U. S. Air Force officers in camp numbered 3,242, and at the time of the evacuation in January 1945, the International Red Cross listed the American strength as 6,844. This was the largest American officers' camp in Germany.

<u>Description</u>

When the first Americans arrived in 1942, the camp consisted of two compounds or enclosures, one for RAF officers and one for RAF NCOs. The rapid increase in strength forced the Germans to build four more compounds, with USAAF personnel taking over the Center, South, West and sharing the North Compound with the British. Adjoining each compound the Germans constructed other enclosures called "vorlagers" in which most of the camp business was transacted and which held such offices as supply, administration and laundry.

Each compound enclosed 15 one-story, wooden barracks or "blocks". These, in turn, were divided into 15 rooms ranging in size from 24 feet by 15 feet to 14 feet by six feet. Occupants slept in double-decker bunks and for every three or four men the Germans provided simple wooden tables, benches and stools. One room, equipped with a cooking range, served as a kitchen. Another, with six porcelain basins, was the washroom. A third, with one urinal and two commodes, was the latrine.

A "Block" could house 80 men comfortably, but with the growth in numbers of PW, rooms designed for eight men began holding 10 and then 12, and the middle of September 1944 saw new PW moving into tents outside the barracks.

Two barbed wire fences 10 feet high and five feet apart surrounded each compound. In between them lay tangled barbed wire concertinas. Paralleling

the barbed wire and 25 feet inside the fence ran a "warning wire" strung on 30-inch wooden posts. The zone between the warning wire and the fence was forbidden territory, entrance to which was punishable by sudden death.

At the corners of the compound and at 50-yard intervals around its perimeter rose 40-foot wooden guard towers holding Germans armed with rifles or machine guns.

U.S. Personnel Lt. Col. Albert P. Clark, Jr., captured on 26 July 1942, became the first Senior American Officer, a position he held until the arrival of Col. Charles G. Goodrich some two months later. The enforced seclusion of individual compounds necessitated the organization of each as an independent PW camp. At the time of the move from Sagan, camp leaders were as follows:

Senior Allied Officer	-	Brigadier General Arthur W. Vanaman
SAO South Compound	-	Col. Charles G. Goodrich
SAO Center Compound	-	Col. Delmar T. Spivey
SAO West Compound	-	Col. Darr H. Alkire
SAO North Compound	-	Lt. Col. Edwin A. Bland

The staff of a compound was organized into two categories:

Main Staff Depts.	Secondary Staff Depts.
a. Adjutant	a. Mail
b. German property	b. Medical
c. German rations	c. Coal
d. Red Cross food	d. Finance
e. Red Cross clothing	e. Canteen
f. Education & Recreation	f. Orderlies, etc.

The basic unit for organization was the barrack building or block. Block staffs were organized to include the same functions as the Compound Staff, and the blocks themselves were sub-divided into squads of 10 men each.

Each compound had a highly organized Security Committee.

German Personnel The original commandant of Stalag Luft 3 was Oberst von Lindeiner, an old-school aristocrat with some 40 years of army service. Courteous and considerate at first sight, he was inclined to fits of uncontrolled rage. Upon one occasion he personally threatened a PW with a pistol. He was, however, more receptive to PW requests than any other commandant.

After the British mass escape of March 1944, Oberst von Lindeiner was replaced by Oberstleutnant Cordes, who had been a PW in World War 1. A short while

later Cordes was succeeded by Oberst Braune, direct and business-like. Stricter than his predecessors, he displayed less sympathy toward PW requests. Nevertheless, he was able to stop misunderstandings such as the one resulting in guards shooting into the compounds. In general, commandants tended to temporize when dealing with PW, or else to avoid granting their requests entirely.

Most disliked by PW were the Abwehr or Security officers - Hauptmann Breuli and his successor Major Kircher.

The Luftwaffe guards were fourth rate troops - either peasants too old for combat duty or young men convalescing after long tours of duty or wounds received at the front. They had almost no contact with PW. In addition to uniformed sentries, soldiers in fatigues were employed by the Germans to scout the interiors of the compounds. These "ferrets" hid under barracks, listened to conversations, looked for tunnels and made themselves generally obnoxious to the PW. The German complement totaled 800.

Occasionally, as after the March 1944 mass escape, Gestapo groups descended upon the camp for a long, thorough search.

<u>Treatment</u>

Because of their status as officers and the fact that their guards were Luftwaffe personnel, the men at Stalag Luft 3 were accorded treatment better than that granted other PW in Germany. Generally, their captors were correct in their adherence to many of the tenets of the Geneva Convention. Friction between captor and captive was constant and inevitable, nevertheless, and the strife is well illustrated by the following example.

On 27 March 1944 the Germans instituted an extra appel (roll call) to occur any time between the regular morning and evening formations. Annoyed by an indignity which they considered unnecessary, PW fought the measure with a passive resistance. They milled about, smoked, failed to stand at attention and made it impossible for the lager officer to take a count. Soon they were dismissed. Later in the day another appel was called. This time the area was lined with German soldiers holding rifles and machine guns in readiness to fire. Discreetly, PW allowed the appel to proceed in an orderly fashion. A few days later, nevertheless, probably as a result of this deliberate protest against German policy, the unwonted extra appel was discontinued.

Since the murder of 50 RAF flyers has been attributed to the Gestapo, acts of atrocious mistreatment

involving the regular Stalag Luft 3 guard complement may be narrowed down to two.

About 2200 hours, 29 December 1943, a guard fired a number of shots into one barrack without excuse or apparent purpose. One bullet passed through the window and seriously wounded the left leg of Lt. Col. John D. Stevenson. Although Col. Stevenson spent the next six months in hospitals, the wound has left him somewhat crippled.

About 1230 hours, 9 April 1944, during an air raid by American bombers, Cpl. Cline O. Miles was standing in the cookhouse doorway. He was facing the interior. Without warning a guard fired at "a man" standing in the doorway. The bullet entered the right shoulderof Cpl. Miles and came out through his mouth, killing him instantly.

Food

German rations, instead of being the equivalent of those furnished depot troops, compared with those received by non-working civilians - the lowest in Germany. While insufficient, these foods provided the bulk of staples, mainly through bread and potatoes. A PWs average daily issue of foods, with caloric content included, follows:

Type of food	Grams	Calories
Potatoes	390	331
Bread	350	910
Meat	11	20
Barley, Oats, Etc.	21	78
Kohlrabi	247	87
Dried Vegetable	14	38
Margarine	31	268
Cheese	10	27
Jam	25	69
Sugar	25	100
TOTALS	1124	1928

A conservative estimate of the caloric requirement of a person sleeping nine hours a day and taking very little exercise is 2,150 calories. German rations, therefore, fell below the minimum requirement for healthy nutrition.

Food came from four other sources: Red Cross parcels, private parcels, occasional canteen purchases and gardens. Of the Red Cross parcels, after the spring of 1943, 40% were American, 25% British, 25% Canadian and 10% miscellaneous such as New Zealand parcels, Christmas parcels and bulk issue from the British colony in Argentina. These were apportioned at the rate of one per man per week during periods of normal supply. If the International Red Cross at Geneva felt that transportation difficulties would prevent the usual delivery, it would notify the camp parcel officer to limit the issue to one-half parcel per man per week. Such a situation arose in September 1944 when all Stalag Luft 3 went on half parcels. Average contents of American and British parcels

were as follows:

American		British	
Food	Weight (Oz.)	Food	Weight (Oz.)
Spam	12	Meat Roll	10
Corned Beef	12	Stew	12
Salmon	8	Cheese	4
Cheese	8	Dried Fruit	8
Dried Fruit	16	Biscuits	10
Biscuits	7	Condensed Milk	14
Klim	16	Margarine	8
Margarine	16	Tea	2
Soluble	4	Sugar	4
Sugar	8	Cocoa	6
Orange Powder	4	Jam	10
Liver Paste	6	Powdered Eggs	2
Chocolate	4	Chocolate	4
		Vegetables	8

Since the kitchen equipment of 10 boilers and two ovens per compound was obviously inadequate, almost all food was prepared by the various room messes in the blocks. These messes obtained from the kitchen only hot water and, four times a week, hot soup. Cooking within the block was performed on a range whose heating surface was three square feet. During winter months, PW were able to use the heating stoves in their rooms as well. With few exceptions, each room messed by itself. All food was pooled, and room cooks were responsible for serving it in digestible and appetizing, if possible, form. Since the stove schedule provided for cooking periods from 3 p.m. to 9 p.m., some rooms ate their main meal in mid-afternoon, while others dined fashionably late. Below is a typical day's menu:

Breakfast - 9 a.m.
    Two slices of German bread with spread
    Coffee (soluble) or tea

Lunch - noon
    Soup (on alternate days)
    Slice of German bread
    Coffee or tea

Supper - 5:30 p.m.
    Potatoes
    One-third can of meat
    Vegetables (twice a week)
    Slice of German bread
    Coffee or tea

Evening snack - 10 p.m.
    Dessert (pie, cake, etc.)
    Coffee or cocoa

A unique PW establishment was Foodacco whose chief function was to provide PW with a means of exchange and a stable barter market where, for example, cocoa could be swapped for cigars. Profits arising from a two per cent commission charge on all transactions was credited to a communal camp fund.

Health

Despite confinement, crowding, lack of medical supplies and poor sanitary facilities, health of PW was astonishingly good.

For trivial ailments, the compounds maintained a first aid room. More serious cases were sent to one of the two sick quarters within the camp. Sick quarters for the South Compound originally consisted of a small building with 24 beds, a staff of three PW doctors and some PW orderlies. This also served the North and West Compounds. The Center Compound had its own dispensary and two PW doctors. On 1 June 1944, the three-compound sick quarters was replaced by a new building with 60 beds.

The Germans furnished very few medical supplies. As a result, PW depended almost wholly on the Red Cross. Large shipments of supplies, including much-needed sulfa drugs, began to arrive in the autumn of 1944. PW were also glad to receive a small fluoroscope and thermometers.

Most common of the minor illnesses were colds, sore throats, influenza, food poisoning and skin diseases. When a PW needed an X-ray or the attentions of a specialist, he was examined by a German doctor. It usually took months to obtain these special attentions. Cases requiring surgery were sent to one of the English hospitals, as a rule Lamsdorf or Obermassfeld. Emergency cases went to a French hospital at Stalag 8C, one mile distant.

Dental care for the North, West and South Compounds was provided by a British dentist and an American dental student. In 14 months, they gave 1,400 treatments to 308 PW from the South Compound alone.

Sanitation was poor. Although PW received a quick delousing upon entry into the camp, they were plagued by bedbugs and other parasites. Since there was no plumbing, both indoor and outdoor latrines added to the sanitation problem in summer. PW successfully fought flies by scrubbing shorts daily, constructing fly traps and screening latrines with ersatz burlap in lieu of wire mesh.

Bathing facilities were extremely limited. In theory the German shower houses could provide each man with a three-minute hot shower weekly. In fact, however, conditions varied from compound to compound and if a PW missed the opportunity to take a hot shower he resorted to a sponge bath with

water he had heated himself - the only other hot water available the year around.

<u>Clothing</u>

In 1943, Germany still issued booty clothing of French, Belgian or English derivation to PW. This practice soon ceased, making both Britons and Americans completely dependent on clothing received from the Red Cross. An exception to the rule was made in the winter of 1943 when the camp authorities obtained 400 old French overcoats from Anglo-American PW.

Gradually, Americans were able to replace their RAF type uniforms with GI enlisted men's uniforms, which proved extremely serviceable. When stock of clothing permitted, each PW was maintained with the following wardrobe:

1 Overcoat
1 Blouse (Jacket)
2 Shirts, Wool or Cotton
1 Pr. Wool Trousers
2 Pr. Winter Underwear
2 Pr. Socks
1 Pr. Gloves
1 Sweater
1 Pr. High Shoes
1 Belt or Suspenders
1 Cap
4 Handerchiefs
1 Blanket (added to 2 German blankets)

<u>Work</u>

Officers were never required to work. To ease the situation in camp, however, they assumed many housekeeping chores such as shoe repairing, distributing food, scrubbing their own rooms and performing general repair work on barracks.

Other chores were carried out by a group of 100 American orderlies whose work was cut to a minimum and whose existence officers tried to make as comfortable as possible under the circumstances.

<u>Pay</u>

The monthly pay scale of officers in Germany was as follows:

F/O and 2d Lt.	72	Reichsmarks
1st Lt.	81	"
Capt.	96	"
Major	108	"
Lt. Col.	120	"
Col.	150	"

Americans adhered closely to the financial policy originated by the British in 1940-42. No money was handled by individual officers but was placed by the accounts officer into individual accounts of each after a sufficient deduction had been made to meet the financial needs of the camp. These deductions, not to exceed 50% of any officer's pay, took

care of laundry, letter forms, airmail postage, entertainments, escape damages and funds transmitted monthly to the NCO camps, which received no pay until July 1944.

Officers at Stalag Luft 3 contributed 33% of their pay to the communal fund, and the entire policy was approved by the War Department on 14 October 1943. Since the British Government unlike the U.S.A., deducted PW pay from army pay, Americans volunteered to carry out all canteen purchases with their own funds, but to maintain joint British-American distribution just as before.

Because of the sudden evacuation from Sagan, Allied PW had no time to meet with German finance authorities and reconcile outstanding Reichsmark balances. The amount due the U.S.A. alone from the German Government totals 2,984,932.75 Reichsmarks.

<u>Mail</u>

Mail from home or sweetheart was the life-blood of PW. Incoming mail was normally received six days a week, without limit as to number of letters or number of sheets per letter. (Germans objected only to V-mail forms.) Incoming letters could travel postage free, but those clipper-posted made record time. Correspondence could be carried on with private persons in any country outside of Germany; Allied, neutral or enemy. Within Germany correspondence with next-of-kin only was permitted. A PW could write one letter per month to next-of-kin in another PW camp or internees' camp.

SOUTH COMPOUND INCOMING MAIL

Month	Letters	Per Capita	Age.
Sep 43	3,190	3	11 weeks
Oct 43	5,392	5	10 "
Nov 43	9,125	9	10 "
Dec 43	24,076	24	8 "
Jan 44	7,680	7	12 "
Feb 44	10,765	9	12 "
Mar 44	11,693	10	12 "
Apr 44	16,355	15	12 "
May 44	15,162	13	13 "
Jun 44	13,558	11	14 "
Jul 44	26,440	20	14 "
Aug 44	14,264	11	15 "
Sep 44	10,277	8	16 "

The travel time reverted to 11-12 weeks in the autumn of 1944, with airmail letters sometimes reaching camp in four to six weeks. All mail to Luftwaffe-held PW was censored in Sagan by a staff of German civilian men and women.

Outgoing mail was limited, except for special correspondence, to three letter forms and four cards per

PW per month. Officers above the rank of major drew six letters and four cards while enlisted men received two letter forms and four cards. Protected personnel received double allotments. PW paid for these correspondence forms and for airmail postage as well.

SOUTH COMPOUND OUTGOING MAIL

Month	Letters	Postage in RMs
Sep 43	3,852	924.50
Oct 43	6,711	2494.60
Nov 43	7,781	2865.86
Dec 43	7,868	2958.00
Jan 44	7,811	2815.30
Feb 44	7,968	2907.10
Mar 44	7,916	3095.80
Apr 44	6,460	3154.90
May 44	8,327	3050.20
Jun 44	10,189	3789.60
Aug 44	8,780	3366.50
Sep 44	8,777	3288.30

Each 60 days, a PW's next-of-kin could mail him a private parcel containing clothing, food and other items not forbidden by German or U.S. Government regulations. These parcels, too, were thoroughly examined by German censors.

Morale

Morale was exceptionally high. PW never allowed themselves to doubt an eventual Allied victory and their spirits soared at news of the European invasion. Cases of demoralization were individual, caused for the most part by reports of infidelities among wives or sweethearts, or lack of mail, or letters in which people failed completely to comprehend PW's predicament. Compound officers succeeded in keeping their charges busy either physically or mentally and in maintaining discipline. The continual arrival of new PW with news of home and the air force also helped to cheer older inmates.

Welfare

The value of the Protecting Power in enforcing the provisions of the Geneva Convention lay principally in the pressure they were able to bring to bear. Although they might have agreed with the PW point of view, they had no means of enforcing their demands upon the Germans, who followed the Geneva Convention only insofar as its provisions coincided with their policies. But the mere existence of a Protecting Power, a third party, had its beneficial effect on German policy.

Direct interview was the only satisfactory traffic with the Protecting Power. Letters usually required six months for answer - if any answer was received. The sequence of events at a routine visit of Protecting Power representatives was as follows: Granting by the German of a few concessions just

prior to the visit; excuses given by the Germans to the representative; conference of representative with compound seniors; conference of representative with Germans. Practical benefits usually amounted to minor concessions from the Germans.

PW of Stalag Luft 3 feel a deep debt of gratitude toward the Red Cross for supplying them with food and clothing, which they considered the two most important things in their PW camp life. Their only complaint is against the Red Cross PW Bulletin for its description of Stalag Luft 3 in terms more appropriately used in depicting life on a college campus than a prison camp.

PW also praised the YMCA for providing them generously with athletic equipment, libraries, public address systems and theatrical materials. With YMCA headquarters established in Sagan, the representative paid many visits to camp.

<u>Religion</u>

On 1 December 1942, the Germans captured Capt. M. E. McDonald with a British Airborne Division in Africa. Because he was "out of the cloth" they did not officially recognize him as a clergyman, nevertheless, he was the accredited chaplain for the camp and conducted services for a large Protestant congregation. He received a quantity of religious literature from the YMCA and friends in Scotland.

In April 1942, Father Philip Goudreau, Order of Mary Immaculate, Quebec, Canada, became the Catholic Chaplain to a group which eventually numbered more than 1,000 PW. Prayer books were received from Geneva and rosary beads from France.

On 12 September 1943, a Christian Science Group was brought together in the South Compound under the direction of 2d Lt. Rudolph K. Grumm, O-749387. His reading material was forwarded by the Church's War Relief Committee, Geneva, as was that of 1st Lt. Robert R. Brunn active in the Center Compound.

Thirteen members of the Church of Jesus Christ of Latter Day Saints, sometimes known as the Mormon Church, held their first meeting in the South Compound on 7 November 1943. 1st Lt. William E. McKell was nominated as presiding Elder and officiated at subsequent weekly meetings. Material was supplied by the European Student Relief Fund, the Red Cross, the YMCA and the Swiss Mission of the Church.

<u>Recreation</u>

Reading was the greatest single activity of PW. The fiction lending library of each compound was enlarged by books received from the YMCA and next-of-kin until it totaled more than 2,000 volumes. Similarly, the compounds' reference libraries grew to include over 500 works of a technical nature.

These books came from the European Student Relief Fund of the YMCA and from PW who had received them from home.

Athletics were second only to reading as the most popular diversion. Camp areas were cleared and made fit playing fields at first for cricket and rugby and later for softball, touch football, badminton, deck tennis and volleyball. In addition, PW took advantage of opportunities for pingpong, wrestling, weight lifting, horizontal and parallel bar work, hockey and swimming in the fire pool. The bulk of athletic equipment was supplied by the YMCA.

The "Luftbandsters", playing on YMCA instruments, could hold its own with any name band in the U.S.A. according to those who heard them give various performances. PW formed junior bands of less experienced players and also a glee club.

Through the services of the YMCA, PW were shown seven films, five somewhat dated Hollywood features and two German musical comedies.

Other activities included card playing, broadcasting music and news over a camp amplifier called "Station KRGY", reading the "Circuit" and "Kriegie Times" journals issued by PW thrice weekly, following world events in the PW news room, attending the Education Department's classes which ranged from Aeronautics to Law, painting, sketching and the inevitable stroll around the compound perimeter track.

Sagan Evacuation

At 2100 hours on 27 January 1945, the various compounds received German orders to move out afoot withing 30 minutes. With an eye on the advancing Red Armies, PW had been preparing two weeks for such a move. Thus the order came as no surprise. In barracks bags, in knotted trousers and on makeshift sleds they packed a minimum of clothing and a maximum of food - usually one parcel per man. Each man abandoned such items as books, letters, camp records and took his overcoat and one blanket. Between 2130 and 2400 hours, all men except some 200 too weak to walk, marched out into the bitter cold and snow in a column of threes - destination unknown. Their guards, drawn from the camp complement, bore rifles and machine pistols. They marched all night, taking ten-minute breaks every hour.

The exodus was harrowing to PW of all compounds but especially those of the South, which made the 55 kilometers from Sagan to Muskau in 27 hours with only four hours sleep. Rations consisted only of bread and margarine obtained from a horse-drawn wagon. PW slept in unheated barns. At Muskau, on

the verge of exhaustion, they were billeted in a blast furnace, which was warm and an empty heating plant, which was cold. Here they were given a 30-hour delay for recuperation. Even so, some 60 men incapable of marching farther had to be left behind. The 25 kilometers from Muskau to Spremberg on 31 January, the South Compound, plus 200 men from the West Compound, went to Stalag 7A at Moosburg. They traveled two days and two nights in locked, unmarked freight cars - 50 men to a car. On 7 February, the Center Compound joined them. The North Compound fell in with the West Compound at Spremberg and on 2 February entrained for Stalag 13D, Nurnberg, which they reached after a trip of two days.

Throughout the march the guards, who drew rations identical with PW's, treated their charges with sympathy and complained at the harshness they all had to undergo. German civilians encountered during the trek were generally considerate, bartering with PW and sometimes supplying them with water.

Stalag 13D Conditions

Conditions at Stalag 13D, where PW stayed for two months, were deplorable. The barracks originally built to house delegates to the Nazi party gatherings at the shrine city, had recently been inhabited by Italian PW who left them filthy. There was no room to exercise, no supplies, nothing to eat out of and practically nothing to eat inasmuch as no Red Cross food parcels were available upon the Americans' arrival. The German ration consisted of 300 grams of bread, 250 grams of potatoes, some dehydrated vegetables and a little margarine. After the first week, sugar was not to be had and soon the margarine supply was exhausted. After three weeks, and in answer to an urgent request, 4,000 Red Cross food parcels arrived from Dulag Luft, Wetzlar. Shortly thereafter, the Swiss came to make arrangements for sending parcels in American convoy, and soon Red Cross parcels began to arrive in GI (Red Cross) trucks.

Throughout this period, large numbers of American PW were pouring into camp - 1,700 from Stalag Luft 4, 150 a day from Dulag Luft and finally some men from Oflag 64.

Sanitation was lamentable. The camp was infested with lice, fleas and bedbugs. Three thousand men, each with only two filthy German blankets, slept on the bare floors. Toilet facilities during the day were satisfactory, but the only night latrine was a can in each sleeping room. Since many men were afflicted with diarrhea, the can had an insufficient capacity and men perforce soiled the floor. Showers were available once every two weeks. Barracks were not heated. Only 200 kilograms of coal were provided for cooking. Morale dropped to its lowest ebb, but Col. Darr H. Alkire succeeded in maintaining discipline.

Nurnberg Evacuation

At 1700 hours on 3 April 1945, the Americans received notice that they were to evacuate the Nurnberg camp and march to Stalag 7A, Moosburg. At this point, the PW took over the organization of the march. They submitted to the German commander plans stipulating that in return for preserving order they were to have full control of the column and to march no more than 20 kilometers a day. The Germans accepted. On 4 April, with each PW in possession of a food parcel, 10,000 Allied PW began the march. While the column was passing a freight marshalling yard near the highway, some P-47s dive-bombed the yard. Two Americans and one Briton were killed and three men seriously wounded. On the following day the column laid out a large replica of an American Air Corps insignia on the road with an arrow pointing in the direction of their march. Thereafter, the column was never strafed. It proceeded to Neumarkt, to Bersheim where 4,500 Red Cross parcels were delivered by truck, then to Mulhauser where more parcels were delivered. On 9 April, the compound column reached the Danube which Col. Alkire flatly refused to cross since it meant exceeding the 20 kilometer-a-day limit. With his refusal the Germans completely lost control of the march and PW began to drop out of the column almost at will. The guards, intimidated by the rapid advance of the American Army, made no serious attempt to stop the disintegration. The main body of the column reached Stalag 7A on 20 April 1945 (See "Influx", Stalag 7A).

\- X X X -

OFLAG 64

(Ground Force Officers)

Location

Oflag 64 was situated in Poland, two and one-half miles northwest of the railroad station in Altburgund (new German name for the old Polish town of Schubin, 53°01' N. - 17°44' E.). The grounds were formerly those of a Polish college.

On 21 January 1945, 1,471 ground force officers and enlisted men left Schubin just ahead of the advancing Russian Army to travel a total of 345 miles, arriving at Oflag 13B, Hammelburg on 9 March 1945.

Strength

Oflag 64 was opened on 6 June 1943 with just a handful of ground force officers. In October of that year, the Red Cross reported 224 American officers and 21 enlisted men there. Almost all of these men had been captured in North Africa and had been held in other camps prior to the opening of Oflag 64. By July 1944, the population had increased to 520 officers and 37 enlisted men. At the time of the evacuation from Poland on 21 January 1945, the camp strength was 1,557.

Description

The camp was composed of a main stone building and six barracks. Only three of these barracks were used until the last few months of the occupation. The buildings were 120 feet long and 40 feet wide. They were subdivided into cubicles seven feet by 10 feet which quartered an average of eight officers. The PW slept in double-tiered wooden bunks equipped with straw mattresses, a pillow, one sheet and a pillow case. The Germans supplied two thin blankets which were totally inadequate for the climate. A large sports ground was available within the compound. The latrines were situated in separate buildings adjoining the barracks, but were of the pit-type at first. Later, latrines equipped with cesspools and pumps were installed, but were insufficient in number.

U.S. Personnel

Colonel Thomas N. Drake was the SAO from its opening on 6 June 1943 until his repatriation on 27 July 1944. Colonel George V. Millett succeeded Colonel Drake and was SAO until the arrival of Colonel Paul R. Goode on 16 October 1944. From that time until the liberation, the camp administration was organized as follows:

Senior American Officer	Colonel Paul R. Goode
Executive Officer	Colonel G. V. Millett
Ass't. Executive Officer	Major K. Benson
Adjutant	Major Merle A. Meacham
Welfare Officer	Lt. Col. J. K. Waters
Senior Medical Officer	Capt. F. M. Burreson

There was also a highly organized Security Committee.

German Personnel

The German personnel consisted of approximately 100 men from the 813th Infantry (Grenadier) Regiment, and four administrative officers. The administration was organized in the following manner:

Camp Commander	:	Oberst Schneider
Second in Command	:	Oberstleutnant Louis
Security Officer	:	Hauptman G. Zimmerman
Welfare Officer	:	Sonderfuhrer H. Theissen
Chief Physician	:	Dr. Pongratz

According to Colonel Drake, the relations between the PW and the Germans were quite impersonal. Hauptman Zimmerman was particularly disliked for his frequent pettiness. He was a Nazi party-member of good standing and often appeared to be able to reverse decisions of Oberst Schneider.

Treatment

The treatment at Oflag 64 was considered better than that of other American PW camps containing ground force personnel. As the camp strength increased, the buildings naturally became more crowded, and comforts experienced in early 1944 disappeared with the shortages of fuel and food all over Germany. According to repatriates who arrived in January 1945, the Germans displayed a definite tendency to provoke incidents in the camp. It appeared that the Germans desired to have as many PW as possible under sentence. As an example, in the summer of 1944 four officers were being marched under guard to the hospital at Gneisen for treatment and were ordered not to use the sidewalk but to walk in the streets of the town. They felt this was humiliating treatment and in violation of the Geneva Convention. They brought this point up to the guards and after some discussion were permitted to use the sidewalks. However, this incident was reported and the four were brought up for trial on the charge of "Obstructing the Functions of the German Reich". The trial was held in October 1944 and the men were acquitted of the charge. However, in December 1944, the four were informed that they would be retried on charges growing out of the incident. The retrial was held on 25 January 1945, and all four officers received the death sentence. They were liberated before the sentence could be carried out.

A similar instance of this tendency to perpetrate incidents occurred on 22 September 1944 when Lt. James R. Schmitz, the Assistant Adjutant, was in the camp office alone and was approached by two unteroffiziers about to post anti-escape posters. Because Lt. Schmitz considered the posters insulting to American officers in that they accused our government "of resorting to gangster warfare up to and within the frontier of the Fatherland" he requested them to wait until he could contact the SAO. Unable to do so, he brought back to the office Lt. Col. Schaefer who discussed the posters with the

Germans. As they were leaving Lt. Schmitz stood in the doorway in token protest. When one unteroffizier approached and touched Lt. Schmitz, he immediately got out of the way. Nevertheless, Lt. Schmitz was accused of blocking the doorway and Lt. Col. Schaefer was accused of interfering with the functions of the German Reich. They were both tried on 28 December 1944 and sentenced to death, but were liberated before the sentence could be carried out.

The treatment grew steadily worse from the Allied invasion until winter. Then as it became obvious to the Germans that defeat was inevitable, many of the guards and camp officials became more lenient, and the treatment improved. There was a noticeable scarcity of true Nazis in the last few days.

Food

From the time the camp opened until the evacuation, the German rations were very poor in both quality and quantity. The Red Cross food parcel became the means of subsistence in the camp and the difference between complete misery and tolerable existence. From 10 October to 3 December 1944, no Red Cross parcels were delivered in camp and the men suffered accordingly. During the period from 20 October to 15 November 1944, all men in camp were checked for weight loss, and the average was nine pounds per man. The German ration during that period was as follows:

Per day each man received:

Meat	35 7/10	Grams
Cooking Oil	9 7/10	"
Margarine	21 4/10	"
Cheese	4 1/2	"
Barley	25	"
Potatoes	353	"
Cabbage	200	"
Carrots	100	"
Dried Vegs.	6 2/5	"

ONE ONLY OF THE FOLLOWING:

Turnips	400	Grams
Sugar	25	"
Sauerkraut	48 2/5	"
Tea (ersatz)	1	"
Jam	25	"
Bread	318	"
Soup Powder	3 1/2	"
Coffee (ersatz)	2 1/2	"

Health

In spite of many hardships due to insufficient food, impure water supplies, and poor sanitation facilities, the health was surprisingly good. The "revier" itself was old, the floors unpainted, the plumbing a constant source of concern among

the doctors. The 30 beds available in the "revier" were usually occupied by men suffering from stomach ailments, colds and other routine complaints. It was not equipped to handle the cases of those seriously ill or badly wounded. These cases were sent to the hospital at Hollstein.

Fortunately for the early arrivals at Oflag 64, RAF doctors who had formerly inhabited the camp left behind about 25 units of Red Cross medical supplies. These sufficed until more supplies were received from the International Red Cross. However, the flow of supplies was inadequate and undependable. By constant nagging, special drugs and emergency items were obtainable from the Germans in rare cases, but the American doctors preferred to isolate themselves from the German doctor as much as possible.

Clothing

Thanks to the Red Cross, clothing was adequate during 1943 and early 1944. However, by November 1944, clothing was so scarce that the Germans demanded that PW turn in all but one uniform. They also demanded field jackets, which were refused. As a result, the guards came through the barracks with fixed bayonets and fired their rifles in the air forcing the men into giving up their jackets. The original excuse for confiscation was that clothing was needed for new PW, but men arrived in Russian, French and British uniforms which were never replaced by American equivalents. Bed clothing was completely inadequate, and many times officers slept two to a bunk in order to "pool" their blankets. The Germans at no time provided sufficient clothing.

Work

The officers at Oflag 64 were not required to do any work except their own fatigue details around camp. These duties were assigned by the SAO's staff. However, 33 of the enlisted men who were sent as orderlies were required to work at a near-by sawmill. Their work was not too hard, and their noon-day rations were slightly better than the camp's.

Pay

In the beginning, officers were paid on a sliding scale according to rank, with lieutenants receiving 60 marks a month. From this 22 marks were deducted for food and 10 for orderly service. The balance was supposed to be used for purchases from the canteen, but since this offered nothing but weak beer and an occasional razor blade, the money was no asset. At no time was an officer permitted to have in his possession more than 30 marks, and an American finance officer was assigned to keep a duplicate set of records on the financial status of each PW. He made arrangements with the German officials to disburse the amounts owed. After a visit on 23 October 1944, the Red Cross reported that camp money disbursal had stopped entirely and the amounts were credited to a special account of each officer.

<u>Mail</u>

The officers received three letter forms and four cards each month. The enlisted men received two letter forms and three cards a month. The SAO received 10 letter forms and 10 cards a month along with necessary letter forms to conduct camp affairs. The Germans checked the number of outgoing letters from each officer a month in the early days. However, it was later noticed that this practice had stopped, and officers were able to borrow mail forms and write as many letters as they wished. There was never any shortage of letter forms and none was ever refused an individual as a punitive measure. The eight censors were all except one enlisted men and ex-residents of the United States. They performed other duties, and for this reason mail was often unnecessarily delayed, sometimes for two weeks. Transit time for letters, including airmail from the U.S.A. to the camp was erratic, varying between 30 and 90 days. Toward the end of the war the mail service grew slower as transportation facilities were harassed by Allied bombers.

<u>Morale</u>

The morale of the men, especially after "D-Day", was exceedingly high. This spirit was reflected in the monthly publication known as the <u>Oflag Item</u>, which was issued from November 1943 to January 1945. By making light of the "Kriegie-Woes" and reviewing the months' activities in the vein of a collegiate newspaper an easy air of comradeship was developed. The "Little Theater of Schubin College" was a huge success. PW produced a total of eight three-act plays, all of which were former Broadway hits. They also produced seven one-act plays, eight musical reviews and one original three-act play. In addition to these activities the men took part in many types of sports. A league was formed for baseball and softball enthusiasts as well as basketball players. Thus, men kept their morale high by keeping occupied.

<u>Welfare</u>

Insofar as the Germans were concerned, welfare consisted of only the barest necessities. All phases of welfare were handled by the International Red Cross, the Protecting Power and the YMCA. As mentioned before, the Red Cross food parcels and clothing took care of two basic requirements of PW. The Protecting Power in its capacity of mediator made seven visits to the camp. The representatives were punctilious about interviewing the American staff in privacy and made a conscientious effort to improve situations about which complaints were made, even though their representations to the German officials were often ignored after their departure.

The athletic and recreational equipment provided by the YMCA contributed a great deal to the welfare of the men. The library at camp was well stocked with a good variety of literature from text books to murder thrillers.

Religion — The religious activities in the camp were very satisfactory. A room was furnished by the Germans and made into an attractive chapel by the men. At one time there were as many as eight chaplains at the camp, but because they felt they were needed elsewhere, they requested transfers to other camps. Only a Protestant and Catholic Chaplain remained.

Recreation — In addition to the many activities mentioned in the paragraph on Morale, there was a great deal of interest in art, crafts and education. Of all recreations, reading seemed to take first place. Many officers availed themselves of numerous text books to improve their knowledge on various subjects. The school was well attended and foreign languages appeared to be favorite subjects.

Many men who had dabbled in art as a hobby took advantage of their leisure to improve their style. Cartoonists appeared from every barrack and new hobbies were developed daily. However, the favorite pastime of all was re-reading letters from home and day-dreaming about the end of the war.

Evacuation — On 21 January 1945, the SAO was informed that the camp was to be evacuated immediately, and that all able-bodied men would fall out to begin the march. The German doctor and the American medical staff hurriedly examined all of the men in the camp, and after a great deal of discussion, agreed to leave behind 86 men under the supervision of Col. Drury. These men were to remain in the hospital until the advancing Russians over-ran the camp. The other 1,471 officers and enlisted men left on foot for the 345 mile trek to Brandenburg.

After the able-bodied men left the camp, the first problem facing the new SAO was to keep the Poles out of the camp because they began a systematic routine of looting. During the first 24 hours several small groups of Germans passed the camp on the same road taken earlier by the column, but they did not enter the camp. Late that evening the Poles reported that Russian tanks had been in the town but had passed on again before they could be informed of the Americans' presence. On the morning of 22 January 1945, both American and Russian flags were raised over the camp and shortly afterward the first Russians appeared on the road. The SAO was told by the tank commanders that they must move on, but that the rear echelon would give PW the best of care. As more and more trucks passed, and no one seemed to have authority to begin the evacuation, the SAO decided to commandeer a truck and driver and return to the Corps headquarters. After sending six

telegrams from that headquarters and discussing the problem at length with the commanding general, Col. Gen. Blov, Col. Drury made evacuation plans.

On 28 January 1945, the men left Schubin by truck and were taken to Rembertow, arriving 31 January 1945. At Rembertow the Russians had taken over a former Polish military school and turned it into a refugee processing center with approximately 5,000 tired, hungry and frightened people of mixed nationalities. In spite of many promises of assistance, it was not until 22 February 1945 that the group boarded a train for Odessa. Meanwhile, several impatient officers had left the camp and proceeded on their own to reach Moscow where they were given air passage back to the United States. The group reached Odessa on 1 March 1945, and were evacuated to the United States by plane and boat.

The 1,471 officers and enlisted men under the command of Oberst Fritz Schneider marched to Exin, Poland (24 kms.), where they were supposed to entrain for a new camp in Brandenburg. However, upon their arrival it was discovered that no arrangements had been made for the journey and the group continued on foot to an estate just outside of Exin where they were quartered for the night in cow barns. The weather was below freezing and the ground was covered with snow. The day's march had been gruelling and 186 men decided to hide in the hay lofts and make their way back to the Russian lines. All of these were successful in their escape, and were able to reach Rembertow where they joined Col. Drury's group.

During the entire 45 days of the march the quarters were, with few exceptions, hay barns, stables, cow sheds or machine shacks. They were often overcrowded, and many were lofts with only one ladder for entrance and exit, thus presenting a great hazard in case of fire. Despite continued protests on the part of Colonel Goode, it was not until 2 February 1945 that the Germans sent a quartering party forward in advance of their arrival. Prior to this time, PW would arrive at their destination at dusk with wet and cold feet and be forced to stand around while hasty arrangements were made for quartering. Frequently fires were not permitted so that shoes and socks could not be dried nor could food be cooked.

The camp sites often lacked adequate drinking water and no shaving or washing facilities were available. No provisions for baths were made during the entire period.

Medical supplies were not provided at all by the Germans until 17 February 1945. After that date only a very limited amount was given.

There had been continuous trouble in providing transportation for the sick and no effort was made to provide proper places for sick call. The ration provided on the march was inadequate. The German ration officer stated that they were receiving the same ration as the German guard company, but this was not true. The average ration for the day was one bowl of turnip soup, a few potatoes, a cup of ersatz coffee or mint tea, a half a slice of brown bread. The only supplement to this diet was an occasional barter with the farmers along the way who wanted cigarettes, soap, fountain pens, etc., until finally 500 Red Cross parcels were obtained on 17 February 1945. These had to be shared by 1,025 men.

The table below gives the number of kilometers the men marched each day:

DATE	DISTANCE (KM)
January 21	24
22	23
23	7
24	9
25	21
26	0
27	18
28	17
29	7
30	12
31	14
February 1	3
2	18
3	0
4	17
5	21
6	22
7	20
8	20
9	13
10	13
11	14
12	24
13	7
14	13
15	0
16	23
17	27
18	8
19	10
20	20
21	0
22	16
23	19
24	23
25	21
26	0
27	16
28	11
March 1 to 5	0
6	9 boarded train arriving at Hammelburg 9 March 1945.

Only 423 officers and 67 enlisted men completed the trek to Oflag 13B, arriving in a state of exhaustion.

Liberation

On 27 March 1945, Colonel Goode was notified that camp 13B would be evacuated that afternoon at 1600 hours. At 1300, American tanks appeared and after a brief consultation, the Germans agreed to surrender the camp immediately. Three of the staff officers and one German officer were selected to carry the white flag of surrender to the American tank column. As they marched out of the gate, an SS private shot Lt. Col. John K. Waters, seriously wounding him. Immediately the tanks started firing and after a few minutes the camp was in the hands of the Americans. However, the spearhead was not prepared to transport so many officers, and it was impossible to remain there and defend the area. Many of the men climbed on the tanks and attempted to get back to the lines that night, but road blocks and mines hampered their progress. The following two days saw nearly all of the men returned to the camp under German guard. Meanwhile the Germans had returned to evacuate the remaining prisoners to southern Germany, and about 500 men were sent to Nurnberg by train. Two days later, the remaining men were marched to Stalag 7A, Moosburg. This trip was approximately 90 miles and it required 15 days to march because of the weakened condition of the men and the constant bombing by the Allied air forces of installations along the way. Many men escaped during this march during the confusion. Upon their arrival at Stalag 7A, Colonel Goode organized the camp of 30,000 PW for their final rescue which occurred 29 April 1945.

- X X X -

RESERVE-LAZARET OBERMASSFELD

(Orthopedic Hospital)

Location Obermassfeld lies in the agricultural and pastural region of Thuringia, nine kilometers south of the city of Meiningen (50°34' N. - 10°24' E.)

Description The main building was a large three-story stone structure erected after World War I as a boys' school. Later it was taken over by the S.A. and then by the Hitler Youth before its conversion into a hospital. Three one-story wood and tar-paper barracks stood in the courtyard to house internal medicine cases, and a fourth barrack was used as an isolation ward. The main installation was divided into rooms comprising patients' wards, medical officers' quarters, two operating theaters - septic and aseptic, a plaster room, X-ray room, orderlies' and guards' quarters. In March 1945, in preparation for an influx of PW from camps near the fighting zones, a French hospital tent was erected near the lazaret proper.

A shortage of water plagued the hospital during the summer of 1944. While there were a sufficient number of washrooms, and showers could theoretically be taken at least once a week, the insufficient water supply actually made the washing situation unsatisfactory. This water shortage was caused by leaks in old underground pipes which were eventually repaired. The number of latrines was insufficient for the hospital when it was at full strength.

The aseptic operating theater became septic in July 1944, probably because of its long use. This condition caused the loss of one life with the result that British medical officers refused to perform any "clean surgery" in the theater. During the winter of 1944-45 the operating theater was closed down completely and operations were carried out in the former sterilizing room. This move was necessitated by a critical fuel shortage which prevented the heating of the large theater. Similarly, enough hot water for the hospital's needs was difficult to obtain. When the coal supply was altogether exhausted, working parties were sent out into the surrounding region to forage for wood. A small shipment of coal, arriving in March 1945, eased the situation somewhat.

Strength Maximum capacity of the hospital building was 360, with the barracks providing space for 140 additional beds. Before the invasion of the continent, patients were almost exclusively British and American air forces personnel shot down on raids over German Europe. Even after the landings on Normandy, few Allied ground

force men were sent to Obermassfeld. Strength averaged 400, at first preponderantly British. Thus on 5 April 1943, the hospital had 10 Americans and 178 Britons. As American participation in the war increased, numbers of American PW patients grew until on 10 March 1945 there were 189 Americans and 264 Britons.

To relieve crowding in the spring of 1943, convalescents were sent to the lazaret at Kloster Haina. When a strength of 560 severely taxed hospital facilities in April 1944, plans were made for recuperating post-operative cases to be transferred to the lazaret at Meiningen - opened in May.

Allied Personnel

Originally run by British PW, Obermassfeld retained its British staff until its liberation. Not until July 1944 were six American medical orderlies reported added to the hospital complement, and the sole American doctor on the staff remained only three months. Charges by some American patients of favoritism and preferential treatment shown by the British staff to British patients were not substantiated by him. Leading members of the staff were:

Lt. Col. A. T. Marrable	- Senior Medical Officer
Major J. B. Sharman	- Assistant SMO
Major Henderson	- Surgeon
Major A. C. Whitcombe	- Executive Officer
Major Kimbell	- Surgery Chief
Major G. Smyth	- Medical Chief
Capt. S. E. Morgan (USA)	- Medical Officer
Capt. B. M. Egan (USA)	- Chaplain

On 7 November 1944 the staff numbered 101, assigned as follows:

British Medical Officers	15
American Medical Officer	1
British Dental Officers	2
British Chaplain	1
American Chaplain	1
British X-Ray Technician	1
British Medical Students	2
British Medical Orderlies	50
American Medical Orderlies	6
British Housekeeping Unit	22

German Personnel

Except for a few occasions when patients were confined in solitary rooms for three or four days because of some trivial infraction of Dr. Falke's rules, PW had no complaints against the Germans. The British Staff welcomed the non-interference and cooperation of the German staff headed by:

Oberstabsarzt Dr. Schuttler	- Chefarzt (1945)
Oberstabsarzt Dr. Falke	- Chefarzt (1943-4)
Oberstabsarzt Dr. Koch	- Asst. Chefarzt
Stabsarzt Dr. Reichel	- Asst. Chefarzt
Major Lumpke	- Abwehr

Treatment In January 1945 Obermassfeld held two Jewish PW who had been unmercifully beaten and were near death as a result. It is probable that this violence occurred prior to their entry to Obermassfeld, where no such mistreatment was ever reported.

Food The German ration plus Red Cross food, which was never lacking, assured all PW of a sufficient diet. Food was cooked in a kitchen which held three large boilers and one cooking range shared by Germans and Allies alike, an arrangement which proved barely satisfactory because of lack of enough equipment. German women prepared the German issue, and PW the Red Cross food. Men who lived in the barracks had hearths on which to cook their own food - enabling them to avoid the strained facilities of the hospital kitchen. Special diets could be prepared for cases urgently in need of such. At the end of August 1944 there was on hand a food supply of

1209 British parcels
2429 American parcels
1851 Canadian parcels
391 Milk parcels
5448 British Invalid parcels
2869 American Invalid parcels

and as late as 10 March 1945 despite shortages encountered elsewhere, Obermassfeld had food stocks to last six weeks at the customary consumption rate of one parcel per man per week.

Health Most patients were seriously wounded with amputations and infected gunfire wounds. The majority came to the hospital directly from combat, either air or ground. They remained at the hospital until the beginning of their convalescence when they were transferred to the Meiningen Reserve Lazaret where their strictly orthopedic treatment was under the supervision of a British specialist and various physical "re-education" teachers.

All medical matters were left in the hands of the British medical officers and little interference was experienced from the German Chefarzt. The drug supply furnished by the Germans covered about 50% of the requirements but by winter 1944 several items, especially plaster bandages, cloth bandages, gauze and cotton wool were no longer available; nor was sterile water. Plaster bandages were used at the rate of 2000 a month and in March 1944 only 1200 were on hand. Seventy Red Cross medical parcels were used per month. Medicines and equipment not furnished by the Germans were obtained from the Red Cross, and at no time was there a shortage so critical that it resulted in handicapping the efforts of the medical staff. Both treatment and equipment were exceptionally good.

Dental treatment and equipment was always satisfactory.

<u>Clothing</u>

As far back as April 1943 the Senior British Officer was requesting that clothing be shipped directly to the Lazaret instead of coming from adjacent Stalag 9C. Yet in September 1944 clothing was still drawn from the stalag. Inasmuch as most patients were aviators who had been shot down, many arrived with their uniforms burned. Extremely few had passed through the Dulag Luft transit camp where they might have been outfitted anew. Nevertheless, the large reserve stock of clothing which should have been on hand in the lazaret was never sent directly from the Red Cross, and the Germans issued practically nothing with the result that Obermassfeld constantly suffered from slight clothing shortage. Each new arrival did, however, receive a shirt and pyjamas upon his admission. The most frequent requests were for shoes - to aid in the construction of protheses - and flannel shirts - to keep pneumonia patients warm and to serve as padding for plaster casts. PW also needed toilet articles such as razors, brushes, laundry soap, toothbrushes, combs and handkerchiefs. Some 900 Red Cross blankets, in addition to those supplied by the Germans, were sufficient to cover all beds satisfactorily.

<u>Work</u>

Medical personnel volunteered for work. Privates who formed the housekeeping detachment considered themselves fortunate to be employed on details which were pleasant compared to those performed by other PW in Germany.

<u>Pay</u>

Patients did not begin to receive pay until they had been in the lazaret for three months. Those who had been shifted from other lazarets where they had stayed fewer than three months, and those who were sent from Obermassfeld to convalescent centers before three months had elapsed, complained about their lack of pay. Their accounts did not become effective until they reached permanent PW camps.

Pay for medical personnel was regularly given in cash until November 1944, when issue of marks or lagergeld was stopped by the High Command. Subsequently, all monetary operations were transacted on "PC2" (Personal Card No. 2). Medical personnel no longer received specie but were credited with amounts due on their individual "PC2".

<u>Mail</u>

Patients were allowed to write three letters and four cards a month; medical personnel, twice that amount. Incoming mail was unlimited. Most of the parcels announced as sent by next-of-kin did not arrive. Those that did were damaged. No Americans stayed in the hospital long enough to receive replies to their letters. Mail from England took three months in transit. The Senior Medical Officer complained that 22 letters sent to the Protecting Power were not acknowledged.

Morale

Morale among the medical personnel, busily engaged in their peacetime profession, was high. Among patients, thanks to the good treatment received, it was no lower than that of patients in hospitals anywhere.

Welfare

In addition to providing Obermassfeld with almost all its food, clothing and more than half its medical supplies, the Red Cross visited the hospital quarterly and submitted comprehensive, if optimistic, reports to the U.S. State Department through neutral channels.

The Protecting Power Delegate inspected the hospital every three months, supported the Senior Medical Officer in his claims against the German commandant with good effect and circulated detailed reports of camp conditions.

The YMCA kept the hospital well stocked with books, games and athletic equipment.

Religion

In April 1943, the only religious services were provided by a chaplain from Meiningen lazaret who visited Obermassfeld once a month. By the beginning of 1944, a Church of England chaplain was assigned to the hospital. Catholics, however, of whom there were about 100 at any given time, requested that a priest be permanently stationed at the hospital. In July 1944, the Swiss, German staff and PW again petitioned higher headquarters for a Catholic chaplain, but it was stated that none was available. In November, the commandant reported that Captain B. M. Egan, a Catholic chaplain in the U.S. Army, would stay and minister unto his fellow PW when he finished the treatment he was undergoing as a patient.

Recreation

Little need for recreation existed, for convalescents were sent to other hospitals as soon as they were fit enough to be transferred. Those strong enough to exercise could play ball games on a field near the hospital. Otherwise patients were not allowed to go out.

Liberation

By 20 March 1945 the Senior Medical Officer had anticipated the arrival of Allied forces and planned accordingly. Since most patients were too weak to be moved, PW in Obermassfeld were liberated at the beginning of April by American troops.

- X X X -

MARLAG UND MILAG NORD

(Naval Personnel)

Location — The camp was situated at Westertimke (53° 51' North latitude - 9° 57' 45" East longitude) 30 miles southwest of Hamburg and 10 miles north of Bremen. It was well placed on sandy ground planted with pine trees. On 10 April 1945, the majority of PW was evacuated toward Lübeck, but many of the personnel who were unable to march remained as a unit until liberated by the British on 14 April.

Strength — Created for the confinement of Navy and Merchant Marine personnel only, the installation under normal conditions had a capacity of 5300 and in emergencies of 6900. According to official figures of the Protecting Power, the strength in April 1944 was 4268 and in December 1944, 4223 with 41 nations and races represented. In April 1945, approximately 1900 RAF officers were removed from Stalag Luft III at Sagan and were accommodated in this camp. In September 1944, a large group of civilian internees was brought in from Gironagny and placed in the Ilag. At no time were there more than 71 Americans from the Navy and Merchant Marine in this camp, and on 2 April 1945 two American Air Corps officers were imprisoned there, the first non-naval American personnel to arrive.

A month before liberation the camp held 35 American Merchant seamen and nine regular service personnel including: Major Peter Ortiz and Lt. Walter W. Taylor of the Marine Corps and Lt. (jg) Richard M. Harris, USNR.

Description — The entire camp, which was constructed in the autumn of 1942 and subsequently added to, consisted of seven lagers as follows: Lager I, Dulag, which was used as an interrogation and transit compound; Lager II, Marlag, housing personnel of the Royal Navy; Lager III, Milag, for the confinement of Merchant Marine personnel of the various nationalities; Lager IV, Milag (Inder), accommodating Indian seamen of the Merchant Navy; Lager V, Wache, for the camp guard; Lager VI, Kommandatur, the administrative officer for the entire establishment; Lager VII, Stabslager, living quarters for the administrative personnel of the entire establishment.

The Marlag Lager for the Navy PW and the Milag Lager for Merchant Marine PW each had two compounds designated as Marlag "O" and Marlag "M" and Milag "O" and Milag "M" for officers and enlisted men respectively. When the 1900 RAF officers arrived, PW from Marlag "M" were transferred to the Ilag compound and the British fliers were accommodated in Marlag "M".

Each compound consisted of several sturdily built one-storied wooden buildings which were well-lighted and heated. There were 29 of them in Marlag and 35 in Milag.

The majority of them were used as barracks for the PW while the others were kitchens and dining rooms, ablution barracks, guard barracks, storehouses, postal section and other administrative buildings. Each building used as living quarters comprised many rooms accommodating 14 to 16 officers or 18 men of other ranks. There were two and three-tiered bunks furnished with pallisses of straw with washable covering. Two blankets were issued each man and some PW had an extra Red Cross blanket. Personnally owned blankets were rare. Cleanliness was the rule and for the most part the barracks were well kept although at times the pallisses were infected with vermin.

The entire camp was surrounded by barbed wire and the Marlag and Milag compounds were also separated by barbed wire. Within the lagers, the compounds for officers and men were also separated by wire. In addition each compound had a barbed wire cattle fence about a yard high placed about four yards inside the outer fencing. PW were not allowed to go beyond the cattle fencing. Placed at the corner of each camp were watchtowers with machine guns and searchlights, which were always turned off during an air raid warning.

German Personnel

At first the camp was commanded by Kapitan zur see Schuhr, a regular German navy officer who was severe but considered by PW as just. After his transfer the personnel was as follows:

Camp Commander	: Fregatten-Kapitan Schmidt
Second in Command	: Korvetten-Kapitan Kogge
Security Officer	: Oberleutnant Schoof
German Physician	: Stabsarzt Dr. Trautman
Accompanying officer of the G.H.C.	: Major Bosenberg

Kapitan Schmidt was short and fat and looked like a pig. He weighed about 220 pounds, was five feet nine inches tall, about 54 years old and had grey hair. The security officer, Oberleutnant Schoof, was about six feet tall, weighed about 150 pounds and had a very thin long nose, dark skin and black hair. The PW did not come into contact with other members of the camp personnel.

When the camp was first formed the camp guard comprised NCOs and men from naval artillery units. These men, between 45 and 55 years, were unfit for frontline service. In addition about 30 members of the German marine forces were distributed throughout the camp as cooks and clerks. Later on the guards at the camp were of the Wehrmacht and wore the uniform of this ground force organization. According to observations by PW there were eight guards around the enlisted men's barracks going on duty at 0730 hours and remaining there until 1800 hours. Armed with pistols, they patrolled the barracks area and sometimes entered them. There were two guards along the inner fence of the enlisted men's compound. Shifts changed every two hours. Twelve guards patrolled as sentries

along the outer fence around the compounds at all times. The guards were old and were for the most part German farmers recently inducted into the Wehrmacht although some of them had been veterans of the first World War. As a rule the guard personnel was changed about every six months. PW traded with the guards whenever they would come into the barracks and talked to them quite openly.

U.S. Personnel

The compounds were administered by English personnel who filled the staff positions. Ph.M. 1/C Charles H. Carter was the American MOC in Marlag "M" and Joseph Ashworth, of the U.S. Merchant Marine Corps, was American MOC in the Milag compound.

The basic unit for organization was the barracks and the barracks' chiefs were all English inasmuch as the number of American PW in the two compounds was so small.

Health

In general the health in the camp was very good. There were a few cases of tuberculosis in the hospital, which was in the Milag section of the camp and was operated by the British, and also a very few cases of dysentery. The American MOC in Marlag "M" acted as the doctor for the Americans. All dental work was done by an English dentist. It was reported by those who had been to the hospital that the treatment was quite good, but the hospital ran short of medical equipment and supplies.

Washing facilities were in a separate building in the camp. In this building were three cold showers which the men could use at any time and 53 water spigots. The men received what was supposed to be a hot shower once a week, but the building where the showers were situated was a quarter of a mile from the camp and three parties of 25 men each would be taken down at one time. Therefore, the men who went in first were the only ones to get a hot shower, because when the others came later the water was cold. The latrine, which was in a separate building, consisted of 47 stools over a hole in the ground. They were cleaned out about once every two weeks. Drinking water was plentiful and was available at all times except the one period of three weeks in December 1944 when the Germans claimed that the pump was broken and needed repair. At that time the water was on only during certain hours of the day.

Food

The usual German ration existed in this camp. Breakfast comprised two slices of bread, half a cup of ersatz coffee and sometimes a small piece of cheese. For dinner the prisoners had soup made out of turnips and potatoes, and for supper each PW was issued three potatoes. About once a month a little horsemeat and sugar was issued. The meager rations were supplemented by Red Cross parcels, the food of which was prepared by PW on the stoves in the barracks.

Clothing The Germans issued no clothing to the PW although there was a great demand for winter overcoats and warm garments. Red Cross shipments were received quite regularly and distribution was made of the necessary clothes to each PW. The English had set up a shop to repair shoes and there was also a tailor shop in the camp. The Germans did not confiscate any uniforms of the prisoners who were allowed to keep whatever clothing they had.

Treatment The treatment of PW was correct. There were no indications of any disciplinary actions having been taken against American PW. The guards were older men and would do favors for the PW for cigarettes. Consequently there was a sort of mutual understanding and as long as the PW did not cause any trouble they were not interfered with by the Germans.

Work & Pay PW from Marlag and Milag never worked outside of the camp, but when they were asked to do so they refused. Seamen 2/C were made to do work within the camp but the Seamen 1/C did nothing except work on cleaning details and KP within the barracks. Those PW who worked received 40 pfennings per day, and according to statements of some they received seven marks 50 pfennings a month. The money was in camp currency and could be spent in the PX operated by the Germans. In November 1944 the Germans stopped issuing camp currency and paid the PW in German marks. No man was ever allowed to have more than 30 marks in his possession.

Recreation In each compound there were sports fields where the PW could play baseball and volley ball. A great deal of equipment was supplied by the Red Cross and YMCA. Other exercise was obtained by walking around in the enclosure during the day, and toward the end of the war the Germans permitted the PW to walk outside the compounds under guard. They would give the guards cigarettes for the privilege of taking these walks and at times would go as far as two and three miles from the camp but never near any town. Plays were put on by the PW in the camp theatre. They also had a band, using instruments issued by the Red Cross and those purchased by the British from the Germans. A well-stocked library (3000 volumes) was run by the British. In regard to education, there were 19 men giving instruction in 25 separate courses, which included languages, mathematics, commercial subjects, vocational, economic and scientific. Classes were very popular and well attended. Textbooks for these courses were obtained from the Red Cross and YMCA.

Mail In general the delivery of mail was very erratic. The average number of letters received per man per month was seven and required as many as 61 days for transit. Parcel post packages required about 43 days in transit. PW received two letter and four card forms per month, while the medical staff received a double ration of the

forms. The Germans were quite regular in issuing these forms and at times additional ones could be obtained from PW who did not desire to use theirs. There were no restrictions on the number of incoming letters a PW could receive and the letters could be kept indefinitely. German civilian girls censored incoming as well as outgoing mail.

Religion

Two small chapels, one for Protestants and the other for Catholics, were in the camp. Protestant church services were held in the morning and evening of every Sunday. In addition prayers were held every night and there was a mid-week "fellowship discussion group" meeting. The YMCA provided hymnals and prayer books and at Christmas time provided hundreds of booklets with Christmas carols. An English chaplain served as minister. A French civilian internee was the Roman Catholic chaplain; Mass and benedictions were held each day.

Welfare

Representatives of the Protecting Power came to the camp about every three months. They made fairly rigid inspections and received oral and written complaints from the Senior British Officers and the Men of Confidence in the individual compounds. The German staff usually accompanied the Swiss representatives when they made a tour of the camp. Complaints about food, clothes, sleeping accommodations, the need for fuel and other matters were turned over to the Germans. In some cases the complaints were acted upon promptly but in other cases, particularly in regard to the coal situation, action was promised but never fulfilled. According to statements of PW, they felt that the Swiss representatives were doing all they possibly could but were handicapped by the Germans in the High Command.

The Red Cross and the YMCA were particularly helpful in regard to the welfare of the PW. Recreational supplies, books and clothing were provided whenever requested, and whenever representatives of these two organizations came to the camp, PW had ready access to them and could usually obtain whatever they requested.

Evacuation & Liberation

On 8 April 1945, the German camp commander notified PW that the camp was to be moved to Lubeck. The few Americans in the camp were to have marched along with the Royal Navy and Merchant Navy personnel. PW who were unable to march were to remain in the camp under German command. The first day out of the camp the column was strafed by British planes and a great deal of confusion resulted, with most of the men going back to the camp. Some Americans escaped and hid out in the woods west of the camp. They spent several days there but when they became sick from drinking stagnant water they decided to give themselves up. Upon their return they found the English in complete control of the camp.

-XXX-

STALAG 2B

(Ground Force Enlisted Men)

Location The camp was situated one and a half miles west of Hammerstein, (53°41' N. - 16°58' 30" E.) west Prussia, on the east side of a highway leading to that city.

Strength In August 1943 the stalag was reported as newly opened to privates of the U.S. ground forces with a strength of 451. The Hammerstein installation acted as a headquarters for work detachments in the region and seldom housed more than one-fifth of the PW credited to it. Thus at the end of May 1944, although the strength was listed as 4807, only 1000 of these were in the enclosure. At its peak in January 1945, the camp strength was put at 7200 Americans, with some 5315 of these out on nine major kommando companies which in turn were subdivided as follows:

Company Lauenberg	- 65 kommandos -	1700 men
Company Stolp	- 40 kommandos -	750 men
Company Rummelsberg	- 28 kommandos -	550 men
Company Köslin	- 25 kommandos -	450 men
Company Falkenberg	- 15 kommandos -	315 men
Company Jastrow	- 25 kommandos -	450 men
Company Dt.Krone	- 30 kommandos -	550 men
Company Schlochau	- 12 kommandos -	200 men
Company Neu Stettin	- 18 kommandos -	350 men

Description The camp sprawled over 25 acres surrounded by the usual two barbed-wire fences. Additional barbed-wire fences formed compounds and sub-compounds. Ten thousand Russians lived in the East Compound, while the other nationalities - 16,000 French, 1600 Serbs, 900 Belgians - and the Americans were segregated by nationalities in the North Compound. Within the American enclosure were the playing field, workshops, dispensary, showers and delouser. At times more than 600 men were quartered in each of the three single-story barracks 15 yards wide and 60 yards long, made available to the Americans. Although this resulted in extremely crowded conditions, it contrasted well with the Russian barracks which held as many as 1000 PW apiece. Barracks were divided in two by a center washroom which had 20 taps. Water fit for drinking was available at all hours except during PW's last two months when it was turned off for part of the day. Bunks were the regulation PW triple-decker types with excelsior mattresses and one German blanket (plus two from the Red Cross) for each. In the front and rear of each barracks was a urinal to be used only at night. Three stoves furnished what heat there was for the front half of each barrack, and two for the rear half. The fuel ration was always insufficient, and in December 1944 was cut to its all-time low of 12 kilos of coal per stove per day. On warm days, the Germans withheld part of the fuel ration.

U.S. Personnel

Pvt. Harry Galler was Man of Confidence from August 1943 until July 1944, when the Germans refused to negotiate with him because they had discovered he was Jewish. Pvt. Galler attributes the German discovery to the activities of a purportedly British PW who called himself Pvt. Leonard B. Cornwall but confided that his real name was Leonard B. England. This man was actively anti-Semitic, possessed a list of American PW who were Jews, spoke fluent German and seemed on friendly terms with the German staff. He was suspected by some PW of being a German stool-pigeon planted in camp to create dissension.

With the resignation of Pvt. Galler, M/Sgt. John M. McMahan became MOC - a position he held until his escape from a marching column on 13 April 1945. Other members of the permanent camp staff were:

Adjutant:	M/Sgt. Robert Ehalt
Red Cross Representative:	Pfc. Gunnar Drangsholt
Mail NCO:	S/Sgt. Edward Volberding
Personal Parcel Distributor:	S/Sgt. Stephen Novak
Recreational Supplies:	Pvt. Henry Wintjen
Educational Department:	Sgt. John Dixon
	Sgt. Eastburn Maynor
Protestant Chaplain:	Cpl. Alfred C. Carroll
	Pvt. Bruce Meads
Catholic Representative:	Pvt. Thomas McGovern
Medical Officers:	Capt. Wilbur McKee
	Capt. Henry Wynsen
	Capt. John Moorman
	Capt. Louis Salerno
	Dr. Bula (Belgian)

A Security Committee also existed.

MOC of the nine major kommando companies were:

Lauenberg:	Cpl. John Kuntz
Stolp:	S/Sgt. Jacob C. Schick
Rummelsberg	Pfc. Paul Sapsara
Köslin	Sgt. Warren Mason
Falkenberg:	Cpl. Kenneth Gastor
Jastrow:	Pvt. Frank De Luca
Dt.Krone:	1st Sgt. Leonard Flaherty
Schlochau:	Pvt. Arnold Trautman
Neu Stettin:	Pvt. Milton Bartelt

German Personnel

Although the German commandant seemed correct in his attitude toward American PW, it is unlikely that the extreme severity of some of his underlings could have existed without his knowledge and consent.

Oberstleutnant Von Bernuth:	Commandant
Oberst Von Keppler:	Commandant
Oberstleutnant Segers:	Executive Officer
Hauptmann Springer:	Kommando Officer
Hauptmann Giesel:	Security Officer

Hauptmann Wagner:	Medical Officer
Unteroffizier Krause:	Chief Censor
Feldwebel Kohler:	Lager NCO
Unteroffizier Wendorf:	Kommando NCO

Of the Germans listed, only the medical officer was liked by PW. The censor was disliked to an extreme, and PW hated Springer, Wendorf and Kohler all three of whom were described as Nazi fanatics who enjoyed wreaking hardships on Americans. Springer is held to be responsible for the killing of men on kommandos.

<u>Treatment</u>

Treatment was worse at Stalag 2B than at any other camp in Germany established for American PW before the Battle of the Bulge. Harshness at the base stalag degenerated into brutality and outright murder on some of the kommandos. Beatings of Americans on kommandos by their German overseers were too numerous to list, but records show that 10 Americans in work detachments were shot to death by their captors.

In the fall of 1943, when Hauptman Springer was seeking men for work details, American NCOs and medical corpsmen stated that according to the Geneva Convention they did not have to work unless they volunteered to do so, and they chose not to volunteer. At this, the German stated that he did not care about the terms of the Geneva Convention and that he would change the rules to suit himself. Thereupon, he demanded that the PW in question fall into line and give their names and numbers for kommando duty. When the Americans insisted on refusing, Hauptmann Springer ordered a bayonet charge against them. At the German guards' obvious disinclination to carry out the command, Hauptmann Springer pushed one of the guards toward an American, with the result that soon all PW were forced to line up as ordered.

Typical of the circumstances surrounding the shootings are the events connected with the deaths of Pfc. Dean Halbert and Pvt. Franklin Reed. On 28 August 1943, these two soldiers had been assigned to a kommando at Gambin, in the district of Stolp. While working in the fields, they asked permission to leave their posts for the purpose of relieving themselves. They remained away from their work until the work detachment guard became suspicious and went looking for them. Some time later he returned them to the place where they had been working and reported the incident to his superior. Both of the kommando guards were then instructed to escort the Americans to the kommando barracks. Shortly after they had departed, several shots were heard by the rest of the Americans on the work detachment. Presently the two guards returned and reported that both Pfc. Halbert and Pvt. Reed had been shot to death for attempting escape. The guards then ordered other American PW to carry the bodies to the barracks.

On another kommando, the Germans shot and killed two Americans, stripped them and placed the bodies in the latrine, where they lay for two days serving as a warning to other PW.

Eight of the killings took place in the latter months of 1943, one in May 1944 and one in December 1944. In almost every case the reason given by the Germans for the shootings was "attempted escape." Witnesses, however, contradict the German reports and state that the shootings were not duty but clear cases of murder.

Food

From the Germans, PW received daily 300 grams of coarse bread and 500 grams of potatoes; twice weekly they received 300 grams of meat and 20 grams of margarine; once a week they drew 50 grams of cheese; marmalade was issued sporadically. All these rations were found in the mid-day meal, which was always in the form of soup. The breakfast ration consisted solely of ersatz coffee. There was no supper.

To supplement the meager German diet, PW relied on Red Cross food. From 12 September 1943 until 1 November 1944, one parcel per man was issued each week. From 1 November until 1 January 1945, the parcel distribution was cut to one-half parcel per man per week because of an insufficient stock. During December 1944 and January 1945, however, carloads of parcels, Christmas parcels included, totaling 101,000 were received. In late January five carloads of parcels were received from Stalag Luft 4 where the Germans said there was no room for them. Later the MOC of Stalag Luft 4 stated that he had never approved the shipment.

Parcels were stored in the lager reserve in Hammerstein and in the headquarters of the various kommando companies. In the stalag proper, they were kept within the "Green Post" compound, between the North and East camps. Many of the parcels arriving at the railroad station were broken open. Whether this damage was due to rough handling in transit or to German pilfering could not be determined. On 19 January 1945, 46,000 parcels were on hand. One month later there were none. The German complement had confiscated 5000, the Wehrmacht 2000, civilians stole 400 and the rest were given to evacuating Americans and other fleeing nationalities passing through the area. During this period five carloads (13,500 parcels) destined either for Stalag 2B or 2D were never received. Their disappearance may be attributed either to German looting or Allied air attacks on trains.

Health

Health was surprisingly good. Aside from minor ailments such as diarrhea or grippe, the main illnesses were malaria, from which some 100 men suffered, and diphtheria, which struck a maximum of five men a month.

Medical supplies in the lazaret were woefully short. PW received no stocks from the Red Cross until June 1944, .

when they got a few parcels in response to two telegrams sent without knowledge of the Germans. Pvt. Drengsholt, the Red Cross representative in camp, had twice been able to wire Switzerland when on business outside the stalag. Within two weeks after the first telegram had been sent, medical supplies were flown to camp. Among the most needed drugs were quinine, atabrine and aspirin. Previous to this time, the Germans had refused to pass on the American medical officer's requisitions, saying that he did not need the supplies. For example, when he asked for 1000 phenobarbitol tablets, the Germans would give him 10, say he now had a supply and would get some more only when his current supply was exhausted. Furthermore, the Germans disliked sending telegrams to the Red Cross in Switzerland for such telegrams gave the impression, they said, that the PW were receiving nothing. Yet, at times the Germans gave only 100 atabrine tablets to some 90 men shaking from malaria and then claimed that the Americans had no right to protest to Geneva about lack of supplies.

Examination of men chosen for kommandos provided the American medical officer with a great deal of difficulty, for the German idea of a PW's fitness for duty differed substantially from the American. Captain McKee tried to hide men who were too sick to go out on work detachments and usually put them in the hospital after falsely diagnosing their cases as grippe or dysentery. Some men, always unwilling to work, sought excuses to forestall their being chosen for kommando duty. The medical officer gave these men all the help he could. He did not, however, permit himself to aid malingerers to the point where it would jeopardize those who were actually sick. Ear, eye, nose, throat, mental, venereal and similar serious cases were sent from Stalag 2B to other hospitals. But PW on kommando sometimes suffered from lack of medication and proper treatment.

One 48-hole latrine, with adequate urinal space, served as many as 1800 PW during the daytime. Since they lacked equipment for many months, PW found it difficult to keep the latrine clean. Twice a day a detail washed it down with hot water.

Bathing facilities were satisfactory. A PW could take three hot showers a week. The shower building was open eight hours a day and contained some 80 shower heads. Men were deloused periodically.

Clothing

The clothing situation was always a source of contention. The Germans insisted they had the right to keep a man's old clothing when he was re-outfitted with Red Cross supplies. This made it necessary for PW to work in rain and mud in their one and only uniform. Eventually the Protecting Power did see that PW were allowed to keep their old clothes.

As in other camps, the Germans never pretended to supply enough clothes and when they were called upon to furnish garments issued wooden shoes, rag-like socks, undershirts spun from processed wood and old overcoats infested with bugs. The Red Cross provided enough of all items except shoes, overcoats, socks, gloves and blankets. The Germans had enough blankets in camp to issue two per PW but instead sent them to Volkssturm troops digging trenches in the vicinity.

In December 1944 the camp received from the Red Cross a shipment of 2380 American uniforms badly needed by 1100 new arrivals. The Germans broke all precedent by demanding that the uniforms be yielded to them and subsequently seized them by force. French PW under German guard loaded trucks which were driven out of camp. Although PW received a receipt for the clothing, they never got a satisfactory explanation. The Man of Confidence complained to the commandant three times and was told that the confiscation order came from the Red Cross. The Protecting Power denied knowledge of any such order and promised an investigation.

Work

Except for housekeeping chores benefiting PW, no work was performed in the stalag. All men fit to work were sent out to kommandos where conditions approximated the following:

A group of 29 Americans were taken under guard to a huge farm 6 kilometers from Stolp, where 12 French PW were already working without guards. Americans were billeted in a section of a large brick-floored barn. Adjoining sections were occupied by pigs, cows and grain. PW slept on double-decker bunks under two blankets. The French had a small building of their own. Guards lived in a small room opening onto the Americans' quarters.

Each day the men rose at 0600 and breakfasted on Red Cross food and on potato soup, bread and hot water (for coffee) which they drew from the farm kitchen. At 0630 they washed their spoons and enamelled bowls and cleaned their "barracks." They shaved and washed themselves in three large wash pans filled from a single spigot which gave only cold water. The outdoor latrine was a three-seater.

At 0700 they rode out to potato fields in horsedrawn wagons driven by coldly hostile German farmhands who would welcome the opportunity to shoot a "kriegie." Under the eyes of a watchful, armed guard they dug potatoes until 1130, when they rode back to the farm for the noon meal. This consisted of Red Cross food supplemented by German vegetable soup. Boarding the wagons at 1300, PW worked until 1630. The evening meal at 1700 consisted of Red Cross food and the farmers issue of soup, potatoes and gravy. After this meal they could sit outdoors in the fenced-in pen (30 feet by eight feet) until 1830. Then the guard locked them in their section for the night.

On Sundays the guard permitted PW to lounge or walk back and forth, in the "yard" all day, but they spent a good deal of their time scrubbing their "barracks" and washing their clothing. Sunday dinner from the farm usually included a meat pudding and cheese.

Once a month each PW received a large Red Cross food box containing four regulation Red Cross parcels. These were transmitted to distant kommandos by rail and to nearby units by Wehrmacht trucks. Parcels were stored in the guard's room until issued. The average tour of duty on a farm kommando lasted indefinitely. On other work detachments it lasted until the specific project has been completed.

Pay

The finance officer collected $17,000 from the Americans in camp. None of this money was returned.

PW who did no work received no pay. Working PW received 70 pfennigs a day in lagergeld which was of little value since it could be spent only on knick-nacks which were seldom available either in the stalag or kommando headquarters.

Mail

Each PW was furnished with two letter forms and four cards per month except for a few months when a shortage, reputedly caused by bombing, cut the issue in half. Medical orderlies received double allotments. Forms were not withheld as punishment. Surface mail to the U.S.A. averaged three and a half month's in transit; airmail, six weeks. Only a spot-check censorship was made by the American staff.

The number of incoming letters was unlimited and PW could retain such mail indefinitely. Surface mail from the U.S.A. took four months to reach camp; airmail, five weeks. All letters were censored at the stalag by Wehrmacht personnel, civilians and SS troops. As a rule, censorship was sloppy. Once a week incoming mail was delivered to kommandos and outgoing mail picked up and brought to the camp for censoring and dispatch. Communication between the men at the stalag and those on kommando was permitted.

Personal parcels generally arrived in good condition about four months after being mailed. Some of these parcels, like a few of the letters, were censored in Berlin. Most, however, were censored at Stalag 2B, where an American always witnessed the censoring. German guards on work detachments made a habit of stealing cigarettes from personal parcels, and at the base camp 90,000 Old Gold and Raleigh cigarettes were confiscated because their packages bore the slogan "For victory - buy war bonds."

Morale

Morale of the Americans as a group was exceptionally high. They were always "cocky." All propaganda efforts by the Germans were ineffective and paradoxically lifted the morale of PW who had schooled themselves to believe

the exact opposite of what they recognized as German propaganda. Discipline was good, with only a few PW causing trouble. PW were largely satisfied with their American camp staff which saw that they were regularly fed and adequately clothed. Only during the period of the evacuation march when PW encountered wretched quarters and lack of food did morale dip.

Welfare

All PW felt extremely grateful to the Red Cross for delivering food, clothing and medical supplies. Had it not been for the Red Cross, states the Man of Confidence, many more men would have died.

The Protecting Power representative visited the camp quarterly and investigated all complaints. Although the visits did not accomplish much, it was felt that the representative had the interests of PW at heart and did as much as he could for them. The May 1944 visit differed from the other in that it seemed to accomplish better results. Kommando killings ceased, except for one in December 1944, but whether this was because of the Protecting Power or coincidence is not known.

The YMCA provided PW with sports equipment, books and musical instruments enough to earn the gratitude of the many men who availed themselves of recreational opportunities.

Religion

The chaplaincy in Stalag 2B was initiated by Pvt. Bruce Meads who arrived in August 1943. When his health broke down in February 1944, leading to his eventual repatriation, he was succeeded by Cpl. Alfred C. Carroll. At first regularly scheduled chapel services were held in any available barracks space. Later permission was granted worshippers to leave the American compound and use the French chapel. With the consent of the abwehr officer, Pvt. Meads began the practice of visiting one kommando each Sunday. Subsequently his assistants visited as many as four kommandos per Sunday.

Catholics attended regular Masses celebrated by a French priest. He and his assistant, Pvt. Thomas McGovern, visited working parties twice monthly. Aside from the services conducted by these representatives, no organized religious activities for kommandos existed.

Recreation

In 1943 and the spring of 1944, PW were locked up in their compound and could only walk in a 50 x 50 yards space in the rear of the three barracks occupied by Americans. In the summer of 1944, after one year in camp, Americans were given access to the athletic field situated in the center of the camp between barracks #8 and #10. Football, softball, basketball and volley ball could be played on this

field simultaneously. Most equipment came from the YMCA and some came from the Germans. The softball field could be used at any time in the evening after 1700 hours; the football field, volley ball and basketball courts were shared with PW of other nationalities.

By November 1944 some 8000 books had been received from the YMCA, Red Cross and European Student Relief Fund. Sgt. Eastburn Meynor was in charge of the library which could be visited any time during the day or evening. A reference library of 2500 books was maintained in addition to the 8000 volumes already mentioned.

A theater built by the French was shared by all. Several original musical comedies were produced by Americans, and since the theater seated only 300 men, five separate performances had to be given to assure each PW of an opportunity to attend. At times the band and theater group, under guard, were permitted to give performances for the benefit of work detachments. The band numbered 18 pieces; all instruments were supplied by the YMCA or Special Services, U.S. Army.

Once three groups totaling 1500 Americans were escorted to motion pictures in Hammerstein - a privilege accorded PW of other nationalities. The Americans spruced up and wore class "A" uniforms putting German officers and soldiers, who were untidy, to shame. This was resented by German civilians and Americans were not taken again to the movies in Hammerstein.

Evacuation & Liberation

On 28 January 1945, PW received German instructions to be ready to evacuate camp at 0800 the following morning. Upon receipt of these instructions, the MOC set up a plan of organization based on 25-man groups and 200-man companies with NCOs in charge. On the day of evacuation, however, PW were moved out of camp in such a manner that the original plan was of little assistance. German guards ordered PW to fall out of the barracks. When 1200 men had assembled on the road, the remaining 500 were allowed to stay in the barracks. A disorganized column of 1200 marched out into the cold and snow. The guards were considerate, and Red Cross food was available. After the first day, the column was broken down into three groups of 400 men each, with NCOs in charge of each group.

For the next three months, the column was on the move, marching an average of 22 kilometers a day six days a week. German rations were neither regular nor adequate. At almost every stop Sgt. McMahan bartered coffee, cigarettes or chocolate for potatoes which he issued to the men. Bread, the most important item, was not issued regularly. When it was needed most, it was never available. The soup was, as a rule, typical, watery German soup, but several times PW got a good,

thick dried-pea soup. Through the activity of some of the key NCOs, Red Cross food was obtained from PW camps passed by the column in the march. Without it, it is doubtful that the majority of men could have finished the march. The ability of the men to steal helped a lot. The weather was atrocious. It always seemed to be either bitter cold or raining or snowing. Quarters were usually unheated barns and stables. Sometimes they slept unsheltered on the ground; and sometimes they were fortunate enough to find a heated barn.

Except for one period when Red Cross food was exhausted and guards became surly, morale of the men remained at a high level. Practically all the men shaved at every opportunity and kept their appearance as neat as possible under the circumstances.

From time to time weak PW would drop out of the column and wait to be picked up by other columns which were on the move. Thus at Dahlen on 6 and 7 March, the column dwindled to some 900 American PW. On 19 March at Tramm, 800 men were sent to work on kommandos, leaving only 133 PW who were joined a week later by the large kommando company from Lauenberg. On 13 April the column was strafed by four Spitfires near Dannenberg. Ten PW were killed. The rest of the column proceeded to Marlag 10C, Westertimke, where they met the men they had left behind at Stalag 2B who had left on 18 February, reached Stalag 10B after an easy three-day trip, and then moved to adjacent Marlag 10C on 16 April. Westertimke was liberated by the British on 28 April 1945.

-XXX-

STALAG 3B

(Ground Force Non-Commissioned Officers)

Location Stalag 3B was situated three-quarters of a mile northwest of Furstenberg, Germany (52.9 N - 14.42 E), which is 60 miles southeast of Berlin and 15 miles south of Frankfurt-on-Oder. The camp lay on the east bank of the Oder Spree Canal, between the canal and the railroad, and was set in an agricultural region.

Strength As of 20 July 1944, this ground forces, enlisted men's camp held, out of a total of 22,522 prisoners, 2903 Americans of whom 2207 were in the camp, 27 in the infirmary and 36 in the hospitals, including three American doctors and 27 NCOs, members of the sanitary personnel. The remaining 600 were in work detachments.

By 18 December 1944, the number of Americans in the camp and its kommandos totaled 4207, 3338 of whom were in the base camp at Furstenberg. Of the 4207 American PW, 3205 were NCOs; three were American medical officers.

The number of army ground force personnel, mostly NCOs, continued to mount in Stalag 3B. Finally, when the Germans decided to move the men westward on 31 January 1945, it had reached 5000.

Description The Furstenberg camp, a typical large stalag, served as the base installation while numerous working kommandos operated within a considerable distance. Also connected with Stalag 3B were a stalag infirmary, a stalag lazaret and a hospital at Gorden.

Stalag 3B is spread out on a plain, two kilometers southwest of the railroad station, and two kilometers from a glassworks. The American camp, which during the early part of 1944 consisted of six wooden barracks, was 350 meters from the entrance to the stalag, at the left of a central avenue. The barracks were set 20 meters apart, perpendicularly to the central avenue. Behind these barracks was a spacious, sandy lot where the PW could walk about freely, play games or prepare individual meals. A small barrack was located in the middle of this lot; it was for the American MOC and his assistant and was used as an American administrative barrack. This small barrack consisted of two rooms, one of which was comfortably furnished and served as the office; the other as a bedroom, with two single wooden beds.

The PW barracks were divided into two parts, each housing, in early 1944, 150 to 190 men or an average of a little over 300 men per barrack. In early 1945, when the men were evacuated, 12 instead of six barracks were provided for the Americans, whose compound measured 300 by 2000 feet, and 450 men instead of 300 lodged in each barrack.

Each half of a barrack was separated from the other by the lavatories, and by a small room which served as an individual kitchen. Two latrines with flushing water were installed at each end, but were only used at night.

Situated on one side of each barrack were a series of triple-decker bunks; the other side consisted of a central passageway and of tables and stools placed near the windows. Light was dim due to the fact that the men's clothing hung from lines stretched in all directions. The barracks were absolutely full; the cubic amount of air was sufficient, but the habitable space was very inadequate. Later on, when more PW moved in, it was necessary to remove some of the tables and install more bunks.

Electric lights were insufficient, making reading at night very trying on the eyes. The barracks were heated by means of three large brick stoves for each half barrack. The quantity of coal furnished the men was insufficient, even for mild winter weather.

The lavatories in the center of each barrack had 24 running water faucets available at all times for the 300-400 men in the barracks. Nearby were large cement tubs for the laundry, but PW had no hot water for that purpose. In the corner of this central laundry, was a stove used exclusively for the preparation of individual dishes.

The kitchen was spacious and well lighted, but lacked utensils.

An additional barrack served as a recreation hall, theatre, church and library. This barrack was entirely built with material from the Red Cross: crates, paper, cans, etc.

U.S. Personnel

Three different enlisted men held the position of MOC at Stalag 3B, serving their terms in the following order: M/Sgt. Clyde M. Bennett, S/Sgt. Arthur S. Taylor and S/Sgt. Joseph C. Gasperich. Sgt. Taylor relieved Sgt. Bennett in May 1944 when the latter departed from camp. Sgt. Gasperich fell heir to the position in August 1944, and served up to and including the evacuation of the camp. Medical officers present in the stalag were Capt. Sidney Brockman, who later left, 1st Lt. Henry W. Hughes and 1st Lt. Stanley M. Awramik, who came in from kommando to replace Capt. Brockman. Cpl. Herman Foster was placed in charge of Red Cross parcels. An American enlisted man, Sgt. Richard M. Gray, acted as chaplain in the American compound, while a Polish padre served as chaplain for the entire camp. Capt. Louis Salerno also served as a medical officer at this camp for a time.

German Personnel

Camp Commandant at Stalag 3B was Oberst Blau, while Oberleutnant Gross served as Lager Officer and Feldwebel Schoen as Lager NCO. The Oberst was an old-line German soldier, rarely seen by PW. Gross, five feet nine inches, 140 pounds, thin, hatchet-faced, femine in appearance and speech, intensely hated by Americans because he constantly bedevilled them. He sometimes kept them out for two hours on appel, hailed them out of the barracks just when they were about to eat, and confiscated their food and cigarettes on shallow pretexts. Schoen, five feet eight inches, 170 pounds, heavy-set, black hair, black-bearded, rough-faced, was reported by PW as a vicious person.

Hauptmann Winkler was the camp security officer. Major Wolfe, the medical officer, rarely had anything to do with PW. The recreation officer, Lt. Von Fricken, was five feet, 11 inches tall, 35 years old, slim, suave and brown-haired. He spoke excellent English. He appeared to be in charge of theatrical activities and said he made frequent trips to other camps. He told Americans that he had managed a W. T. Grant store in an eastern state and that he was forced to enter the Wehrmacht while visiting Germany. He cursed the Germans while talking to the PW and although he was sometimes openly ridiculed by the PW, who did not salute him nor come to attention when he entered their barracks, he apparently did not ask that they be disciplined. Some PW could not decide whether he was a German or American spy. Von Fricken also told another story: He had represented the Gestapo for 12 years in the United States, and boasted that he got out of the country two days before the FBI would have caught him.

Treatment

It was reported that Hauptmann Winkler, Oberst Blau and Lager Officer Gross never abided to a great degree by the Geneva Convention. They always claimed that they were giving the PW all that the German High Command permitted them and would take orders and recommendations from no one else except the High Command.

The PW had difficulty in submitting themselves to the extremely strict discipline of the camp. German camp authorities, from the Commandant down to the lowest-ranking officer, were very narrow-minded and obstinate to all proposals with regard to an easier running of the camp. It was, therefore, difficult for the PW to acclimate themselves.

The most serious problem encountered by the PW in Stalag 3B was undoubtedly that of the continual repetition of searches and the confiscation of such articles as cigarettes, clothing and food.

There were no atrocities.

Food

In early 1944 there were no serious complaints about the food ration. Cooking was done by Americans who did a good job in accordance with American taste. In addition

to the German rations, PW received a regular supply of Red Cross parcels, amounting to one per man per week. Food at this time was plentiful and PW appeared well nourished.

Meals were prepared under the supervision of an American NCO who was held in great esteem by the other PW. At first, when Red Cross parcels had not yet been received at the camp, the basic food rations furnished by the American authorities were carefully weighed by the American head cook, but when Red Cross parcels began to arrive the German rations were no longer weighed. However, the rations varied little at this time, except for sugar and potatoes which at times were reduced in quantity by one-third.

The average German basic food ration for two weeks and for 26 men was as follows:

Meat	8,500 gr.	Marmalade	8,050 gr.
Margarine	10,025 gr.	Pastes	2,510 gr.
Cheese	1,485 gr.	Cereals	935 gr.
Bread	12,090 gr.	Potatoes	728,000 gr.
Sugar	10,400 gr.		

PW complained of the poor quality of the potatoes, of which 20-40% frequently had to be thrown away. Furthermore, oftentimes peas received by the PW were infested with worms.

In the kitchen there was a stove which used exclusively for preparing individual meals. This stove was added by the camp commandant to make up for the insufficient number of individual stoves in the barracks. The lack of dishes, forks and knives was noticeable, however, the PW did not complain greatly over this and manufactured their own utensils.

During the latter part of 1944, the following meals could generally be provided each day from the German rations: ersatz tea or coffee for breakfast, a litre of soup for dinner, a dry ration of about one-half pound loaf of bread divided among six men and a pound of margarine for 30 men, together with a few potatoes. This amounted to about six potatoes, three spoonfuls of sugar, three spoonfuls of jam and 300 grams of bread per man per week (an average loaf of bread weighed 1500 grams). In addition, the Germans issued dehydrated rutabaga soup five times a week, potato soup once a week and grain or vegetable soup once a week. These dehydrated soups were frequently full of maggots.

During the period 10 September to 18 December 1944, the PW received only one Red Cross parcel each. Aside from rare next-of-kin parcels, they lived solely on German rations which had deteriorated to rutabaga soup, bread, potatoes (12 to a man per week), and ersatz coffee or tea. They were constantly hungry and the food situation was not alleviated until 18 December when each PW received one parcel and thereafter a half parcel a week.

In December 1944, the Germans commenced dumping the Red Cross food parcels out of the cans into dishes. The Germans controlled this procedure while the Americans watched, and five Germans were intercepted stealing chocolate, raisins and cigarettes from the parcels. Each barrack leader assigned his own men on detail to watch and after that nothing was stolen. A protest to the Protecting Power was lodged on the opening of the parcels, but the Swiss replied that the Germans were within their rights as the contents of the parcels were given to PW in an edible state. During this time, the commandant would not permit a prisoner to receive his cigarettes from his next-of-kin parcels. The cigarettes were removed from the NOK parcels and placed into a storeroom and distributed three packs weekly along with five packs from the Red Cross parcels. However, no PW was to have more than five packs of cigarettes in his possession.

Private cooking was hampered through lack of fuel and the fact that the stoves were too large and practically useless for cooking.

Food was sufficient when backed up with Red Cross parcels but the men endured hardships if this supplement was lacking. One PW had the following to say regarding the German ration: "A lot of us became sick from eating rotten food but we had to eat to live. They fed us lots less than we could eat."

In September 1943, after the PW received Red Cross parcels, they experienced their first "shake-down" inspection by the Germans. The pretext was that PW had too many cans of coffee and too many cigarettes and had supposedly started a black market among the citizens of Furstenberg, who in turn shipped supplies to the Berlin black market. This was untrue but the Germans confiscated all cans of coffee in excess of one can per man, cigarettes in excess of two packs and any extra quantity of margarine and meat. A month later, the same thing occurred and any extra coffee and food was confiscated. During these searches the guards stole many articles not supposed to be confiscated.

On 31 January 1945, the PW were evacuated from Stalag 3B. They were provided with no food at the beginning of the march or the following day when they stopped at their first bivouac area. They received no food until the afternoon of the third day when they received one-fifth of a loaf of bread per man. Throughout the march they were given very little water and for two days they had no water whatsoever. For the entire seven days of the march they drew one and one-quarter loaf of bread per man and one-eighth of a #2½ can of cheese for eight men at one time. This was the entire German ration for the march.

In May 1944, following an unsuccessful escape attempt, Gestapo agents visited Stalag 3B and staged a thorough

search. PW were kept outside quarters during the search and when they returned to the barracks they discovered that food had been removed from many of the Red Cross parcels. This food was not returned.

Health

First Lt. Henry W. Hughes and 1st Lt. Stanley M. Awramik were in charge of the camp's infirmary. Lt. Hughes was permitted daily to visit the American patients at the camp's lazaret where the patients were attended by American medical orderlies. Conditions at the lazaret were said to be quite satisfactory though there was no definite ward or bed space reserved for the Americans. All the surgical work was performed by a Russian PW surgeon who was very capable. Other American doctors, Capt. Sidney Brockman and Capt. Louis Salerno, also served at Stalag 3B.

German drug and medical supplies were rationed and Americans had to use principally Red Cross supplies. Dental facilities were insufficient, with only one dentist, an Italian, in charge of the entire camp. There was a lack of material, especially for fillings. The men had difficulty in being treated as there was always a long waiting list.

All mental cases from Stalag 3B were sent to the mental home at Gorden near Braunschweig. The Senior American Medical Officer, Lt. Hughes, was permitted regular visits to the hospital to ascertain the well-being of the patients.

In December 1944 a new military hospital, consisting of three new brick and cement barracks, was made available in the camp. The surgical installation was complete, with rooms for dressing wounds, septic and antiseptic operation rooms, consultation room, laboratories, pharmacy and lounge for doctors and members of the sanitary personnel. The only complaint concerning the military hospital was that the rooms were inadequately heated, except for the room of post-operative cases and the one occupied by fever patients. In December 1944, 90 patients were in the military hospital, including a few serious cases (1 case of perforating appendicitis, 1 case of chronic nephritis and 1 case of tuberculosis of the bones); stomach ulcers were common in the stalag. The large number of anemia cases was due, according to the doctor, to undernourishment. Tonics for the undernourished as well as milk for the fever patients were needed. Cases of gastritis, cholecystitis and rheumatism were also frequent.

A small epidemic of diphtheria broke out in the camp in November 1944. In December 1944, there were three diphtheria patients and six germ carriers.

In conclusion, it can be said that the health of the men at Stalag 3B was good, and that the cooperation between the Germans and the American doctors in caring

for patients was excellent. There was practically no interference from the Germans with regard to the actual medical attendance and nursing of the sick in the camp. Although at times the medical supply was low, it always proved to be sufficient.

Clothing

In February 1944 the clothing situation in the base camp was good, due mostly to the arrival of shipments from the Red Cross. At this time, however, men on labor detachments were in need of clothing, such as working outfits. Each man owned a uniform and a few extra pieces. The same held true for the labor detachments, but in this case, extra clothing was necessary. Each man also owned a pair of shoes; a second pair was issued only when the first pair was obviously beyond wear.

In November 1944, PW felt they needed 2000 blankets, 8000 pairs of wool socks, 1500 pairs small-sized shoes, 4000 pairs of gloves and 1000 pairs of shoe soles, leather, nails and heels. They complained at this time of the confiscation of American clothing by the Germans in September, when 161 articles of clothing were discovered missing after a German search. The camp commandant stated that the clothing, and other articles confiscated, had come into the camp illegally and were justly confiscated. Furthermore, it was reported by the MOC that military clothing (jackets and trousers) were confiscated by the German security department from men arriving from other stalags, before admittance to Stalag 3B. The commandant stated that the clothing which was confiscated was excessive to the clothing marked on the men's clothing cards and that it must be considered as illegally obtained.

Clothes were taken from the warehouses of the Americans on the pretext that they must serve to clothe prisoners newly arrived at transit camps. The following objects were confiscated on 18 November 1944: 1604 belts, 340 pairs of stockings, 221 shirts, 517 sweaters, 1200 wool caps and 1140 shoe laces. The Americans had to turn over 1000 coats on 25 November 1944. On 4 December they were asked for 1000 pairs of shoes. After bargaining it was finally decided that they had to turn over to the Germans 100 pairs of shoes and 60 packages of food.

During early December the Germans requested the Americans to relinquish their field jackets. When the Americans refused the Germans backed up their demands with entrance into camp of reserve soldiers who, together with the guards, fixed bayonets and fired some shots into the air. However, almost simultaneously the PW, following the orders of MOC Casperich who had been warned of the expected seizure, ripped and tore the jackets beyond use because it was suspected the enemy wanted them for their own soldiers.

Generally speaking, at this time (in spite of the seizures) the American PW were well equipped; they lacked only coats and small tunics. In summary, it can be said that the PW were properly clothed at all times, but it must be noted that the Germans did not issue any clothing and that the men were kept warm only by the Red Cross clothing shipments into the camp.

Work

Five kommando detachments were dependent on Stalag 3B. In February 1944, 668 soldiers were employed in the construction of a power plant at No. 1 (Trattendorf); 14 volunteer NCOs were doing agricultural work at No. 2 (Schorbus); 67 soldiers were digging, building embankments and doing similar work for German railroads at No. 3 (Markisch-Heide); 27 NCOs were doing agricultural work at No. 4 (Schuhlen); and 14 NCOs were employed in agriculture at No. 7 (Roitz).

All NCOs were working voluntarily; no pressure was applied to make them work on kommandos. In the base camp, only the members of the sanitary personnel and a few hundred volunteers worked. Work was the hardest at Kommandos No. 1 and No. 3, where civilian overseers were sometimes extremely harsh.

Pay

Whether at the base camp or at the kommandos, workers received a minimum of 70 pfennings per day. The members of the sanitary personnel received 30 marks per month; the senior medical officer 96 marks. These amounts corresponded to German army pay, but were paid in "lagergeld" instead of German currency. The printing of the "lagergeld" stopped in the fall of 1944, when amounts due PW were supposedly credited to their accounts by the German Finance Office.

Mail

American PW received two letter forms and four postcards each month. There was no limit to the number of letters they could receive. Medical officers and members of the sanitary personnel were entitled to twice the amount above-mentioned. Letters took from three to four months to reach the United States after leaving the camp, and a reply took approximately the same length of time. The correspondence was censored in Berlin; the period of time elapsing between the arrival of a letter and its release by censorship was not in excess of a week.

In November 1944, all outgoing PW mail was stopped for a fortnight because one American had written an anonymous letter to a false address, insulting the German Reich, its Fuhrer and the camp authorities. As this man's name was never disclosed to the Germans the whole camp was punished by the above-mentioned measure taken by camp authorities.

Americans complained most about the fact that their families were regularly sending NOK packages and yet comparatively few were received during their incarceration.

Morale

Morale in Stalag 3B was good. PW were satisfied with the way the camp was being run by their elected officers, and eagerly awaited the day of liberation. As they were sure of an Allied victory, it can be said that the major detriment to their morale was the occasional lack of food.

Welfare

The American Red Cross and the YMCA performed an admirable task in looking after the welfare of the American PW. Art, sporting and recreational equipment furnished to the PW by the YMCA was gratefully accepted and put to good use. Morale was boosted by messages transmitted from their families to PW by the YMCA delegates.

Red Cross food kept the men from going hungry; and Red Cross clothing, from freezing. Influenza would have been widespread among the men in the winter had not the Red Cross supplied the PW both with blankets and medicines.

Approximately every three months, delegates of the International Red Cross and the Protecting Power visited the camp, at which time they made investigations of the conditions and listened to the complaints of the PW. Strong protests were made to the Germans when room was found for improvement in the existing conditions. Many attempts were made to better PW life, even though sometimes the delegates were powerless to aid the Americans. Representatives made reports to the State Department on the care of our PW by the Detaining Power.

"I'll never forget the Red Cross or the YMCA" (a common statement of gratitude made by the PW at Stalag 3B), is testimonial to their interest in the welfare of American PW.

Religion

One barrack provided space for a theatre at one end, a chapel on the other and a library in the center. The inside of the chapel was built entirely by the PW with material from the Red Cross: crates, paper, cans, etc. The chapel was attractively decorated by numerous PW draftsmen and painters.

A Polish Catholic priest, Father Walter Samolewicz, interned at Ilag 7Z (Tittmoning), held divine services at the camp. Private Richard Gray, a member of the sanitary personnel, acted as Protestant chaplain. PW were quite satisfied with this arrangement.

Germans never interfered with religious activities.

Recreation

As mentioned above, a large barrack housed a theatre, a library and a chapel. Concerts and lectures were held in this building. The library contained 10,600 books, many of which were sent to labor detachments. Cpl. Edward P. Tryor was librarian.

Exercise was obtained through occasional walks, baseball, football, basketball, volleyball and other sports, equipment for which was furnished by the YMCA. Indoors, PW played table tennis, cards, checkers and other games. They established a glee club and choir as well as a 17-piece orchestra. Instruments were furnished by the YMCA. Original productions were presented semi-monthly or monthly in the theatre built by the PW. Twice-weekly quiz contests helped to enliven the monotonous routine. Art equipment was also furnished by the YMCA for those who desired to work along that line.

Educational courses were offered in German, Agriculture and Spanish for the benefit of the PW. The school, however, was not well attended.

Until late 1944, beer could sometimes be bought by PW at the canteen, which usually was very low on other stock.

Evacuation On 31 January 1945, 5000 PW from Stalag 3B were marched west on two hours' notice. They had not expected the move. Roads were jammed with refugees and troops, and PW at Stalag 3B had expected to be left there until overrun by the Russians. At 1500 hours they were told to be ready to move in two hours. Actually, it was three or four hours later before they left the camp, and then they spent two more hours outside before the movement got underway. Each man had one-half of a Red Cross parcel issued three or four days before the march started, but no food was on hand at the start of the march. Although ample stocks of Red Cross parcels were kept at Guben, a few miles away, the Germans made no effort to bring them to Stalag 3B for distribution. On the first day the column marched until 1700 hours, 1 February, 24 consecutive hours from the time they had been alerted to move. This long march was made through snow, ice and deep puddles. PW were then jammed into small barns to sleep. The next seven days they completed their march to Stalag 3A (Luckenwalde), 108 kilometers west of Furstenberg, arriving 7 February 1945. For food during the march they had a total of one-half loaf of bread and one-half pound of cheese per man plus one ration of soup distributed once to one-half the men. Horse carts followed the column and picked up PW too sick to keep up with the column. On the march the guards were guilty of no brutality, and sympathized with PW.

Liberation The PW remained in Stalag 3A until 22 April, when the camp was liberated by the Russians. Stalag 3A was turned over to the Americans on 6 May at which time Lt. Col. Walter M. Oakes and a Col. Harte of the American PW took over the camp.

-XXX-

STALAG 7A.

(Ground Force Enlisted Men
Air Force Officer Evacuees)

Location — Stalag 7A was in Bavaria 35 kilometers northeast of Munich and one kilometer north of Moosburg (48°27' North Latitude, 11°57' East Longitude).

Strength — This installation served several purposes: It was the camp for NCO's of the U. S. Air Force until 13 October 1943 when all 1900 were transferred to Stalag 17B. It was the transit camp from which officers and men of the ground forces captured in Africa and Italy were routed to permanent camps. It was headquarters for working parties of ground force privates who numbered 270 in September 1943, dropped to nil the following month and rose to 1100 in July 1944. As Germany collapsed in the spring of 1945, it became the final gathering place for no fewer than 7948 officers and 6944 enlisted men moved from other PW camps.

Description — Situated in a flat area surrounded by hills, the camp was roughly a square divided into three main compounds which in turn were subdivised into small stockades. The Nordlager held newly arrived PW two days while they were searched, medically examined and deloused. The Suedlager held only Russians. The Hauptlager housed PW of other nationalities - French, Polish, Jugoslav (Serb), British and American. Although nationalities were segregated by compounds, intercommunication existed. No effort was made to keep transient American PW from the permanent inmates. Seven guard towers and the usual double barbed wire fence formed the camps perimeter.

Barracks were rectangular wooden buildings divided into two sections, A and B, by a central room used for washing and eating. In it were a water faucet, and water pump and some tables. The barracks chief and assistant had a small corner room to themselves. PW slept on triple-deck wooden bunks and gunny-sack mattresses filled with excelsior. Gradually the number of men per barracks increased from 150 to 400. Men slept on tables, floors and the ground.

U. S. Personnel — Because of the camp's shifting population, leaders were changed frequently. Among them were:

MOC Cpl. Charles Daramus	February 1943
MOC S/Sgt. Earl Benson	March 1943
MOC S/Sgt. Clyde M. Bennett	March 1943
MOC S/Sgt. Kenneth J. Kurtenbach	July-Oct 1943
MOC M/Sgt. John H. McMahon	June-Sept 1943
MOC S/Sgt. James P. Caparel	Oct 1943 - Feb 1944
MOC T/Sgt. Philip M. Beeman	Feb 1944 - Apr 1945

SAO Col. A. Y. Smith (AAF) Feb - Mar 1945
SAO Col. Paul R. Goode April 1945

Chaplain 1st Lt. Eugene L. Daniel Feb 1944 - Apr 45

Major Fred H. Beaumont, Medical Corps
Captain Gordan Keppel, Medical Corps
Captain Louis Salerno, Medical Corps
1st Lt. James Godfrey, Medical Corps
Captain Garrold R. Hungester, Medical Corps

German Personnel

The guard was drawn from the Fourth Company of the 512th Landesschuetzen Battalion. Four officers and 200 men were employed on general duties. Ten sonderfuehrers with the rank of officers acted as interpreters. Twenty civilian men and 20 civilian women were employed as clerks in the camp. This complement was increased in April 1945 with the arrival of the entire camp staff and guard personnel of Stalag Luft 3, Nurnberg. Control of the camp, however, remained in the hands of the regular Stalag 7A staff:

Commandant	- Oberst Burger
Asst. Commandant	- Oberstleutnant Wohler
Security officer	- Hauptman Baumler
Doctor	- Oberfeldarzt Dr. Zeitzler
Lager officer	- Hauptman Malheuim
Parcel officer	- Sonderfuehrer Kluge

It has been reported by some PW that Burger, Malheuim and Kluge, a fanatic of the worst sort, were shot three days after the camp's liberation.

Treatment

German treatment was barely correct. In addition to harsh living conditions caused by extreme overcrowding, instances of mistreatment occasionally cropped up. Thus, at one time the Germans tried to segregate all Jews among U. S. PW, calling them in from work detachments and allotting them a separate barrack. The MOC lodged a protest with the Protecting Power immediately. When questioned, camp authorities stated that the action was taken for the Jews' own protection against possible civilian acts of violence. Eventually, the attempt at segregation failed and Jews were not distinguished from other American PW.

At the Munich kommando, guards jabbed PW with bayonets and hit them with rifle butts. In the base camp an NCO reported being kicked, then being mistaken for a Frenchman and choked during an argument and later handcuffed after an escape attempt. Once an American, using a hole in the fence instead of the open gate to go from one compound to another, was shot at but not hit. In April 1943 a Russian was shot on the compound wire and left hanging there wounded. An Englishman went to lift him off the wire and was shot but recovered. The Russian died.

In July 1943, 500 Americans without overcoats were forced to stand in formation for five hours in a heavy rain. The reasons, said the Germans, was that the Americans had not been falling out at exactly 0800. During the first two weeks of August, the camp discipline officer had the PW fall out for roll call at 2100, 2400 and 0300. They were punished thus because many Americans had been escaping. PW showed no annoyance and displayed such good morale that the Germans discontinued the practice, especially since both sides knew that the PW could sleep all day but the guards could not.

Sonderfuehrer Kluge once marched 1100 PW for a whole day without food through Nurnberg so they could see the devastation wrought by Allied bombing.

In September 1943 when PW ventured out of the barracks to watch the bombing of Munich, Germans came into the compound with dogs, one of which jumped into a window and was stabbed by a retreating American. During the Regensburg raid when PW were again outside their barracks contrary to orders, a German night fighter flying over the camp reported that someone in the American compound was signaling with a mirror. After that PW were notified that anyone outside the barracks during an air raid would be shot. One night a JU 88 with lights on made two runs over the camp and dropped cement blocks. Germans then started propagandizing to the effect that the Allies were bombing their own PW camps.

Food

Here too PW depended on Red Cross food for sustenance and nourishment. Until September 1944, each PW drew his full parcel per week, and a two months' reserve was kept on hand in camp. Then the ration was cut to half a parcel per man per week and the reserve not allowed to exceed one month's supply. With the influx of PW in the beginning of 1945, stocks fell to an all time low. PW feared a complete collapse in the delivery of Red Cross food. Fortunately, this fear never materialized.

In July 1943, the MOC persuaded the Germans to issue each man a spoon and crockery plate. Cooking utensils were improvised from whatever materials could be found. Fifteen or 20 men formed mess groups, pooled their Red Cross rations and took turns in preparing them. They cooked over the small barrack's stove. Each barrack had two men on the chow detail, and the space around each stove was therefore quite crowded. At 0630 the detail brought hot water from the compound kitchen. Breakfast usually consisted of coffee and a few biscuits only. At 1130 they brought the German dinner ration - usually potatoes boiled in their

jackets - from the kitchen. Sometimes spinach-type greens or barley soup were added. Five men divided one loaf of coarse German-issue bread. For supper at 1700, PW drew more potatoes. On Sundays they received greens with morsels of meat. Twice a week they had a small piece of margarine. At first, French cooks prepared the food in the compound kitchen, but since Americans thought some of the victuals disappeared in the process, they later installed their own cooks.

Health

Health was good. Several American doctors, captured early in the African and Italian campaigns accompanied PW to Stalag 7A and were able to remain with them until their transfer to permanent camps. The camp also had some British doctors and some French. Men reported to the dispensary and if deemed ill enough for hospitalization were kept in the compound infirmary which could accomodate 120 patients in 10 rooms. More serious cases went to the German camp lazaret outside the compound. This installation consisted of eight barrack-type buildings, two of which were equipped for surgical operations.

Allied doctors complained of a serious shortage of medical supplies. At first they used German drugs and such equipment as they could get. Later the Red Cross sent supplies which alleviated the shortage but did not satisfy the doctors' demands.

Despite delousings, lice and fleas troubled PW a great deal. Americans, however, unlike the Russians, never contracted typhus. For a time they suffered from skin diseases brought about by uncleanliness; washing facilities were completely unsatisfactory and a man was extremely lucky to take a shower every 15 days.

Latrines were always a source of contention between PW and camp authorities. Complaint was constantly made that the pits were emptied only when they threatened to overflow and that there was no chloride of lime to neutralize the odor which permeated the surrounding area.

Emergency dental treatment could be obtained in the German lazaret.

Clothing

Since the Germans issued practically no clothing and the flow of needy transients through camp was heavy, the clothing shortage was always acute. From February 1943 on, the reports of the Protecting Power repeatedly carried such paragraphs as the following: The general condition of clothing is very bad. The American Red Cross should send out clothing in sufficient quantities as the cold season is approaching. Great coats and whole uniforms are badly wanted. The supply of uniforms issued by the Detaining Power is 12

mainly old French or British uniforms in a state of mending which leaves no hope for long wear.

Clothing from the Red Cross did arrive, but not in sufficient quantity to provide for equipping newly captured PW who were wearing only the clothes in which they were captured and sometimes not even those. It was observed by a Man of Confidence that four warehouses in camp contained many new English overcoats and battle-dress outfits as well as many articles of American clothing taken from PW as they entered the camp or left it. These included aviators' leather jackets, American coveralls, combat jackets, pants, shoes, hats and shirts. It was believed by the Man of Confidence that the clothing in storage was more than enough to alleviate the suffering of both American and British PW, yet all pleas and efforts to have the Germans ameliorate the situation were to no avail.

Work

The original group of air force PW - comprised almost exclusively of NCO's - was not ordered to work, nevertheless, before going to Stalag 17B many volunteered for kommando duty merely to get on the other side of the compounds barbed wire and have more liberty. On the other hand, Germans insisted that ground force privates be assigned to labor details. Camp authorities tried to have PW volunteer for duties - a practice which the MOC advised against except in the case of farm work, which was less unpleasant than other kommando duty.

Attached to the camp were as many as 83 work detachments ranging in size from four men (usually sent out to farms) to 900 men. The three main kommandos were situated in Munich, Augsburg and Landshutt. After the heavy bombing of Munich on October 4, 1944, a work detachment of some 1400 PW was formed. This party consisted of 60% Americans and 40% British. It left the Stalag at 0500 and returned at 2000. PW traveled in cattle cars from Moosburg station, standing up all the way to Munich and back. The time spent in the train going to and returning from work was three and one-half hours. During their eight working hours a day, PW cleared debris, filled bomb craters and dismantled damaged rails. Men received two meals at Munich and their regular ration at the camp. In the event of air attacks, adequate shelter was provided. There were instances of Germans pricking with bayonets and hitting them with rifle butts to make them work faster and harder.

A model farm kommando was described as follows: Twenty PW live in a farmhouse of five rooms, including a room with a stove for the cooking of Red Cross food. They sleep in three of the rooms in double-tier beds with straw mattresses and eiderdowns. Bathing and toilet facilities are primitive but similar to those used by their employer. The

men sometimes eat with the farmer for whom they work and their diet, supplemented with Red Cross food, is good. Medical supplies for minor injuries are on hand and a civilian doctor takes sick parade twice a week. PW each possess two work uniforms, a dress uniform and two pair of shoes. Fourteen of the men are free on Sundays; the others do the essential farmwork, namely feeding cattle and cleaning stables. Razor blades, beer and matches are available. PW have neither time nor facilities for sports. The mail situation is satisfactory except for the pilfering of parcels en route from the stalag to the detachment.

On only three occasions was the Man of Confidence permitted to visit kommando camps for inspection. Although he turned in complaints, no improvement in conditions resulted.

Pay

In March 1943, it was reported that the matter of paying officers had not yet been settled between PW and camp authorities. In the same month, an American enlisted man on kommando was paid the equivalent of $13.00 a month. Another worker revealed that the wage rate of .70 Reichmarks a day. In July this was increased to .90 Reichmarks a day.

In April 1944, an advance of 50 Reichmarks was made to officer PW of the Allies, but in April 1945, the Senior British officer stated that officers were not being paid and that they had not received any pay statements for seven months. Similarly, the 1400 man kommando working daily in the debris of Munich was not paid because the labor performed by them was considered by the Germans to be "emergency" labor to which anyone resident in the Reich was subject without pay.

In October 1944 it was announced that PW pay, which up to that time had been in camp money or "lagergeld" would henceforth be in Reichmarks.

Mail

During their stay at camp, transient PW were allowed to send one postcard, usually their first, in which they informed next-of-kin of their German PW number and address. PW permanently at 7A drew two post cards and two letter forms per month. Incoming mail, censored at camp, was unlimited in quantity but sporadic in arrival, especially at kommandos, which received no incoming mail for months at a time. Both outgoing and incoming letters took four months in transit, as did personal parcels. The flow of such parcels was light.

On 10 November 1944, four French PW were employed to unload coal into a bunker of the German barracks situated in the vicinity of the camp. They found

that a large number of both official and private letters and cards were scattered in the coal. They picked up several loose letters as well as bunches tied together in small packages. Part of the letter included official letters addressed to the spokesmen of the different nationalities represented in the camp, coming from the Red Cross, the YMCA and other organizations. The next morning the French, British and American spokesmen went to the Commandant's office to protest and demand explanations as well as the restitution of the mail after inspection of the bunker in question. The following day, the camp commandant made it known that he would take charge of the affair personally. After a hasty censorship, a considerable number of letters (two sacks weighing 88 pounds apiece) were delivered to PW. These letters dated from the months of May, June and July 1944. It was impossible to say how long they had been in the coal. The commandant stated that an error had been made and that punishment would be inflicted, but that no letter had been burned.

The assistant American MOC was under the impression that mail - including outgoing letters - definitely had been burned. This impression was strengthened after the incident when the Germans issued additional new letter forms.

<u>Morale</u>

Initially morale was high. Air force NCO's repeatedly made breaks from camp, and before their transfer to Stalag 17B showed their hostility toward the Germans by often refusing to salute, by failing to come to attention when a German officer entered the barracks and by their careless, slouching, hands-in-pocket walk.

After their sojourn in camps in Italy, ground force PW captured in 1942-43 were pleasantly surprised by the treatment accorded them in Stalag 7A which had been a model camp for several years.

In spite of a succession of able camp leaders, morale slumped when the camp grew so crowded that PW had neither decent living quarters, nor satisfactory sanitary facilities nor sufficient clothing. Early in 1944 the MOC reported that stealing among PW was common and that fights were inevitable. However, except for a period of three weeks in December 1944, the strongest morale factor - food - was available. In the spring of 1945, although the camp was more crowded than ever, morale did not slump. Red Cross food kept coming through, and the arrival of officers with strong, experienced SAO's did much to prevent the spirit of PW from disintegrating.

Welfare

A representative of the Protecting Power made a routine visit to the camp every six months. In addition he would make a special trip whenever summoned. NCO's were permitted to talk to him privately, but despite oral and written protests about both general and specific affairs of the camp, very little improvement was ever effected. The representatives repeatedly said that his hands were tied and there was nothing he could do about it. One NCO felt that the representatives were characterized by indifference and inertia until the arrival of American officers in the camp. Subsequently, their attitude changed for the better.

PW were indebted to the Red Cross for almost all their food, clothing and medical supplies. While food parcels arrived regularly and in sufficient quantity most of the time, the camp suffered a constant clothing shortage since the stocks shipped from Geneva were not enough to equip the many thousands of transient PW who passed through the camp every few months.

The first groups of PW arriving in camp reported the presence of recreational and athletic equipment which had come from the YMCA. Later, however, as the stalag evolved into a transit camp and work camp, need for such equipment was less evident and little was received.

Religion

In 1943-44, Camp chaplain was 1st Lt. Eugene L. Daniel who won the admiration of both Americans and British. He had complete liberty to look after PW in the stalag, and once a month went to visit the two work detachments near Munich. He also received permission to visit the Wehrkreis PW hospital. In addition to Chaplain Daniel, Captain Arkell of the Church of England held services for Protestants.

Roman Catholics were permitted to attend weekly masses celebrated by French priests.

Jews were for a time segregated in separate barracks. Otherwise they were not discriminated against. Nor were they offered any religious services.

Conditions on kommandos varied. A few were visited by PW chaplains or attended local services, but most had no opportunity for religious observances.

Recreation

Before their transfer to 17A, the air force NCO's main diversions were baseball and bridge. They also played a good deal of volley ball. For a time they had a basketball court, but tore down the backboards for fuel. They also played horseshoes. A Camp baseball league had many games between the "POWs", "Wildcats", "Bomber Aces", "Luftgangsters",

and so on. At first they were allowed to use the soccer field behind their compound, a privilege later denied them. PW lacked sufficient space for recreation, especially toward the end when the compound was so completely overcrowded that Italians were sleeping in tents on the baseball diamond.

The original study program included classes in Spanish, German, French, auto mechanics, economics, bookkeeping, accounting, and mathematics. The YMCA furnished the books for these courses.

A theater kept its 1943 participants interested and its audience amused. Plays were given in a room between two barracks, and because of the limited accommodations, a show could have quite an extended run. The program was well arranged to provide continued and varied entertainment. One of the plays was "Our Town". Another was one written by the director of the group and called, "Uncle Sam Wants You". The German censor cut some of the jokes from this piece, but he did not understand most of them. The camp commandant attended one performance. There were also a minstrel show and some singing performances. When the camp became so crowded during the fall of 1943, a group of men used to go from barracks to barracks to sing each night. The band was short of instruments.

In 1944 and 1945, conditions deteriorated. Ground force enlisted men indulged in little or no sports or recreation either because there was too little equipment for the transients or because as regular members of kommandos they were too tired after the day's work to play.

Influx

On 2 February 2000 officers of the South Compound, Stalag Luft 3, reached Stalag 7A, followed on 7 February by 2000 more from the Center Compound. They were placed in the Nordlager from which small groups were taken to be searched, deloused and sent to the main camp. No facilities were provided for washing, sanitation, cooking and only straw spread over the floors of the barracks served as bedding. In somewhat less than a week, all personnel had moved to the main camp, where conditions were little better

Over 300 men were housed in barracks normally holding fewer than 200 men. In order to provide bunks for this number in each building, the Germans arranged three-decker in groups of four, thus accommodating 12 PW per unit. The barracks had no heat and as a result were damp, cold and unhealthful. The German administration was unprepared for the influx of new personnel and seemed completely disorganized. German rations were unbelievably poor;

no inside sanitary facilities existed and there was no hot water. The 2000 PW of the Center Compound were quartered in two adjacent but separate stockades some distance from the enclosure holding their mates from the South Compound. At the rear of the barracks in each of the two stockades, a small open area - barely large enough to hold the various units for counting - was available for exercise. Aside from this, no facilities were provided for physical training or athletics. Nor was there any recreational material other than books in a traveling library provided by the YMCA.

In March the Germans provided boilers and fuel enough to allow each man to draw a pint of hot water twice daily. In order to improve the quantity and quality of German rations issued to Americans, Colonel Archibald Y. Smith, SAO, made a continuous effort to place an American officer and several enlisted men in the German kitchen. This was finally accomplished 24 March and henceforward rations improved steadily. The German administration also consented to allow groups of 50 men under guard to gather small quantities of firewood in the area adjacent to the camp. These improvements, although falling far short of the provisions of the Geneva Convention, helped a great deal to improve the mental and physical state of all the PW. During all of this period Red Cross food, initially on a half-parcel basis, was increased to full parcels and the health of the PW remained remarkably good. By this time, too, news of the Allied advances acted as a tonic on the men.

The first of April saw many PW from other camps throughout Germany evacuated to the vicinity of Stalag 7A to prevent their recapture by Allied forces pressing toward the center of the Reich. This influx brought about a state of unbelievable overcrowding and confusion. Members of the former South Compound were moved en masse into the enclosure occupied by the Center Compound. Thus 4000 PW lived in an area which had been unable to support 2000 satisfactorily. Large tents were erected in whatever space was available; straw was provided as bedding. It was not uncommon to see men sleeping on blankets in foxholes. Col. Paul R. Goode became SAO upon the arrival of officers from Oflag 64 in mid-April. Air Force officers from Nurnberg arrived on 19 April. During the last 10 days of April it was felt that all PW would be left in camps, following the agreement between the German Government and the Allies, and preparations were made accordingly. However, fear that the Germans would move PW to the Salzburg redoubt and there hold them as hostages was never absent.

Liberation

On 27 April two representatives of the Protecting Power arrived at Moosburg to attend and facilitate the transfer of the PW camp from German to American authority. On the 28th it was learned from Oberst Burger, the commandant, that order was to be assured by assigning PW officers to various PW groups. Moreover, Col. Burger kept the entire German administrative staff in camp, as well as the complete guard staff. Col. Burger had not yet received from the German military authorities a reply to his question concerning the avoidance of fighting in the vicinity of the camp. The commandant asked the two Swiss to act as intermediaries between himself and the Men of Confidence.

After a conference with the Men of Confidence, the two Swiss were recalled to the commandant. It appeared that the unexpectedly rapid advance of the American forces in the region necessitated an immediate conference between the camp authorities, represented by Oberst Braune, and the local German Army Corps Commandant in order to propose the exclusion of fighting from the Moosburg region. The proposal, made by Oberst Braune and the Swiss representative, was accepted in view of Article 7 of the Geneva Convention. Appropriate instructions were given to the commander of the division in the sector in question, and the proposal was formulated for presentation to the advancing Americans. According to this proposal, an area of a few kilometers around Moosburg would have to be declared a neutral zone.

At dawn on the 29th, the American and British Men of Confidence, the Swiss representative and an officer from the SS fighting division in the region drove in a white Red Cross car to the American lines. They were stopped by two tanks commanded by a colonel who drove them to the commanding general. After a long discussion with the German spokesman, the general declared the proposal unfavorable and unacceptable. The German returned to his divisional headquarters and the Swiss then drove to camp with the Men of Confidence.

At 1000, immediately after their arrival, the battle started. The ensuing fight lasted some two and a half hours, during which a shell hit one of the camp barracks injuring 12 of the guards and killing one. PW remained calm although tank shots, machine guns and small arms fire could be heard. Half an hour after the fighting abated, Combat Team A of the 14th Armored Division appeared at the camp entrance. The guards, unresisting, were disarmed. PW burst out rejoicing but did not try to leave camp. The supervision of the camp automatically went to the Men of Confidence, and an official transfer did not take place.

By instruction of the American military commander, part of the German administrative personnel remained at their posts. The remainder, including the guards, were taken as PW. The Swiss reported that treatment of German camp authorities and guards by American troops was correct.

- X X X -

STALAG 9B

(Ground Force Privates
Captured in the "Bulge")

<u>Location</u>

Stalag 9B was situated in the outskirts of Bad Orb (50°14' N. - 9°22' E.) in the Hessen-Nassau region of Prussia, 51 kilometers northwest of Frankfurt-on-Main.

<u>Strength</u>

On 17 December 1944, 985 PW captured during the first two days of the German counter-offensive, were marched for four days from Belgium into Germany. During this march, they received food and water only once. The walking wounded received no attention except such first aid as American medical personnel in the column could give them. They reached Gerolstein and were packed into boxcars, 60 men to the car. The cars were so small that the men could not lie down. PW entered the cars on 21 December and did not get out until 26 December. En route, they were fed only once. Eight men seeking to escape jumped into a field and were killed by an exploding land mine. The German sergeant in charge, enraged that anyone had attempted escape, began shooting wildly. Although he knew that every car was densely packed with PW, he fired a round through the door of a car, killing an American soldier. The day after Christmas, the men arrived at Bad Orb.

On 25 January the camp reached its peak with 4070 American enlisted men. The following day 1275 NCO's were transferred to Stalag 9A, Ziegenhain. On 26 February 1000 privates left Stalag 12A, Limburg, for Bad Orb. They marched in a column which averaged 25 miles a day. On leaving, they were given one-half a loaf of bread and a small cheese for the five-day march. No medical supplies were available; men who collapsed were left behind under guard. PW had no blankets and some had only a shirt and pair of trousers for clothing. Their arrival, plus that of other PW, brought the camp strength to 3333 on 1 April 1945.

<u>Description</u>

From 290 to 500 PW were jammed into barracks of the usual one-story wood and tarpaper types, divided into two sections with the washroom in the middle. Washroom facilities consisted of one cold water tap and one latrine hole emptying into an adjacent cesspool which had to be shoveled out every few days. Each half of the barracks contained a stove. Throughout the winter the fuel ration was two arm loads of wood per stove per day, providing heat for only one hour a day. Bunks, when there were bunks,

were triple-deckers arranged in groups of four. Three barracks were completely bare of bunks and two others had only half the number needed with the result that 1500 men were sleeping on the floors. PW who were fortunate received one blanket each, yet at the camp's liberation some 30 PW still lacked any covering whatsoever. To keep warm, men huddled together in groups of three and four. All barracks were in a state of disrepair; roofs leaked; windows were broken; lighting was either unsatisfactory or lacking completely. Very few barracks had tables and chairs. Some bunks had mattresses and some barrack floors were covered with straw, which PW used in lieu of toilet paper. The outdoor latrines had some forty seats - a number totally insufficient for the needs of 4000 men. Every building was infested with bedbugs, fleas, lice and other vermin.

<u>U.S. Personnel</u> Pfc. J. C. F. Kasten was Man of Confidence, assisted by Pvt. Edmund Pfennenstiel who spoke German fluently. When Pfc. Kasten was sent out on a kommando working party, the barracks leaders suggested that Pvt. Pfennenstiel succeed him. Pvt. Pfennenstiel refused to take the post, however, until the barracks leaders had consulted PW in their charge and gained their approval. Subsequently, he was an extremely able MOC. His assistant was Pfc. Ben F. Dodge. Other important members of the staff were:

Captain O. C. Buxton	Medical Corps
1st Lt. J. P. Sutherland	Medical Corps
Captain M. A. Eder	Dental Corps
1st Lt. S. R. Neel	Chaplain
1st Lt. E. J. Hurley	Chaplain

<u>German Personnel</u> Noteworthy members of the German complement are listed below:

Oberst Sieber	Commandant
Oberstleutnant Waerg	Deputy Commandant
Hauptmann Horn	Camp Officer
Hauptmann Kuhle	Lager Officer
Sonderfuhrer Bonnkirch	Welfare Officer
Gefreiter Weiss	Interpreter
Pvt. Wolfgang Dethe	Mess Guard

It was Hauptmann Kuhle who permitted American PW to replace Russians in the camp kitchen and Pvt. Dethe who cajoled them illegally to appropriate extra rations. Gefreiter Weiss, at great personal risk, informed the MOC as to the progress of the war and daily located the position of advancing American troops on maps which he smuggled in to the American PW.

After a 23 March 1945 visit the Swiss Delegate reported, "In spite of the fact that it is difficult to obtain any kind of material to improve conditions, it is most strongly felt that the camp commander with his staff have no interest whatsoever in the welfare of the prisoners of war. This is clearly shown by the fact that although he made many promises on our last visit, he has not even tried to ameliorate conditions and is apt to blame the Allies for these conditions due to their constant bombing."

Treatment

In a report describing Stalags 9A, 9C and 9B, which he visited 13 March 1945, the Representative of the International Red Cross stated, "The situation may be considered very serious. The personal impression which one gets from an inspection tour of these camps cannot be described. One discovers distress and famine in their most terrible forms. Most of the prisoners who have come here from the territories of the East, and those who still continue to come, are nothing but skin and bones. Very many of them are suffering from acute diarrhea with bloody phlegm due to their complete exhaustion. Pneumonia, dorsal and bronchial cases are very common.

The prisoners who have been in camp for a long time are often also so thin that those whom one had known previously can hardly be recognized.

These prisoners, in rags, covered with filth and infested with vermin, live crowded together in barracks, when they do not lie under tents, squeezed together on the ground on a thin pallet of dirty straw or two or three per cot, or on benches and tables. Some of them are scarcely able to get up, or else they fall in a swoon as they did when they tried to get up when the Representative was passing through. They do not move, even at meal time, when they are presented with their inadequate German rations (for example 9B has been completely without salt for weeks).

Food

When the Americans arrived the Kitchen was in charge of Russian PW under the lax supervision of German guards. Sanitary conditions in the kitchen were foul and the soup prepared was practically inedible. When the MOC was permitted to substitute American PW for the Russian help, there resulted a considerable improvement in the preparation of the meager prison fare. The eight bushels of potatoes which German Pvt. Bathe enabled the Americans to steal was most necessary since the German ration was terribly slight. It consisted of 300 grams of bread, 550 grams of potatoes, 30 grams of horse meat, 1/2 litre of tea and 1/2 litre of soup made from putrid greens. The greens made the men sick, and the MOC intervened

to have the allotment of greens changed to oatmeal. Later, even this small ration was cut so that at the end of their stay PW were receiving only 210 grams of bread and 290 grams of potatoes per day. The MOC was convinced that a larger ration was available and attributes its non-distribution to Oberst Sieber, the commandant. The full ration listed above was the minimum German civilian ration minus fresh vegetables, eggs and whole milk. No German soldier was so ill fed.

A thousand men lacked eating utensils of any kind - either spoons, forks or bowls. They ate out of their helmets or old tin cans or pails - anything on which they could put their hands.

Only one shipment of Red Cross food reached camp, 2300 parcels on 10 March 1945. Failure of another shipment to arrive from Geneva was attributed to the chaotic transportation conditions within Germany.

The German rations had a paper value of 1400 calories. Actually, the caloric content was even further lowered by the waste in using products of inferior quality. Since a completely inactive man needs at least 1700 calories to live, it is apparent that PW were slowly starving to death.

<u>Health</u>

In the month between 28 February and 1 April, 32 Americans died of malnutrition and pneumonia. Medical attention was in the care of the two American medical officers and 10 American medical orderlies. On 23 March the infirmary held 72 patients, 22 of whom were pneumonia cases. The others suffered from malnutrition and dysentery. Influenza, grippe and bronchitis were common throughout the camp. No medical parcels were received from the Red Cross and the extreme scarcity of medicines furnished by the Germans contributed to deaths of PW who otherwise might have been saved. The MOC considered it fortunate in light of the exposure, starvation and lack of medical facilities, that more PW did not die.

<u>Clothing</u>

Instead of issuing clothing, the German confiscated it from PW. Upon being captured many men were forced to give up everything they were not wearing, such extra items as shoes, overshoes, blankets and gloves. Some had only shirts and trousers, no jackets. Others lacked shoes and bundled their feet in rags. At Limburg and elsewhere en route from the front, Germans took Americans' overcoats with the result that as late as the last week of March one-fifth of the PW had none.

No clothing came from the Red Cross because of the transportation breakdown.

<u>Work</u>

On 8 February 350 of the physically fit PW were sent to a work detachment in the Leipzig district. Other men at the camp were forced to carry out the stalag housekeeping chores. Until Pvt. Pfennenstiel became MOC, German guards had marched into the camp and taken the first men in sight for necessary camp details. This resulted in considerable inequity since they not infrequently took the same men time after time. The MOC arranged to take care of all details through men physically fit to work and subsequently furnished a daily work roster to the Germans.

<u>Pay</u>

In December 1944 en route to Bad Orb, PW were lined up at Waxweiler and forced to give up all money in their possession. About $10,000 was taken from the 985 men by the German lieutenant in charge and no receipts given.

Since the issue of "lagergeld" had been abolished, no money was paid to officer or NCO's. The amount due them was credited by the Germans to their accounts every month, to be settled at the war's end. Non-working privates received no pay.

<u>Mail</u>

No incoming mail was received. The issue of letter-forms was irregular and haphazard, but each PW was permitted to mail home a form postcard informing NOK of his status.

<u>Morale</u>

Morale fell rapidly under the brutalizing conditions and by March the majority of men were absolutely broken in spirit, crushed and apathetic. The Swiss delegate emphasized the fact that even American and British PW asked for food like beggars.

<u>Welfare</u>

The Protecting Power inspectors visited the camp on 24 January and 23 March 1945, each time reporting the atrocious camp conditions and extracting promises from the commandant.

The International Red Cross representative wrote an extremely strong report decrying camp conditions as he saw them on 10 March 1945. That more Red Cross food and supplies did not reach camp must be attributed to the disruption of German transport.

For similar reasons, the YMCA was never able to visit the camp nor to supply recreational equipment.

<u>Religion</u>

Until 25 January, no room was available for either Catholic or Protestant services, although two chaplains were present in the camp. In February, however, the chaplains held regular services for both denominations and received the cooperation of German camp authorities.

When the MOC refused to single out Jews for segregation, a German officer selected those American PW who he thought were Jews and put them in a separate

barracks. No other discrimination was made against them.

Recreation From the end of December to the middle of January, PW were allowed to leave the barracks only between 0830 and 1700 hours; the rest of the time they were locked in. Outdoor recreation was non-existent because of PW's weakness. The British lazaret at Bad Soden sent over 32 books - the only volumes obtainable.

Proposed Evacuation Being informed of the rapid advance of the American forces, Pvt. Pfannenstiel began to prepare a camp organization to meet the contingencies of their arrival. Secretly, with the aid of the barrack leaders, he selected 500 of the most reliable men in the camp and made them military police, whose authority was to begin when the American troops arrived in the vicinity, at which time they were to maintain control and order within the camp. About the third week in March, the district commander ordered that 1500 of the men in Stalag 9B be marched eastward to another camp. When he received this order, subject protested that to march the men in their semi-starved condition was impossible. He realized that the Americans were close and wished to prevent the march by any means possible. The district commander met his protest by reducing the number demanded to 1000. Subject was told to choose the 1000 best fitted for the march. He then went to the German medical officer in charge of the camp and pointed out that there were a number of diphtheria and possibly typhus cases in the camp and that to march them off might spread an epidemic through the area covered by the march. He was successful in convincing the doctor who proceeded to slap a ten-day quarantine on the camp. By this means subject was able to prevent the movement of any of the American Pa/W until they were rescued by American forces.

Liberation Subject was attending church services in the camp at 1415 hours on Easter Sunday, 1 April 1945, when he was called out of the church. He suspected at this time that the Americans might be closing in on the camp. Sent by the camp commander to Bad Orb, a hospital town, he was taken to the major in command of the town hospitals. The major proposed that subject take a white flag and proceed to meet the American troops and guarantee the surrender of the town. This proposal strongly accorded with the wishes of the townspeople. Subject felt that an American soldier wandering around alone behind German lines carrying a white flag might have some trouble so he refused to go unless he was accompanied by two unarmed German officers. The major named two officers and with them subject proceeded toward the edge of town. By this time an American unit, rumored to be one of great size and power, had occupied the hill overlooking the town. As subject's party reached the edge of the town, it was stopped by the German, Major Fulkmann,

charged with the military defense of the town. Fulkmann denied having made any arrangement with the medical major for its surrender and refused to permit the party to proceed until he had consulted with the medical major.

At this time the German garrison opened up with small arms fire against the American position on the hill, and the Americans answered with machine guns. Subject's party was caught between the two fires. The German officer with him then walked down the street and told him to follow and keep cool. In the meantime the American firing, which had started high over his head, was getting lower and lower. Without much time to spare, the German officer and he managed to duck into an underground hospital. During the night the medical major and the major in command of the garrison met at the hospital to consult on what to do. In the meantime the Americans began firing artillery shells into the town. They dropped one shell regularly every 15 minutes. The medical major persuaded the garrison major that resistance was hopeless and the latter agreed to withdraw his troops. The withdrawal took place during the night and the next morning Pvt. Pfannenstiel's party again went forward with their white flag to meet the Americans.

They made contact on the edge of the town with Capt. Langley, commander of an American reconnaissance group of 200 men that had run 60 miles ahead of the main body of the American forces, and hours ahead of its own ammunition supply. By the time that the group entered Bad Orb with its tank guns and anti-tank weapons pointing fiercely in all directions, there was not a single round of artillery ammunition available to be fired from any of the guns. Subject borrowed a car and returned with some of the American soldiers to Stalag 9B. There everything was in order, the German guard unit remained and the camp commander turned over the control of the camp to the Americans. At about noon, American units of the main body began to pass through the town, and when they learned of the pitiful condition of the American Ps/W at Stalag 9B, the units, as they passed through, emptied their PX stores and sent them up to the prisoners. After several days, the American personnel at Stalag 9B were evacuated to camp Lucky Strike near Le Havre.

- X X X -

OFLAG 13 B

(Transit Camp For Evacuees)

<u>Location</u>

Oflag 13 B was situated in a rural district just outside of Hammelburg, Germany (50°05' N. - 9°54' E.), and formed a part of a complex consisting of other prisoner of war camps within a German military training center.

<u>Strength</u>

Approximately 300 American officers opened the camp on 11 January 1945, and by the time the Protecting Power visited the camp on 23 January 1945, the strength had increased to 453 officers, 12 non-commissioned officers and 18 privates. All of these men were captured on the Western Front between the 15th and 22nd of December 1944. By 25 March 1945, the strength had increased to 1291 officers and 127 enlisted men which included the 423 officers and 67 enlisted men who arrived from Oflag 64 at Schubin, Poland.

<u>Description</u>

The American compound was formerly occupied by Serbian officers and consisted of seven stone barracks of antiquated types. Soon after the opening of the camp as an American Oflag, the buildings received some badly needed repairs which made them livable. Approximately 200 men were crowded into each five-room barrack, and although ventilation and daylight were adequate, each room contained only two drop lights of 15 watt bulbs. During the extremely cold weather, the men tried to keep from freezing by putting on all available clothing and huddling around the one stove furnished to each room. For each stove, the Germans issued 48 coal briquets for three days. These briquets measured about 5" x 3" x 3". As a result of this small ration, the barrack temperature averaged about 30 degrees. At the insistence of the SAO, small details were permitted to "scrounge" for pieces of wood to supplement the fuel supply.

Wash rooms did not exist and the officers had to carry water from the kitchen faucet to the few wash basins supplied to each room. No hot water was available for washing because of the fuel shortage, and the delousing plant was not in operation for three full months. Toilet facilities were completely inadequate in type and number. Complaints about this were handled by the Protecting Power and some improvement was achieved.

<u>U.S. Personnel</u>

Upon the opening of the camp, Colonel Charles C. Cavender became the SAO, and he appointed Major Albert L. Berndt as the SNO. There were no other officers appointed to hold definite offices. However, when the evacuated officers of Oflag 64 arrived at the compound, Colonel Paul R. Goode

became the SAO and organized the camp on the same basis as the compound at Schubin, Poland. He used the Oflag 64 staff, but retained Major Berndt as the SMO.

<u>German Personnel</u> The German camp commander was Generalmajor von Goeckel, who had as his executive officer Oberst Giese. However, the block commander for the American officers' section was Hauptmann Fuchs. General von Goeckel was the commander of the entire military installation and delegated most of the prisoner of war administration to Oberst Giese.

<u>Treatment</u> Treatment was only fair. It must be pointed out the the camp was opened at the time of Germany's last offensive, the "Belgian Bulge". Soon after the opening of the camp it was apparent that this thrust was destined to fail, and strong feeling of tension between the American and German personnel existed. There were many Allied air raids in the vicinity, and the air alert system at the camp was rigid.

When an air alert was sounded, all POW were required to hurry to their barracks and were given only three minutes in which to clear the open areas between buildings. One evening a warning signal was given and about an hour later the second alarm was sounded. At this moment, four American officers were standing at the fence talking to some Serbian officers and were slow in leaving the fence. Just as they reached the steps of their barrack, and before the termination of the three-minute period, a guard saw them and fired at them. He was about 75 yards away, but he hit one of the officers in the back, piercing his lung and chest. The officer died the following day of the wounds.

When more and more air raids occurred and the rigidity of the air alert rules remained the same, it became necessary for the men to be confined to their barracks for six and seven hours at a time. The SAO complained to the German commandant that the lack of indoor toilet facilities and the long periods of confinement were detrimental to the health of the men. The commandant later rescinded the order, and gave permission for the men to go to the latrine. The following day, one of the officers left the building and walked toward the latrine. A guard yelled something at him in German which the PW did not understand, and the guard immediately shot him in the back of the head. This incident was witnessed by the camp commandant, General von Goeckel, Colonel Goode, and Major Berndt as they were approaching the area. When they reached the officer he was dead and the guard merely stated he did not know about the new rule.

There was one particular rule which caused a great deal of dissension between the Germans and Americans. The commandant issued orders that all Americans were required to salute all German officers first, regardless of their rank. Naturally, this rule was violated on many occasions and was always a subject of discussion between the SAO and the German officials. After the arrival of the officers from Oflag 64, the commandant was persuaded to revoke the order.

Food

When the camp first opened the ration had a "paper value" content of 1770 calories per day. This was below the normal requirement for men getting plenty of sleep and performing no work. The ration was cut several times until it contained only 1070 calories a day. Officers were allowed to purchase supplementary rations from the canteen when supplies were available. These usually consisted of cabbage, carrots and beets. There were no Red Cross packages delivered during the entire period, but the Serbian officers insisted on sharing with the American officers on a per capita basis all of the Red Cross food parcels received by Serbs. In all, approximately 1500 parcels were given to the Americans during the three months of the camp's operation.

The kitchen used by the Americans was suitably equipped, and the German rations were used to the best advantage. The extreme shortage of fuel hampered the preparation of the food, but after the wood-forage details were formed, this situation was improved.

The normal daily menu consisted of one-tenth of a loaf of bread, one cup of ersatz coffee, one bowl of barley soup, and one serving of a vegetable a day. About three times a week a small piece of margarine was issued, and occasionally a tablespoon of sugar. Toward the end of March, many officers were in a dangerous condition due to malnutrition, and the SMO credited the generosity of the Serbian officers with the saving of many lives.

Health

The health of the officers was not good. Many of the men arrived at the Oflag with wounds from the battlefield. Nearly all of them had been marched many miles in bitterly cold weather with insufficient food and rest. Few PW arrived at the camp in vehicles. The lack of a proper diet prevented quick recoveries from such minor ailments as colds, dysentery, trench feet and influenza. Therefore, men with serious wounds and illnesses had little chance of recovery without the assistance of the Serbian compound.

When the 27 medical officers of the compound were captured, their equipment and supplies were confiscated. However, some few drugs and instruments had been concealed and were smuggled into the camp. The 20-bed dispensary was on the second floor of a good brick building which also housed the medical personnel and the first-aid room. All of the rooms were well-lighted and clean. Every effort was made by the medical personnel to make the patients as comfortable as possible. The men who were seriously ill were treated in the adjoining lazaret which was a part of the Serbian Oflag. The Serbian lazaret contained 450 beds, and although there too the equipment was not good, the Serbian doctors had been in prison for about four years and were experienced in successfully treating a variety of "kriegy" ailments with makeshift medicines and equipment. Fortunately, surgical equipment was quite good; the head of the staff was a famous surgeon of outstanding ability.

Soon after the Americans arrived, the SMO of the Serbian compound assigned 60 beds for the exclusive use of Americans, and since "invalid" rations were issued there in addition to the other advantages offered, the men who were admitted to the lazaret had a better chance for recovery.

<u>Clothing</u>

There was no German stock of clothing and no Red Cross clothing was received while the camp was in operation. In the beginning, most of the men had complete uniforms, but lacked extra socks, sweaters and jackets. Shoes were in need of repair at all times and no repair equipment was furnished. Because of extreme cold and lack of fuel, the clothing shortage became a bitter hardship for everyone, and life at Oflag 13 B was reduced to getting enough food to keep well and finding ways and means to keep warm.

<u>Work</u>

The officers performed no work except camp details assigned by the SAO.

<u>Pay</u>

At the time the men were captured, their money was confiscated and a receipt given to each individual. Since there was no pay scale worked out, the men purchased supplies from the canteen on a debit and credit system, using their receipts as collateral. Prices in the canteen were exceptionally high, but by clever manipulation the officers were able to purchase adequate amounts when items were put on sale.

<u>Mail</u>

The outgoing mail was satisfactorily handled, and the usual three letter forms and three post cards per month were issued. However, no incoming mail was received during the camp's operation.

Morale — Morale at this camp was not high. When compared with long-established camps, there was little semblance of organization. The extremely bad conditions seemed to create a feeling of futility and carelessness. Several officers reported that this situation was improved after the arrival of the evacuees from Oflag 64. The example of military discipline, courtesy and personal cleanliness displayed by men who had been forced to march 345 miles through sub-zero and zero weather did a great deal toward raising the morale of the other officers. However, the complete lack of mail and the almost certain knowledge that their families had not been notified of their safety due to the large number of captives, contributed a great deal to the low morale of the PW.

Welfare — The first visit of the Protecting Power was made by accident. The Detaining Power had not notified the Protecting Power of the existence of the camp but on 22 January 1945, representatives of the Swiss legation arrived to inspect Stalag 13-C, and the adjoining Serbian compound in accordance with previous arrangements. When informed by the commandant of the Oflag 's opening, the representatives' request to visit the camp was approved. At that time there were many shortages. Many requisitions were made on the International Red Cross, but supplies were not received prior to the liberation of the camp. Another visit of the Protecting Power was made on 25 March 1945 when acute shortages were reported to the Red Cross again. No YMCA or Red Cross equipment was received by the camp, and the only benefits were received through the courtesy of the Serbian compound.

Religion — There were seven Protestant chaplains and two Roman Catholic priests in the camp, but since the room provided by the Germans for religious services was not heated attendance was small. Religious articles necessary for Catholic services were not available until the last of March.

Recreation — There was one room set aside as a "day-room", but again the lack of heating facilities prevented its becoming popular. The Serbians donated two ping-pong tables, cards and checker-boards while a small group of Australians located nearby donated a piano and some musical instruments. The "jam-session" became the only form of amusement which stimulated morale. For outdoor activity, there was room for only one sport...horse-shoe pitching, and this had few devotees. The lack of books, theatrical equipment, sports kits and art equipment made the dullness of captivity a constant source of discomfort.

Evacuation

On 27 March 1945, the SAO was notified that the camp would be evacuated that afternoon at 1600. At 1300, American tanks appeared and after a short consultation with the German officials, the SAO decided to surrender the camp to the task force. This force was 50 miles ahead of the main body of American troops and there were no facilities to transport the PW from the camp except on the tanks. The SAO divided the men into three groups: those who were not physically able to make the trip; those who would be able to walk beside the tanks; and those who would have to ride. Out of about 500 who tried to march, only 30 got through to the American lines. Those who rode on the tanks ran into strong enemy opposition, and all were either killed or recaptured. The following day some 500 were moved out by train to Nurnberg. All of the remaining able-bodied men were marched the 90 miles to Stalag 7A, Moosburg. The men who were sick in the lazaret and the infirmary along with the medical staff, remained behind.

Liberation

After the main evacuation from Hammelburg, the Germans left only a token guard around the camp to pick up the American stragglers from the first "liberation", and to guard the Serbians who were not evacuated. The guard company that had made the march from Schubin, Poland, with the members of Oflag 64 was used for the movement of the troops to Nurnberg. The remaining guards were all Volkssturm, and were responsible for gathering the American stragglers together in a compound adjoining the main American compound. As soon as they collected a group of 50 or 75, evacuation marches would begin.

On 3 April 1945, a German hauptmann arrived at the camp, and asked the SMO for four of the most seriously wounded prisoners to be designated for transfer to the town of Bad Kissingen where the Germans had supposedly converted 25 resort hotels into 300-bed hospitals. The German officer reported that Bad Kissingen was to be made an open city because Frau Goebbels was living in the town. The SMO protested the movement of these men because it might impair their chances for recovery. When this protest was over-ruled by the German officer, the SMO requested to be permitted to go to the American lines and inform the commanders that the city was "open". This permission was refused, and at midnight four wounded men were taken in a truck to the resort town. The following day, two more evacuations took place involving about 20 sick and wounded officers. After the second trip that day, the driver evidently became nervous over the proximity of the American troops and failed to return to the camp although he had been ordered to evacuate at least 20 more PW during the day.

On 6 April 1945, the 14th Armored Division entered the town of Hammelburg in great force and fired on all remaining buildings, carefully avoiding the camp. However, two large shells believed fired by the Germans did explode in the camp area. There were no casualties during the entire liberation, and the evacuation of the PW was arranged for in an orderly way. By this time only a handful of German guards remained, and they were turned over to CIC units which had accompanied the spearhead.

- X X X -

STALAG 17B

(Air Force Non-Commissioned Officers)

Location

Stalag 17B was situated 100 meters northwest of Gneixendorf, a village which is six kilometers northwest of Krems, Austria (48°27' N - 15°39' E). The surrounding area was populated mostly by peasants who raised cattle and did truck farming. The camp itself was in use as a concentration camp from 1938 until 1940 when it began receiving French and Poles as the first PW.

Strength

On 13 October 1943, 1350 non-commissioned officers of the air forces were transferred from Stalag 7A to Stalag 17B, which already contained PW from France, Italy, Russia, Yugoslavia and various smaller nations. At the time of the first Protecting Power visit on 12 January 1944, the strength had increased to 2667. From then until the last days of the war a constant stream of non-commissioned officers arrived from Dulag Luft and strength reached 4237 in spite of protestations to the Detaining Power about the over-crowded conditions.

The entire camp contained 29,794 prisoners of war of various nationalities.

Description

The Americans occupied five compounds, each of which measured 175 yards by 75 yards and contained four double barracks 100 by 240 feet. The barracks were built to accommodate approximately 240 men, but at least 400 men were crowded into them after the first three months of occupancy. Each double barrack contained a washroom of six basins in the center of the building. The beds in the barracks were triple-decked, and each tier had four compartments with one man to a compartment, making a total of 12 men in each group. Each single barrack had a stove to supply heat and cooking facilities for approximately 200 men. The fuel ration for a week was 54 pounds of coal. Because of the lack of heating and an insufficient number of blankets, the men slept two to a bunk for added warmth. Lighting facilities were very poor, and many light bulbs were missing at all times.

Aside from the nine double barracks used for housing purposes, one barrack was reserved for the infirmary and the medical personnel's quarters. Half of a barrack was the library, another half for the MOC and his staff, a half for the theater, a half for Red Cross food distribution and a half for the meeting room. In addition, one barrack was used as a repair shop for shoes and clothing. Four additional barracks were added in early 1944, but two others were torn down because they were considered by the Germans to be too close to the fence, thus making it possible for PW to build tunnels for escape purposes. One of these buildings had been used as a gymnasium, and the other as

a chapel. Latrines were open pit-type and were situated away from the barracks.

Two separate wire fences charged with electricity surrounded the area, and four watchtowers equipped with machine guns were placed at strategic points. At night street lights were used in addition to the searchlights from the guard towers to illuminate the area.

U.S. Personnel

Staff Sergeant Kenneth J. Kurtenbach was MOC from the opening of the camp until its evacuation. Major Fred H. Beaumont was the SAO and the medical officer, but took no active part in the camp organization. Captain Stephen W. Kane was the only chaplain and acted in an advisory capacity whenever called upon. There also existed a security committee. Sgt. Kurtenbach carried on the administration with the following organization:

S/Sgt. Charles M. Belmer	Adjutant
T/Sgt. Alexander M. Haddon	School Director
S/Sgt. David H. Woo	Mail Supervisor
S/Sgt. Gerald H. Tucker	Mail Supervisor
S/Sgt. Samuel E. Underwood	Theater Supervisor
S/Sgt. Edward W. Weisenberg	Sports Supervisor

The medical staff consisted of:

Major Fred H. Beaumont
Captain Carrold H. Nungester
Captain Thomas E. Corcoran
Captain Paul G. Jacobs

German Personnel

The German personnel changed somewhat during the camp's existence, but for most of the time, the following men were in control in the positions indicated:

Oberst Kuhn	Commandant
Major Wenglorz	Security Officer
Major Eigl (Luftwaffe)	Lager Officer
Oberstabsarzt Dr. Pilger	Doctor

The blame for the bad conditions which existed at this camp has been placed on Oberst Kuhn who was both unreasonable and uncooperative. Four months elapsed after the opening of the compound before the MOC was granted an interview with the commandant to register protests, and weeks would pass before written requests were acknowledged. Frequently, orders would be issued to the MOC verbally and would never be confirmed in writing. Some cooperation was obtained from Major Eigl, but since there was friction between him (Luftwaffe) and the other German officers (Wehrmacht), his authority was extremely limited.

Treatment

The treatment at Stalag 17B was never considered good, and was at times even brutal. An example of extreme brutality occurred in early 1944. Two men attempting to escape were discovered in an out-of-bounds area ad-

adjoining the compound. As soon as they were discovered, they threw up their hands indicating their surrender. They were shot while their hands were thus upraised. One of the men died immediately, but the other was only injured in the leg. After he fell a guard ran to within 20 feet of him and fired again. The guards then turned toward the barracks and fired wild shots in that direction. One shot entered a barrack and seriously wounded an American who was lying in his bunk. Permission was denied the Americans by the Germans to bring the body of the dead man into the compound for burial, and medical treatment for the injured man in the outer zone was delayed several hours.

One PW was mentally sick when he was taken to the hospital where no provisions were made to handle cases of this type. In a moment of insanity the PW jumped from a window and ran to the fence, followed by a French doctor and orderlies who shouted to the guard not to shoot him. He was dressed in hospital pajamas which should have indicated to the guard that he was mentally unbalanced even if the doctor had not called the warning. As the patient climbed over the fence the guard shot him in the heart.

There were about 30 recorded cases of guards striking PW with bayonets, pistols and rifle butt. Protests to the commandant were always useless. In fact, on one occasion the commandant is reported to have stated that men were lucky to get off so lightly.

On another occasion an order was issued that all PW take everything that they wanted to keep and stand on the parade ground as if they were leaving camp. Nothing was touched in the barracks during the search that ensued. The same procedure was followed on the next day, and still nothing was touched. The third day, most of the PW left behind many articles of food, clothing and comfort equipment. On this occasion, German troops entered the compound with wagons and took away any and all articles left in the barracks during the parade. The Protecting Power described this act as plunder to the German commandant who finally promised to return the items, but this proved to be an almost impossible task.

Food

The normal ration issued to a PW for one week was as follows:

Bread	:	2425 grams
Fat	:	218 grams (68 grams were cooking fat. The remaininder for spread.)
Potatoes	:	(Vary up to 2800 grams. For the decrease in potatoes another leguminous plant was substitutded.)
Beets or raisins	:	1750 grams
Starch foods	:	150 grams

Cottage cheese	:		94 grams
Sugar	:		175 grams
Marmalade	:		175 grams
Ersatz coffee	:		12 grams
Vegetables	:		450 grams
Salt	:	(approx.)	140 grams
Raisins	:		120 grams
Dried Vegetables	:		43 grams

An average daily menu would contain the following:

3 potatoes	½ cup of ersatz coffee
1 cup of soup	3 grams of margarine
22 grams of bread	

Vegetables were issued only when available and within the limits of the quanities available to German civilians.

When reserve supplies of Red Cross parcels were received in the camp, the German authorities reduced their issue ration. Even though protests were made to the commandant by the MOC and the Protecting Power, this practice continued. As soon as the Red Cross supplies would be exhausted, the normal ration would again be issued.

For the first three months absolutely no eating utensils were supplied. At the end of that time, one bowl and one spoon were given to each third man. PW were able to make bowls and spoons from Klim cans, which also served as drinking mugs.

On 17 October 1944, some one broke into the kitchen and stole 275 packages of cigarettes and 35 standard Red Cross parcels complete. Since the keys to the kitchen were held by the Germans it was obvious that they were responsible for the theft. However the commandant did not satisfy the MOC with his report of the investigation.

Toward the last of September 1944, the MOC received a telegram from the International Red Cross that three carloads of food, clothing and comfort supplies would arrive in a few days. These cars did in fact arrive the first of October, but the commandant neither notified the MOC nor had the cards unloaded. Instead, the cars were rerouted to another city where the contents were stored in a military park. Representatives of the IRC arrived a few days later and informed the MOC that the commandant had orders to reroute the shipment for "military reasons." Upon inspection of the cars in the nearby town, only a few of the cases proved to have been pilfered. Although there were only 3000 parcels on hand in the camp, the delivery of these cars was delayed two weeks. On 9 December two more carloads arrived and the shipment was 13 cases short. On 13 December four more cars arrived, of which one car was sixteen cases short, nine other cases pillaged, and one car with two cases missing. Seals on all four cars were broken.

Except for these incidents, the Red Cross supplies arrived in good condition.

Health

In general, health of the PW was good. They maintained their weight until the last month or so before the evacuation; they were active in games and sports, and stayed mentally healthy by keeping busy. Approximately 150 attended sick call each day with skin diseases, upper-respiratory infections and stomach ailments. About 30% of all cases at sick call were for skin diseases attributed to the conditions under which they lived. The acute shortage of water (available four hours each day), lack of hot water, lack of laundry facilities, and over-crowded sleeping conditions created many health problems, but improvements were always noticed during the summer months when the men could be outdoors a great deal of the time.

The average daily strength of the revier was 70, while the adjoining Lagerlazaret cared for approximately 40, who were victims of the more serious cases of shrapnel, flak and gun wounds. Conditions there were very satisfactory in equipment, medical, clinical and surgical attendance. X-ray and consultation services were available, and were supervised by very competent medical officers who were prisoners of war of nationalities other than American.

The revier originally consisted of two ordinary barracks and two sectional "knock-down" temporary buildings. These also housed the medical personnel as previously stated. The construction was not weather tight and heating in cold weather was impossible. During most of the cold weather the water pipes froze, but the installation of a new stove in one of the buildings enabled the hospital staff to furnish an invalid diet to each patient and sufficient hot water for a bath on admission and discharge as well as once a week during his stay. The fuel supply was inadequate for these standards, but supplementary fuel was supplied by men who volunteered for wood forage details.

The two temporary buildings were set aside for isolation wards of infectious patients, but because of their poor condition, they were used only in cases of dire need.

The management of the revier was solely in the hands of the American medical PW without any interference from German authorities. A German medical officer was assigned to supervise the revier, but his daily visits concerned administrative problems only.

Clothing

The clothing condition in the camp was not unsatisfactory in the beginning because most of the men had received adequate issues when they passed through Dulag Luft. However, after the confiscation referred to in the paragraph on "Treatment," shortages became acute.

There were never sufficient blankets. The two thin cotton blankets issued by the Germans were described as "tablecloths" by many repatriates, and although the Red Cross furnished many American GI blankets, the strength increased so rapidly that only two-thirds of the men were fortunate enough to be issued one.

As in other camps, the leather flying jackets which most of the men wore at the time of their capture were taken away, but after repeated protests, some of these were returned. Shoes were a problem in the early stages, but the repair shop operated by PW alleviated the condition to some extent. The Serbian shoes issued when GI shoes were not available from the stock Red Cross supplies proved to be inadequate in quality to withstand the cold and mud.

<u>Work</u> Since all of the men at this camp were non-commissioned officers, they were not required to work.

<u>Pay</u> The monthly rate of pay for the PW was RM 7.50, or approximately $1.53. However, the men received this money in cash only on a few occasions. The Germans stated that the pay was to reimburse the German government for the razor blades, soap, matches, pencils, paper, etc., which were sometimes available in the canteen.

<u>Mail</u> The number of mail forms issued to each prisoner varied at different times from two mail forms and two postcards to four mail forms and three postcards. There was no record of mail forms being withheld for disciplinary reasons, and apparently no check was made on the number of communications written by each PW. However, on one occasion, forms were not issued, reportedly because the printer had been bombed out. Two weeks later, a Protecting Power visit was announced and 10,000 forms were issued immediately.

Incoming mail was very irregular and considered unsatisfactory by the PW. Since all of their mail had to be processed through Stalag Luft 3, censorship often delayed it four and five weeks. Surface letters required an average of four months for delivery as against three months for air mail. Surprisingly enough, personal parcels often arrived in two months, but the average time in transit was three to five months. In August 1944, no parcels arrived in the camp, but the following month 685 were received.

When parcels were delivered to the camp, a list of the recipients was posted in the barracks. These men were required to line up outside the delivery room. Before the PW could take possession of his parcel, the German guard would open the parcel, take everything out, and punch holes in any tinned foods. PW were permitted to keep the containers, however. No items were ever confiscated from these parcels as far as could be ascertained.

Morale The morale of PW at this camp was good as a result of two factors: the successes of the Allied armies in the field, and the recreational and educational opportunities within the camp. There was no serious trouble among the PW, and the unimportant fights and disputes which occasionally occurred seemed to spring from a desire to break the monotony. These incidents were quickly over and forgotten.

The leadership of the MOC and his staff is credited with the maintenance of high morale throughout the existence of the camp.

Welfare Representatives of the International Red Cross Committee and the Protecting Power visited the camp approximately every three months, and always transmitted the complaints of the MOC to the German authorities in a strong manner. On many occasions, the Representatives reported unsatisfactory conditions at the camp to the State Department, and made every attempt to correct such conditions at the time of the visits.

The dispatch of Red Cross parcels to the camps was prompt, and all delays in supplies reaching PW was blamed on the German authorities. On several occasions insufficient clothing supplies were dispatched, but this was usually due to an increase in the strength after the requisition had been received in Geneva.

Requisitions to the YMCA for sports equipment and books were always promptly filled. The only delay incurred on the requests was in getting the approval of transmission from the German commandant.

Religion Even though repeated requests for additional chaplains were made to the German authorities, Captain Stephan W. Kane carried the full ecclesiastical burden for the camp. The PW cooperated with Father Kane in converting a barrack into a chapel for the religious services. Father Kane held daily services for the Catholics of the camp, and offered additional services for the Protestant PW. His untiring efforts in behalf of the men contributed a great deal to the good morale and discipline of the camp.

Recreation The large recreation area in the camp to which the men had access during most of the daylight hours permitted them to enjoy a number of sports. Basketball, volley ball, baseball, boxing and track meets were among the favorite outdoor exercises. In addition, some enterprising PW built a miniature golf course and used hockey sticks and handballs as equipment. Competitive spirit was high after barrack leagues and teams were formed. In addition to these activities, the PW took great pride in the excellent band which gave frequent concerts and which played for the theatrical efforts of the "Cardboard Players." During the colder months,

the PW depended a great deal on card games, checkers, chess, and other indoor games, as well as reading material from the well-stocked library. A complete public address system with speakers in each barrack inspired the organization of a "radio station" (WPBS) which furnished scheduled programs of music and information.

The most outstanding effort in field of recreation was the educational program organized by T/Sgt. Alexander M. Haddon with the following aims and objectives:

(1) To keep men mentally alert
(2) To offer accredited instruction
(3) To help men to plan for post-war educational and vocational activities.

Sgt. Haddon was assisted by a staff composed of instructors, librarians, a secretary, and office help. Classes in Mathematics, Law, Photography, Music, Economics, American History, Shorthand, Auto Mechanics, English, Spanish, German and French were given to the students. The school was held in a building containing the fiction and technical libraries. Six separate classrooms accommodating 40 men were used for instruction, and furniture consisted of benches, tables and blackboards. Because the limited supply of technical books prevented a check-out system, tables and benches were furnished for reference work.

Interests which were not handled in the scheduled classes named above were provided for in evening discussion groups. These were usually journalism, farm management and live-stock farming, and were directed by men who had had successful experience in the fields. These evening discussion groups were particularly popular during the spring and summer months when they could be held outdoors after the supper hour.

When the school was first started, attendance registered 1369, but gradually enthusiasm dropped until the average attendance was 980. This was the average attendance figure during the school's operation.

Evacuation

On 8 April 1945, 4000 of the PW at Stalag 17B began an 18-day march of 281 miles to Braunau, Austria. The remaining 200 men were too ill to make the march and were left behind in the hospital. These men were liberated on 9 May 1945 by the Russians.

The marching column was divided into eight groups of 500 with an American leader in charge of each group guarded by about 20 German Volkssturm guards and two dogs. Red Cross parcels were issued to each man in sufficient amounts to last about seven days. During the 18-day march, the column averaged 20 kilometers each day. At the end of the day, they were forced to bivouac in open fields regardless of the weather. On

three occasions, the men were quartered in cow barns. The only food furnished to PW by the German authorities was barley soup and bread. Trading with the German and Austrian civilians became the main source of sustenance after the Red Cross parcel supplies were exhausted. The destination of the column was a Russian prison camp 4 kilometers north of Braunau. Upon arrival the PW cut down pine trees and made small huts since there was no housing available. Roaming guards patrolled the area and the woods surrounding the area, but no escape attempts were made because it was apparent that the liberation forces were in the immediate vicinity.

The day after their arrival at the new site, Red Cross parcels were issued to every PW. A second issue was made a few days later of one parcel for every fifth man.

Liberation

On 3 May 1945 the camp was liberated when six men of the 13th Armored Division arrived in three jeeps and easily captured the remaining guards who numbered 205. Other units of the 13th Armored followed shortly and organized the evacuation of the PW by C-47 to France on 9 May 1945.

-XXX-

Family of

Henry Eugene Maul

The Maul Family

1941

Mary Jane, Henry Eugene, Virginia Lee
Henry Charles, Bertha Marie

Dad as a child...

As a baby, Dad won a
Most Beautiful Baby Contest

Dad
April 1924

Dad and sister, Virginia
April 1929

Dad
1934

1942
Age 18
Army Class 26-42
Boeing School of Aeronautics

1949
Age 26
Wedding Day

Childhood Homes

1930-1945
719 Franklin Ave
Alton, Illinois

This home was built in 1930.
My dad's family moved in when he was 6 years old.

1945-1949
1408 Liberty St
Alton, Illinois

My dad's parents moved from Franklin to Liberty about 1945.
My parents were married in 1949.

Mom and Dad's Wedding

September 12, 1949

Mary Jane Maul Hinton, Patricia Collins, Virginia Lee Maul Munger, Mom, Dad, Paul Munger, George Collins, Bernard Snyder, ?

Patricia & George Collins Children

The Maul Girls

Diana, Shelia, Cindy

Cindy, Shelia, Diana
1956

Cindy, Shelia, Diana
1959

The Maul Girls

Shelia, Diana, Cindy
1974

Diana, Cindy, Shelia
1992

Diana, Shelia, Cindy
1986

Cindy, Diana, Shelia
2020

Diana, Cindy, Shelia
1987

S/Sgt. Henry Eugene “Gene” Maul

Mom and Dad

1992

Research Sources

American Air Museum in Britain. americanairmuseum.com.

American Heritage Center (AHC). “Prisoner of War Diaries.” Nov. 2015, ahcwyo.org.

Cerbone, Cheryl. “American Ex-Prisoners of War Organization.” axpow.org.

Civil Affairs Division; War Crimes Branch, War Department. “Stalag Luft III, in the Matter of Killings or Executions of Prisoners of War.” Archives.gov.

Critical Past, LLC. “Red Cross Supplies Being Distributed to Liberated Allied Prisoners in Moosburg, Germany during World War II.” criticalpast.com.

Durand, Arthur A. “Stalag Luft III: The Secret Story.” Louisiana State University Press, 1999.

Fold3 - Historical Military Records. fold3.com.

Historical Society, Emmitsburg Areas. “World War II Honor Roll.” Emmitsburg.net.

Maul, Hinton, Nash, Lucker, Burk, Fohrman, Snyder Familes.

McCutcheon, Bill. “Death March from Stalag Luft 4 during WWII,” “Stalag Luft 3 POW Camp Including the Great Escape,” “WW2 History of the 392nd Bomb Group at Wendling and German POW Stalag Luft Camps for Airmen.” b24.net.

Messenger, Charles. “Stalag Luft III : The German POW Camp That Inspired the Great Escape: Rare Photographs from Wartime Archives.” Greenhill Books, 2019.

Richard, Oscar. “Kriegie: An American POW in Germany.” Louisiana State University Press, 2000.

Rose, Len. “Stalag Luft VI and IV.” stalagluft4.org.

Simmons, Kenneth W. “Kriegie: Prisoner of War.” Cpsia, 2019.

Smith, Mary, and Barbara Freer. "Stalag Luft I Photos," "The Kriegies," "Stalag Luft IV Photos." merkki.com.

Smithsonian Air and Space Magazine. smithsonianmag.com

The U.S. National Archives and Records Administration.

Tuck, Howard, and Great Britain. "Stalag Luft III : An Official History of the "Great Escape, POW Camp : An Official Account." Frontline Books, 2016.

Victor F. Gammon, "Not All Glory: True Accounts of RAF Airmen Taken Prisoner in Europe." 1939-45. 2014, military-history.fandom.com. The March (1945).

War Department. Office of the Provost Marshal General. American Prisoner of War Information Bureau. Records Branch. ca. 1942-9/18/1947. "American POWs in Germany, November 1, 1945." US National Archives Research Catalog, Military Intelligence Service War Department, 1942, catalog.archives.gov.

War Department. Office of the Quartermaster General. Memorial Division. Identification Branch. ca. 1942-ca. 1947. "Missing Air Crew Report Number 4566." US National Archives Research Catalog, War Department, Office Quartermaster General, 1942, catalog.archives.gov.

War History Online. "Stalag Luft III." warhistoryonline.com.

Wartime Memories Project. "The Wartime Memories Project – Tell Us Your Story." wartimememoriesproject.com.

Wikipedia. wikipedia.org, 2014.

WWII Forums. "Media | WWII Forums." ww2f.com.

Zhou, Jing. "B-17 Bomber Flying Fortress – The Queen of the Skies." b17flyingfortress.de.

Notes